D1690828

Global Perspectives on Higher Education and Lifelong Learners

The global expansion of participation rates in higher education continues more or less unabated. However, while the concept of *lifelong learning* has figured prominently in national and international educational policy discourse for more than three decades, its implications for the field of higher education has remained relatively underdeveloped.

This book focuses on a particular dimension of lifelong learning: higher education for those who have not progressed directly from school to higher education. Some will embark on undergraduate programmes as mature students, part-time and/or distance students; others wish to return to higher education after having completed (or not completed) a previous academic programme, while increasing numbers participate in postgraduate and continuing studies for a complex mix of professional and personal reasons.

Adopting a comparative and international longitudinal perspective which goes beyond a snapshot view by building on the cases of a core group of ten OECD countries, this timely book investigates the ways in which important new developments impacting on higher education crystallise around the lifelong learning agenda:

- new technology and open source resources;
- the changing role of the state and market in higher education;
- the blurring of public and private boundaries;
- issues of equity and access in a time of global economic turmoil;
- the increased emphasis on research and international league tables;
- the changing nature of education; and
- the complex interaction of international, national and regional expectations which governments and other stakeholders have of universities and other public and private institutions of higher education.

While focusing on the situation in Canada, the USA, Japan, Australia, New Zealand and a wide variety of European countries, the book also assesses the issues from the perspective of developing countries.

Maria Slowey is Director of Higher Education Research and Development at Dublin City University, Ireland.

Hans G. Schuetze is a Professor Emeritus and former Director, Centre for Policy Studies in Higher Education and Training, University of British Columbia in Vancouver, Canada.

Global Perspectives on Higher Education and Lifelong Learners

Edited by Maria Slowey and
Hans G. Schuetze

Routledge
Taylor & Francis Group
LONDON AND NEW YORK

First published 2012
by Routledge
2 Park Square, Milton Park, Abingdon, Oxon OX14 4RN

Simultaneously published in the USA and Canada
by Routledge
711 Third Avenue, New York, NY 10017

Routledge is an imprint of the Taylor & Francis Group, an informa business

© 2012 selection and editorial material, M. Slowey and H. Schuetze; individual chapters, the contributors

The right of the editors to be identified as the authors of the editorial material, and of the authors for their individual chapters, has been asserted in accordance with sections 77 and 78 of the Copyright, Designs and Patents Act 1988.

All rights reserved. No part of this book may be reprinted or reproduced or utilised in any form or by any electronic, mechanical, or other means, now known or hereafter invented, including photocopying and recording, or in any information storage or retrieval system, without permission in writing from the publishers.

Trademark notice: Product or corporate names may be trademarks or registered trademarks, and are used only for identification and explanation without intent to infringe.

British Library Cataloguing in Publication Data
A catalogue record for this book is available from the British Library

Library of Congress Cataloging in Publication Data
Global perspectives on higher education and lifelong learners / [edited by] Hans Schuetze, Maria Slowey.
    p. cm.
  1. Adult education–OECD countries–Case studies. 2. Adult college students–OECD countries–Case studies. 3. Education, Higher–OECD countries–Case studies. 4. Education and globalization–OECD countries–Case studies. I. Schützte, Hans Georg. II. Slowey, Maria.
  LC5215.G573 2012
  374–dc23   2011041278

ISBN: 978-0-415-67507-9 (hbk)
ISBN: 978-0-203-12249-5 (ebk)

Typeset in Galliard
by HWA Text and Data Management, London

Printed and bound in Great Britain by the MPG Books Group

Contents

List of figures   viii
List of tables   ix
List of contributors   x

PART I
Comparative perspectives   1

1 All change – no change? Lifelong learners and higher education revisited   3
MARIA SLOWEY AND HANS G. SCHUETZE

PART II
Europe   23

2 Austria: non-traditional students in the 2000s   25
HANS PECHAR AND ANGELA WROBLEWSKI

3 Germany: from individual talent to institutional permeability: changing policies for non-traditional access routes in German higher education   43
ANDRÄ WOLTER

4 Ireland: lifelong learning and higher education in Ireland: turbulent times   60
MARIA SLOWEY

5 Portugal: higher education and lifelong education in Portugal   82
ALBERTO AMARAL AND MADALENA FONSECA

6 Sweden: higher education and lifelong learning in Sweden 97
CAMILLA THUNBORG AND AGNIESZKA BRON

7 United Kingdom: universities and lifelong learning in the UK – adults as losers, but who are the winners? 112
MICHAEL OSBORNE AND MUIR HOUSTON

PART III
North America 133

8 Canada: large archipelago, small bridges and infrequent ferries: lifelong learning and Canadian higher education 135
HANS G. SCHUETZE

9 Mexico: great expectations, scattered approaches, disjointed results: the rocky road to lifelong learning in Mexican higher education 157
GERMÁN ÁLVAREZ-MENDIOLA

10 United States of America: adult higher education and lifelong learning in the USA: perplexing contradictions 173
CAROL E. KASWORM

PART IV
Pacific – Australia, Japan and New Zealand 193

11 Australia: intensifying performance and learner-centredness in Australian higher education 195
HARSH SURI AND DAVID BECKETT

12 Japan: lifelong learning and higher education in Japan 217
SHINICHI YAMAMOTO

13 New Zealand: lifelong learning and higher education in Aotearoa New Zealand 230
BRIAN FINDSEN

PART V
Perspectives from two 'BRICS' countries — 249

14 South Africa: higher education in lifelong learning in a middle-income country: but by the grace of champions? — 251
SHIRLEY WALTERS

15 Brazil: lifelong learning and the role of the university in Brazil: some reflections — 266
ANA CANEN

PART VI
Epilogue — 279

16 Afterword: a look around the corner — 281
MARIA SLOWEY AND HANS G. SCHUETZE

Index — 289

Figures

2.1	Development of student numbers in Austria	33
4.1	General government balance and gross debt (% of GDP)	63
4.2	Unemployment rate by level of education	64
6.1	The Swedish education system	98
11.1	Higher education revenue proportion by sector	200
12.1	University entrants aged 25 years and older	221
12.2	Unemployment rate 1973–2010	222
12.3	University enrolment: implications of demographic trends and projections for the future	226
12.4	Numbers of learners in different types of programmes	228
16.1	Higher education in the broader landscape of lifelong learning	287

Tables

1.1	Case study countries and themes 1987–2011	11
2.1	Employment of students during term	35
4.1	Enrolment trends in universities in Ireland by mode and level of study	68
4.2	Enrolment trends in institutes of technology (IoTs) in Ireland by mode and level of study	69
4.3	Age distribution of full-time new entrants to universities and institutes of technology in Ireland	73
5.1	Higher education level attained (percentage of active population 15–64 years)	83
5.2	Unemployment rate by education level and age group	85
5.3	Enrolments by subsystem	86
5.4	Relative distribution of graduates, by field of education, Portugal	87
5.5	Access of first year students as mature students aged 23 years and over	93
7.1	Young (18 and 19 years at entry) full-time participation in UK higher education by schooling, social class and neighbourhood	121
7.2	Mature student participation in HE by no previous HE experience and neighbourhood in first degree and in all undergraduate level courses from 1997/98 to 2007/08	122
10.1	Undergraduate students in institutions of higher education in the USA by age, employment intensity, and dependency status	180
10.2	Engagement of undergraduate students in distance education in institutions of higher education in the USA	182
10.3	Percentages of students who work and workers who study; self-defined identity of undergraduate students aged 24 or older in institutions of higher education in the USA (1999–2000)	183
12.1	Number and type of higher education institutions and students in Japan	220

Contributors

Germán Álvarez-Mendiola works for the Center for Research and Advanced Studies in Mexico. His field of research is higher education, especially educational policies, private sector and lifelong learning. He coordinates the collection 'Library of Higher Education' of the National Association of Universities and Higher Education Institutions.

Alberto Amaral is Professor at the University of Porto, a former Rector of the University of Porto (1986–1998) and of CIPES and President of the Portuguese Quality Agency and former Director of CIPES. He is editor and co-editor of several books and published papers on higher education policies.

David Beckett is an Associate Professor and Associate Dean, in the Melbourne Graduate School of Education, at the University of Melbourne. He publishes in adults' workplace and lifelong learning, and also in philosophy of education.

Agnieszka Bron is a Professor and holds the Chair of Education at the Stockholm University, Sweden. She has published extensively on subjects such as biographical learning (ethnicity, gender, informal learning and work) and comparative studies (blue-collar workers' access to post-secondary education, and non-traditional students). Among others she is a co-founder of the European Society for Research in the Education of Adults.

Ana Canen is a Professor in the Department of Educational Studies at the Federal University of Rio de Janeiro (UFRJ). She also is a Researcher for the Brazilian Research Council (CNPq). Her research interests are multicultural and comparative education, institutional evaluation and teacher education.

Brian Findsen is a Professor of Education in the Faculty of Education at the University of Waikato. He was previously Professor and Head of Adult Education at Glasgow University. He has published extensively in the field of adult education and lifelong learning, with a particular interest in learning for older adults.

Madalena Fonseca is a geographer, an Assistant Professor for economic geography at the University of Porto, Portugal and researcher at the Centre for Research on Higher Education Policies (CIPES). At present she is the general secretary of the Portuguese Agency for Accreditation and Assessment of Higher Education (A3ES) in Lisbon.

Muir Houston is a member of the Social Justice, Place and Lifelong Education Research group in the School of Education at the University of Glasgow. He previously held posts at Stirling and the West of Scotland. His research interests include the student experience in higher education, adult education and the development of aspirations in young people.

Carol E. Kasworm is W. Dallas Herring Professor in the Department of Leadership and Policy in Adult and Higher Education in North Carolina State University. She has published extensively on adult learners in higher education. She has held many leadership roles including the American Association of Adult and Continuing Education and Continuing Education Hall of Fame.

Michael Osborne is Professor of Adult and Lifelong Learning at the University of Glasgow. He is Director of the Centre for Research and Development in Adult and Lifelong Learning within the School of Education and Co-director of the PASCAL Observatory on Place Management, Social Capital and Lifelong Learning.

Hans Pechar is a Professor in the Faculty for Interdisciplinary Studies (IFF), University of Klagenfurt, and Head of the Department of Science Communications and Higher Education Research. The focus of his research is comparative higher education and the economics of higher education. From 1999 to 2003 he was a member of the Board of Governors of the Consortium of Higher Education Researchers (CHER). He has published extensively on higher education, including recent publications on the Bologna Process, the knowledge society, comparative critical policy analysis and accountability.

Hans G. Schuetze is a Professor Emeritus and former Director of the Centre for Policy Studies in Higher Education and Training, University of British Columbia in Vancouver, Canada. Since 1994 he has been an Honorary Senior Research Fellow at the University of Glasgow, Scotland. He is a Distinguished Member of the Canadian Society for the Study of Higher Education and a member of CHER and CIES as well as of the Deutscher Juristentag (German Lawyers' Association). His publications are on the subject of educational policy, legal and economic issues in education, higher and adult education, lifelong learning, and work and learning, most of them from a comparative perspective.

Maria Slowey is Professor and Director of Higher Education Research and Development at Dublin City University where, from 2004 to 2009, she was also Vice-President for Learning Innovation. She was previously Professor and Director of Adult and Continuing Education and Vice-Dean Research at the University of Glasgow. She has engaged extensively with national and international policy analysis and development in the fields of adult and higher education at national and international levels, including work with UNESCO, the OECD, the EC and the Higher Education Funding Councils of England and Scotland. In 2009 she was conferred with the award of Academician of the British Academy of Social Sciences.

Harsh Suri is a Lecturer in the Centre for the Study of Higher Education at the University of Melbourne. She publishes in research methods in education and policy issues in higher education.

Camilla Thunborg is an Associate Professor in the University of Stockholm with particular interest in adult participation in education and training.

Shirley Walters is Director of the Division for Lifelong Learning and Professor of Adult and Continuing Education at the University of Western Cape, South Africa. She was Chair of the committee responsible for oversight of the national Qualifications Framework for South Africa and has published extensively on the topic of adult education and equity issues.

Andrä Wolter is Professor of Higher Education Research, Humboldt University, Berlin. From 1993 to 2010 he was Professor for Policy Studies in Education, Dresden University and also, from 2004 to 2006, head of the higher education research department, Higher Education Information System (HIS), Hanover. His main research fields relate to higher education, lifelong learning and monitoring procedures in education.

Angela Wroblewski is researcher with the Faculty for Interdisciplinary Studies (IFF), University of Klagenfurt, Austria and the Department of Science Communications and Higher Education Research.

Shinichi Yamamoto is a Professor and the Director of Research Institute for Higher Education in Hiroshima University, Japan. After graduation from the University of Tokyo in 1972, he started working for the Ministry of Education in Japan as a bureaucrat. After serving there for 20 years, he joined academia and worked for the University of Tsukuba before moving to Hiroshima University in 2006. His main concern is higher education systems including policy, finance, and teaching/research.

Part I
Comparative perspectives

Chapter 1

All change – no change?
Lifelong learners and higher education revisited

Maria Slowey and Hans G. Schuetze

Introduction: *Plus ça change, plus c'est la même chose?*

Globally, higher education systems have undergone substantial transformation since the time of our first look at adult learners in higher education (OECD 1987). Notably, the pace of change in most systems has accelerated over the last decade with increasing diversification in the composition of the student body, types of higher education institutions, forms of provision and funding mechanisms. The reform of higher education has been a dominant theme in national and international policy discourse with a focus amongst other considerations on changing higher education governance, financing, structures and *modi operandi* in order to make institutions more 'relevant' to the needs of labour markets, more 'efficient', more transparent and accountable, and more international and competitive. As the participation rates in OECD countries increased significantly, equity issues and widening access for under-represented sections of the population tended to be relegated to second order consideration.

Global trends are, of course, mediated at the level of national public policy by complex political, historical, cultural and economic conditions. This is why we believe that there is much insight to be gained from an examination of the ways in which a common international topic is interpreted across different countries. The idea of *lifelong learning* is one such theme, having been widely promulgated for decades by international organizations such as UNESCO, OECD and the EU as an organizing principle or 'master plan' for a potentially new approach to teaching and learning.

The concept is contested and open to widely different interpretations, as discussed in our earlier book (Schuetze and Slowey 2000). At its core, however, lifelong learning is built around two axes: a vertical one which relates to the truism that people learn not just while they are young, but over the whole of their lives; and a horizontal axis which relates to the fact that active and purposeful learning takes place not only in formal educational institutions such as schools or universities, but also in the workplace, in the community, in different social environments as well as through individual non-formal study.

However, while the concept of lifelong learning featured prominently in national and international educational policy discourse, the implications of this concept for *higher education* remained underdeveloped. Some types of institutions in the post-secondary system gradually changed to accommodate lifelong learners, but overall, higher education has been slow to adapt its mission, structures and understanding of knowledge and learning – in short, its culture – to the demands for a more open, flexible and egalitarian system. This generally slow pace of change seems somewhat surprising in the light of calls from employers for an educated, flexible and adaptable work force, the aspirations of governments to develop 'knowledge-based economies' and 'learning societies' and, in many OECD countries, significant demographic shifts associated with ageing populations. Two factors contribute to this slow progress towards a lifelong learning system. First, there is the recognition that a system of lifelong learning requires complex processes of articulation and coordination as well as far-reaching changes to the formal education system and the ways the workplace and other social organizations are designed, organized and used as learning places. Second, however, the complexity of the concept masks a fundamental conflict between, on the one hand, a model of lifelong learning derived from principles of social justice and equity, and on the other, a model based on a human capital perspective (Coffield 2000; Rubenson and Schuetze 2000; Slowey and Watson 2003; Fagerlind and Stromqvist 2004; Schuetze and Slowey 2003; Schuetze 2006; Schuetze and Casey 2006; Field 2006; Jarvis 2009; Rubenson 2009). In relation to higher education, the dominance of the neoliberal perspective has, inevitably, resulted in the latter perspective being preeminent.

By adopting a common analytic framework and a comparative and international approach, this book aims to go beyond the level of generality in order to uncover just how these competing agendas play out in practice at national levels. Specifically, our interest is in higher education for those who have not progressed directly from school to higher education, but who are engaged – in one way or another – in broader economic, social and civic life outside the academy. Some embark on undergraduate programmes as mature students, part-time and/or distance students; others wish to return to higher education after having completed (or not completed) a programme leading to a first degree or other post-secondary qualification, while increasing numbers participate in postgraduate and continuing studies for a complex mix of professional, personal and social purposes. In different ways they are all lifelong learners.

Additionally, by building on a core group of ten OECD countries involved in two previous studies (OECD 1987; Schuetze and Slowey 2000) we are in a position to go beyond a snapshot view, providing a cumulative *longitudinal* perspective. This allows us to address important new developments which affect the way in which higher education systems have responded (or not) to the lifelong learning agenda, including: the changing role of the state; the marketization of higher education; the blurring of public and private boundaries; issues of equity and access in a time of global economic turmoil; the increased emphasis on research and international league tables; the changing nature of the education and associated forms of knowledge defined as 'higher'; new technology and open source materials; and the complex interaction of international, national and regional expectations which governments and other stakeholders have of higher education.

This chapter is divided into four parts. The first provides an overview of global changes in higher education which have particular relevance for lifelong learning. The second outlines our methodology and the main themes to be explored in-depth in the country case studies in this book. The third examines the patterns – both congruent and contradictory – emerging from qualitative reviews of developments in lifelong learning alongside the (growing) phenomenon of international quantitative indicators of various kinds. The final part draws the themes together, locating higher education in the much broader landscape of lifelong learning.

Global developments

The classic role of universities in the formation and social reproduction of the next generation remains their most fundamental function, yet *systems* of higher education as a whole have changed dramatically in terms of the scale, the structure, the composition of the student body, patterns of governance, stakeholder involvement, the growth in graduate education and the emphasis on research (Marginson and van der Wende 2006; Altbach, Reisberg and Rumbley 2009; Schuetze and Slowey 2009; Scott 2009). As a result, universities and other institutions of higher education have become significant economic, social and cultural players at local, regional, national and global levels and the subject of increasing attention at national and international policy levels – as is, for example, reflected in the findings of a comprehensive review of higher education policies in 24 countries (OECD 2008).

There has also been a steady growth in the resources invested in higher education, and even where public budgets ceased to grow (or were reduced due to the crisis of the banking and financial services systems at the end of the first decade of the twenty-first century), institutions sought to diversify their income sources and make up for losses by increasing tuition and other fees, cutting scholarships and services, or, where these measures did not suffice to fill the gap, by cutting student enrolments and programmes (Douglass 2010). In many countries this reflects an ideological shift towards increased marketization and privatization of elements of higher education – with consequent blurring of the boundaries between public and private dimensions (Marginson 2007; Enders and Jongbloed 2007;

Ball and Youdell 2008; Altbach and Levy 2005; Altbach, Reisberg and Rumbley 2009).

The higher education system indeed grew exponentially: globally, student numbers have doubled in less than a decade and a half, from 68 million in 1991 to 132 million in 2004 (OECD 2008). Despite the major challenges facing the higher education systems of poor countries, most also experienced expansion. A study of middle income countries involved in the UNESCO World Education Indicators (WEI) Programme showed the significantly larger volume of students graduating from these countries than in the 30 OECD member states combined (UNESCO 2007). In 2006, for example, China had more tertiary graduates (2.4 million) than the top three OECD countries combined – the United States (1.4 million), Japan (0.6 million) and France (0.3 million).

In exploring the topic of lifelong learning in higher education, three factors need to be taken into consideration when looking behind these headline higher education participation figures. Firstly, one of the key comparative indicators of levels of participation is the Age Participation Rate (APR). This measures the proportion of the population of the typical school-leaving age cohort which progresses to higher education. By definition, this refers to young people, and only rarely are such measures used to explore levels of participation by adults in higher education. Secondly, much of the expansion in higher education over the last two decades has taken place in non-university institutions such as polytechnics, community colleges, further education colleges and the like. The statistics therefore generally do not refer only to universities, but to participation across all types of higher education institutions. Thirdly, international statistics usually refer to full-time undergraduate entrants, whereas mature students are more likely to be found on part-time, distance, post-experience and non-credit programmes.

As the country chapters (except for Mexico and Brazil) show, the term lifelong learning is so ubiquitous in national policies that it is easy to forget that the concept and principle were first developed – and strongly advocated – by international organizations, not by individual countries. In fact, a brief glance 'at national educational documents is all that is needed to appreciate the extraordinary success the supranational organizations have had in setting the agenda for lifelong learning' (Rubenson 2009: 129).

As developed and discussed by UNESCO and OECD in the 1970s the concept of lifelong learning – building on radical education ideas emanating from the adult education tradition – was associated with notions of 'de-schooling' and student protests which criticized the traditional education system as being closed and elitist, especially the universities (for example, Field 2006; Osborne and Thomas 2003; Schuetze and Casey 2006; Osborne, Gallacher and Crossan 2007; Desjardin and Rubenson 2009). Sometimes referred to as the 'first generation' of lifelong learning, the underlying principles were characterized by a mix of social justice objectives relating to participation and inclusion – including the provision of second chance opportunities for people to return to education as adult students. Educational opportunity was seen as the foundation for participation in social and civic life, and therefore of critical importance in fostering a vibrant democracy, as well as preparation for employment.

The concept then experienced a revival in the 1990s in a different guise. This 'second generation' of lifelong learning was shaped by a neoliberal agenda in which lifelong learning was viewed as a key educational mechanism to underpin the development of the 'knowledge economy'. This new economy, it was argued, required a well-trained, flexible and adaptable workforce, with associated investment from enterprise and individual workers in continuing training and learning. As in its earlier incarnation, there were variations in emphasis between the major international organizations, with UNESCO stressing individual development and enrichment as well as the wider economic objectives of lifelong learning (UNESCO 1996). In contrast, the OECD (1996) and later the European Union (2000) and the World Bank (2003) placed the main emphasis on human resource and employment dimensions, with considerations of equity and social justice as secondary concerns. Lifelong learning was thus highlighted as a potential tool in the drive for 'modernization' and 'development' with the economic imperative of education and training being to the fore.

The active advocacy of lifelong learning by international organizations stood in contrast to their ability to implement a lifelong learning policy in the member countries. With the exception of the EU, which can legislate on matters for which it has the mandate, international organizations have no direct instrument of implementation. Nevertheless, higher education institutions were subject to, and arguably complicit with, the growing use of policy-steering mechanisms (Neave 2004). Thus, despite the fact that universities and other institutions of higher education in the various countries emerged from different traditions, and took on different organizational forms as they played their role in nation building, analyses of the contemporary trends in higher education suggest there is evidence of increasing convergence. Reviews of empirical literature reveal a high degree of global isomorphism in terms of aspiration, content, expansion and patterns of enrolment from the medieval roots of the university through to contemporary times (Meyer 2000; Schofer and Meyer 2005).

In Europe, for example, the major EU policy driver in relation to higher education builds on the original *Bologna Declaration* (1999). At a meeting in Prague in 2001, higher education ministers adopted (at least rhetorically) the promotion of lifelong learning as one of their joint policy objectives.

Lifelong learning is proclaimed to be an essential element of the European Higher Education Area. In the future Europe, built upon a knowledge-based society and economy, or so the rhetoric has it, lifelong learning strategies are necessary to face the challenges of competitiveness and the use of new technologies to improve social cohesion, equal opportunities and the quality of life (European Ministers in Charge of Higher Education, European Union 2001).

By 2011, with 47 countries involved, Bologna became *the* key mechanism to achieve a European Higher Education Area (EHEA), a Europe-wide framework of understanding with a view to greater transparency and commonality of the structure of qualifications – including opportunities for credit transfer through ECTS (European Credit Transfer System).

Other regions of the world also moved rapidly in a similar direction: for example, regional groupings such as the Latin American and Caribbean Area for Higher Education (ENLACES), the African Union Harmonisation Strategy, and the Southeast Asian Ministers of Education Organisation, also seek further cross-global recognition for their qualifications. A memorandum signed by the EU and Ministers from Latin America and the Caribbean is one such example. *Inter alia* this memorandum recognized the 'importance to society of high quality education and training and broad access to lifelong learning provided by higher education' and agreed to 'promote distance education, constantly bearing in mind the need to maintain an optimum balance between class-room teaching and distance education. It will explore, where appropriate, the potential for cooperation in the validation and recognition of distance learning in a transnational context having due regard to quality assurance' (EULAC, 2000: 2).

These moves to harmonization could be seen as fostering new managerialism, new governance structures and paving the way for further marketization in higher education in Europe and elsewhere (UNESCO 2005; Hackl 2009). However, as higher education policy remains a national responsibility, change is brought about through indirect mechanisms. To take the EU again as an example, policy is steered through engagement with stakeholders and networks of experts, showcasing 'good practice' and inviting member countries to report on their policies and monitor progress. This 'open method of coordination' is notably efficient as a steering mechanism in shaping national policies by the use of informal mechanisms such as peer pressure (Cort 2009). Policy steering can, however, also be accompanied by targeted funding and it is important, especially in times of financial stringency in many countries, not to underestimate 'the power of the purse' and the considerable financial leverage provided by EU-funded higher education programmes (Batory and Lindstrom 2011).

Despite competing interpretations, and the inherent complexity of translating the concept into practice, we thus find that the interrelationship of lifelong learning and higher education has in fact grown in prominence in international educational policy discourse since our 2000 analysis. In 2008, for example, a survey of higher education institutions in Europe found that over half (54 per cent) of institutions claimed to have set in place a strategy for lifelong learning, with a further 25 per cent indicating that one was in preparation (Davies and Feutrie 2008; also, Jackobi and Rusconi 2008). However, as Davies and Feutrie pointed out, the limitations of the survey meant that they were unable to ascertain the extent to which these were genuine strategies – with associated plans for actual implementation – as opposed to mere aspirations, or just rhetorical 'slogans'.

This example raises a key question. With all its obvious limitations, why has the (woolly) concept of lifelong learning proved to be so enduring? We explored the topic in some depth in 2000, yet here we are, a decade later, in a changed global environment, with lifelong learning still, apparently, a live topic in the policy arena – at least for rich countries.

While lifelong learning is a global theme, the context in which it is translated – or not – into practice is within nation states. An important approach to finding some answer(s) to these questions is thus through a brief overview of international experiences.

Overview of country case studies

In one of his last papers, Burton Clark emphasized the importance of analysing higher education systems and institutions from an *international perspective*, seeing the time as being 'long overdue for researchers and practitioners alike to escape nationalistic tunnel vision as fully as possible' (2007: 321).

While higher education systems are subject to common economic, social and demographic pressures resulting in increasing levels of participation by adults in higher education, evidence from our earlier comparative study suggests that the differentials *between* countries appear remarkably persistent over time. In 2000, building on our earlier OECD study (1987) we developed a three-fold grouping of countries along a continuum relating to the levels of adult participation in higher education.

1. Countries with relatively high levels of participation by adult learners and demonstrating a relatively high degree of flexibility in relation to entry criteria and study patterns: this category included Sweden and the United States.
2. Countries where there were significant, but lower, proportions of adult learners across the system as a whole, and where adult students were frequently located in open universities or dedicated centres of adult or continuing education within 'mainstream' institutions: this category included Australia, Canada, New Zealand and the UK.
3. Countries with low levels of adult participation in higher education: this category included Austria, Germany, Ireland and Japan.

In this book, twelve years later, we wanted to include the *same* ten OECD countries as in 1987 and 2000 as this makes possible a longitudinal view of developments over a 25-year period. From a global perspective, however, we were sensitive to the limitations set by this focus on OECD – by definition, richer – countries. We have, therefore, added four more countries: Portugal, Brazil, Mexico and South Africa. In terms of the stage of development and per capita income, they represent two from the so-called BRICS group of countries (Brazil and South Africa) and two countries from southern Europe and North America (Portugal and Mexico). These additions open up new perspectives and permit comparisons with countries that represent different traditions, developments and economic realities.

Table 1.1 summarizes the main themes addressed in our sequence of country case studies over a period of substantial change in the scale, shape and, arguably, the role of higher education globally. The main purpose of this third book is to depict, analyse and compare developments in the specific arena of lifelong learning in these 14 countries over the last decade. As in the two first books, such a comparison is not undertaken on the basis of precise statistics about enrolments, participation, drop-out, completion rates and the like, but rather qualitative and critical analysis of approaches, policies and longer term developments, based on available data, policy documents and research studies.

In the 2000 book we adopted a 'dual lens' approach with, at the macro level, a focus on the relationship of lifelong learning and systems of higher education; and, at the micro level, a focus on learners and institutions. This dual lens also provides the perspective in this book, facilitating longitudinal as well as comparative analysis.

The authors of the country chapters, all experienced researchers in the field, are well placed to address the common themes identified in Table 1.1 in the *particular historical, social and economic context* of the country in which they are based. In relation to the international context, since the time of our 2000 book there has been significant development in statistics and composite indices which seek to measure, on a comparative basis, particular aspects of our topic. As a conceptual approach, lifelong learning, if nothing else, challenged the established education system by changing the focus from a supply-dominated to a learner-orientated perspective. In order to define and measure progress, this necessitates a whole new perspective on data and indicators. Ideally, such an information infrastructure would need

> to comprise comparable indicators not only of the contexts, inputs, process and multiple outcomes of formal education as well as non-formal and informal learning across the lifespan, but the information also needs to be collected and presented at several levels of aggregation.
> (Tuijnman 2003: 481)

At national and international levels, attempts indeed have been made to respond to this challenge. Examples include the *Global Report on Adult*

Table 1.1 Case study countries and themes 1987–2011

Year of publication, title, publisher	Countries	Main themes and analytic questions
1987, Adults in Higher Education (OECD)	Europe Austria Germany Ireland Sweden UK (England) North America Canada USA Pacific countries Australia Japan New Zealand	• Public policy on higher education. • The 'adultification' of the university (the 'graying of the campus'). • Typology of adults in universities. • Participation of adult students, aged 25 and older. • Criteria for enhancement of adult participation. • Classification of country higher education systems according to adult participation.
2000, Higher Education and Lifelong Learners: International Perspectives on Change (Routledge)	Same as 1987	• Changes in the environment for higher education. • Diversification and proliferation of vocationally-orientated higher education institutions. • Broadening the focus beyond universities to include all higher education institutions. • The massive increase in participation in the 1990s, including 'non-traditional' students. • Shift of focus from 'adult/mature' and 'non-traditional' students to (i) 'under-represented groups' and (ii) lifelong learners.
2012, Global Perspectives on Higher Education and Lifelong Learners (Routledge)	Same as 1987 Augmented by perspectives from southern Europe and North America (Portugal and Mexico); and, two BRICS countries (Brazil and South Africa)	• How relevant is the concept of lifelong learning to early 21st-century higher education? Who are the lifelong learners in higher education? • How have the equality, widening participation and social justice dimensions of lifelong learning in higher education been affected by the dominant economic drivers of the last decade? • What is the impact of new developments in technology-enhanced, blended and e-learning approaches on flexible forms of higher education provision?

Education and Learning (UNESCO 2009), work by OECD on the social outcomes of learning (2007 and 2010) and the development of the European Lifelong Learning Index (ELLI) (2009). The latter builds on a Composite Learning Index developed by the Canadian Council on Learning (Schuetze, Chapter 8) and draws on a range of statistical and survey data to develop an index along the four dimensions developed by UNESCO in its 1996 report *Learning: The Treasure Within*: (i) 'learning to know', (ii) 'learning to do', (iii) 'learning to live together', and (iv) 'learning to be'. The ELLI is an index that 'reflects a starting point towards being able to capture, measure and compare this concept of lifelong learning across European countries' (Hoskins, Cartwright and Schoof 2010: 10). This index uses a range of existing statistical data that relate to different aspects of lifelong learning. Some of these are obvious, for example, the proportion of the 20–24 age group participating in post-secondary education, the level of higher education attainment of adults, and drop-out rates from secondary education. Others appear rather marginal, or make little sense given the ubiquity of the internet. Nonetheless, in times of global competition and the interest of many in rankings of all kinds, these data-driven indices are enjoying a growing popularity deflecting, as the country case studies show, from the reality that an information system of lifelong learning is still very much in its infancy. In terms of outcomes, the overall ELLI index results show broad groupings similar in fact to those we identified for our European countries in 1987 and 2000, with Sweden and Denmark being 'the most successful countries in Europe at implementing the idea of lifelong and lifewide learning' (ibid.: 9).

While such developments signal the continuing importance of the topic of lifelong learning from an international policy perspective, given the controversy surrounding the collection of basic statistics from well-established, mainstream formal education, a holistic and comprehensive framework of lifelong learning statistics and indicators is already the subject of debate (Planas and Preston 2010). At a minimum, such indicators pose two basic challenges, concerning firstly questions about the validity of the underlying data; and, secondly, the fact that they take into account only those aspects which can be easily measured.

Working to a common framework, qualitative case studies allow authors to look behind such broad-brush statistics, providing new analytic insights to key questions relating to lifelong learners and higher education. How relevant is the concept of lifelong learning to higher education in the early twenty-first century? How are lifelong learners defined in different countries? How have the equality, widening participation and social justice dimensions of lifelong learning in higher education been affected by the dominant neoliberal economic ideologies of the last decade? What is the impact of new developments in technology-enhanced, blended and e-learning approaches on flexible forms of higher education provision?

The relevance of the concept of lifelong learning to higher education in the early twenty-first century

If, as discussed above, lifelong learning does indeed continue to feature in the international policy discourse, what about its application to higher education at national levels?

Four main conceptions of lifelong learning emerge from the country chapters.

- The first focuses on the *life stage* of the learner. This perspective addresses the significant proportion of students who do not progress directly from initial education (school) to higher education, but who come to study after a period of engagement in economic, social and/ or civic life. There is a close association with age at entry to higher education (older than the average) which is then used in many countries as a proxy for 'lifelong learners'.
- The second focuses on the *mode of study* – including part-time, open learning, distance education and e-learning opportunities. Students studying on such part-time or flexible bases are used in some countries as a proxy for 'lifelong learners'.
- The third focuses on the *type of programme* – often with a continuing professional development (CPD) orientation, or in partnership with employers, such as Masters programmes, non-credit, adult and community courses. Many countries report an expansion of post-experience courses, often on a full cost basis, or on the periphery of universities and other higher education institutions.
- The fourth focuses on the *organization of provision* – including specialist institutions ('open universities' of various types), centres with dedicated missions for continuing education (often full-cost units within public institutions) and, in some countries, the rapid expansion of private providers (which are often disproportionately attended by learners from under-represented and non-traditional groups).

The addition of Portugal, Mexico, Brazil and South Africa to the original group of ten countries provides invaluable new perspectives. Lifelong learning in higher education is not high on the agenda of the latter three countries as their primary focus is on dealing with enormous inequalities in initial levels of education – in Mexico, for example, in 2005 the average years of education received by the poorest decile of the population was only 3.2 (Álvarez-Mendiola, Chapter 9). In contrast, in Sweden, with high levels of education and mass participation in higher education, the goal of lifelong learning in higher education is 'continuously being implemented' (Bron and Thunborg, Chapter 6). Despite the enormous challenges faced by poor countries, however, they have much to contribute to conceptual thinking on the topic.

In Brazil, for example, equity-orientated policies may help contribute to the development of 'an original and culturally based Latin American project that contributes to a new lifelong learning vision' (Canen, Chapter 15), while the experience of young and old people in South Africa dealing with HIV and AIDS in their families 'calls into question what it means to be an "adult" and shifts the focus from mere chronological age' (Walters, Chapter 14).

The chapters on Portugal, Mexico and Brazil also highlight an emerging trend, whereby measures to increase levels of participation by under-represented groups of learners to higher education, without supporting this expansion through adequate public funds, mean that the latter groups of learners tend to be disproportionately represented in a private sector of variable quality (for example, Amaral and Fonseca, Chapter 5).

While all countries show expansion in their systems, much of the recent growth in higher education has taken place in institutions other than universities. In many countries, for example the UK, adult students are predominantly located in these newer institutions which, typically, have a particular mission to work in collaboration with local and regional communities, and to strengthen links with employers (Osborne and Houston, Chapter 7). These trends can been seen as part of more general developments in higher education, including the shift from Mode I to Mode II forms of knowledge (Gibbons, Nowotny and Scott 2000) and from 'knowing what' to 'knowing how' (Barnett, 2005) – with, in general, a stronger impact on newer and non-university institutions. In this context, in Australia for example, the theme of lifelong learning remains 'implicit', but the breadth and overuse of the concept have meant that, in practice, it has been replaced by the notion of the 'knowledge economy' (Beckett and Suri, Chapter 11).

While various elements of flexibility, relevance and a commitment to teaching are of the greatest importance to many lifelong learners, the growing emphasis on national and international league tables over the first decade of the twenty-first century tends to reinforce differentiation and the hierarchical positioning of research-intensive, elite universities compared with the broader spectrum of higher education institutions. In practice, as for example in the case of Austria, adult students and others from under-represented groups find it easier to gain access to lower status and non-university institutions, and are less well represented in elite universities (Pechar and Wroblewski, Chapter 2). From equity and other perspectives, however, is this necessarily a 'problem' as long as individuals gain access to the form of higher education which best suits their needs and abilities?

Typology of lifelong learners in higher education in the early twenty-first century

Just as lifelong learning is open to different interpretations, as the country case studies show, lifelong learners are also a very heterogeneous group ranging from senior professionals, already well qualified and highly paid, who are attending post-experience post-graduate programmes to update and broaden their professional knowledge and skills, to adult learners with few, if any, previous qualifications, entering higher education programmes for a variety of reasons for the first time.

It is important to attempt to develop a typology of sub-categories of lifelong learners to give both a focus and an indication of the complexity of the terrain in the analysis that follows. This is not an exhaustive listing; moreover, individual learners may well belong to overlapping categories, with motivations often only vaguely articulated. Nevertheless, we believe that the following typology reflects the majority of lifelong learning groups identified in the country chapters.

Emerging from the case studies we identify three aspects to consider in any such categorization: the nature of the entry/admission qualification; the access route; and the primary motivation for higher education study.

(i) Second chance learners: Those without traditional formal entry qualifications (such as *Abitur*, A-Levels, *Baccalaureate*, Leaving Certificate, High School Diploma or the like), who enter higher education via a special entrance examination or assessment, and who are usually coming to higher education later in life on a *second chance* basis.

(ii) Equity groups: Those who are from socio-economic or other groups which are *under-represented* in higher education and the focus of national or institutional equity policies – relating, for example, to gender, to those from working-class or particular socio-economic backgrounds, to indigenous people, to migrants, to people living in remote rural areas or to those with disabilities.

(iii) Deferrers: Those who *defer* entry into higher education, following completion of secondary education and gaining appropriate qualifications because they decided at that stage to enter employment or pursue other activities such as voluntary work, travel, community engagement or family responsibilities.

(iv) Recurrent learners: Those – an increasing number as many chapters show – who have a first degree or diploma who are *recurrent learners* returning to higher education for a further, usually higher, degree. Some of these use recently established national frameworks of qualifications in many countries, and/or recognition of prior learning (RPL) to *change direction* between, for example, a vocational route and an academic route. Such learners have a variety of motivations ranging from those who judge they need an additional or different qualification for employment and professional purposes, to those who have a continuing interest and love of learning for its own sake.

(v) Returners: Those who take advantage of the flexibility in the higher education structures of some countries, to *drop-in* to higher education,

having 'dropped-out' or deferred at an earlier stage for a variety of reasons. Such learners often see their higher education experience as woven into the fabric of their lives, rather than being discrete and finite.
(vi) Refreshers: Overlapping with a number of the above sub-categories, there are those who, as professionals and with or without traditional educational qualifications, enrol in continuing education programmes to *refresh* their knowledge and skills.
(vii) Learners in later life: Finally, reflecting the demographic trends in many of the richer countries, there are the *third age* (or, increasingly, *fourth age*) learners, who, from a wide variety of educational and social backgrounds enrol in (mainly) non-credit higher education programmes for personal development purposes.

While the balance varies between countries, examples of all of the above are found to different degrees. In Japan, for example, the last version above, liberal learning in later life, traditionally formed the dominant conception of lifelong learning in higher education (Yamamoto, Chapter 12). In New Zealand, Ireland and the UK on the other hand, lifelong learners and adult learners are still often used as synonyms for each other (Slowey, Chapter 4; Osborne and Houston, Chapter 7; Findsen, Chapter 13).

Flexibility and the broader landscape of lifelong learning

Flexibility is one of the most dominant themes in the country case studies as it facilitates, in different ways, lifelong learning – flexibility in terms of entry routes, modes of study, accumulation of credits over place and time, financial support, and linkages and pathways enabling mobility between different sectors of education and training.

Part-time study is core to the notion of flexibility. Yet some systems still do not recognize the reality of part-time undergraduate study (Austria) while others, such as the UK and Canada, with longstanding traditions of part-time provision, have seen a decline in undergraduate part-time numbers. Overall, despite the rhetoric of lifelong learning, despite the significant developments in technology-enhanced learning, and despite the fact that part-time learners (as officially defined) constitute around one-fifth of all students in higher education (OECD 2009, Table C1.6), in practice their experience appears to remain marginal in many countries.

The use of new learning technologies is widespread in the broader field of lifelong learning, as we envisaged in 2000. Is this an example of continuing studies blazing a pedagogically innovative trail for 'mainstream' higher education provision? Or does this perhaps represent a form of ghettoization for those perceived as 'second-class' cohorts of learners?

The country case studies show increasing – in some, very extensive – use of new technology in higher education teaching and learning. Yet, in the main this is used to enhance the learning of mainstream, full-time students. Outside the USA and Sweden, we see little evidence of the 'blurring of boundaries' between full- and part-time students, as anticipated in our two previous studies. At the undergraduate level, the resourcing and organizational model of most higher education systems remains orientated towards the traditional, full-time student. On the other hand, the patterns of study of some cohorts of young students are altering, as they increasingly combine study with significant employment commitments and as, for some, higher education comes to be viewed as an activity to be pursued over the lifecourse.

Outlook

Many of the policy initiatives undertaken in the name of lifelong learning have indeed included a focus on making higher education more accessible – including to sections of the population that traditionally have been under-represented (if not actually excluded) from higher education. Undoubtedly, the move in rich countries towards mass higher education has resulted in a degree of progress in increasing equity of access (Clancy and Goestellec 2007). However, as the country case studies in this book show, the primary motivation was the aim of creating more productive 'human capital' for the new knowledge-based economies, rather than for equity reasons or for higher education as an individual right. Access thus remains an unresolved issue. Even if it does appear, as in Jericho of old, that many of the walls have 'come tumbling down' there are still barriers, invisible but effective, which constrain access and the development of a genuine cultural shift towards supporting lifelong learners (Bourgeois, Duke, Guyot and Merrill 1999; Schuetze 2001; Taylor, Barr and Steele 2002).

As Watson (2009) points out, most of the criteria which dominated the quest to define 'world class' universities over the first decade of the twenty-first century, effectively excluded factors which are 'vital for the support of lifelong learning' such as teaching quality, widening participation and social mobility, services to business and communities, and other contributions to civil society. Working from a common analytic framework, the fourteen country case studies in this book make a distinctive contribution towards identifying just what such a system might look like, along with identifying the barriers towards its achievement. This involves, we believe, profound epistemological, academic and pedagogical challenges for universities, and other institutions of higher education – amounting, in effect, to a paradigm shift. Despite increased levels of participation and significant evidence of raised awareness of inter-cultural sensitivities, most countries in this book echo the experience of Australia that 'admission procedures, teaching practices and assessment methods would be instantly recognizable to students of the 1960s and doubtless earlier' (Beckett and Suri, Chapter 11).

Accommodating learning needs and choices by lifelong learners, whether called 'non-traditional students' or members of 'under-represented groups', cannot be provided in the way 'extra-mural departments' accommodated the demand from learners 'outside the walls' some 100 years ago: rather, lifelong learners are (and will be in greater numbers) *within* the walls and demanding fundamental change of higher education *from within*. This clearly will not happen without tensions and struggles. In revisiting the topic of lifelong learners in higher education we raise the question *all change – no change?* The following chapters provide a clear response. Without 'all change', lifelong learners will indeed remain marginal – to the great loss not just of individuals and communities, but also to the vibrancy of higher education and its relevance to important global issues of the twenty-first century.

References

Altbach, P.G. and Levy, D.C. (2005) *Private Higher Education: A Global Revolution*, Rotterdam: Sense.

Altbach, P.G., Reisberg, L. and Rumbley, L.E. (2009) *Trends in Global Higher Education: Tracking an Academic Revolution*, Boston: Boston College CIHE.

Ball, S. and Youdell, D. (2008) *Hidden Privatisation*, Research Report, Brussels: Education International.

Barnett, R. (2005) *Reshaping the University: New Relationships between Research, Scholarship and Teaching*, Maidenhead and New York: SRHE/Open University Press.

Batory, A. and Lindstrom, N. (2011) 'The power of the purse: supranational entrepreneurship, financial incentives, and European higher education policy', *Governance: An International Journal of Policy, Administration, and Institutions*, 24 (2): 311–329.

Bologna Declaration (1999) http://www.aic.lv/ace/ace_disk/Bologna/maindoc/bologna_declaration.pdf (accessed 1 June 2011).

Bourgeois, E., Duke, C., Guyot, J.L. and Merrill, B. (1999) *The Adult University*, Buckingham: Open University Press.

Clancy, P. and Goestellec, G. (2007) 'Exploring access and equity in higher education: policy and performance in a comparative perspective', *Higher Education Quarterly* 61 (2): 136–154.

Clark, B. (2007) 'A note on pursuing things that work', in P. Gumport (ed.) *Sociology of Higher Education: Contributions and Their Contexts*, Baltimore: Johns Hopkins University Press.

Coffield, F. (ed.) (2000) *Differing Visions of the Learning Society*, Bristol: Policy Press.

Cort, P. (2009) 'The open method of coordination in vocational education and training: a triangle of EU governance', in R. Desjardins & K. Rubenson (eds) *Research of vs research for Education Policy*, Saarbrücken: VDM, pp. 170–184.

Davies, P. and Feutrie, M. (2008) 'University lifelong learning to lifelong learning universities', in *Bologna Handbook: No 8, June 2006*, Berlin: Raabe and the European Universities Association.

Douglass, J. A. (2010) 'Higher education budgets and the global recession – tracking varied national responses and their consequences', Center for Studies in Higher Education, University of California at Berkeley: Research and Occasional Paper Series CSHE 4.2010.

Enders, J. and Jongbloed, B. (eds) (2007) *Public–Private Dynamics in Higher Education*, Reihe: Science Studies.

European Union (2000) *Memorandum on Lifelong Learning*, Brussels: Commission of the European Union.

European Union (2001) *Towards the European Higher Education Area: Communiqué of the Meeting of European Ministers in Charge of Higher Education*, Prague, 29 May, Brussels: Commission of the European Union.

European Union Latin American Council (EULAC) (2000) http://www.international. ac.uk/resources/CARIBBEAN%20MINISTERIAL%20CONFERENCE%20 ON.pdf (accessed 1 June 2011).

Fagerlind, I. and Stromqvist, G. (eds) (2004) *Reforming Higher Education in the Nordic Countries*, Paris: International Institute for Educational Planning.

Field, J. (2006). *Lifelong Learning and the New Educational Order*, 2nd edn, Stoke-on-Trent: Trentham Books.

Gibbons, M., Nowotny, H. and Scott, P. (2000) *Rethinking Science: Knowledge Production in an Age of Uncertainty*, London: Polity Press.

Hackl, E. (2009) 'Reconceptualising public responsibility and public good in the European higher education area', paper presented to the 6th International Workshop on Higher Education Reforms, Centre for Research and Advanced Studies, Department of Educational Research, Mexico City, November 9–11.

Hoskins, B., Cartwright, F. and Schoof, U. (2010) *Making Lifelong Learning Tangible! The ELLI Index – Europe 2010*, Gutersloh: Bertsmann Stifung.

Jackobi, A.P. and Rusconi, A. (2008) *Opening of Higher Education? A Lifelong Learning Perspective on the Bologna Process*, Berlin: Social Science Research Centre.

Jarvis, P. (2009) 'Lifelong learning: a social ambiguity', in P. Jarvis (ed.) *The Routledge International Handbook of Lifelong Learning*. London: Routledge, pp. 9–18.

Marginson, S. (2007) 'The public/private division in higher education: a global revision', *Higher Education* 53, 307–333.

Marginson, S. and van der Wende, M. (2006) *Globalisation and Higher Education*, Paris: OECD.

Meyer, J. (2000) 'Globalization: sources and effects on national states and societies', *International Sociology*, 15 (2): 233–248.

Neave, G. (2004) 'Higher education policy as orthodoxy: being one tale of doxological drift, political intention and changing circumstances', in P. Teixeira, B. Jongbloed, D. Dill and A. Amaral (eds) *Markets in Higher Education: Rhetoric or Reality?* Dordrecht: Kluwer Academic Publishers, pp. 127–160.

OECD (1987) *Adults in Higher Education*, Paris: OECD.

OECD (1996) *Lifelong Learning for All*, Paris: OECD.

OECD (2007) *Understanding the Social Outcomes of Learning: Synthesis Report*, Paris: OECD.

OECD (2008) *Tertiary Education for the Knowledge Society*, Paris: OECD.

OECD (2009) *Education at a Glance*, Paris: OECD.

OECD (2010) *Improving Health and Social Cohesion through Education: Synthesis Report*, Paris: OECD.

Osborne, M. and Thomas, E. (eds) (2003) *Lifelong Learning in a Changing Continent*, Leicester: National Institute of Adult Continuing Education.

Osborne, M., Gallacher, J. and Crossan, B. (eds) (2007) *Researching Widening Access to Lifelong Learning: Issues and Approaches in International Research*, London: Routledge.

Planas, J. and Preston, J. (2010) *A Dangerous Obsession? Rethinking National Indices of Lifelong Learning and Competitiveness*, London: Centre for Learning and Life Chances in Knowledge Economies and Societies, Institute of Education.

Rubenson, K. (2009) 'Lifelong learning in an era of transnational governance', in R. Desjardins and K. Rubenson (eds) *Research of vs Research for Education Policy*, Saarbrücken: VDM, pp. 129–146.

Rubenson, K. and Schuetze, H.G. (2000) 'Lifelong learning for the knowledge society: demand, supply and policy dilemmas', in K. Rubenson and H.G. Schuetze (eds) *Transition to the Knowledge Society: Policies and Strategies for Individual Participation and Learning*, Vancouver: UBC (Institute for European Studies).

Schofer, E. and Meyer, J.M. (2005) *The World-Wide Expansion of Higher Education*, CDDRL Working Papers 32: Stanford University.

Schuetze, H.G. (2001) 'Tumbling walls, changing landscapes – "Non-traditional students" and lifelong learners in higher education', in H.G. Schuetze (ed.) 'And the walls came tumbling down' – Higher Education and non-traditional students, papers from the International Symposium on Non-Traditional Learners in Higher Education, Vancouver: Centre for Policy Studies in Higher Education and Training, pp. 17–31.

Schuetze, H.G. (2006) 'International concepts and agendas of lifelong learning', *Compare* 36 (3) 289–306.

Schuetze, H.G., and Casey, C. (2006) 'Models and meanings of lifelong learning: progress and barriers on the way to the learning society', *Compare* 36(3), 279–287.

Schuetze, H.G. and Slowey, M. (eds) (2000) *Higher Education and Lifelong Learners: International Perspectives on Change*, London and New York: RoutledgeFalmer.

Schuetze, H.G. and Slowey, M. (2003) 'Participation and exclusion – a comparative analysis of non-traditional and lifelong learners in systems of mass higher education', *Higher Education* 44, 309–327.

Schuetze, H.G. and Slowey, M. (2009) Special Edition on Higher Education Reform and Access, *Journal of Adult and Continuing Education* 15.2.

Scott, P. (2009) *Access in Higher Education in Europe and North America: Trends and Developments*, Bucharest: CEPES/UNESCO.

Slowey, M. and Watson, D. (eds) (2003) *Higher Education and the Lifecourse*, Maidenhead: SRHE/ Open University Press.

Taylor, R., Barr, J. and Steele, T. (2002) *For a Radical Higher Education: After Postmodernism*, Buckingham: SRHE and Open University Press.

Tuijnman, A. (2003) 'Measuring lifelong learning for the new economy', *Compare* 33(4), 471–482.

UNESCO (1996) *Learning: The Treasure Within*, Paris: UNESCO.

UNESCO (2005) *Implications of WTO/GATS on Higher Education in Asia and the Pacific*, UNESCO Forum Occasional Paper Series Paper No.8, Paris: UNESCO.

UNESCO (2007) *Education Counts: Benchmarking Progress in 19 WEI Countries*, Paris: UNESCO Institute for Statistics.

UNESCO (2009) *UNESCO Global Report on Adult Education and Learning*, Hamburg: UNESCO.
Watson, D. (2009) 'Universities and lifelong learning', in P. Jarvis (ed.) *The Routledge International Handbook of Lifelong Learning*, London: Routledge, pp. 102–113.
World Bank (2003) *Lifelong Learning in the Global Knowledge Economy: Challenges for Developing Countires*, Washington DC: World Bank.

Part II
Europe

Chapter 2

Austria
Non-traditional students in the 2000s

Hans Pechar and Angela Wroblewski

Introduction

Ten years ago, we gave an account of the situation of non-traditional students in Austrian higher education (Pechar and Wroblewski 2000). We defined non-traditional students by the following characteristics:

- alternative routes of access to higher education (the regular route to higher education is via graduation from the Gymnasium, however, there are alternatives for students with occupational experience that are taken by a small minority);
- delayed entrance to higher education;
- part-time study, mainly due to working while studying.

We mainly focused on part-time students because this was, by far, the largest group. However, our paradoxical finding was that this group was largely invisible, because there was (and still is) no official part-time status at Austrian universities. Although the majority of students study part-time, they are considered to be full-time students. Our conclusion was that this myth of the full-time student resulted in the neglect of the needs of non-traditional students in general and working part-time students in particular. The structure of Austrian higher education – the legal definition of students, the way courses were offered, the nature of student aid – did not do justice to the needs of this group of students.

In this chapter we will follow-up on these considerations and discuss the impact of the recent changes in higher education policy on the conditions of non-traditional students, in particular working part-time students. We will also discuss to what extent the awareness of the underlying principles of lifelong learning has increased in universities.

The last decade brought many changes to Austrian higher education:

- a major reform in university governance (Federal Ministry for Science and Research 2011);

- the implementation of the Bologna reform;
- the introduction of tuition fees;
- the establishment of new sectors of higher education (private university sector, and the establishment of a new University for Continuing Education).

In the first section we will discuss the rationale for these policy changes and we devise some hypotheses on the possible impact of these changes on the conditions for non-traditional students. In the second section we present a statistical portrait of non-traditional students and discuss the extent to which the data support our hypothesis. Our conclusions point to a mismatch between traditional and modernized elements in Austrian higher education.

Policy changes in the 2000s

University governance

The reform of university governance triggered the most fervent controversy of the last decade. The traditional governance pattern at Austrian universities was characterized by a dualism between administrative and academic responsibilities. On the one hand the university was a state agency and subject to centralized decision making by legislation and state bureaucracy; on the other hand the academic oligarchy was in charge of all issues regarding teaching and research – each chair holder controlling his/her own specialized field of research. The university as an organization was weak. The rector was regarded as *primus inter pares* to represent the university, not to govern, let alone manage it.

Academics regarded it as a cultural obligation of the enlightened secular state (*Kulturstaat*) to provide beneficial circumstances for academic life. The state was seen mainly as a power to protect the integrity and autonomy of universities, not as a potential threat to their independence. The implicit precondition for this pattern of dual governance was mutual trust and respect between the state bureaucracy and senior academics. This tacit agreement was seriously disturbed during the expansion of universities starting in the 1960s and the attempts of the government to make higher education more relevant to the economy.

Starting in the 1990s, the government abandoned the *Kulturstaat* tradition and instead embraced the Anglo-Saxon policies of new public management (NPM). The first major step to apply NPM successfully to higher education was the establishment of *Fachhochschulen* in 1993 (Pratt and Hackl 1999; Pechar 2004). It was much more difficult to apply the NPM approach to universities. A first reform proposal by the government was strongly rejected by the academic community and resulted in a compromise (University Organisation Act 1993) that was only a cautious step towards more institutional autonomy (Pechar and Pellert 1998).

The most important consequence of this new university act was the emergence of a new type of rector who – compared with the former rectors – had significantly increased responsibilities. It was mainly this group that advocated for more efficient management structures. In the early 2000s the government continued with a governance reform that aimed for full legal entity of universities (Titscher et al. 2000). In 2002 a new Organizational Act (Universities Act 2002) was passed by Parliament, in 2004 it became operative.

Universities are no longer state agencies, but they remain in the domain of the public law ('legal persons under public law'). The federal government keeps the responsibility for basic funding, but universities are relieved of the fiscal regulations of the federal budget and receive a lump-sum budget under their own discretion. Resources are allocated on the basis of performance contracts. Each university has a governing board that elects the rector. The rector is no longer 'first among equals' but a manager who is more independent of collegial academic bodies than before. Academics are no longer civil servants but employed by private contracts.

The new organizational law is probably the most far-reaching reform since 1849, when Austria embraced the Humboldtian model. It has – among other effects – severe consequences for the culture of teaching and learning. In the 'old regime' this culture was characterized by a laissez-faire style that allowed students to determine the pace of their studies, e.g. they could decide to take an examination at the end of the course or to delay this decision to a later semester – potentially an open-ended process. Because of the flexibility associated with that system there was no necessity to provide specific support for working students or students with specific needs. The laissez-faire conditions for students were matched by laissez-faire conditions for academics. Neither of the two sides had formal obligations vis-à-vis the other in the way it occurs in the higher education systems of the Anglo-Saxon world. Monitoring the progress of students was not considered an obligation of the university and its instructors. Such monitoring was even seen as illegitimate and inconsistent with the spirit of the Humboldtian university, ignoring the fact 'that Humboldt's ideals were created for a university at which at most 1 per cent of a given age group studied, and therefore bear little relation to the realities of present-day mass higher education, especially in German-speaking Europe' (Ash 2006: 248).

The laissez-faire culture was persistent because neither students nor academics were interested in changing it. Both enjoyed the large amount of freedom it granted to them, and under the old governance regime rectors had neither a responsibility for nor influence on teaching. This changed under the new governance regime. Now the university management has a strong interest in an efficient use of resources, hence they try to substitute the laissez-faire attitudes by stricter rules. Rectors have a direct interest in reducing the duration of studies, because this duration plays a role in the formula for the allocation of the budget. Gradually the old laissez-faire practices are displaced by stricter rules. The changing attitudes of university managers are also reflected in their support for the Bologna Process. From their perspective the new European study architecture is an excellent opportunity to abandon the laissez-faire culture of teaching and learning.

Bologna Process

At the European level the Bologna Process is considered a success story. Indeed, in 1999 not even the most optimistic proponents of this reform would have thought that this concept would prevail so fast (Pechar 2007). In Austria too, Bologna was implemented quite successfully, at least at a superficial level. With the exception of medicine, law and teacher training, all disciplines have introduced the new study architecture. By now (winter term 2009/10) 75 per cent of all studies taken by first year students are bachelor studies. However, beneath this success with the most visible and ostensible goals of the Bologna Process we can discover some serious problems. There is some indication that the Bologna Process was implemented in a superficial way (Ash 2006).

The introduction of the bachelor's degree was much more than the addition of a new degree; it replaces the single tier by a two-tier logic (Clark 1983: 49). For centuries, the single-tier logic has shaped the attitudes of students and teachers and the expectations of employers at the level of the labour market. Hence, implementation of the Bologna Process marked a dramatic change for Austrian higher education and it seems that some advocates of the Bologna Process underestimated the magnitude of this change.

The Bologna reform was mainly promoted by the government and the university managers. In contrast, academics and students predominantly rejected this reform. Objections to its emphasis on employability are deeply rooted in the Humboldtian tradition that tends to depreciate practical and applied knowledge. The opponents were quite successful in assimilating the new degree to the traditional one-tier framework. In many cases the reform was implemented in a way that contradicts the spirit of the Bologna declaration. In some cases, bachelor's programmes are set up by simply dividing a *Diplomstudiengang* (the old type of one-tier master's programme, taken after completion of secondary school) into two parts. The curriculum of the bachelor's programme is not shaped by the logic of a two-tier system, but remains rooted in one-tier logic.

Moreover, the bachelor is often not regarded as a degree in its own right, but rather as an 'intermediate degree' on the way to the master's. More than 80 per cent of bachelor graduates from universities start a master course within a year and so did 62 per cent of graduates from *Fachhochschulen* (Unger et al. 2010b).

The transition towards a two-tier system is a matter not only of the content of the curriculum, but also of the style and culture of teaching and learning. In higher education systems with a long tradition of two tiers it is understood that the culture of undergraduate education differs from that of graduate programmes. The Humboldtian idea of 'unity of teaching and research' is not applied at the undergraduate level, but to graduate – mainly PhD – programmes. In the German-speaking countries the idea of 'unity of teaching and research' is still regarded as the essence of any kind of higher education. Any move towards a more structured curriculum with explicit obligations for both students and teachers is pejoratively called 'Verschulung' – a move towards a school-like curriculum that eliminates the differences in the learning cultures of schools and universities. Moreover, the objective of modularizing and of achieving graduation by accumulating credits points for modules is not compatible with a preference for extensive comprehensive examinations. Hence, although ECTS[1] is being increasingly introduced, it is often used in a very formal, superficial way.

The acid test of successful implementation of the Bologna architecture will be the acceptance of the bachelor's degree in the labour market. So far, the status of the bachelor's degree is still vague and employers are rather sceptical. Ironically, although employers' associations are among the most vigorous advocates of the new study architecture – because they strive for a shorter study duration – individual employers still tend to prefer a master's degree. It does not help to overcome this scepticism that the government, which is one of the most important employers of graduates in Austria, does not yet recognize the bachelor's degree for high level civil service positions.

Tuition fees

In the early 1970s tuition fees were abolished and for the last decades of the 20th century higher education was regarded as a pure public good. It was seen as the responsibility of the state to provide and fund all higher education. Commencing in the 1990s, the lack of public resources again stirred a debate on the need for possible additional revenue from private sources. In 2001, tuition fees amounting to €363 per semester were introduced. In 2008 another policy change occurred. Tuition fees have not been completely abolished but they were redesigned as a surcharge for students who exceed the standard duration of study courses. However, many exceptions – in particular for working students – have the effect that only a minority of students (22 per cent) are paying fees (Unger *et al.* 2010a: 377).

The fee policy gave rise to a heated debate about whether fees function as a social barrier for students from low income families. There is no empirical evidence to social selection due to fees. The €363 fee per semester was relatively low. In addition, students who are eligible for student aid were exempt from fees. However, the 'flat fees' introduced by the government for all enrolled students did not differentiate between full-time and part-time students.

In the first year when fees were introduced, enrolment figures declined by more than 20 per cent. However, this decline can be explained in terms of the exit of non-active 'paper students' who under previous laissez-faire conditions stayed enrolled for various reasons. Estimates based on examination statistics concluded that the number of active students – defined as students who took at least one examination during a period of two years – remained stable (Pechar and Wroblewski 2002). When fees were charged for the first time, there was about an 8 per cent decline in the number of first-year enrolments. However, this decline was compensated for in the following years with first-year enrolments higher than expected.

Establishment of a private university sector

The private university sector in Austrian higher education is a very recent phenomenon. Until the 1990s Austria restricted ownership of universities to the Federal government. Private universities then were regarded as inconsistent with the goal to provide a homogenous higher education system of high quality. However, during the 1990s, a dramatic internationalization of higher education took place. Austrian policy makers suddenly were confronted with the emergence of new providers, a booming market of degree courses offered by non-traditional institutions, and the establishment of branch campuses of foreign institutions and franchising arrangements. Many of those developments exceeded and undermined national regulations. It became evident that in this new environment attempts to maintain a public monopoly would be counter-productive. Hence, at the end of the 1990s the Austrian government decided to legalize a private sector. It was legally established in 1999 (*Universitäts-Akkreditierungsgesetz*), and the first private university was accredited in 2000 by the Accreditation Council (*Akkreditierungsrat*).

The private sector is small and is likely to stay so in the foreseeable future. From a comparative perspective, it can be classified as 'marginal' (Geiger 1986). Overall, the accredited institutions offer a wide range of different fields of study. Most private universities have successfully found niches of their own in carefully defining their subject fields as well as in providing good support to their students. One surprising development is the emergence of 'provincial' universities which legally are private institutions but depend heavily on public subsidies from the provinces. The intensity and quality of research is still highly heterogeneous between the accredited private institutions.

Establishment of a University of Continuous Education

For several years, a commitment to lifelong learning has been an issue in education policy. Higher education is no exception. However, a closer look reveals a limited understanding of this concept. Most frequently, lifelong learning is identified with continuing education (Sünkel and Westphal 2011). A commitment to lifelong learning is thus interpreted as support for more attention and more resources to education and training after completed initial education. In that sense, for many years Austrian universities have extended their non-degree offerings in continuing education, mainly for university graduates, but increasingly also for other target groups. For Austrian universities, which are not allowed to decide on fees for degree courses, offering continuing education has the appeal that this activity is an opportunity to generate additional income.

As a consequence the range of courses in academic continuous training expanded. In addition, a special university for continuous training, the Danube University Krems, was founded in 1994. It is the first university specializing in continuing education in Austria; it is funded by the Federal Government, a province (Niederösterreich) and tuition fees. Since 2004, the university is based on a specific act (Federal Law on the University for Continuing Education Krems) and has the status of a public university – with the special task of offering only continuing education.

The university comprises five faculties (Health and Medicine, Communication and Globalization, Business and Law, Education and Media, Arts, Culture and Building) and 16 departments. Student figures at the Danube University increased steadily, from 1,270 students in 2000/01 to 5,049 students in 2009/10.

Impact on study conditions

The description so far has revealed that despite the foundation of the University Krems, lifelong learning was no priority in higher education policy. Our assessment of the impact of the policy changes portrayed above will focus on the conditions of non-traditional students. We will formulate some hypotheses and in the following section we will check whether the available data confirm these hypotheses.

Our main hypothesis is that the policy changes have complicated the situation for students with reduced time budgets because of employment, childcare or health problems. The main reason is that the laissez-faire characteristics of study conditions at Austrian universities were reduced. As we have seen, the Bologna Process, in particular at the bachelor level, has introduced more structured study programmes as in the old study architecture. Since the new governance model simultaneously has established strong incentives for university leadership to reduce the duration of studies, the university management was eager to take the implementation of the Bologna architecture as an opportunity to eliminate at least some of the traditional laissez-faire characteristics.

That has mixed outcomes for students. On the one hand, a better structure of study programmes can be regarded as a facilitation for students, in particular for academically weaker students who have problems in mastering complex and diffuse tasks. From that perspective, the introduction of more structured study programmes can be regarded as a kind of 'normalization', a reduction of an Austrian 'exceptionalism' that is at odds with mass higher education. On the other hand a tighter study structure makes it more difficult for students to act as part-time students in a system where they are formerly regarded as full-time students. The new Bologna study architecture puts at risk the delicate balance between negligence and freedom that made it easier for students to arrange conflicting tasks even if a formal structure of part-time study did not exist.

In addition, the temporary introduction of tuition fees increased the stress for working students. Since no part-time option was available, students who effectively did study only part-time still had to pay full fees. Obviously, such an arrangement is a strong incentive to shorten the duration of study in order to minimize the total amount of fees. For that reason, many students tried to reduce their employment. However, the nature of student aid in Austria puts limits on that strategy. Since stipends are limited and student loans are not available, many students had to work for economic reasons, even if that had the consequence that they were enrolled for a longer period and paid a higher amount of fees.

Our initial analysis in 2000 was based on a specifically conducted survey. For our present analysis we have to rely on existing data (official statistics and results of a regularly conducted Austrian student survey). To put comparisons over time on a legitimate basis we refer to these data sources and not to our own survey from 1998. The official statistics that are provided in the next section give only an incomplete picture of the impact of the policy change on the study conditions because official statistics do not contain information about factors that constitute non-traditional students (e.g. children, employment, etc.). Thus, student surveys are the main source of information about living and studying conditions of students. However, there is another source of evidence, even if it is inherently sketchy and difficult to quantify: the attitudes of students to the policies which we have described, in particular their resistance to the Bologna Process. Again, no methodically sound survey exists on that issue, but there are many sporadic signs of discontent that finally erupted in a powerful protest movement during autumn and winter 2009.

A statistical portrait of students in the 2000s

The development of enrolments at Austrian universities during the last decade is characterized by a continuous increase of student figures (with a temporary decline after the introduction of student fees in 2001/02), an increasing female participation, and a restructuring of the higher education sector due to the upgrading of former colleges of education to *Pädagogische Hochschulen* and an ongoing expansion of *Fachhochschulen* (Figure 2.1).[2]

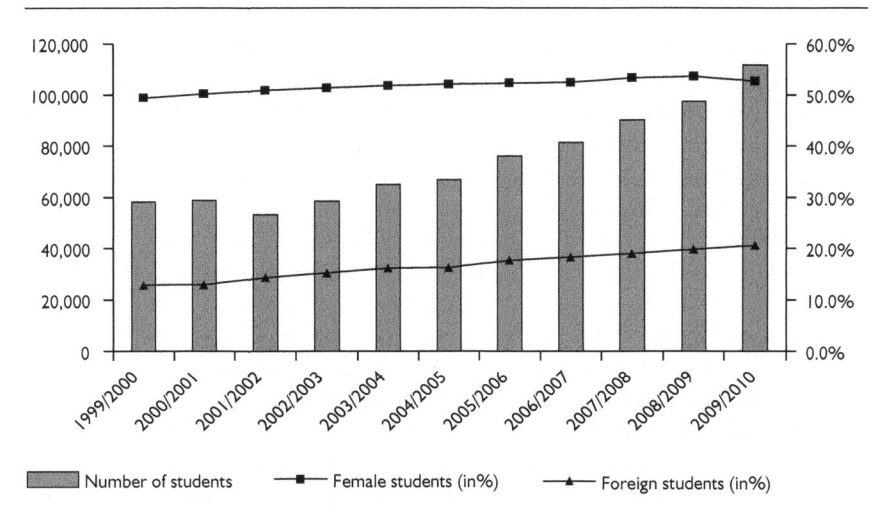

Figure 2.1 Development of student numbers in Austria (1999/2000 to 2009/10)

In 2009 about 300,000 regular students were enrolled at public higher education institutions in Austria. The vast majority (about 246,000 students) were at universities: about 8,000 students were enrolled at universities of arts, 36,000 at *Fachhochschulen* and 8,000 at *Pädagogische Hochschulen*. *Fachhochschulen* accounted for most of the increase in student figures as the number of students increased from about 10,000 (winter term 1999/2000) to 36,000 (winter term 2009/10). If we consider the whole tertiary sector, by now 40 per cent of the Austrian resident population aged 18 to 21 enters higher education (male: 36 per cent, female: 45 per cent). This means an increase of 10 percentage points compared with 1999/2000.

Access to higher education is still biased by social origin. The probability that the child of an academic enters higher education is four times higher than that for a child of a person who completed an apprenticeship (Unger *et al.* 2010a: 60f). Fifty-four per cent of all students at universities are female. However, there is a high degree of gender segregation in the university system as 80 per cent of students at *Pädagogische Hochschulen* but only 45 per cent of students at *Fachhochschulen* are female. Also the gender segregation within subjects remains stable – women are still an exception in technical studies.

Students with alternative entrance qualifications

Until the end of the 1990s the university entrance qualification for the majority of first year students was the final certificate of upper secondary education (*Matura*, the Austrian equivalent to the German *Abitur*). This changed due to the increasing share of foreign students and as a consequence of the expansion of *Fachhochschulen*.

The share of students with alternative university entrance qualifications (*Berufsreifeprüfung* or *Studienberechtigungsprüfung* for people with apprenticeship or other forms of secondary education) increased at universities from 3.5 per cent in 2000/01 to 5.9 per cent in 2009/10. In absolute terms the number of students with alternative entrance qualification quadrupled within 10 years (224 students had an alternative entrance qualification in 1999/00, but the figure in 2009/10 was 990). The share of students with foreign A-levels also increased significantly (from 13 per cent in 2000/01 to 20 per cent in 2009/10). As a consequence the significance of traditional access routes (upper secondary general school) declined. At *Fachhochschulen* the situation is a bit different: in 2009/10 most students graduated from upper secondary vocational schools (46 per cent) and only one-third attended an upper secondary general school. Alternative entrance qualifications are slightly more important compared with universities (7.2 per cent), and other entrance qualifications (e.g. an entrance examination) are more frequent (6.3 per cent).

Late beginners and senior students

The age structure of students at research universities didn't change during the last decade (Unger *et al.* 2010a: 43). First year students are on average between 20 and 21 years old. At universities of arts, beginners are on average one year older and here the average age increased by 1.5 years since 2000/01. Students at *Fachhochschulen* are the oldest with an average entrance age of 25.2 years. At *Fachhochschulen* the average age of first year students increased in the same period by about 2 years. This is mainly due to the increase in the number of places for working students. At the moment (winter semester 2009/10) one-third of student places at *Fachhochschulen* are designed for students in regular employment.

The number of senior students (women aged 55+, men aged 60+) declined significantly after the introduction of student fees in 2001 (from about 4,500 in 2000/01 to 2,300 in 2001/02). In the following years the absolute number of senior students remained stable with a recent increase in the winter semester 2009/10 (about 3,000 senior students).

Working students

As no official part-time status exists for working students, information about employment of students is only available on the basis of surveys.[3] Since the end of the 1990s employment of students during term has increased. While in 1998 more than half of all students were not employed during term, in 2002 only one-third and in 2006 and 2009 about 40 per cent didn't work. The share of students in full-time employment remained stable (about 10 per cent). The increase in employment rates is mainly due to an increase in

Table 2.1 Employment of students during term

	1998	2002	2006	2009
Continuous employment during term	31.5%	49.0%	41.9%	44.7%
Temporary employment during term	15.8%	17.6%	17.7%	16.5%
No employment during term	52.7%	33.4%	40.4%	38.8%
Total	100.0%	100.0%	100.0%	100.0%

Sources: Austrian student surveys 1998 (Wroblewski et al. 1999), 2002 (Wroblewski and Unger 2003), 2006 (Unger and Wroblewski 2007) and 2009 (Unger et al. 2010a).

minor employment.[4] In 2002 one-third of working students were in minor employment whereas in 2009 their share amounts to 42 per cent (Table 2.1).

Although the extent of employment varies, the overall picture didn't change. Therefore we refer in the following mainly to actual data (2009, Unger et al. 2010a) to describe the situation of non-traditional students. Employment is highly correlated with age, in particular continuous employment during term increases from 20 per cent among the youngest students to 71 per cent among students older than 30. Furthermore the extent of employment rises with age. Working students up to 20 years old work on average 10 hours a week while the average working week of older students comprises 33 hours.

Working students in the youngest cohort work mainly in minor employment (63 per cent) or as an intern (4 per cent). Working students older than 30 have employment contracts as employees (51 per cent), officials (21 per cent) or are self-employed/free-lancers (14 per cent). Atypical employment (like minor employment or internships) plays hardly any role (17 per cent).

Employment rate and extent of employment vary significantly between bachelor and master students. Thirty-eight per cent of bachelor students work during term regularly, 17 per cent work occasionally and 45 per cent do not work at all. On the contrary, 55 per cent of master students work regularly during term and 17 per cent are temporarily employed. Hence, only 29 per cent of master students do not work during term. The differences in employment between bachelor and master students are on the one hand due to the different age structure. However, the main reason is the different organization of study as bachelor studies are more strictly organized (they require more attendance time at university, are based on a tight schedule, etc.).

The share of working students is to a lesser extent determined by social origin. While 42 per cent of students from upper class families do not work during term and 41 per cent work regularly, only about one-third of students with a working-class background do not work during term and 52 per cent are employed continuously. The effect of social background on employment status is moderated by the existing system of state student assistance which is mainly means tested. Forty-three per cent of working-class students receive state student assistance, as do 30 per cent of students coming from lower middle class families compared with 8 per cent of upper class students.

Employment of students is mainly motivated by financial necessity: 76 per cent of working students agree with the statement 'Employment is necessary to make a living'. There is no significant difference by gender or between bachelor and master students. Despite financial necessity, 47 per cent of working students are also employed in order to gain professional experience and 39 per cent hope they will benefit from their working experience in future job searches. The motive to gain professional experience is more important to master students (59 per cent) than to bachelor students (46 per cent).

As mentioned above, the form of employment differs between younger and older students and between bachelor and master students. The older students are the most likely to have 'regular jobs' not jobs that might be considered 'typical for students'. How students assess the relationship between employment and study gives strong support for that assumption: the jobs of master students are more challenging and are more often related to the field of study. Master students also state more often that they benefit in their studies from their work experience. On the other hand, bachelor students work more often in jobs that require no specific qualifications. They also would like more often to reduce job engagement in favour of study. No difference between master and bachelor students exists in the assessment of job flexibility and problems to reconcile employment and study. It is worth noting that more than half of working students are flexible to schedule their working time according to their need (e.g. their university schedule). It seems that the possibility to reconcile study and work is more a result of flexibility in the labour market than a consequence of specific target group-oriented offers by the university.

About one out of five students enter higher education with regular work experience (defined as employment for at least one year, at least 20 hours a week). This applies more to men than women (23 per cent of men and 19 per cent of women). The share of first year students with work experience varies significantly by social background. Thirty-seven per cent of working class students have work experience before enrolment but only 9 per cent of upper class students (lower middle class: 24 per cent; upper middle class: 15 per cent). Students with work experience are overrepresented at *Fachhochschulen* (36 per cent) and especially in courses for working students (61 per cent).

Study motives

Although lifelong learning is not a very prominent topic in higher education policy, it is a relevant study motive especially for master students. The relevant motive structure is different for first grade students (bachelor students and students in old diploma degree programmes) and master students. Furthermore there are differences between the higher education sectors. The most important motive for enrolment is interest in the subject – this holds for about 90 per cent of all students regardless of higher education sector and/or type of study. Labour market orientation is mentioned in both groups in second place, however for master students to increase labour market prospects is even more important (master students: 88 per cent; bachelor students: 70 per cent). Among first grade students, labour market orientation plays a more important role for students at *Fachhochschulen* (83 per cent).

As already mentioned, an important motive for starting a master course is the low reputation of a bachelor degree. About 70 per cent of master students – especially those from universities – agree that a bachelor is not enough to gain an attractive labour market position. Furthermore 53 per cent of master students defines the master degree course as a kind of further education (compared with 20 per cent of first grade students). Further education is most important for students in courses for working students at *Fachhochschulen* (73 per cent). Another motive that is mainly relevant for students with work experience is vocational re-orientation. This motive is mentioned by 20 per cent of bachelor students, especially at *Pädagogische Hochschulen* (34 per cent) and by working students at *Fachhochschulen* (39 per cent).

Students with children

During the last decade the share of students with children declined from 12 per cent in 1998 or 11 per cent in 2002 to 7 per cent in 2006 and 9 per cent in 2009. In 2009, 7 per cent of bachelor students and 9 per cent of master students had children.

The decline in the share of students with children may be caused by a complex set of intervening factors. The introduction of fees might be one explanation because students with only a few study activities decided to exmatriculate. The implementation of the Bologna system might also have some influence because bachelor studies are more strictly organized and include less scope for flexibility. Therefore the reconciliation problem is reinforced. On the other hand, the age at first birth in general has increased continuously in Austria. On average, women are 28 years old when they give birth for the first time (2010, Source: Statistics Austria), in 1991 the average was 25 years. A study for Germany revealed that female as well as male students plan to have their first child after graduation when they are settled in a 'good job' (Middendorff 2003).

Furthermore the situation for students with children changed during the last decade because of more engagement of universities in providing support for childcare. Since the end of the 1990s, measures to help reconcile study and childcare were introduced stepwise. In 1999 a career/family compatibility service centre opened at the Federal Ministry for Science and Research and a three-year 'Childcare in Universities' project was launched (Czernohorszky

2003). In the beginning, the Ministry financed initial pilot projects and created structures to anchor this topic in the universities (e.g. the establishment of 'childcare officers' which gave university staff and students with children a voice at the university). Furthermore some universities (Vienna, Graz, Salzburg and Linz) received EU-project funding to set up campus childcare facilities. These projects were subsequently continued and financed by the universities at the end of the initial funding period and served as role models for other universities. In the meantime, all public universities in Austria now either provide at least some childcare facilities or have established a childcare information centre.

Students with special needs

A specific group of students that is highly affected by the missing part-time status are handicapped students or students with chronic diseases. In 2009 (Unger *et al.* 2010a), 1 per cent of all students defined themselves as handicapped, 12 per cent were chronically ill and 7 per cent reported another impairment. Seventy per cent of affected students reported that they are impaired in their study because of their health status. In the following we define students who are physically or mentally impaired and who are consequently impaired in their studies as the relevant group. This group consists of 14 per cent of all students.

The University Act 2002 contains specific regulations for students who are registered as handicapped (e.g. they hold a handicapped ID for which one may apply in case the impairment amounts to at least 50 per cent). For these students the regular duration of studies is doubled (which is important if they receive a scholarship) and they are entitled to adapted conditions for exams if needed. Because of anticipated stigmatizing effects when looking for a job, students try to avoid applying for an ID. Therefore only 4 per cent of all students who belong to the relevant group hold a handicapped ID, which represents 0.5 per cent of all students. However, if students with diseases do not hold a special ID (e.g. to avoid stigmatizing effects in case of job search after graduation) they are not entitled to any support. The degree of support for such students depends on the engagement of the representative of handicapped students at the university and the significance that the university management devotes to the topic (Wroblewski and Laimer 2010).

Students in new sectors of higher education

The description so far has focused on regular students who form the core of the official statistics and the population of student surveys. Students attending university courses who are registered as 'special' students are therefore not considered in official statistics or student surveys. The same holds for students at private universities. In official higher education statistics in Austria, only the absolute number of students in university courses by gender are reported. The number of participants in university courses of continuing education increased significantly during the last decade (from about 7,000 in 2000/01 to 14,400 in 2009/10). More than one-third of students in university courses are enrolled at the Danube University Krems.

In 2009/10, 5,829 students were enrolled at private universities in Austria. The private university sector has expanded during recent years (2005/06: 3,608 students). The share of foreign students is higher than in the public sector (37 per cent versus 21 per cent).

Conclusions

Austrian higher education has arrived at an interesting crossroads: the modernization efforts of the last decade have provoked significant resistance from academics and students, but some of this refusal is due to an incomplete and incoherent implementation of these reforms. It is neither feasible nor desirable to move backwards to the traditional laissez-faire model. Massification has irrevocably changed higher education; and Austrian universities, like many of their European counterparts, have significant problems adapting to that reality. However, during the last decade there were considerable steps in that direction, such as the new governance model and the implementation of a new study architecture. In other areas – such as admissions, part-time studies, student aid – no significant change has occurred.

Thus we observe an incoherent system with a mismatch between traditional and modernized elements. One example of such mismatch is that policy makers emphasize the responsibility of universities to reduce dropout rates and duration of studies, but do not allow them to limit admission of students according to the places available. Another kind of mismatch occurs when the new study architecture emphasizes stricter rules that actually reduce the traditional laissez-faire features of Austrian education without providing a part-time functional equivalent for students who are not in a position to study on a full-time basis. One might summarize that despite the recent severe changes in the higher education system, higher education policy is still oriented towards the 'traditional student', who studies full time at a public university immediately after graduation from high school.

We can increasingly find discussions that reveal a deeper understanding of lifelong learning at the conceptual level, namely as a concept that breaks with the traditional segmentation of learning phases during a person's biography (Schnabl and Gasser 2011). Considered in that way, lifelong learning would not just strengthen an additional sector beyond initial education and training, but it would also restructure the culture of learning in existing institutions (including universities) for a new paradigm that regards learning as a lifelong activity. Such an approach would mainly have two consequences:

- It would firstly require to open universities – including their degree courses – for new target groups. Higher education institutions would need to re-think their concept of necessary requirements for entrance (Pechar 2009). At present, access to higher education is basically limited to students who have graduated from upper secondary schools. A lifelong learning approach would approve other qualifications as well and ideally develop procedures for recognizing informal prior learning.
- It would secondly require reconsideration of the traditional classification and subdivision of learning periods over the life course. The late teens and early twenties would remain the main target group for universities, but it would become normal for a person to change between periods of study and periods of employment. The initial education and the first degree would remain the foundation of a tertiary qualification, but it would be regularly updated by sub-degree and occasionally also degree courses. Such an approach would allow a shorter time for initial education.

There are many barriers in the present Austrian higher education system that constrain a policy change in that direction. Most important, the present legal regulations on access prevent universities from exerting any influence on the composition of their student body. As school leavers who graduate with a Matura are entitled to enrol on any course in any university, universities are left with no discretion over admissions. This is a major difference between universities and all other sectors of higher education. Only the former are denied the right to control admission of students. This is a bizarre reversion of the internationally established relation between prestige and selectivity of higher education sectors. Usually, the higher the prestige of a sector or institution, the more selective is admission to higher education. It is an exception in Austria that the most prestigious institutions are open whereas all others are selective.

The conflict about this 'no admission' policy has become very intense during the last decade and it is probably the most divisive question in higher education policy. Advocates of no admission defend this policy on equity grounds, but it is obvious that this concept embodies a very special notion of equity. Access to universities is framed as a privilege for a special group that can be considered as a kind of 'estate'. The 'educational estate' is treated equitably but everybody who does not belong to that estate is excluded. This type of 'openness' and 'equity' is the opposite of an equitable approach to lifelong learning that opens up to new target groups for higher education. Representatives of universities have repeatedly argued that it is impossible to realize the idea of recognizing prior learning if institutions cannot admit their own students (Österreichische Universitätenkonferenz 2008). In other words, a comprehensive approach to lifelong learning requires the entitlement system to be substituted by university entrance selection.

Notes

1 The European Credit Transfer System is an important aspect of the Bologna Process which aims at facilitating student mobility. ECTS credits are based on the workload students need in order to achieve expected learning outcomes. In most cases 60 ECTS credits are attached to a full-time academic year.
2 A note on terminology: *Pädagogische Hochschulen* is often translated as 'Universities of Education' and *Fachhochschulen* as 'Universities of Applied Science'. We stick to the German term because both sectors are regarded as non-university sectors.
3 Surveys of students have a long tradition in Austria. The first survey was conducted in 1974. The surveys we refer to took place in 1998, 2002, 2006 and 2009. All of them are based on a stratified random sample. The surveys in 1998 and 2002 were postal surveys (paper and pencil), in 2006 and 2009 the surveys were conducted as online surveys. Due to these changes in survey design and some changes in question wording, the survey results are only comparable with caution. The survey population is regular students at public universities. As a consequence the survey population doesn't cover irregular students (e.g. students in further training courses) or students at private universities. In 2009 about 40,000 students participated in the survey.
4 'Minor employment' is defined as monthly income which does not exceed €366.33 (2010). Income up to this threshold coincides with the eligibility for student assistance and family allowance. Minimum income workers are covered by accident insurance but not by health insurance or pension insurance. They might voluntarily obtain health insurance and pension insurance.

References

Ash, M.G. (2006) 'Bachelor of what, master of whom? The Humboldt myth and historical transformations of higher education in German-speaking Europe and the US', *European Journal of Education*, 41: 245–267.
Clark, B.R. (1983) *The Higher Education System. Academic Organization in Cross-National Perspective*, Berkeley and Los Angeles: UC Press.
Czernohorszky, E. (2003) 'Maßnahmen zur Vereinbarkeit von Beruf und Privatem: Arbeitsgruppe Kinderbetreuung an Universitäten' (Reconciliation policies: working group childcare at universities), in: Schaller-Steidl, R. and Neuwirth, B. (eds) *Frauenförderung in Wissenschaft und Forschung. Konzepte, Strukturen, Praktiken*, Vienna: Verlag Österreich: 347–359.
Federal Ministry for Science and Research (2011) *Austrian Universitites Act 2002*, Vienna. Available at http://www.bmwf.gv.at/fileadmin/user_upload/wissenschaft/recht/englisch/E_UG.pdf
Geiger, R. (1986) *Private Sectors in Higher Education. Structure, Function, and Change in Eight Countries*, Ann Arbor: University of Michigan Press.
Middendorff, E. (2003) *Kinder eingeplant? Lebensentwürfe Studierender und ihre Einstellung zum Studium mit Kind*, Hannover: HIS Kurz-Information.
Österreichische Universitätenkonferenz (Universities Austria) (2008) *Stellungnahme zum Konsultationspapier – Nationaler Qualifikationsrahmen für Österreich (Comment on the consultation paper – National qualifications framework for Austria)*, Vienna: REKO. Online. Available at http://www.reko.ac.at/upload/uniko-NQR-Stellungnahme.Endversion_Juni.2008__1_.pdf> (accessed 8 March 2011).

Pechar, H. (2004) 'Austrian higher education meets the knowledge society', *Canadian Journal of Higher Education*, 34: 55–72.
Pechar, H. (2007) 'The Bologna Process: a European response to global competition in higher education', *Canadian Journal of Higher Education*, 37: 107–123.
Pechar, H. (2009) 'Can research universities survive without control over admission? Reflections on Austria's exceptionalism in higher education policy', *Journal of Adult & Continuing Education*, 15: 142–154.
Pechar, H. and Pellert, A. (1998) 'Managing change: organisational reform in Austrian universities', *Higher Education Policy* 11: 141–151.
Pechar, H. and Wroblewski, A. (2000) 'The enduring myth of the full-time student: an exploration of the reality of participation patterns in Austrian universities', in: Schuetze, H.G. and Slowey, M. (eds) *Higher Education and Lifelong Learners. International Perspectives on Change*, London/New York: Routledge/Falmer: 27–47.
Pechar, H. and Wroblewski, A. (2002) *Retrospektive Schätzung studienaktiver Studierender an Universitäten der Wissenschaften für den Zeitraum 1996/97–2000/01 (Estimation in retrospect of the number of active students at universities 1996/97–2000/01)*, Wien: Federal Ministry for Science, Education and Culture.
Pratt, J. and Hackl, E. (1999) 'Breaking the mould in Austrian higher education', *Higher Education Review*, 32: 34–54.
Schnabl, C. and Gasser, C. (2011) 'Lifelong Learning – Anspruch und Wirklichkeit an österreichischen Universitäten' (Lifelong Learning – Demand and reality at Austrian universities), in: Tomaschek, N. and Gornik, E. (eds) *The Lifelong Learning University*, Münster: Waxmann: 167–179.
Sünkel, H. and Westphal, E. (2011) 'Lifelong Learning und die Österreichische Universitätenkonferenz', in: Tomaschek, N. and Gornik, E. (eds) *The Lifelong Learning University*, Münster: Waxmann: 161–166.
Titscher, S., Winckler, G., Biedermann, H., Gatterbauer, H., Laske, S., Moser, R., Strehl, F., Wojda, F. and Wulz H. (eds) (2000) *Universitäten im Wettbewerb. Zur Neustrukturierung österreichischer Universitäten (Universities in competition. The restructuring of Austrian universities)*, München/Mering: Rainer Hampp Verlag.
Unger, M. and Wroblewski, A. (2007) *Studierenden-Sozialerhebung 2006 (Austrian Student Survey 2006)*, Vienna: Federal Ministry for Science and Research.
Unger, M., Angel, S. and Dünser, L. (2010b) *Umstieg vom Bachelor- auf das Masterstudium (Transition from Bachelor to Master)*, Vienna: Federal Ministry for Science and Research.
Unger, M., Zaussinger, S., Angel, S., Dünser, L., Grabher, A., Hartl, J., Paulinger, G., Brandl, J., Wejwar, P. and Gottwald, R. (2010a) *Studierenden-Sozialerhebung 2009 (Austrian Student Survey 2009)*, Vienna: Federal Ministry for Science and Research.
Wroblewski, A. and Laimer, A. (2010) *Studierende mit gesundheitlichen Beeinträchtigungen. Teil B: Fallstudien an Universitäten und Fachhochschulen (Students with special needs, part B: case studies at universities and Fachhochschulen)*, Vienna: Federal Ministry for Science and Research.
Wroblewski, A. and Unger, M. (2003) *Studierenden-Sozialerhebung 2003 (Austrian Student Survey 2003)*, Vienna: Federal Ministry for Education, Science and Culture.
Wroblewski, A., Unger, M. and Schmutzer-Hollensteiner, E. (1999) *Bericht zur sozialen Lage der Studierenden (Report on the social situation of students)*, Vienna: Federal Ministry for Science and Transport.

Chapter 3

Germany
From individual talent to institutional permeability: changing policies for non-traditional access routes in German higher education

Andrä Wolter

Introduction

Among lifelong learners in higher education, non-traditional students form a key group along with participants in continuing higher education programmes (Schuetze and Slowey 2000, 2002). After a long period of marginalization (as described in Wolter 2000) the issue of access for non-traditional students has become a more prominent topic in German higher education policy during the last decade. Since the 1970s, access policy has primarily focused on formal admission procedures for the regular route to higher education, in particular for those who finish the grammar school track (*Gymnasium*) with the usual university entry qualification, the German *Abitur*. For more than four decades the main access issue has been the almost continuous growth of student demand that has caused the predominant restrictive limitation policy (*Numerus clausus*). The proportion of new entrants increased more than fivefold between 1960 and 1990 from around 6 to 30 per cent with a subsequent rise to more than 45 per cent by 2010 – without parallel growth in the number of study places. This discrepancy has resulted in considerable capacity bottlenecks in many institutions or courses. Against this backdrop, political or institutional interest in opening up access for non-traditional students was rather slack for a long time.

Despite the continuous growth in enrolment this constellation has changed over the last few years. New initiatives have been taken, and new programmes and regulations have been established to extend opportunities for non-traditional students (Nickel and Leusing 2009). In the following sections the systemic context of access for either traditional or non-traditional students (and what is meant by the term non-traditional in the particular German context) will be described as well as the reasons for the new policy concern for more open access. Furthermore, the current state of development will be analysed in a more detailed way, including the obstacles and difficulties in implementing new concepts of access policy. Germany may be an example of a 'delayed' country in relation to the implementation of a lifelong learning policy in higher education. Unlike other comparable countries, the massive expansion in the participation in higher education has taken place primarily by the extension and heterogenization of traditional students and only to a very limited extent by the establishment of new non-traditional paths to higher education (Teichler and Wolter 2004).

The institutional context of higher education in Germany: access routes, institutional structures and reform measures

To understand the current changes in the access policy, in particular for non-traditional students, it is necessary to be aware of some specific features of the German education system. Different from some other countries, in which access to universities depends primarily on the institutional decision to admit an applicant based on a multi-stage selection procedure, access in Germany is based in principle on the precondition of having a formal study entitlement that is normally acquired by the *Abitur*, the successful final examination of the *Gymnasium*. Additional selection at the stage of admission is carried out primarily in institutions and courses with capacity limits, and only among those with a formal study entitlement. Hence, the main selection does not take place at the level of entrance to higher education but as a continuous process within the school system, in particular in secondary education.

Germany is a federal state in which the responsibility for education, particularly for the school system, is traditionally institutionalized at state level (*Länder*). This is the reason for some varieties in the school sector (including vocational schools) and, after the recent so-called federalism reform, also in higher education, even if there is a certain degree of convergence largely due to the efforts of an interstate coordination institution, the Conference of the State Ministers for Education (*Kultusministerkonferenz*, KMK). Secondary education is not organized as a comprehensive system but as a highly segmented tracking system in which the central transition stage is between primary and secondary school, that means between the 4th and 5th grade at the age of ten (in a few states at grade seven). The *Gymnasium* is one of various tracks students can take after primary school. There are some varieties in the structure of secondary education between the 16 German *Länder* but the *Gymnasium* exists in all of them and, nationally, about 40 per cent of all pupils attend this track.

The second important stage in secondary education is between the lower and upper level. The main path to the *Abitur* (the final high school exam) leads through the upper or senior level of the grammar schools which are 'generally educating' – not vocationally orientated – (*gymnasiale Oberstufe*) that now lasts for two years. Access to this level is not only possible from the lower level of the *Gymnasium* (grades five and seven to nine and ten) but also from other secondary school types if individual school achievement justifies such a transition. Some *Länder* have introduced a vocationally orientated senior level of the grammar school (called *berufliches Gymnasium* or *Fachgymnasium*), in this case three years, as a special provision for those who did not attend the lower level of the *Gymnasium*. At present, about 35 per cent of all graduates who leave the school system have completed the *Abitur*, the large majority via the general route; but there are large differences in this proportion between the *Länder*.

Those school-leavers who do not transfer to the upper level of the *Gymnasium* – either to its general or vocational form – normally move on to institutions of vocational training. Germany has a well-established system of vocational training separate from higher education. Vocational education is offered in two ways, both of which usually take three years: first, and this is the main route, as an apprenticeship as a part of the so-called dual system which combines part-time vocational school with practical on-the-job training at the place of work; and second, as full-time vocational school (*Berufsfachschule*) which exists in different forms offering a complete or only basic vocational training. The dual vocational training is often seen as the reason for the availability of a qualified workforce in Germany, as the backbone of Germany's international industrial strength. The full-time option is more typical for service professions.

Among those who finish their school career with the *Abitur*, a minority continue with vocational education – a few of whom may still enrol after finishing vocational training. Altogether approximately 60 per cent of a typical age cohort take up one of the various provisions in vocational education, mostly in the dual system. With some exceptions, certificates of vocational training do not entitle students to go on to higher education (unless this is with the *Abitur*). But they open access to upper secondary vocational schools (*Fachoberschule, Berufsoberschule*), the completion of which gives access to non-university higher education, sometimes even to the university sector.

Two historical heritages linked with the predominant structures of access to higher education are a real burden for the wider participation of non-traditional students. First, there is the almost exclusive tie between study entitlement and grammar school education (*gymnasiale Bildung*). According to the German notion of education (in the meaning of personal cultivation), the mission of the *Gymnasium* embraces the attainment of the necessary study proficiency (*Studierfähigkeit*), documented in the maturity certificate, so that the ability to study and the *Abitur* are often considered to be the same thing. From this point of view, a person without proof of maturity is not able to study successfully. Second, the institutional segmentation between different educational routes that evolved throughout the 19th century has been historically justified by the differentiation between two different types of knowledge: theoretical, cognitive knowledge gained through *gymnasiale Bildung*, and practical experiential knowledge gained through vocational training and experience. This differentiation has led to an excessive contrast between general and vocational education – the 'German education schism' (Baethge 2007) which has theoretically legitimized the myth of the German *Gymnasium* and the exclusion of vocational learning from access to higher education, in particular in the university sector.

During the 19th century, the antagonism between general and vocational training and the construction of an access route to university study only from the *Gymnasium* reflected the low degree of institutionalization of vocational training under pre-industrial conditions. In this historical context the privilege of the *Gymnasium* to exclusively grant entry to academia was understandable. As a consequence of this, the so-called second educational route, consisting of partly evening, partly day schools both leading to the regular *Abitur*, has often been considered to be the only legitimate way to university for adults with vocational competencies but without study entitlement. However, in the meantime the historically evolved identification of study entitlement, the ability to study and *gymnasiale Bildung* has become more and more obsolete because it does not reflect the fundamental changes in the qualification requirements and achievements of the vocational and continuing education system.

The second pillar of the German higher education system, the *Fachhochschulen*, non-university institutions (despite the fact that they call themselves universities of applied sciences), have established an access route of their own. About 40 per cent of all new entrants to higher education enrol at this institution (and about 60 per cent in the university sector). It is possible to obtain access to this institution by the *Abitur* too, and about half of all new entrants choose this path. The other half comes via the upper secondary vocational schools already mentioned such as *Fachoberschulen* or *Berufsoberschulen* or from further education colleges. *Fachhochschulen* provide more work-related programmes in a limited number of subjects such as engineering, social work or business administration (and of course, in a variety of specialized programmes). Whereas previously universities and *Fachhochschulen* awarded distinct degrees, all institutions now offer bachelors and masters degrees as a result of the Bologna process. In some *Länder* another type of institution exists, the *Berufsakademie*. This type provides double-qualifying courses (so-called dual courses) with a bachelors degree and a professional proficiency. Access to this type of institution usually requires the maturity certificate.

For the last 10 to 15 years German higher education has been entangled in a massive process of change, even a transformation of sorts (Wolter 2004). Numerous reform processes have been taking place simultaneously and have overlapped, and the concept of opening up higher education for non-traditional students is a (small) part of this very broad reform agenda. Here we will focus on three centrally important trends. The first embraces a broad range of reforms concerning the structure and organization of studies including the degrees. This has been caused primarily by the Bologna process, the European project to establish a common, or at least more common, architecture of studies among European countries. For Germany, this reform indicates a deep break with the traditional model of courses and studying by adopting such standards as two consecutive degrees, modularization, credit points or a shorter duration of studies (now mainly three instead of previously four to five years until the first degree). This bundle of reforms has provoked a very lively and controversial public debate about the intended and non-intended side-effects of these measures (Teichler 2005, 2008).

The second trend comprises a similarly heterogeneous spectrum of reforms concerning the mechanisms of governance and steering at the level between state and institution, and that within institutions (Kehm and Lanzendorf 2005; Schimank and Lange 2009; Wolter 2007a). The main concern of this so-called new steering model is the reduction of detailed state control in favour of wider institutional self-steering by strengthening the university management, introducing new steering procedures such as target agreements or the reinforcement of competition particularly in allocation processes (e.g. by performance- or indicator-based procedures). In the long term these measures might have a far greater importance for the future development of higher education than the study reforms because of their impact on the *modus operandi* of the total institution. Unfortunately, lifelong learning orientated indicators play only a minor role in the new funding and allocation procedures so that there are not really any additional incentives for higher education institutions to extend their activities in this area.

A third reform worth mentioning is the development and implementation of measures for stronger vertical differentiation of higher education (Kehm and Pasternack 2009; Teichler 2009). Traditionally, German higher education has been considered as an example of a publicly organized system with a low degree of vertical, and often also of horizontal, differentiation. This more or less homogeneous system based on the assumption that institutions have the same status and reputation, and *grosso modo* show the same quality, is now faced with several challenges of more differentiation. In the first instance this has taken the form of a competitive programme to select and to promote 'excellent' universities. This so-called 'excellence initiative' has resulted in increasing pressure on institutions to cultivate their strengths and eliminate their weaknesses in order to compete with other institutions. Regrettably, adopting lifelong learning structures, opening up for non-traditional students and promoting continuing education have often been eyed suspiciously as detrimental to the achievement of academic excellence.

Non-traditional students and lifelong learners in German higher education

In many countries the expansion of higher education has led to a more heterogeneous student body in terms of gender, social background, migration status and other characteristics (Schuetze and Slowey 2000). This change has often included the increasing participation of non-traditional students. Since the 1980s a growing political and academic interest in this group could be observed (OECD 1987), but it has always been difficult to define precisely what is meant by the concept of non-traditional students, in particular in an international-comparative perspective. The names of the group also vary – often the terms adult or mature students are used for non-traditional students. To understand the particular German notion of non-traditional students it is useful to distinguish five different meanings (Kasworm 1993):

1. *Age*: A widespread but simple approach defines non-traditional students in line with a specific chronological age, mostly older than 25 at the time of enrolment. In this context, opening up access to higher education means primarily achieving a mixture of ages in the composition of the student body.
2. *Participation*: According to this approach, non-traditional students are target groups who are underrepresented in their participation in higher education, e.g. students with a working-class background, with a disability, or from migrant or indigenous families. Therefore, an open access policy means a compensatory strategy to raise social inclusion and to reduce social inequality in the participation rates and patterns.
3. *Life-course*: This concept refers to the stages of the – in the case of non-traditional students – mostly winding biographical paths to higher education, often embracing not only a school career but also more or less extended periods of vocational training and work experience, or often with a family biography. From this perspective, policy would aim to promote the degree of experiential diversity in the student body; and this approach would be in line with the biographical discourse in continuing and higher education research.
4. *Access and admission*: In many countries, non-traditional students often come to higher education by means of alternative routes. Often, non-traditional students come to university at a later point in time ('delayed') after a special admission procedure or via recognition of prior vocational training or work experience. In this case opening up access means to increase the permeability between vocational (including continuing) education and higher education.
5. *Modes of studying*: According to this approach, non-traditional learners are primarily those who study in non-traditional forms such as part-time, distance or parallel to work. To promote non-traditional students then from this perspective means to organize courses and studies in a more flexible and demand orientated way.

In accordance with these various approaches six groups of participants can be distinguished that basically cover the notion of non-traditional students in German higher education:

1 *Second educational route*: This category embraces those students who at first leave school without the *Abitur* but complete vocational training afterwards and then attend one of the options of the grammar school for adults (*Abendgymnasium, Kolleg*) after a period of work experience. This hybrid group is traditional in their formal study entitlement acquired in the school system but non-traditional in their biographical sequences. In the terminology of the OECD (1987) study these students are 'second chancers'. Currently, about 3 per cent of all new entrants in higher education institutions take this route.

2 *Third educational route*: Those without the *Abitur* who are admitted by one of the special admission procedures at university level are subsumed under the category 'third educational route' (*Dritter Bildungsweg*). They are also 'second chancers' but via an alternative non-school route. Different to the second educational route just mentioned that has been regulated by school laws, the third route is subject to higher education legislation. This group is the core of non-traditional students in the German understanding.

3 *Double-qualified school leavers*: Those students who at first obtain the *Abitur* but transfer to vocational training afterwards before moving on to higher education are also a hybrid group embracing a traditional study entitlement with an interposed training sequence. The main objective of these students is to improve their future labour market prospects by a vocational competence and degree. Categorized in the OECD (1987) study as 'deferrers', they comprise about 5 per cent of all first year students.

4 *Non-traditional study provisions*: Independent of their formal qualification and entitlement, students can practise different forms of studying, e.g. distance or part-time. Whereas in Germany only a very small amount of such flexible provision is formally organized, the number of de facto part-time students is considerable; about 20 per cent study in such an informal way (Isserstedt *et al.* 2010: 313). Because of this the number of non-traditional students would be highly overestimated if the definition referred to the form of provision.

5 *Participants in continuing higher education*: Another group often subsumed under non-traditional includes participants in continuing higher education provision. Most of them have already earned a first degree, so they re-enter higher education (that is why the OECD study called them 'returners') for different purposes: sometimes to pursue an advanced degree, a special professional qualification or an individual interest. Such provision can be institutionalized at three levels: as a regular course of studies leading to a regular degree (mostly a masters), as a non-degree programme (often with its own certificate) or as a public provision with a rather general orientation (e.g. so-called PUSH provisions promoting the *p*ublic *u*nderstanding of *s*ciences and *h*umanities). In Germany, a

well-established and highly diversified market for continuing education exists outside universities, even for graduates. Therefore, the share of higher education institutions in the total continuing education provision is very modest – about 5 per cent of all participation cases in continuing education are registered in higher education (Wolter 2007b).
6 *Senior students*: Students who enrol after retirement are a further and steadily increasing group of non-traditional students. They can enrol in regular courses or in specific programmes, sometimes at special institutions (e.g. Universities of the Third Age). These people do not normally aspire to a formal professional qualification even if their target is sometimes a formal degree; they study rather for personal fulfilment and interest (Wolter 2007b).

The political and academic focus as far as non-traditional students in German higher education are concerned, is upon the 'third educational route', despite the fact that all these different groups represent different types of lifelong learners. The issue of non-traditional students strictly defined is linked very closely to the topic of permeability between vocational training and higher education (Wolter 2010). According to this narrow definition, non-traditional students are mainly those entering higher education through particular institutional admission procedures, based on the vocational proficiencies and personal competencies these students have developed during their life-course. In the frame of reference set up by the five concepts mentioned above, this definition refers to the third criterion, the special arrangements of access and admission, in combination with the fourth approach – the winding life-course – because these students have to fulfil the requirements of a vocational biography and work experience before achieving access to higher education.

In the meantime, every German state has initiated a special admission procedure, mostly at a very minimal level. The particular forms of this access route vary between the *Länder*, also a consequence of German educational federalism. Some *Länder* have a long tradition of access for non-traditional students (for example Lower Saxony, which institutionalized such an opportunity 40 years ago). Other *Länder* have carried out measures only recently to open up access. The current state of regulation across the whole of Germany is not really transparent, one of the reasons being the parallel existence of multiple procedures in some states. According to a document of the Federal Conference of the Educational Ministers (KMK 2010) there are at least 30 different regulations in the 16 German *Länder* converging in four basic models (Nickel and Leusing 2009).

- The first widespread and oldest model is that of a formal entry examination before admission – often called an admission examination or aptitude test (*Zulassungs* or *Eignungsprüfung*).

- The second model is that of a conditional admission (*Probestudium*) which means that applicants can enrol for a certain time (for example two to four terms) without any kind of entrance exam but they have to prove their ability to study on the basis of their study progress including several tests.
- The third and most recent model is the automatic granting of admission to those qualified professionals who have completed a further education programme as a craftsman or an industry masters or another examination at the level of further education colleges (for example as a technician).
- Beside these models, in some *Länder* there is the additional procedure of the so-called talent exam (*Begabtenprüfung*). This is an individual self-taught examination standardized at *Abitur* level.

State regulations also differ in the determination of the level of educational achievement, age, duration of work experience, examination standards and demands (if there is a formal test) and also the results of the entire procedure, in particular the entitlement to study at a university or *Fachhochschule*, or which subject or course.

Bologna, Copenhagen and the increasing need for a qualified workforce: changing access policies for non-traditional students

An admission procedure for non-traditional students, for those with individual talent but without the traditional maturity exam, was established for the first time during the 1920s (Wolter 1990). The role model for this gate to university was not the qualified worker or professional but the gifted individual or extraordinary personality who did not have a regular opportunity to attend a grammar school through no fault of his or her own. This narrow path to university implied a very strict selection procedure at entrance level based on certain standards, the norm for which was the maturity exam. Vocational qualifications and work experience did not have any significance. Until recently this role model of the gifted personality was the decisive concept for this extremely selective access route.

Since the 1960s some new ideas and concepts have emerged. However, they have not had any great political or practical relevance. As a part of the reform movement in German higher education policy in the late 1960s and early 1970s, the idea of the social opening of the university via non-traditional access routes came up in order to address social inequality in participation in higher education. The enormous social disparities in study opportunities (Wolter 2009, 2011) have often been the reason for compensatory strategies, and opening up access has always been one of these. But this approach considerably overestimated the structural and quantitative importance of this access route which was rather marginal (for some statistics see below). From the perspective of social equity, non-traditional access paths have always fulfilled merely the function of an individual valve – and not of a socially opening compensatory mechanism.

In the early 1990s a lively debate about the equivalence between general and vocational education arose because, at this time, the supply of apprenticeships on the market for vocational training was larger than the demand. The impression was widespread that vocational training was increasingly less attractive than general academic education. Opening up access for non-traditional students was considered to be a means for upgrading vocational training and making this option more attractive. But then from the mid-1990s the demand for apprenticeships by far exceeded the supply; and the political and economic interest in opening up access, in particular from the German employers' associations, declined considerably for some years. Since 2008 the supply–demand balance has changed a little because of demographically smaller age cohorts.

These various justifications and reasons for a broader non-traditional access route have co-existed for some decades, but until recently have led only to very modest organizational changes. Since the end of the 1990s three new lines of argument have evolved and created a new dynamic in the policy discourse about non-traditional students and lifelong learners in German higher education. This development has provoked a significant shift from a more individual to a definitely structural perspective. This includes, firstly, the introduction of the idea of lifelong learning as an element of the Bologna process; secondly, the greater importance of the concept of permeability between vocational and higher education as a part of the Copenhagen process (as well as a part of Bologna and the European Qualification Frame); and thirdly, the perception of a growing gap in the supply of a highly qualified workforce on the labour market.

Between the Bologna conference and declaration (1999) and the last follow-up conference in Leuven (2009), many additional action lines have been drawn up. Hence, in the meantime, lifelong learning has become a central part of the Bologna process, although a rather programmatic one. The original Bologna declaration mentioned the notion of lifelong learning peripherally at most. Two years later, the Prague communiqué (2001) introduced a new item on the Bologna agenda with the expression 'lifelong learning as an essential element of the European Higher Education Area', but still in a very vague way. The next step was the Berlin communiqué (2003), which specified the idea of lifelong learning in higher education as the 'recognition of prior learning' and more permeability of access to higher education with such expressions as a 'wide range of flexible learning paths' or 'lifelong learning paths into and within higher education'. Since Berlin, a fixed association exists between both these concepts – lifelong learning and recognition of prior learning.

This connection was reinforced by the following Bologna conferences from Bergen (2005) to Leuven (2009). The Leuven communiqué (2009) explicitly linked the notion of lifelong learning with the objective of widening participation. As a result, lifelong learning embraces mainly four elements in the context of Bologna (Banscherus 2010): (1) the recognition of prior learning, (2) the widening of non-traditional access routes, (3) the realization of flexible learning paths and course provisions such as part-time or distance studies, and (4) the creation of supporting systems such as counselling or financial support. It is true that the adoption of the idea of lifelong learning into the Bologna process seems to be very selective and does not comprise the full meaning of this concept – for example, continuing higher education opportunities have not been a central concern of the Bologna process up to now. Furthermore, lifelong learning has not really been a topic of high priority on the current national Bologna agendas. But it is fair to say that the issue of non-traditional students has experienced a strong tail wind through the Bologna process, at least in German higher education policy.

The issues of recognition and permeability have a more prominent place on the agenda of the parallel Copenhagen process in the field of vocational training and education. Bologna and Copenhagen converge in the particular issue of permeability between vocational training and higher education and in the targeted instruments for more permeability. The Copenhagen declaration (from November 2002) ascribed great importance to the topic of recognition of competences and qualifications, primarily in order to promote mobility between different countries, but also to increase permeability. Even more elaborately, the subsequent Maastricht communiqué (from December 2004) postulates that 'the parity of esteem and links between vocational education and training (VET) and general education, in particular with higher education, need to be fostered by innovative strategies and instruments'. The development of a European Qualifications Framework (EQF) for Lifelong Learning as well as the implementation of the European Credit Transfer System for VET (ECVET) are regarded as appropriate instruments for more transparency and permeability, including the transition from work to higher education and embracing the validation of non-formal and informal learning.

The basic idea substantiating the EQF and the corresponding National Qualification Frames is that the learning outcomes and individually available competencies (and not primarily the formal certificate) should be decisive for what will be acknowledged as the level of qualification. Although there is a wide programmatic consensus on these issues, there are differences in their national priority and in the ways these concepts have been implemented under specific national conditions. This idea introduces a mechanism of opening and permeability into highly regulated systems such as the German one based primarily on formal entitlements. In this frame of reference one of the most important experimental programmes in German educational policy, the so-called ANKOM programme (2006–2009), was placed exactly on the interface between vocational and further education on the one hand and higher education on the other. Even if only a few institutions (with selected courses) participated in the programme, it was the most ambitious project building bridges between vocational and higher education. The specific new approach of the programme was to concentrate on the recognition of competencies, acquired primarily through further education programmes, as equivalent with certain *study* requirements – and not with *access* requirements (Corradi *et al.* 2006; Stamm-Riemer *et al.* 2008, 2011).

The last but not least important impulse for the new concern about non-traditional students has its roots in the increasing fear of a growing lack of a highly qualified workforce, caused primarily by the demographic decline of the age cohorts entering the labour market and employment system in the future. Furthermore, the demographic development interferes with the continuous change in the qualification structure of the national labour force. This change consists of two secular trends that are linked with each other. The first trend is the relatively constant transformation of the economy from an industrial structure to a post-industrial, service-based society. This change has been accompanied by a shift in the internal structure of the tertiary sector from the primary to the secondary knowledge-based sector of the service sector. This change constitutes the empirical basis for speaking of a knowledge-based economy.

This change has had a clear impact on qualification requirements – the second trend, which Ulrich Teichler (1991) described as the trend 'towards a highly qualified society'. There has been a relatively continuous process of upgrading in the national labour force resulting in a substitution of low qualified work by human capital intensive work. The most obvious indicator for this process is the changing composition of employment. Whereas the proportion of employers with few if any qualifications has diminished by more than half during recent decades, the share of employees with a vocational training certificate has increased significantly, and the share of those with a higher education degree has already more than quadrupled. Recent projections of the future demand for the labour force (Bonin *et al.* 2007; Helmrich and Zika 2010) have shown that both these trends will probably continue over the next two decades. The demographic change creates a high replacement need for the rising number of retiring graduates, and the structural change creates an additional demand.

As a consequence of this, the proportion of highly skilled persons will continue to rise, although probably not with the same speed or scale as in the past. And this growing demand will be more and more confronted with a decline in the supply of graduates because of the demographic downturn. This prospect has elicited serious concern that the future need for graduates will exceed the supply leaving higher education institutions. There are three main strategies to close the predicted gap between the supply and demand of graduates. The first thought includes measures to increase participation by the regular way to university – that means in grammar school education. The second comprises measures to reduce the drop-out rate or – vice versa – to improve the success rate of students during their university careers. And the third strategy consists of initiatives to increase the permeability between vocational training and higher education and to widen non-traditional access routes. Therefore it can be observed that there is currently something of a coincidence between European policy to raise the permeability of access to university, and the predicted future development of the economic demand for a highly qualified workforce.

The current state of non-traditional access in German higher education

Against this backdrop, a political consensus has been reached between the state, trade unions and employers' associations, and also some stakeholders, in the area of higher education policy in order to widen access routes for new target groups, particularly for vocationally qualified adults. In March 2009, the Conference of the State Ministers of Education (KMK) agreed an arrangement supported by the federal government to coordinate the very inconsistent present state regulations and to increase the permeability of access to higher education for non-traditional students (KMK 2009). This decision was of great importance because it was the first time that the German *Länder* – with federal approval – agreed on such a far-reaching document. Currently, the *Länder* are faced with the implementation of this agreement into state law. All in all, the new agreement is a step in the right direction and may overcome the very disparate previous state regulations, but it is still restrictive in some respects.

According to this KMK decision, all those who have passed a formal further education course (at the level of a technician, a craftsman or industrial Masters) are given a general study entitlement – without an additional test or examination – for all institutions and programmes (except a very few with additional aptitude tests, such as arts), although this is limited by the widespread *numerus clausus*. Those who have completed regular initial vocational training and have worked on the job for at least three years can take a study entitlement for a particular subject or programme – on the condition that there is a substantial affinity between the profession learned previously and the chosen study programme or subject. However, this is exactly where there is a serious restriction: the spectrum of apprenticeship-based occupations and the diversity of courses and programmes in higher education do not fit together. Such a link between the former occupation and the desired course of study rules out the opportunity to correct early decisions on the choice of career at a later point.

There are no data available that tell us anything about the success of the still quite new regulations. The available data refer to the *status-quo* ante (based on the year 2008). According to these data (Autorengruppe Bildungsberichterstattung 2010: 291) the importance of non-traditional access routes has been very modest so far.

- About 95 per cent of all new entrants to the university sector had the general entrance entitlement, the *Abitur*, including those with an *Abitur* from one of the second educational route institutions (2.1 per cent). In the *Fachhochschulen* sector about 55 per cent had the *Abitur* and another 35 per cent came from one of the vocational schools described above (most from the *Fachoberschule*).
- Only 0.6 per cent of all new entrants in universities came via the third educational route, the core of non-traditional students in Germany. In the *Fachhochschulen* sector the proportion of the third educational route is a little greater (1.8 per cent). In both sectors together, not more than 1.1 per cent of first year students are non-traditional ones. At least, however, the proportion of non-traditional students has doubled since 1995. The proportion varies between the states, between institutions and also between subjects. Some *Länder* (e.g. Lower Saxony), institutions (e.g. the Distance University in Hagen) and subjects (e.g. economics, education, social sciences) show a larger share.

Conclusions

Compared with the situation ten years ago, there has been some significant progress in terms of policies, legal regulations and, to a limited extent, in institutional practice concerning access for non-traditional students. Most of the political stakeholders agree at least thetorically with the strategy to implement lifelong learning structures in higher education. However, it seems that the general political insight into the necessity of an open access policy has made more progress than, in particular, the acceptance by and the implementation activities of most of the higher education institutions. This discrepancy has resulted in the still very low level of participation. It is fair to say that the structure of access in German higher education continues to be very *Abitur*-centred, and non-traditional access routes have played only a very marginal role up to now.

There are various reasons for this: the non-transparent and not really flexible admission procedures, the pronounced conservatism of universities because of their concern about increasing capacity bottlenecks and about individual deficits in the study proficiency of non-traditional applicants, and the considerable lack of flexible study structures. The prevailing mode of full-time and on-site studies and the lack of dual courses with work and study in parallel indicate a general deficit in institutional and curricular flexibility. This lack of flexibility in the organization of studies is one of the main obstacles for the participation of non-traditional students in German higher education. Despite some measures to open up access and admission carried out in recent years, it is fair to emphasize that studies are not very conducive to the specific needs of students with a non-traditional biography. To put it another way, these deficits and difficulties illustrate the two most important action strategies for increasing the proportion of non-traditional students: more flexible admission procedures (including recognition) and more flexible study provision (including supportive measures such as counselling).

But it is realistic to expect that in the near future the institutional obstacles, the interest-based political resistance of some stakeholders, and the scepticism and hesitation particularly on the part of the universities will not disappear. Even further in the future, institutional interest in procedures of opening up will be limited because of the concern over maintaining academic excellence. The resistance of the grammar school contingent against widened access opportunities in addition to the *Abitur* will continue (with the argument of study skills). The competition between vocational training and higher education for new recruits will probably grow because the long-term need for a more highly qualified labour force will increase. Therefore, in future the qualitative relevance of non-traditional access routes in German higher education may also be higher than their quantitative importance.

References

Autorengruppe Bildungsberichterstattung (2010) *Bildung in Deutschland 2010* (Education in Germany 2010), Bielefeld: Bertelsmann.

Baethge, M. (2007) 'Das deutsche Bildungs-Schisma: Welche Probleme ein vorindustrielles Bildungssystem in einer nachindustriellen Gesellschaft hat?' (The German Educational Schism), in D. Lemmermöhle and M. Hasselhorn (eds) *Bildung – Lernen*, Göttingen: Wallstein.

Banscherus, U. (2010) 'Lebenslanges Lernen im Bologna-Prozess' (Lifelong Learning in the Bologna Process), in A. Wolter, G. Wiesner and C. Koepernik (eds) *Der lernende Mensch in der Wissensgesellschaft*, München: Juventa.

Bonin, H., Schneider, M., Qunike, H. and Arens (2007) *Zukunft von Bildung und Arbeit. Perspektiven von Arbeitskräftebedarf und -angebot bis 2020* (The Future of Education and Work), Bonn: Bundesministerium für Bildung und Forschung.

Corradi, C., Evans, N. and Valk, A. (eds) (2006) *Recognising Experiential Learning. Practices in European Universities*, Tartu: University Press.

Helmrich, R. and Zika, G. (eds) (2010) *Beruf und Qualifikation in der Zukunft* (The Future of Profession and Qualification), Bielefeld: Bertelsmann.

Isserstedt, W., Middendorff, E., Kandulla, M., Borchert, L. and Leszczensky, M. (2010) *Die wirtschaftliche und soziale Lage der Studierenden in der Bundesrepublik Deutschland 2009* (The Economic and Social Situation of Students in Germany 2010), Bonn/Berlin: Bundesministerium für Bildung und Forschung.

Kasworm, C.E. (1993) 'Adult higher education from an international perspective', *Higher Education*, 25: 411–423.

Kehm, B. and Lanzendorf, U. (2005) 'Ein neues Governance-Regime für die Hochschulen – mehr Markt und weniger Selbststeuerung?' (A New

Governance Regime for Higher Education) in U. Teichler and R. Tippelt (eds) *Hochschullandschaft im Wandel*, Zeitschrift für Pädagogik, 50: 41–56. Beiheft.

Kehm, B. and Pasternack, P. (2009) 'The German "Excellence Initiative" and its role in restructuring the national higher education landscape', in D. Palfreyman and T. Tapper (eds) *Structuring Mass Higher Education. The Role of Elite Institutions*, London: Routledge.

KMK, Kultusministerkonferenz (2009) *Hochschulzugang für beruflich qualifizierte Bewerber ohne schulische Hochschulzugangsberechtigung* (Access to Higher Education for Vocationally Qualified People), Beschluss der Kultusministerkonferenz vom 06.03.2009.

KMK, Kultusministerkonferenz (2010) *Synoptische Darstellung der in den Ländern bestehenden Möglichkeiten des Hochschulzugangs für beruflich qualifizierte Bewerber ohne schulische Hochschulzugangsberechtigung auf der Grundlage hochschulrechtlicher Regelungen* (Overview about the Regulations for the Admission of Vocationally Qualified People to Higher Education in the German States), Stand Juli 2010.

Nickel, S. and Leusing, B. (2009) *Studieren ohne Abitur: Entwicklungspotenziale in Bund und Ländern* (Studying without *Abitur*), Gütersloh: Centrum für Hochschulentwicklung.

OECD (1987) *Adults in Higher Education*, Paris: OECD.

Schimank, U. and Lange, S. (2009) 'Germany: a latecomer to new public management', in C. Paradeise, E. Reale, I. Bleiklie and E. Ferlie (eds) *University Governance. Western Europe Comparative Perspectives*, Heidelberg: Springer.

Schuetze, H.G. and Slowey, M. (eds) (2000) *Higher Education and Lifelong Learners. International Perspectives on Change*, London: Routledge.

Schuetze, H.G. and Slowey, M. (2002) 'Participation and exclusion: a comparative analysis of non-traditional students and lifelong learners in higher education', *Higher Education*, 44: 309–327.

Stamm-Riemer, I., Loroff, C. and Hartmann, E.(eds) (2011) *Anrechnungsmodelle. Generalisierte Ergebnisse der ANKOM-Initiative* (Models of Recognition), Hannover: Hochschul-Informations-System.

Stamm-Riemer, I., Loroff, C., Minks, K.-H. and Freitag (eds) (2008) *Die Entwicklung von Anrechnungsmodellen. Zu Äquivalenzpotenzialen von beruflicher und hochschulischer Bildung* (The Development of Recognition Models), Hannover: Hochschul-Informations-System.

Teichler, U. (1991) 'Towards a highly educated society', *Higher Education Policy*, 4 (4): 11–20.

Teichler, U. (2005) *Hochschulsysteme und Hochschulpolitik. Quantitative und strukturelle Dynamiken, Differenzierungen und der Bologna-Prozess* (Higher Education Systems and Policy), Münster: Waxmann.

Teichler, U. (2008) *Der Jargon der Nützlichkeit. Zur Employability-Diskussion im Bologna-Prozess* (The Jargon of Utilitarism: The Employability Debate in the Bologna Process), Das Hochschulwesen, 56 (3): 68–79.

Teichler, U. (2009) 'Between over-diversification and over-homogenization: five decades of search for a creative fabric of higher education', in B. Kehm and B. Stensaker (eds) *University Rankings, Diversity, and the New Landscape of Higher Education*, Rotterdam: Sense Publishers.

Teichler, U. and Wolter, A. (2004) *Zugangswege und Studienangebote für nicht-traditionelle Studierende* (Access Routes and Study Provisions for Non-traditional Students), Die Hochschule, 13(2): 64–80.
Wolter, A. (1990) 'Die symbolische Macht des *Abiturs*' (The Symbolic Significance of the *Abitur*), in N. Kluge *et al.* (eds) *Vom Lehrling zum Akademiker – Neue Wege des Hochschulzugangs für berufserfahrene Erwachsene*, Oldenburg: BIS.
Wolter, A. (2000) 'Non-traditional students in German higher education – situation, profiles, policies and perspectives', in H.G. Schuetze and M. Slowey (eds) *Higher Education and Lifelong Learners. International Perspectives on Change*, London: Routledge.
Wolter, A. (2004) 'From state control to competition. German higher education transformed', *The Canadian Journal of Higher Education*, 34 (3): 73–104.
Wolter, A. (2007a) 'From the academic republic to the managerial university. The implementation of new governance structures in German higher education', in University of Tsukuba (ed.) *Reforms of Higher Education in Six Countries. Commonalities and Differences*, Tokyo: University of Tsukuba.
Wolter, A. (2007b) 'Diversifizierung des Weiterbildungsmarktes und Nachfrage nach akademischer Weiterbildung in Deutschland' (The Diversification of the Market for Continuing Education and the Social Demand for Continuing Higher Education in Germany), *Österreichische Zeitschrift für Hochschulentwicklung*, 2 (1): 14–29.
Wolter, A. (2009) 'Expanding graduate employment and mobilizing social demand for higher education: recent developments and policy debates in Germany', *Journal of Adult and Continuing Education*, 15(2): 187–203.
Wolter, A. (2010) 'Zur Durchlässigkeit zwischen beruflicher Bildung und Hochschule' (About Permeability between Vocational Training and Higher Education), in K. Birkelbach, A. Bolder and K. Düsseldorf (eds) *Berufliche Bildung in Zeiten des Wandels*, Hohengehren: Schneider.
Wolter, A. (2011) 'Hochschulzugang und soziale Ungleichheit in Deutschland' (Access to Higher Education and Social Inequality in Germany), in Heinrich-Böll-Stiftung (ed.) *Öffnung der Hochschule – Chancengerechtigkeit, Diversität, Integration*, Berlin: Heinrich-Böll-Stiftung.

Chapter 4

Ireland

Lifelong learning and higher education in Ireland: turbulent times

Maria Slowey

Introduction

In the middle of the 19th century, John Henry Newman was assigned the task of securing university education in Ireland for the Catholic population. It is true that his specific mission was not an immediate success – partly because it seems his skills did not lie in organization and administration, partly because he was regarded with a degree of suspicion by some of the Irish bishops (he was not only English, but he was also a convert) and partly because of the inadequate scale of the middle-class (male) Catholic population from which students would be drawn. It did, however, provide him with the opportunity to elaborate his vision of the role of the university. Newman's 'Nine discourses delivered to the Catholics of Dublin' and 'Occasional lectures and essays addressed to the members of the Catholic university' were subsequently brought together and published in full in 1873 as *The Idea of a University: Defined and Illustrated* (Newman 1913).

At the heart of Newman's vision was a view of the university as

> a place where enquiry is pushed forward and discoveries perfected and verified, and rashness rendered innocuous and error exposed by the collision of mind with mind and knowledge with knowledge.
>
> (Newman 1913)

In line with international trends, since the 1970s higher education policy in Ireland has been dominated by a broad aim to increase levels of participation within a diversified 'system' of mass higher education. In this context, wider debate about the distinctive nature of the educational and intellectual purposes of higher education tended to take second place. Around a century and a half after Newman, the chapter on Ireland in our previous book (Schuetze and Slowey 2000) could point to remarkable growth with a participation rate of around 50 per cent and more third level entry places per capita than most OECD countries (Collins 2000). Participation rates continued to increase so that by 2010 the number of new entrants to higher education was ten times that of the 1960s – an estimated 65% of the relevant age cohort (Hyland 2011).

But what about the 'vision' for higher education? To what extent was Newman's image of the university as a place for the dynamic and creative engagement of 'mind and mind' and 'knowledge with knowledge' visible in such a totally different social and economic environment? Coinciding with the end of a roller coaster 'boom to bust' decade in Spring 2011 – just a few months after the arrival in Ireland of the International Monetary Fund and the European Central Bank on an international mission to 'bail out' the Irish economy – a Strategy Group established by the Government published (after some delay) its report *National Strategy for Higher Education to 2030* (hereafter the National Strategy for Higher Education) (DES 2011a).

The language of this report reflected the dominant global policy discourse of the early 21st century, with a primary focus on higher education's role in relation to the knowledge economy and knowledge society.

> Higher education is the key to economic recovery in the short-term and to longer-term prosperity. Our economy depends on – and will continue to depend on – knowledge and its application in products, processes and services that are exported.
>
> (DES 2011a: 29)

Within this context, the concept of *lifelong learning* was indeed prominent, with no less than a dozen references scattered throughout the report. Although not formally defined, in the main, lifelong learning tended to be linked to the upskilling agenda and related policy strategies aimed at encouraging more flexible and responsive forms of higher education provision.

> ... the period of this strategy demands that Ireland's higher education system become much more flexible in provision in both time and place, and that it facilitates transfer and progression through all levels of the system. There remain significant challenges in this area: successive reports have recognized the relatively poor performance of our system in the area of lifelong learning, while the requirement for upgrading and changing of employee skills and competencies is becoming ever greater. Changes to system funding and operation will be needed in order to enable the institutions to respond to these needs by increasing the variety and diversity of their provision and improvements in the interface between higher education and further education and training will be necessary to support enhanced progression opportunities.
>
> (DES 2011a: 13)

Few of the underlying notions – flexibility of time and place, transfer and progression, equity of funding for different modes of study and the like – were new. They were, in fact, long familiar in work on higher education and lifelong learning – as explored, for example, in our 2000 volume (Schuetze and Slowey 2000). The national environment, however, had been transformed dramatically by the collapse of the financial system and the consequent economic shock waves. It is in this context, therefore, that this chapter explores the experience of one small state in relation to lifelong learning, with particular reference to issues of equity and access for adult learners to higher education. The chapter is structured in four parts. The first locates higher education policy in Ireland within the broader socio-economic environment. The second outlines general patterns of participation in higher education. The third explores two particular dimensions of lifelong learning in higher education in Ireland. The final part points to some fundamental educational challenges which the transformation to a genuinely lifelong learning approach would pose for the system.

Shifting sands

While a ten-year period from 2000 to 2010 is too short a phase in which to make causal inferences, it is a reasonable period over which broad trends can be identified. In considering developments in relation to higher education in Ireland, the first decade of this millennium coincided with a period of such significant economic upheaval – from modest growth, to unsustainable boom, to sudden and dramatic collapse of the national economy – that it provides the dominant backdrop for consideration of issues around lifelong learning in higher education in Ireland.

There were many indicators of the transformation of Ireland over this period, but perhaps the most culturally and socially symbolic was the socio-demographic change associated with migration patterns. At the start of the decade, Ireland was, as it traditionally had been, a country of net emigration, driven largely by the lack of employment opportunities. By the middle of the decade, however, as the economy and associated work opportunities boomed, Ireland was transformed into a country of net immigration – including Irish citizens returning and the 'new Irish' from different parts of the world, and, in particular, from the new accession states to the EU. The figures are striking: in 1990 official figures show that 23,000 more people emigrated than immigrated; by 2000 this trend was totally reversed so that 25,000 more people immigrated than emigrated, reaching a peak in 2006 with net migration into Ireland of around 72,000 people (Munck 2011). From 2009, however, the balance was swinging back with around 8,000 more people leaving Ireland than entering (ibid.). This reversal had resulted, by the end of the decade, in tragic consequences for many individuals, and communities and jobs were lost at an astonishing speed. Figure 4.1 illustrates the context in which public policy, including that relating to higher education, was perilously located. While for most of the decade government balances were comfortably above GDP, from 2007, the public finances started to decline rapidly.

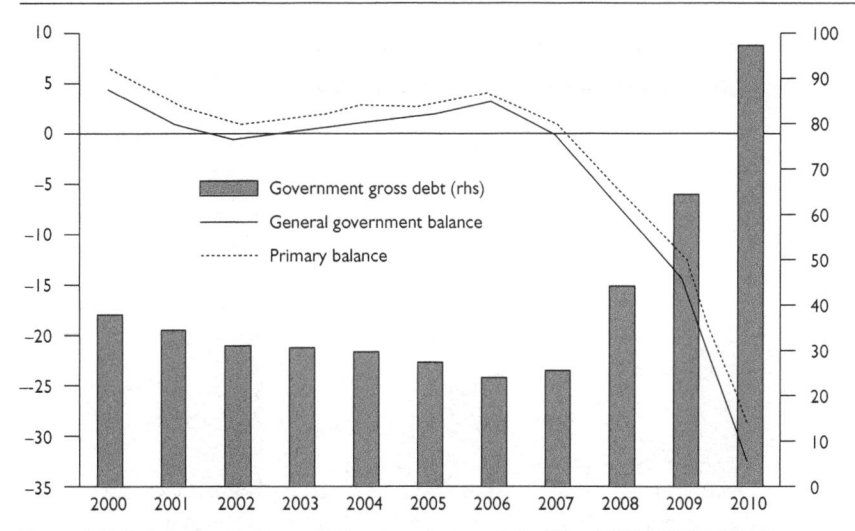

Figure 4.1 General government balance and gross debt (% of GDP) 2000–2010
Source: European Commission (2011, Figure 17).

So by 2010, Ireland was, to public dismay, once again a country of net emigration. The official level of unemployment, in the region of 14 per cent, would have been higher had not a new generation of people left the country in search of work elsewhere. While all social groups were affected, as Figure 4.2 shows, those with the lowest level of qualifications – inevitably those from poor and working-class backgrounds – were hit the hardest.

This is not the place to go into the complex, contested, explanations of the factors underpinning a decade of such dramatically shifting sands. Undoubtedly, however, the significant growth of inward foreign direct investment over the previous decade had a profound effect on the economic and employment structure of Ireland. While transnational regulation was important, even in a globalized environment, national strategies also had significant impact in terms of 'constructing the specific balance between the global-led, local-led, and nationally mediated modes of integration into the global economy' (O'Riain 2000: 187). O'Riain made the case that a period of growth enjoyed by Ireland in the 1990s was associated with the emergence of what he termed the Flexible Developmental State (FDS).

In practice, as subsequent critiques highlighted, in certain crucial areas, in particular the financial and planning sectors, 'flexible' became translated into 'light touch' which, in effect, became 'no regulation', with, as will be discussed further below, far-reaching consequences for education and social policy. In a passionate account of the collapse of the Irish economy, the Deputy Editor of the *Irish Times* argued in his book *Ship of Fools* that the key underpinning factor in the causal link lay in a political culture which created a 'lethal cocktail' of lack of regulation of banking coupled with a spiralling property development sector (O'Toole 2009).

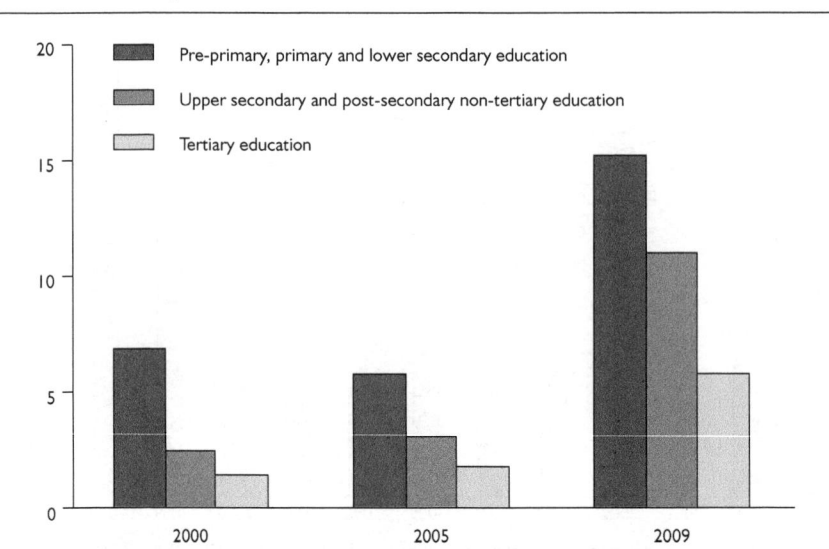

Figure 4.2 Unemployment rate by level of education (2000–2009)
Source: adapted from European Commission (2011, Figure 37).

If state intervention in the regulation of aspects of the management of the economy and environment was weak, engagement by the state in shaping higher education became if anything stronger. Partly, as in other parts of Europe, this was through the promulgation of educational initiatives such as the Bologna Process (Neave 2004). But most significantly, it was through the step change increase in research funding made available on a competitive bidding basis by Science Foundation Ireland (SFI) and the Higher Education Authority (HEA) Programme for Research in Third Level Education (PRTLI). An analysis of the resistance by Irish academics to the intrusion of the 'evaluative state' suggests that, paradoxically, it was the state's first major attempt to address the lack of investment in research infrastructure over decades that fundamentally altered the relations between the state and the universities (the relationship between the state and other parts of the higher education system, such as the institutes of technology, was structurally different) (Clancy 2007a). This new research funding environment, Clancy argues, 'heralded the introduction of unbridled market principles into the steering of higher education and represented government's most serious attempt to exert control over the internal workings of the university' (Clancy 2007a: 116).

Higher education in Ireland

It is within this rapidly changing socio-political and economic context that discussion of the issues of lifelong learning and equity in higher education in recent times needs to be located. Over the period in question the fundamental structure of the system did not change greatly. The Higher

Education Act of 1997 had set in place the constitutional arrangements for the seven universities – Trinity College (Dublin University), the four constituent colleges of the National University of Ireland (the University Colleges of Dublin, Cork, Galway and Maynooth) and two new universities (Dublin City and Limerick). In addition, the system comprised Ireland's largest tertiary institution of higher education in terms of student numbers (Dublin Institute of Technology), 15 institutes of technology (IoTs) as well as a number of specialist colleges (including Colleges of Education which remained autonomous, although linked to various universities for validation purposes). In 2006, the Institutes of Technology Act transferred responsibility for oversight of the funding of this sector to the HEA. There was also a small, but growing, private higher education sector.

Higher education in Ireland sees itself as being engaged actively with the Bologna Process: it is one of the first countries to be 'compliant' with Bologna, and was the first country to request the European Universities Association (EUA) to undertake an expert sectoral review of the seven universities (HEA 2005a). A National Framework of Qualifications (NFQ) was established with the aim of ultimately mapping all education and training qualifications on a 1 to 10 spectrum from basic literacy and numeracy through to doctoral level. The Framework was speedily implemented in the institute of technology sector and was verified as compatible with Bologna in 2006. It took some time for the universities to engage, partly because of debates about the appropriateness of a learning outcomes approach for higher education. However, towards the end of the decade all major university awards had also been mapped on to the National Framework (IUQB 2007). In terms of quality assurance, again there was evolution in the system as a number of separate bodies were established to deal with different aspects of quality. Following a governmental decree, implemented with some haste because of the financial crisis, to reduce the number of 'quangos' (quasi-autonomous non-governmental organizations), at the end of 2010 the Irish Universities Quality Board was set to become part of a new body – Qualifications and Quality Assurance Ireland – formed from a merger with the National Qualifications Authority of Ireland, and the Higher and Further Education and Training Councils.

While the *structure* of the system remained largely unchanged over the decade, in terms of *teaching* and *research* the system altered in three important respects. Firstly, despite demographic changes and falling numbers of school leavers, the steady growth in student numbers continued in the early part of the decade: overall enrolment increased by 17 per cent between 2000/2001 and 2004/2005; and undergraduate enrolment increased by 7 per cent (HEA 2006). Secondly, there was a significant change in the relative balance between undergraduate and postgraduate students, with disproportionate increases in the numbers of students on postgraduate programmes. To take one striking example, between 2006/2007 and 2007/2008 full-time postgraduate enrolments in the institute of technology sector increased by 43 per cent, while numbers on undergraduate programmes declined by nearly 10 per cent over the previous five years (HEA 2009a). Thirdly, as mentioned above, there was a sea change in the level of investment in research, in particular, in the STEM subjects (science, technology, engineering and mathematics).

Speaking at a seminar on the *Delivery of the Strategy for Higher Education* at the Royal Irish Academy in May 2011, the achievements of the Irish system were highlighted by the Minister of Education and Skills, Ruairi Quinn. In relation to participation, he referred to a study carried out by the Economic and Financial Ministers of the EC which

> attests to the ability of our higher education system to maintain high levels of participation and quality through difficult circumstances. In that study we were ranked first both in terms of graduates per 1,000 inhabitants and in terms of how international employers rate our graduates.
>
> (DES 2011b: 1)

In relation to research output, Ireland's performance had progressed in leaps and bounds – described by the Minister in his speech as 'meteoric' – and was now 'ranked within the top 20 nations in the world across all research fields, and Irish research institutions feature within the top 1 per cent in the world in 18 key fields' (DES 2011b: 3). As discussed above, a complex 'steering' model of research investment was used to achieve this outcome. Competitive proposals were subject to international peer scrutiny, with a strong emphasis on collaboration between researchers across different institutions (and with relevant industrial partners). Even allowing for Ireland's advantage in being English speaking, and the profile of its ancient university, Trinity College Dublin (dating from 1592), the higher education system clearly performed well on a comparative basis. As the Minister pointed out, notwithstanding

> reservations about the crudeness of international rankings, it is also very significant that eight Irish institutions feature in the top 500 in global rankings out of more than 15,000 universities worldwide. Per capita, Ireland has the 8th highest number of high-ranking institutions and we are ahead of the UK and the US (on a per capita basis) on this metric.
>
> (DES 2011b: 2)

This level of output had been achieved despite historically relatively low levels of investment: thus, for example, investment per student enrolment in Trinity College Dublin (Ireland's highest ranked university internationally) was less than a sixth that of universities in the USA with comparable outputs (Hazelkorn 2011).

The decade 2000–2010, as Table 4.1 shows, was a period of sustained growth in participation in universities in Ireland. Women students continued to constitute the majority of new entrants (around 59 per cent) although the gendered division of knowledge highlighted in the 2000 analysis remained largely unchanged (Collins 2000). Part-time students (a proxy for an access dimension of lifelong learning) constituted around 10 per cent of undergraduate enrolments. As discussed further below, a strong policy steer – reinforced by several international reviews over this period – recommended an increase in both the numbers *and* the proportion of part-time students. However, after a period of modest growth to 2004, part-time undergraduate numbers in fact started to decline, with a substantial (18 per cent) drop between the academic years 2008/09 and 2009/10, and an overall reduction in the proportion of undergraduates defined as part-time over the period 2000 to 2009. Some of this variation may reflect statistical blips arising from the introduction of a new statistical methodology. However, a more likely explanation lay in the level of fees charged for part-time study, making it a relatively unattractive option.

This period also saw sustained growth in postgraduate enrolments in Irish universities: the relative proportion studying on a part-time basis increased from 30.3 per cent of new entrants in 2003/4 to 34.5 per cent in 2009/2010. The overall growth in postgraduate numbers reflected both increasing demand, and a National Development Plan which – in seeking to position Ireland as a leading knowledge economy – reaffirmed an objective to double the number of doctoral students in the system (Department of Enterprise, Trade and Employment 2006). The Irish Universities Association and other bodies worked together around the notion of 'Fourth Level Ireland' which sought to increase both the quantity and quality of doctoral education (IUA 2005).

The patterns in the other part of the binary system, the institute of technology sector, reflect some slightly different trends (Table 4.2). Providing shorter cycle, more vocationally orientated programmes, the institutes were widely regarded as having contributed to Ireland's attractiveness for inward investment. However, demographic trends, increased competition from the university sector, combined with (for some years) booming employment opportunities, resulted in a significant decrease in part-time enrolments in this sector.

The factors which shaped higher education in Ireland over this period were common to most economically developed countries. An analysis of five major policy documents published over a short period (2009–2011) in Ireland, England, Scotland, Wales and Northern Ireland (the 'North Atlantic Isles') identified six generic global drivers, mediated by national and regional cultural, historical and economic conditions: the move to mass higher education; widening participation and increasing social inclusion; internationalization; the knowledge society; neoliberalism and 'cost sharing'; and fiscal pressures (Scott 2011). These drivers, which provide the context for considerations of lifelong learning, equity and access, reflect, of course, a transformed world from that in which Newman was developing his vision.

Table 4.1 Enrolment trends in universities in Ireland by mode and level of study (2000–2009)

	2000/1	2001/2	2002/3	2003/4	2004/5	2005/6	2006/7	2007/8	2008/9	2009/10
Undergraduate										
Full-time	60,013	61,804	63,209	64,531	65,300	66,834	68,039	70,064	73,089	76,956
Part-time	5,831	7,148	7,504	7,204	9,727	8,742	8,506	8,016	7,535	6,176
Total undergraduate enrolment	65,844	68,952	70,713	71,735	75,027	75,576	76,545	74,480	80,633	83,132
Postgraduate										
Full-time	11,226	12,536	14,078	15,350	15,339	15,688	16,224	16,569	18,128	19,480
Part-time	5,992	6,795	7,338	6,689	6,977	7,573	7,950	8,502	9,138	10,272
Total postgraduate enrolment	7,218	19,331	21,416	22,039	22,316	23,261	24,174	25,071	27,266	29,752
Overall enrolment	83,062	88,283	92,129	93,774	97,343	98,837	100,719	103,551	107,899	112,884

Note: Enrolments in the category 'undergraduate' in the university sector are on honours degree courses ranked Level 8 or above on the National Framework of Qualifications.

Source: adapted from HEA (2006: Table 1.1) and HEA (2010a: Table 1.2).

Table 4.2 Enrolment trends in institutes of technology (IoTs) in Ireland by mode and level of study (2003–2009)

	2003/4	2004/5	2005/6	2006/7	2007/8	2008/9	2009/10	% change 08/09–09/10
Undergraduate								
Full-time	51,798	50,424	51,517	51,322	49,048	51,892	56,893	9.6%
Part-time	16,088	14,088	13,228	–	12,997	12,921	12,921	0.0%
Total undergraduate enrolment	67,886	64,512	64,745	51,322	62,045	64,813	69,814	7.7%
Postgraduate								
Full-time	1,194	1,235	1,325	1,565	2,238	2,572	2,939	14.3%
Part-time	1,125	982	1,316	–	2,471	2,104	2,529	20.2%
Total postgraduate enrolment	2,319	2,217	2,614	1,565	4,709	4,676	5,468	16.9%
Overall enrolment	70,205	66,729	67,386	52,887	66,754	69,489	75,282	8.3%

Note: about 55% (2009/2010) of enrolments in the category 'undergraduate' in the IoT sector are on certificate, diploma, ordinary degree courses ranked Level 7 or below on the Irish National Qualifications Framework, with the balance on Level 8 honours degrees.

Source: adapted from HEA (2006: Table 1.2) and HEA (2010a: Table 1.3). Figures prior to 2003 not available in this form.

Interpretations of lifelong learning in higher education in Ireland

As discussed above, the rhetoric of lifelong learning featured prominently in Irish policy discourse – particularly in the *National Strategy for Higher Education 2030*. As discussed in Chapter 1, competing interpretations of lifelong learning reflect tensions evident in, for example, the impetus for the European Year of Lifelong Learning (1996) between, on the one hand a narrow skills agenda, and on the other, a broader vision of 'learning to foster a democratic, informed and participative society' (Watson and Taylor 1998: 21). These tensions not only continue, but are exacerbated by the global economic crisis. Common ground can, however, be found.

To take one concrete example: the idea of awarding recognition for prior learning (RPL) is particularly interesting as the arguments in favour straddle both the skills *and* the democratizing agendas. Thus in Ireland, RPL is promoted both by *Aontas* (the national adult education association, with a strong involvement from community based adult education groups) and by *Forfas* (the national skills development agency). While not in widespread use in higher education, pilot work is in progress through initiatives such as an Education in Employment Project on RPL, a university sector Framework Implementation Network (FIN) and a Roadmap for Employment–Academic Partnerships (REAP).

In 2005, the Department of Enterprise, Trade and Employment commissioned a report to underpin the development of a National Skills Strategy. The subsequent report presented a view of the skills required for the labour market over the period to 2020, with the aim of positioning Ireland as a knowledge-based economy (Expert Group on Future Skills Needs 2007). This report set out highly specific targets, including the objective that 48 per cent of the labour force should achieve NFQ (National Framework of Qualifications) Levels 6 to 10 (from National Certificate to PhD). In order to achieve this objective, an additional 500,000 individuals within the labour market (employed and unemployed) would need to progress by at 'least one level' on the NFQ. This would be achieved partly by additional participation in colleges, institutes of technology and universities, but also partly through recognition of non-formal and non-certificated learning. As highlighted in a subsequent report from the Expert Group on Future Skills Needs:

> The growing emphasis on lifelong learning and upskilling in Ireland and internationally has given increased prominence to the potential of Recognition of Prior Learning (RPL) as a mechanism that can contribute to a range of social and economic goals. Over the past decade, education and training policy has increasingly recognized that learning and its resulting value is a 'whole-of-life' experience that encompasses formal, non-formal and informal learning as well as experiential learning.
>
> (Expert Group on Future Skills Needs 2011: 14–15)

While there is no denying the dominance of the skills conception of lifelong learning in higher education in Ireland as in most other European countries (Davies and Feutrie 2008), several other interpretations of lifelong learning are also evident. Two themes of particular interest are selected here for more detailed consideration. Theme one: lifelong learning associated with equity and widening access; and theme two: lifelong learning associated with innovative modes of study.

Theme one: lifelong learning, equity, and widening access

In 2008, the National Office of Equity and Access of the Higher Education Authority published a *National Plan for Equality of Access to Higher Education 2008–2013* (hereafter, the National Plan for Access) (HEA 2008). The preparation of the document involved consultation with a wide range of interested parties, and built on several previous national reports. The National Plan for Access pointed out that the objective of promoting access to higher education had a 'long history in Irish education policy'. Since the early 1970s, 'promoting the attainment of equality of opportunity in higher education was included among the core functions of the Higher Education Authority, when it was established in 1971' (HEA 2008: 108).

The National Plan for Access included ambitious objectives and targets, which, it was claimed, represented 'the strategic consensus on Irish higher education access policy at this time' (ibid.: 10).

> We have now reached a point in our national educational development where the achievement of further growth in higher education will require continuing progress in relation to widening access. This means that the achievement of our national objectives in relation to upskilling the population will require further success in extending higher education opportunities to groups that have traditionally been under-represented in higher education. This fact, that our economic sustainability is increasingly dependent on the learning achievements and skills of all citizens, is a very concrete illustration of the interdependence of our national social and economic objectives.
>
> (HEA 2008: 10)

Lifelong learning featured second of five 'high-level goals' identified in the National Plan for Access:

1 Institution-wide approaches to access
2 Enhancing access through lifelong learning
3 Investment in widening participation in higher education
4 Modernization of student supports
5 Widening participation in higher education for people with disabilities.

Each of these goals was elaborated through specific objectives and supporting actions. In the case of lifelong learning, the overarching objectives pointed to the way in which this complex concept was to be operationalized in practical policy terms in the National Plan for Access. The lifelong learning objectives focused on three main areas: (a) the development of a broader range of entry routes; (b) a significant expansion of part-time/flexible courses; and (c) measures to address the student support implications of lifelong learning. From this policy perspective, lifelong learning was thus seen as an integral dimension of a widening access strategy: offering opportunities for non-traditional learners (of all ages).

Throughout the decade, national policy sought to encourage the development of institutional and collaborative initiatives aimed at reaching out to schools catering for students from socio-economically disadvantaged sections of the population, as well as other initiatives aimed at target groups such as travellers, new immigrants, learners with disabilities and mature students. The omission of a focus on gender inequality, however, was striking although not surprising as women represented a majority of students in higher education over the decade. Where gender equality was raised, the focus tended to be on 'the problem for boys' education' despite the continuing gendered nature of participation across disciplines and significant differences in relation to academic staff – a point taken up by an EUA peer review team review of the sector which indicated that they

> would like to draw attention of the universities to the gender composition of their staff, especially at senior levels. Only a small minority of universities mentioned this as an issue during the review process, although it appears to be emerging as a system-wide policy issue.
>
> (HEA 2005a: 23)

The National Strategy for Access sought to encourage widening access through two broad mechanisms: individual and institutional. The former approach targeted financial and other supports at individual learners in designated groups, while the latter provided incentives for institutions to develop a range of outreach initiatives and post-entry academic and personal support for non-traditional learners. Thus, for example, means tested maintenance grants for full-time students formed a key element of national policy – providing support for approximately 36 per cent of full-time students in higher education. At an institutional level, through Targeted Initiatives and a Strategic Innovation Fund, the Higher Education Authority supported the development of access programmes and a creative range of pre- and post-entry activities, including outreach to schools in areas of multiple disadvantage, adult learning organizations, community groups and the like.

Most institutions also put in place educational guidance experts to work with adults who were considering entering higher education as mature

Table 4.3 Age distribution of full-time new entrants to universities and institutes of technology in Ireland (% of total 2009–2010)

	Universities	Institutes of technology
17 and under	6.8	6.7
18	39.3	31.6
19	32.9	27.6
20	6.1	8.9
21	2.4	4.0
22	1.3	2.4
23	0.9	1.5
24	1.6	2.4
25–29	4.1	6.2
30 and over	4.6	8.9
Total	21,906	18,910

Source: adapted from HEA (2010a, Tables 6.5 and 6.6).

students. As had been noted in our 2000 volume and in several international reviews, the Irish higher education system was characterized by 'very young undergraduates' with, in 2003, around 84 per cent of entrants to full-time undergraduate programmes aged 19 or under and students still from 'largely "standard" backgrounds' (HEA 2005b: 13, 23). By the end of the decade, the picture had become rather more complex. In Ireland, the formal definition of mature students relates to those aged 23 or over on entry. In academic terms, this means individuals can seek admission with a range of alternative qualifications (access certificates, portfolios and the like) to those required of school leavers – which are based on Leaving Certificate points, with disciplines in high demand being subject to a highly competitive 'points race'. As the figures in Table 4.3 indicate, not only did mature students represent a small proportion of all new entrants in 2009, but they were also grouped in the younger end of the age continuum – both in the universities (less than 5 per cent of new entrants were over 30 years of age) and institutes of technology (less than 10 per cent). In terms of performance, a national study of progression to the next year of study found that mature students were 'substantially' more likely to remain on their course than younger students on Level 6 and 7 programmes, with little or no marked difference between the age groups on Level 8 courses (HEA 2010b: 37).

So, if little substantial progress can be discerned in relation to access by adult students to full-time study, what about outcomes for other target groups? Given the fact that educational inequalities are deeply rooted in broader socio-economic inequalities, and the associated difficulty of demonstrating cause and effect in such a complex area, it is only possible to look at indirect and/

or qualitative indicators of outcomes. One approach is to examine the impact at the *meso* level of a particular institution. In 2011, Dublin City University celebrated 21 years of a pioneering initiative aimed at increasing participation in higher education from Ballymun, one of the most disadvantaged areas of Dublin. The entry qualifications of such students differed from the entry profile of the majority of students in terms of grades in the Leaving Certificate; however, an evaluation of outcomes over 21 years,showed that Access students were not only as likely to complete their programmes as other students, but a comparison of their final degree performance showed a similar spread of grades to the 'standard' cohort (DCU 2011).

A second approach to identifying impact is at the *macro* level of the system. Since 1980, the HEA has undertaken five national studies of the socio-economic background of new entrants to higher education (most recently, O'Connell *et al.* 2006). In 2007, Clancy, the researcher responsible for the design of the original HEA study and author of most subsequent reports, undertook a comparative review of the available evidence with a view to ascertaining whether, in the context of the expansion of higher education, there was any evidence of increasing levels of equality in terms of the social composition of the student body (Clancy and Goestellec 2007). The conclusion in relation to Ireland (and several other countries) was that, although stark inequalities indeed remained, 'there has been a significant reduction in the odds ratios suggesting that there has been a significant reduction in socio-economic group inequalities' (ibid.: 151).

For those who have direct experience of working with non-traditional learners of different kinds in higher education, the finding that they perform well comes as no surprise. Such students are likely to be particularly motivated as they have to overcome a wide range of structural barriers – social, cultural and economic – in order to participate in higher education. Educational inequality is integrally connected to deep-rooted socio-economic inequalities which cannot be solved in isolation by higher education; nevertheless, innovative responses on the part of higher education systems and institutions *can* indeed open up life-changing opportunities for individuals who would otherwise have been excluded.

Theme two: lifelong learning and innovative modes of study

In 2003, the Irish Department of Education and Science invited the OECD secretariat to undertake a review of the Irish higher education system 'to evaluate the performance of the sector and recommend how it can better meet Ireland's strategic objectives' (final report, OECD 2006: 2). In making the connection between widening participation and lifelong learning, the review team placed particular emphasis on redressing the relatively low levels of participation in part-time and distance learning in Ireland. They highlighted obvious disincentives in the system both for individuals (who had to pay fees) and for institutions (because of a lack of clarity in how they were being compensated for admitting such students). In recommending that part-time numbers be 'significantly increased as a proportion of total students in higher education', the review team also draw attention to the fact that continuing education (which takes place largely in the evenings) should be 'fully integrated into institutional life rather than being often regarded as a separate and distinctive operation employing different staff' if it is to feed into mainstream programmes and be given the due recognition deserved by this type of provision (OECD 2006: 31).

The fact that part-time study – and by extension, part-time students – was a Cinderella area of higher education came as no surprise to those interested in adult education in Ireland. From the time of the initial study on which the selection of countries in this volume is based (OECD 1987), Ireland ranked in the lowest grouping in terms of the proportion of part-time students. This pattern was highlighted at the start of the decade in the White Paper *Learning for Life* published in 2000 (Department of Education and Science 2000) which *inter alia* proposed the establishment of a targeted strategic fund to support flexible provision for adult learners and, specifically, the extension of the 'free fee' scheme (whereby all full-time students only paid a registration charge, but no fees) to part-time students (who were liable for fees) from particular socio-economic backgrounds. However, as repeated analyses demonstrated, little progress was made in practice (Collins 2000; Fleming 2004; Healy and Slowey 2006; Darmody and Fleming 2009; Morgan and Slowey 2009).

As mentioned above, the aim of increasing the numbers of part-time and distance students featured prominently in the National Strategy for Access as an important component of lifelong learning. The report, yet again, commented on the fact that, while Ireland had achieved a remarkable expansion of higher education opportunities for school-leaving students, the fact that the overwhelming proportion gained admission via the 'traditional' Leaving Certificate route represented a weakness. It was recommended that steps should be taken to encourage alternative admission routes, supporting the lifelong learning agenda through a 'significant' expansion of part-time and flexible courses.

Nevertheless, as the figures in Tables 4.1 and 4.2 show, at undergraduate level the numbers of part-time learners actually *declined* in both the universities and the institutes of technology. The issue of part-time opportunities thus again featured prominently in the National Strategy for Higher Education which commented that Ireland's 'current low level of part-time study opportunities limits the accessibility of higher education for working adults and adults with caring responsibilities. It also limits the study options available to traditional school leavers, who may prefer or need to combine work and part-time study' (Department of Education and Skills 2011a: 46). The Strategy also pointed out that Ireland's poor performance in lifelong learning and the inflexibility of higher education were among the strongest concerns to emerge through the consultations and the submissions received by the Strategy Group ... While there has been considerable expansion of higher education opportunities in recent years, this expansion has mainly been in the provision of full-time opportunities focused primarily on entrants from upper second-level education. Irish higher education students have the narrowest age-range across all OECD countries reflecting the current unresponsiveness of Irish higher education to the skills needs of adults in the population.

(Department of Education and Skills 2011a: 46)

The recommendation to treat part-time study for institutional funding purposes pro rata to full-time study was accepted by the Minister and was to be introduced in a phased manner over a number of years. While undoubtedly a positive step from an access and equity perspective, three realities remain: firstly, part-time students pay fees while the (re)introduction of fees for full-time students remains a political minefield; secondly, this step was taken at a time of the severest of cutbacks in public investment, so in the end may make little or no real difference to the income received by institutions; and thirdly, in this context, part-time higher education is in danger of being reduced to little more than a possible mechanism in the search to drive down costs while catering for increasing demand.

Competing rationales also underpinned much of the related discussion about open and distance learning (ODL). An Advisory Group, set up by the HEA and chaired by an international expert, Malcolm Skilbeck, developed a plan which, amongst other things, proposed the establishment of a National Open and Distance Learning Office within the HEA (2009b). However, the official response from the HEA concluded that, while this was unlikely 'in the current economic climate, it is clear that the HEA will have to take a leading role in this area, not least because of the centrality of funding reforms and the need to incorporate the concept of flexible learning into the accountability and performance funding metrics' (HEA 2009c: 9).

Ireland's underperformance in ODL and flexible learning up to now has been characterised by fragmentation and a lack of co-ordination, where there are numerous 'pockets of innovation' without the desirable institutional and systemic change. The development of a coherent national approach to open and flexible delivery of higher education will require leadership and co-ordination.

(HEA 2009c: 9)

And there was indeed evidence of many 'pockets of innovation' at the regional, institutional and course level in incorporating technology into the learning environment. In 2009, the Dublin Region Higher Education

Alliance (DRHEA) undertook an audit of e-learning activity across its member institutions: four universities and four institutes of technology, comprising more than half of the national higher education sector. All eight institutions supported e-learning with a Virtual Learning Environment (VLE) with reported levels of usage being 'extremely high' and growing annually (DRHEA 2009). In addition, the audit found a wide range of learning technologies incorporated into mainstream teaching, including: audio/podcasting, video, collaborative learning tools, resource development tools, Web 2.0 tools, SMART technologies, assessment, synchronous learning and portfolio tools.

It is recognized, however, that critical mass and scale can be difficult to achieve in a small country. There is thus a strong focus in this, as in many related policy initiatives, on encouraging cross-institutional collaboration, co-operation and consolidation. While the rationale may be largely instrumental, in terms of increasing efficiency and use of scarce resources, collaboration is in fact also a fundamental prerequisite for the development of a dynamic system of lifelong learning.

Conclusion: lifelong learning and the challenge of democratizing access to knowledge

At the start of this tumultuous decade the social inequality of the intake to universities in Ireland was – as in most countries – stark: there was effective saturation of students from higher professional backgrounds (almost 100 per cent) and employer and managerial backgrounds (about 80 per cent) as compared with a small minority of those from semi-skilled and unskilled backgrounds (Clancy 2001). In addition, the opportunities for people to return to study when adults on either a full-time, part-time or flexible basis, were limited. In the middle of the decade, at the peak of the economic boom, there was indeed a significant increase in investment in higher education, some of which was targeted at increasing access and educational innovation, but the bulk of which went to support (badly needed) research infrastructure. Over this period, Ireland also started to feature prominently in certain international indicators from bodies such as OECD, the World Bank and UNESCO. The story revealed by these indicators, however, was by no means uniform in terms of educational and social progress (Jacobson *et al.* 2006; Clancy 2007b; Downes and Gilligan 2007; Ryan 2007). In 2005, at a time when Irish people were ranked as the second wealthiest in the world (with a per capita GDP of $37,738) and the country ranked twelfth in terms of Gross National Income (which excludes multi-national profit repatriations), Ireland remained a very unequal society: on a composite UN development measure of levels of inequality, Ireland came near the bottom (16th out of 18 countries and just above the USA and Italy) (Healy and Slowey 2006; Wilkinson and Pickett 2009).

Thus the issues raised at the turn of the millennium remained pertinent:

> The challenge to the Irish economy may not be to the development process as much as to *egalitarianism* within the society and economy.
> (O'Riain 2000: 187, emphasis added)

Remaining equally pertinent were the observations on higher education in Ireland in our 2000 volume. Collins argued then that the adult learning critique posed to universities is to

> move them from a position in which the student is the target of a knowledge delivery system to one in which the student is actively engaged in constructing knowledge through reflective practice; from one which removes the learner from a real world situation to one which relies on the real world situation as the learning agenda; from a concern with access to one of emancipation; and to one which recognizes the multi-disciplinary, open systemic nature of knowledge.
> (Collins 2000: 81)

Perhaps it is this approach, rather than a revisiting of Newman, which points the direction to a genuinely lifelong learning form of higher education for the 21st century? As historian of higher education Sheldon Rothblatt points out, Newman was a teacher 'motivated by a pastoral conception of pedagogy', a theologian 'concerned with sin and redemption' and a moralist 'bothered by the dissolution of authority in Liberal England' (Rothblatt 1989: 23). Newman's view of knowledge, and what 'constitutes a universe of education', is thus very different to what most would wish for in contemporary higher education.

On the other hand, if higher education reform and innovation is simply reduced to notions of flexible systems of entry, study and progression (ideas which were around in Newman's time, and which 'horrified' him about the new University of London), the real challenge of lifelong learning concerning the democratization of access to knowledge is in danger of being overlooked.

Viewing lifelong learning in this broader perspective would not only benefit those seeking to gain the chance to participate in higher education, but could also change the culture and experience for *all* students, altering the dynamic of the relationship between higher education and wider civil society.

References

Clancy, P. (2001) *College Entry in Focus: a Fourth National Survey of Access to Higher Education*, Dublin: Higher Education Authority.

Clancy, P. (2007a) 'Education', in S. O'Sullivan (ed.) *Contemporary Ireland: A Sociological Map*, Dublin, University College Dublin Press, pp. 101–119.

Clancy, P. (2007b) 'Resisting the evaluative state: irish academics win the battle but lose the war', in J. Enders and F. Van Vught, Twente: Centre for Higher Education Policy Studies.

Clancy, P. and Goestellec, G. (2007) 'Exploring access and equity in higher education: policy and performance in a comparative perspective', *Higher Education Quarterly*, 61 (2): 136–154.

Collins, T. (2000) 'Ireland: adult learner and non-traditional students in Irish higher education', in H.G. Schuetze and M. Slowey (eds) *Higher Education and Lifelong Learners: International Perspectives on Change*, London: RoutledgeFalmer.

Darmody, M. and Fleming, B. (2009) '"The balancing act" – Irish part-time undergraduate students in higher education', *Irish Educational Studies*, 28 (1): 67–83.

Davies, P. and Feutrie, M. (2008) 'University lifelong learning to lifelong learning universities', Bologna Handbook, No 8. Berlin: Raabe Academic Publishers.

DCU, Dublin City University (2011) *The Access Programme at DCU 20 Years on*, Dublin: DCU.

Department of Education and Science (2000) *Learning for Life: White Paper on Adult Education*, Dublin, Stationery Office.

Department of Enterprise, Trade and Employment (2006) *Strategy for Science, Technology and Innovation*, Dublin: DETE.

Department of Finance (2006) *National Development Plan 2007–2013: Transforming Ireland – A Better Quality of Life for All*, Dublin, Stationery Office.

DES, Department for Education and Skills (2011a) *National Strategy for Higher Education*, Dublin: Stationery Office.

DES, Department for Education and Skills (2011b) *Delivery of the Strategy for Higher Education*, speech by Minister of Education and Skills Royal Irish Academy, 30 May 2011. http://www.education.i.e./robots/view.jsp?pcategory=10861&language=EN&ecategory=11469&link=link001&doc=5318 (accessed 16 June 2011).

Downes, P. and Gilligan, A.L. (eds) (2007) *Beyond Educational Disadvantage*, Dublin: Institute of Public Administration.

DRHEA, Dublin Region Higher Education Alliance (2009) *Enhancement of Learning: Enabling eLearning and Blended Learning*, DRHE report available online <www.drhea.i.e./enhancement_audit.php> (accessed 16 June 2011).

European Commission (2011) *The Economic Adjustment Programme for Ireland*, Directorate-General for Economic and Financial Affairs, Brussels: European Commission.

Expert Group on Future Skills Needs (2007) *Tomorrow's Skills: Towards a National Skills Strategy* (5th Report) Dublin: Stationery Office.

Expert Group on Future Skills Needs (2011) *The Role of RPL in the Context of the National Skills Strategy Upskilling Objectives*, Dublin: Stationery Office.

Fleming, T. (2004) 'The state of adult education' in *The Adult Learner: 2004*, Dublin, AONTAS, pp. 9–17.

Hazelkorn, E. (2011) *Rankings and the Reshaping of Higher Education: The Battle for World-Class Excellence*, Basingstoke: Palgrave Macmillan.

HEA (2005a) *Review of Quality Assurance in Irish Universities – Sectoral Report*, Dublin: Higher Education Authority and the Irish Universities Quality Board.

HEA (2005b) *Key Facts and Figures*, Dublin: Higher Education Authority.

HEA (2006) *Key Facts and Figures*, Dublin: Higher Education Authority.

HEA (2008) *National Plan for Equality of Access to Higher Education 2008–2013*, Dublin: Higher Education Authority.
HEA (2009a) *Key Facts and Figures*, Dublin: Higher Education Authority.
HEA (2009b) *New Directions for Open and Distance Learning in Ireland*, Report Advisory Group chaired by Malcolm Skillbeck to the HEA, Dublin: Higher Education Authority.
HEA (2009c) *Open and Flexible Learning: HEA Position Paper*, Dublin: Higher Education Authority.
HEA (2010a) *Key Facts and Figures*, Dublin: Higher Education Authority.
HEA (2010b) *A Study of Progression in Irish Higher Education*, Dublin: Higher Education Authority.
Healy, T. and Slowey, M. (2006) 'Social exclusion and adult engagement in lifelong learning – some comparative implications for European states based on Ireland's Celtic Tiger Experience', *Compare*, 36 (3): 359–378.
Holmes, M. (ed.) (2005) *Ireland and the European Union: Nice, Enlargement and the Future of Europe*, Manchester: Manchester University Press.
Hyland, A. (2011) *Entry to Higher Education in Ireland in the 21st Century*, Dublin: National Council on Curriculum and Assessment and the Higher Education Authority.
IUA, Irish Universities Association (2005) *Reform of the 3rd Level and Creation of 4th Level Ireland: Securing Competitive Advantage in the 21st Century*, Dublin: Irish Universities Association.
IUQB, Irish Universities Quality Board (2007) *Progress Report on the Bologna Process*, Dublin: Irish Universities Quality Board.
Jacobson, D., Kirby, P. and O'Broin, D. (eds) (2006) *Taming the Tiger: Social Exclusion in a Globalised Ireland*, Dublin: tasc/New Island.
Morgan, M. and Slowey, M (2009) 'Higher education in the broader educational landscape: widening the perspective on equity and access in Ireland, *Journal of Adult Continuing Education*, 15 (2): 204–219.
Munck, R. (2011) 'Ireland in the world, the world in Ireland', in B. Fanning and R. Munck (eds) *Globalization, Migration and Social Transformation: Ireland in Europe and the World*, Farnham: Ashgate.
Neave, G. (2004) 'Higher education policy as orthodoxy: being one tale of doxological drift, political intention and changing circumstances', in P. Teixeira, B. Jongbloed, D. Dill and A. Amaral (eds) *Markets in Higher Education: Rhetoric or Reality?* Dordrecht: Kluwer Academic Publishers, pp. 127–160.
Newman, J.H. (1913 ed.) *The Idea of a University: Defined and Illustrated*, London: Longmans, Green and Co.
O'Connell, P.J., Clancy, D. and McCoy, S. (2006) *Who Went to College in 2004? A National Survey of New Entrants to Higher Education*, Dublin: Higher Education Authority.
OECD (1987) *Adults in Higher Education*, Paris: OECD.
OECD (2006) *Reviews of National Policies for Higher Education – Higher Education in Ireland*, Paris: OECD.
O'Riain, S. (2000) 'The flexible developmental state: globalization, information technology, and the "Celtic Tiger"', *Politics and Society*, 28 (2): 57–193.
O'Toole, F. (2009) *Ship of Fools: How Stupidity and Corruption Sank the Celtic Tiger*, London: Faber.

Rothblatt, S. (1989) *The Idea of a University and its Antithesis*, Seminar on the Sociology of Culture 7–9 October, Victoria: La Trobe University.

Ryan, A. (2007) 'What if education mattered?', in B. Connolly, T. Fleming, D. McCormack and A. Ryan (eds) *Radical Learning for Liberation* 2, Maynooth: Maynooth Adult and Community Education, pp. 131–140.

Schuetze, H.G. and Slowey, M. (eds) (2000) *Higher Education and Lifelong Learners: International Perspectives on Change*, London: RoutledgeFalmer.

Scott, P. (2011) 'Higher education reform in the Atlantic isles: similarities and differences' presentation in seminar series 'Higher Education in Challenging Times: Questioning the Unquestioned', Dublin: Dublin City University, 18 May.

Watson, D. and Taylor, R. (1998) *Lifelong Learning and the University: A Post-Dearing Agenda*, London: Falmer Press.

Wilkinson, D. and Pickett, K. (2009) *The Spirit Level: Why Equality is Better for Everyone*, London: Allen Lane.

Chapter 5

Portugal
Higher education and lifelong education in Portugal

Alberto Amaral and Madalena Fonseca

Introduction

Portuguese higher education indicators are still strongly affected by the politics of the former political regime which was a dictatorship for several decades. Education was not a priority of the dictator Salazar and at the time of the 1974 revolution there was an elite higher education system with a gross participation rate of only about 7 per cent (Amaral *et al.* 2005), with most of the Portuguese population having a low education level. A high percentage of the population was part of a rural society and the country's weak industrial development was in general based on a labour force characterized by low salaries, low literacy levels and few advanced skills. Therefore, when Portugal became a member of the EU in 1986, the country suffered from a considerable handicap in education and training.

Following the revolution, education has been assumed to be a major political priority and enrolments in higher education increased sharply from 30,000 students in the 1960s, to nearly 400,000 students by the end of the 20th century (MCTES 2006). This very fast development of higher education has led to a high duality in Portuguese society (ibid.), with a well-educated younger population living side by side with an older generation with low education levels.

Educational attainment in Portugal has risen significantly in recent decades although disparities with other OECD and EU countries have persisted. The percentage of adults with at least upper secondary education was 28 per cent in 2008, one of the lowest in the OECD and the EU19 (average values, respectively, 71 and 72 per cent[1]). However, the difference between the 25–34 age cohort (47 per cent) and the 55–64 age cohort (13 per cent) shows this shortfall is being rapidly advanced. The percentage of adults (25–64 years) with higher education has increased from 9 per cent in 2000 to 14 per cent in 2008, still much lower than average values from OECD countries (28 per cent), or EU19 countries (25 per cent). However, the gap was narrower for younger cohorts, both for higher education and for upper secondary education attainment (OECD 2010, pp. 35–36). The net entry rate into higher education (Type A programmes) was 81 per cent in 2008, the third highest in OECD and EU19 countries (OECD 2010, p. 48). This indicator 'provides an indication of the accessibility of tertiary education as well as the perceived value of attending tertiary programmes' (ibid., p. 78); it corresponds to the probability that a young person will enter tertiary education in her/his lifetime if current age-specific entry rates continue (ibid., p. 53).

Recent education policies in Portugal have had as their main objectives broadening access, in particular of adult population and lifelong learning in formal and non-formal education; the development of vocational study programmes; and quality assurance. Higher education has shown evidence of a better performance or at least its main macro indicators show a clear improvement, while upper secondary education indicators remained beneath the set goals.

The country-specific context of higher education

Portugal has a resident population of about 10.6 million inhabitants. Consistently declining birth rates associated with increasing life expectancy have resulted in an ageing population, which created problems for the welfare system and a decline of the number of traditional candidates for higher education. Over the last two decades, the number of young people in the population of Portugal (0–24 years old) fell by about 313,000, while the older generation (≥ 65 years) increased by more than 500,000 (EUROSTAT). So far, the effects of immigration have not compensated for this phenomenon.

As result of the long period of dictatorship that neglected education, the present average level of education of the Portuguese population is thus still quite low, despite the efforts made after the revolution (Table 5.1). Portugal has relied on a development strategy based on labour-intensive activities, supported by a labour force with low salaries and low levels of education and skills, a situation that has not changed after the accession to the EU, as financial incentives were mainly used to attract foreign, labour intensive industries. The labour market continued to offer employment for people with low education levels, which did not provide incentives for young people from families with lower social capital to invest in higher levels of education.

Table 5.1 Higher education level attained (percentage of active population 15–64 years)

	2000	2005	2009
Basic education or less	77.3	70.5	65.9
Secondary education	12.8	15.4	17.8
Higher education	9.9	14.1	16.2

Source: Observatório de Emprego e Formação Profissional, 2010.

Globalization is now forcing Portugal to pay a very heavy price for this strategy.

The possibility of getting employment without a high level of qualification has promoted early entrance into the labour market. Portugal has an excessive percentage of young people who have abandoned the education system to enter the labour market. Although this situation has improved in recent years, in 2009, 31.2 per cent of young people (18–24 years old) left the education system without completing at least upper secondary education, more than twice the share of the EU27 (14.4 per cent) (EUROSTAT). So far, Portugal has not been able – at least until 2008 – to achieve the OECD and EU19 average value for the graduation rate at upper secondary level in spite of a significant improvement from 52 per cent in 1997 to 63 per cent in 2008 (average for OECD, 80 per cent; for the EU19, 83 per cent while some European countries have graduation rates higher than 90 per cent). Great efforts have been made meanwhile to widen upper secondary graduation to students outside the typical age of graduation with second chance/adult education programmes.

An economic development model that did not promote the need to attain higher education levels explains why Portugal has traditionally had a low participation in education activities. In 2007, more than three-quarters of the adult population – nearly 80 per cent – (25–64 years old) neither participated in formal or non-formal education nor looked for information on learning activities, against the OECD average of 52 per cent (OECD 2010, p. 83). The participation rate of the adult population in formal and non-formal education – 26 per cent – was lower than the OECD and EU19 averages (41 per cent and 37 per cent). For the younger cohorts, both males and females, the share was higher – 39 per cent and 41 per cent – but still below OECD and EU19 average values (between 46 and 51 per cent). In Portugal, participation in education has a number of characteristics: those with higher education are much more likely to participate in lifelong learning; more younger people participate than older people; high-skilled white-collar workers have higher rates of participation than less qualified employees. The low participation in lifelong learning in Portugal reflects the absence of a 'training culture' and how training has been 'remedial, rather than preventive' (Guichard and Larre 2006, p. 13).

Recently, the economic situation has deteriorated significantly, as a result of excessive public deficits in the wake of the worldwide recession, in a context where the low education level of the labour force militates against the capacity of Portugal to compete and promote its economic development. Levels of unemployment have consistently increased. Unemployment is more severe for young people and for people without a higher education qualification (Table 5.2), although in 2010/2011 unemployment rates are becoming quite significant even for higher education graduates with many graduates looking for employment abroad.

Table 5.2 Unemployment rate by education level and age group

	2000	2005	2009
Basic education or less	4.0	7.9	10.2
Secondary education	4.7	8.2	9.7
Higher education	3.2	6.4	6.6
15–24 years	8.7	16.4	20.2
25–54 years	3.6	7.4	9.4
55–64 years	3.3	6.3	7.9

Source: Observatório de Emprego e Formação Profissional, 2010.

In 2008, unemployment rates of people with higher education in Portugal, although lower than the average unemployment rate in the country, were still higher than the average in OECD and EU19 countries (OECD 2010). On the contrary, unemployment rates for people with lower levels of education (lower than ISCED 3c) were lower in Portugal than average values for OECD and EU19 countries. These data reveal the structural problems of the Portuguese labour market and its vulnerable economic base, strongly specialized in labour-intensive industries able to offer jobs for non-qualified workers. Moreover, there have been no relevant changes in the last 10 years and employment rates for lower levels of education remained unchanged between 1997 and 2007, but higher than in OECD and EU19 countries (OECD 2010, p. 113).

Labour cost differentials are relevant. The labour costs of an experienced graduate in Portugal are not significantly different from those in the other OECD countries, but compared with the costs of a recent graduate are more than twice as high (OECD 2010, p. 173). There are higher private than public returns to higher education in Portugal, compared with other OECD countries, which can be a strong incentive to invest in education, although also an indicator that widening access is needed. However, considering the labour costs differentials analysed before, young people are not always encouraged to pursue schooling since they have no great expectations in the short run. The general upgrading of education levels of the younger cohorts, combined with the low participation of adults in lifelong education, indicate the duality of education levels of the Portuguese population will persist for some time.

Overview of the national higher education system

After the 1974 revolution, a difficult economic situation and political turmoil resulted in intervention by the IMF. The World Bank also played an important role in helping to define and finance education policies. It was under the influence of the World Bank that the public polytechnic

Table 5.3 Enrolments by subsystem (2008–2009)

Sub-system		First year enrolments (first time)		Total enrolments	
		Total	%	Total	%
Public	University	54 243	46.0	175 465	47.0
	Polytechnic	35 033	29.7	106 973	28.7
Private	University	18 956	16.1	60 755	16.3
	Polytechnic	9 606	8.2	29 809	8.0
Total		117 838	100.0	373 002	100.0

Source: GPEARI (2011a).

subsystem was implemented and expanded to provide the human resources demanded by the economy. The World Bank assumed that Portugal would play a role as provider of specialized manpower for manufacturing industries, services and agriculture (Teixeira, Amaral and Rosa 2003). Therefore, the Portuguese higher education system has become binary, with universities and polytechnics, and includes public and private institutions (Table 5.3).

Upper secondary programmes in Portugal, as in other OECD countries, were traditionally designed to prepare students for higher education, and Portugal has indeed a very high entry rate into higher education (Type A) in spite of the already mentioned under-performance at upper secondary school level. Post-secondary (non-higher education) vocational programmes have been expanding in the last few years, even if still at lower level than in other European countries. There is also evidence of a growing offer by Higher Education Institutions of higher education Type B programmes as well as part-time, evening courses or e- and b-learning systems, trying to meet or even encourage demand from non-traditional, older students (Amaral and Magalhães 2009).

Portugal has registered a higher education graduation rate 45.3 per cent (Type A), above the OECD and EU19 average of about 38 per cent, which corresponds to the estimated percentage of an age cohort that will complete higher education, based on the current patterns of graduation. This graduation rate has increased from 15 per cent in 1995, to 23 per cent in 2000, before reaching the present rate of 45.3 per cent, while the graduation rate for higher education Type B programmes remained very low and quite unchanged (2 per cent in 2008, compared with the OECD average of 8 per cent). Completion rates in higher education in Portugal (72 per cent) meet the OECD and EU19 averages (69 per cent and 80 per cent respectively) as well as the rate of dropout or interruption of studies, which corresponded to 28 per cent in Portugal, compared with 31 per cent for the OECD and 30 per cent for the EU19.

It is possible to conclude that macro indicators for higher education indicate that Portugal is performing quite well when compared with OECD

Table 5.4 Relative distribution of graduates, by field of education (2008) Portugal

		Portugal (1)	OECD average (2)	EU19 average (3)	Potugal/ OECD comparison = (1)/(2)	Portugual/ EU19 comparison =(1)/(3)
Health and welfare	5A/6	17.6	13.5	14.3	1.31	1.24
	5B	69.7	17.6	18.9	3.97	3.68
Life sciences, physical sciences and agriculture	5A/6	7.9	7.0	7.2	1.13	1.09
	5B	0.4	3.3	3.4	0.11	0.11
Mathematics and computer science	5A/6	7.2	4.8	5.2	1.49	1.40
	5B	0.6	4.3	2.5	0.13	0.22
Humanities, arts and education	5A/6	16.0	25.0	24.2	0.64	0.66
	5B	10.2	21.4	22.8	0.48	0.45
Social sciences, business, law and services	5A/6	32.9	37.3	36.4	0.88	0.90
	5B	15.4	37.0	34.5	0.42	0.45
Engineering, manufacturing and construction	5A/6	18.3	12.0	12.6	1.52	1.45
	5B	3.8	12.2	10.8	0.31	0.35

Source: OECD 2010.

and EU19 averages despite the significant percentage of young people not completing upper secondary education. Although additional education beyond compulsory schooling provides important long-term returns for individuals, which should motivate people to enter higher education to get a degree instead of entering the labour market just after completing secondary education, in Portugal there are still important problems at the level of upper secondary education, which exhibits weak macro indicators, and in the transition from upper secondary education to higher education.

The relative distribution of graduates, by field of education, in Portugal, in 2008, shows a great imbalance of the relative weight of higher education Type A and Type B programmes. Type B programmes are underdeveloped in Portugal, with the exception of Health and Welfare where the proportion of graduates in Type B programmes is 4 times the average share in OECD and EU19 countries (Table 5.4). This can be explained by an overwhelming expansion of nursing study programmes in recent years, which are attracting students that could not obtain a place to study medicine, the most popular programme in universities (Fonseca *et al.*, forthcoming). All the other fields have a deficit in graduates of Type B programmes, especially in the life sciences, physical sciences and agriculture, mathematics and computer science and engineering, and manufacturing and construction. Since there are many programmes of three-year Type A programmes in traditional universities, vocationally-orientated programmes have difficulty in attracting candidates and the labour market does not favour vocationally trained graduates.

Access to higher education in Portugal is governed by a system of quotas (*numerus clausus*) that applies to every study programme in universities or polytechnics, public or private (Teixeira *et al.*, 2009). Even for study programmes in very low demand, which never fill the available vacancies, there is a *numerus clausus*. Each student competes for a place in a public institution by indicating six possible combinations of institution/study programme in order of preference, relying on an application grade that is a weighted combination of the student's upper secondary school grades and grades obtained in national examinations for core scientific areas. Because such supply constraints apply to all study programmes, students are encouraged to behave strategically and choose the programmes where they have better chances of being admitted. There is a considerable mismatch between offer and demand in both types of institutions, scientific areas and geographical locations (Fonseca *et al.*, forthcoming).

An analysis of the family background of higher education students (socio-economic groups of both parents, and educational attainment of both parents and the family income level) reveals a second negative aspect of the Portuguese higher education system (Tavares *et al.* 2008). Indeed, it is clear that Portugal is still far from having equitable access to higher education as students with parents holding a higher education degree are about ten times more likely to enter than students from families with low educational backgrounds (ibid.). There is also a considerable influence of family background on the choice students make between university and polytechnic degrees, with university enrolment being clearly favoured by students from households with higher education backgrounds (ibid.). For instance, the percentage of fathers holding a higher education degree was much higher for university students than for polytechnic students, and the same holds true for the schooling level of mothers (ibid.).

Family income also has an influence over the patterns of choice of students, with polytechnics enrolling the highest percentage of students from families with lower financial resources (Tavares *et al.* 2008).

The implementation of a student social support system in Portuguese higher education was initiated after the April 1974 revolution. In the early 1990s student support policies became entangled with the government's attempts to increase cost sharing by raising tuition fees that until then were merely symbolic (about €6 at current rates) as their value had been kept frozen since the 1940s. A more neoliberal Parliament passed Law 37/03, of 22 August, allowing higher education institutions to set the value of tuition fees between a minimum of 1.3 times the minimum monthly wage and a maximum determined by updating its 1941 frozen value relative to inflation.

At present, the student social support system includes direct and indirect support mechanisms, irrespective of the enrolling institution (public or private, university or polytechnic). Direct support consists of means-tested grants (scholarships) for needy students who demonstrate academic merit. The government has also implemented a loan system in parallel with the system of scholarships. The initial reaction of students to loans was negative, as they were afraid this would open the way to progressively converting the traditional grant system into a loan system. However, the initial mistrust seems to have disappeared and the number of students using this alternative has increased from 1,524 in December 2007 to 11,108 in December 2009 (DGES 2010).

Expenditure on higher education in Portugal has grown significantly both in absolute and per capita values. The index of change between 2000 and 2007 (100 in 2000) was 170 for the absolute expenditure and 158 for the per capita expenditure (OECD 2010, p. 207). These values are significantly higher than the average for OECD countries and indicate that the Portuguese higher education system is moving towards the OECD form. The expenditure on education as a percentage of GDP is also approaching the average values for the OECD and EU19, with a special focus on higher education (OECD 2010, p. 217). In Portugal, the share of public sources for higher education funding changed from 92.5 per cent in 2000, to 70.0 per cent in 2007, approaching the OECD average of 69.1 per cent and lower than the EU 19 average of 79.4 per cent (OECD 2010, p. 235). There is a wide range of values for the different countries, with the UK being the European country with the lowest share of 35.8 per cent. In this framework, tuition fees play an important role. According to the OECD report *Education at a Glance 2010*, Portugal fits in Model 4 for countries with a low level of tuition fees and less developed student support systems which corresponds to a relatively higher burden on the families than in other countries, even those with higher levels of tuition fees (OECD 2010, pp. 251–252).

Lifelong education policies

Lifelong learning in Portugal only became more visible after Parliament passed the Comprehensive Law on the Education System (CLES) in 1986. The CLES defined professional training as an important objective in the overall structure of the educational system, and established a framework of training activities designed to promote the participation of working people, for the purposes of both professional enhancement and professional conversion. As far as non-formal educational activities were concerned, the law emphasized the development of technological aptitudes and technical knowledge, which would foster adult adaptation to contemporary life. The legislation explicitly assumes the connection between education and professional activity, which thus requires the education system to prepare students for the transition to the labour market. However, some problems remained to be solved, such as the lack of clear articulation between education and professional training, and the inadequacy of efforts in relation to transition to the labour market.

Since 1979, adult students (those over 25) have been allowed to enrol in higher education courses in any Portuguese university or polytechnic without the full secondary school diploma, provided that they have passed an examination – either the regular entrance examination or an 'ad hoc' examination. Special laws were passed directed at students who were also in employment.

However, most of the more determined policy measures orientated towards lifelong learning were to a large extent the result of expectations or demands from the European Union. Portugal's accession to the European Community in 1986 can be seen as a turning point in the country's participation in lifelong learning, mainly as a result of activities developed with support from the European Social Fund (ESF). This became the main source of financing for training systems, and indeed the main inspiration behind the organization of national training policies.

In 1996, a National Commission for Lifelong Education and Learning was established by a decision of the Council of Ministers in a joint effort by the Ministers of Education and Employment to improve the articulation between their respective areas. The commission has set broad lines of development, even if they scarcely refer to higher education:

1 To pay special attention to a significant part of the population with low skills. The objective was that 50 per cent of the active population would have at least 10 years of schooling in 2006 (this refers to about 900,000 workers).
2 To fight against dropout and educational exclusion, in relation to issues of access, exclusion and qualitative improvements in the educational system.
3 To strengthen the links between education and training by developing a system of accreditation of the different types of professional training and lifelong education, coordinating the different types of institutions providing these services and giving more emphasis to the professional dimension in educational training.

The Commission emphasized the need for co-ordination through the adoption of several measures: to consider the transition to the labour market as a dimension of the educational system, the establishment of a common language, standards, and norms for training programmes, as well as their co-ordinated organization and an emphasis on recurrent education.

The Council of Ministers also decided to hold regular meetings of a small group of ministers with portfolios that impinged on policies for human resource development. Some other political moves reflected the national commission's demand for more co-ordinated action. One example was the elaboration of the Portuguese National Employment Programme following the European summit in Luxembourg in late 1997. Some specific objectives were defined, such as an increase in recurrent and continuing education and improved labour market connections. The programme also recognized the importance of lifelong learning, and created a special sub-programme, entitled 'Endurance', which aimed to provide information and orientation, as well as technical and financial support, to projects to create new opportunities for open and distance education.

Up to the present, the role of employers and their economic associations has been very limited in terms of lifelong learning activities. Nevertheless, some signs have been made by entrepreneurial organizations, aiming to play a more active role in terms of continuing education. A document from one industrial association (1995) claimed that activities devoted to lifelong professional training should become an increasing responsibility of the employees and their organizations. However, these experiences have almost been restricted to some MBA programmes.

More recent initiatives

The Portuguese government has more recently adopted some relevant measures and initiatives, including:

a New Opportunity Programmes
b Technological Specialization Courses
c Non-traditional adult students
d Performance-based contracts.

The 'New Opportunity Programme', launched in 2005, was mainly funded through the European Social Fund in the Human Potential Thematic Operational Programme of the National Strategic Reference Framework (NSRF). The first enrolments in this programme were in 2007; it includes actions aiming at improving the qualifications of the Portuguese population and developing lifelong learning. Besides the global goals of the Lisbon Agenda, the programme has some specific objectives, such as increasing the offer of vocational education in upper secondary education, offering a new opportunity to students who leave the education system before completing their basic education, integrating vocational courses in upper secondary schools that traditionally only provided general courses leading to higher education, implementing a system for the recognition and certification of competencies and offering new vocational training opportunities to adults with low qualifications. Almost 650,000 individuals were involved in the years up to 2010 in the different sub-programmes (www.novasoportunidades.gov.pt).

Technological Specialization Courses (CETs) are short-cycle programmes preparing students for employment although also providing preparation for access to higher education first cycle study programmes. CETs can be provided both at the level of secondary education and by higher education institutions at post-secondary level. After completing a CET, students are awarded a specialization diploma corresponding to level 5 of the European Qualifications Framework. The number of students enrolled in CETs has constantly increased (20 times in 4 years) and 86 per cent of them enrolled in the polytechnic subsystem. Male students predominate (69.4 per cent). Most students concentrate in the areas of Engineering and Transforming Industries (32 per cent), followed by Social Sciences, Commerce and Law (22 per cent) and Sciences, Mathematics and Informatics (19 per cent) (GPEARI 2011b).

A third important measure in the most recent Portuguese policies has been lowering the qualification age – from 25 to 23 years – to enter higher education without having completed upper secondary education. Special admission examinations at national level were abolished and responsibility for selecting students was fully transferred to higher education institutions. The quantitative results of this policy were spectacular, as the number of first year mature students jumped suddenly from 551 (over-25-year-olds) in 2004/05 to 10,856 (over-23-year-olds) in 2006/2007 (Amaral and Magalhães 2009).

It is relevant to emphasize that most mature students initially enrolled in the private sector (60.4 per cent in 2006/07) although in later years this has been reversed (48.7 per cent in 2007/08 and 48.8 per cent in 2008/09) (Table 5.5). However, when the percentage of mature students is measured against the total number of students in each subsystem it is evident that they represent a far more important phenomenon for the private sector (29.3 per cent of total first year enrolments in 2006/07) than for the public sector (8.3 per cent of total enrolments in 2006/07). Mature students are only a minor proportion of total enrolments in public universities (4.3 per cent in 2006/07).

As the number of young people has been progressively decreasing due to consistently declining birth rates, the number of traditional candidates to higher education has also steadily declined, promoting increasing competition for students among higher education institutions. The private sector was the most affected by this phenomenon. Indeed, for some private universities non-traditional first year students represented over 60 per cent of total first year enrolments in 2006/07 (Amaral and Magalhães 2009). Apparently there is a pattern of concentration of the public sector (or at least public universities) on the market for more traditional students, while the private institutions may try to survive by assuming an increasing role in the 'less traditional' educational market, including lifelong education.

Another interesting aspect is the relative weight of male and female students. While traditional students show a consistently higher proportion of females (56.9 per cent of first year students enrolled in 2009/10 using the traditional access route were females) the reverse situation is observed

Table 5.5 Access of first year students as mature students aged 23 years and over

Subsystem	2006–2007			2007–2008			2008–2009		
	Total	≥ 23 years	% ≥ 23 years	Total	≥ 23 years	% ≥ 23 years	Total	≥ 23 years	% ≥ 23 years
Public sector	51,218	4,257	8.3%	59,354	6,039	10.2%	60,290	5,373	8.9%
Universities	29,737	1,271	4.3%	32,760	2,083	6.4%	33,500	1,887	5.6%
Polytechnics	21,481	2,986	13.9%	26,594	3,956	14.9%	26,790	3,486	13.0%
Private sector	22,266	6,599	29.6%	23,785	5,734	24.1%	21,610	5,116	23.7%
Universities	15,033	4,820	32.1%	15,963	3,723	23.3%	15,311	3,421	22.3%
Polytechnics	7,233	1,779	24.6%	7,822	2,011	25.7%	6,299	1,695	26.9%
Total	73,484	10,856	14.8%	83,139	11,773	14.2%	81,900	10,489	12.8%

Source: GPEARI 2011c.

for non-traditional students (23.7 per cent female students from CETs and 46.4 per cent female students as ≥ 23 years old). Consequently, the overall balance in favour of female students when total enrolments are considered shows a slight tendency to decrease as new entrance routes are being promoted.

It is interesting to observe that, unlike the position in Portugal, there are more non-traditional female students than male students in Norway. A possible explanation is that in Portugal most non-traditional students are people entering the labour market without completing formal upper secondary education and returning to complete their education, while in Norway most non-traditional students are probably females returning to the system after spending a period taking care of their children.

In January 2010, the Ministry for Science, Technology and Higher Education signed performance-based contracts with all the public universities and public polytechnics, granting institutions additional funding against an increase in the number of graduates produced by the public sector. These contracts are valid until the end of the academic year 2013/14 and the main overall target is the provision of study programmes aiming specifically at adult students and at students already employed who want to upgrade their qualifications. Among others, the contracts foresee, in what concerns universities, an increase of 67,000 graduates over the next four years, 35 per cent being in Sciences, Technologies and Engineering and 20 per cent in Medicine, Health and Life Sciences and Technologies, an increase in Medicine vacancies as well as an increase in Masters programmes, evening and e-learning courses and an increase of 3,500 in the number of awarded PhDs. As for polytechnics, the contracts foresee an increase of 40,000 graduates over the next 4 years, the reinforcement of the number of post-secondary CETs, as well as of vocational Masters, mainly provided in evening courses. The number of new programmes will correspond to 34 per cent of CETs, 52 per cent of Professional Post-graduations and 13 per cent cycles offered in evening courses.

Discussion and conclusions

Portugal is at present facing a very difficult challenge. Portugal became a member of the EU in January 1986 with a very low average education level amongst its population. While the formal higher education system developed very fast, initiatives aiming at the further qualification of the labour force have been fairly ineffective, despite 25 years of European integration and financial support from structural funds.

The fast development of the formal higher education system combined with the apparent inefficiency of lifelong activities has resulted in the duality of Portuguese society, which becomes quite visible after segmenting the overall population into finer age intervals. For instance, while the share of the

Portuguese population with university education is low (about 11 per cent), only about half of the OECD average, a high proportion of young people (20 to 25 years of age) reach a level on a *par* with those in the Netherlands, Germany and Norway. Another example of this duality is visible, for instance, in the 12 per cent growth rate of the share of new science and technology PhDs per thousand of population aged 25–34 years for the period 1998–99, compared with no growth at all at the European Union level, or in the 16 per cent average annual growth rate of scientific publications per million of population from 1995 to 2000 that was below 3 per cent in the EU (MCTES 2006).

What can be observed is the effort made by Portugal to catch up with the other EU member countries, which has produced the young generation of highly trained and competent people prepared by higher education for entering the labour market. However, the labour market that for many years had been based on a combination of low salaries with low skills, was slow to react. This has led to a mismatch, as on the one hand higher education produces more highly skilled people than is required in the current labour market while on the other hand, unemployment is rising steadily for people with lower levels of literacy as economic globalisation has led to a decrease in the demand for unskilled labour.

Recent policy measures have been taken in order to intensify the efficiency of the education system. However, the slow transformation of the labour market and the present economic difficulties indicate that Portugal is entering a very painful adaptation period with young educated people already presenting themselves in popular protest ballads as 'the generation without remuneration', wondering why it is necessary to be educated to become a slave. At the same time government has at last been trying to solve part of the equation by promoting the qualification of a labour force desperately needing more advanced skills. It remains to be seen if this effort is too little and was made too late.

The implementation of the Bologna process is also providing pressure for change at the level of higher education. Higher education institutions have already adapted their study programmes to the Bologna process. Most of the new programmes have seen their normal course duration shortened from four or five years to only three years, while a very large number of second-cycle programmes (Masters) are now on offer. However, it is as yet too early to draw conclusions about the effect of these changes on the employability of graduates, the average time to graduation or even to what extent the shorter duration of first degrees will attract more students.

Note

1 EUROSTAT data shows 29.9 per cent for Portugal, 72.0 per cent for EU27 and 68.8 per cent for EU15.

References

Amaral, A. and Magalhães, A. (2009) 'Access policies: between institutional competition and the search for equality of opportunities', *Journal of Adult and Continuing Education*, 15, 2: 155–169.

Amaral, A., Rosa, M. and Veiga, A. (2005) 'Institutional internationalisation strategies in a context of state inefficiency', in J. Huisman and M. van der Wende (eds) *On Cooperation and Competition* II. Bonn: Lemmens Verlags, pp. 249–275.

DGES (2010) http://www.dges.mctes.pt/NR/rdonlyres/DB16C19A-3C9A-4D42-A538-20A9DE823C74/4002/linha_ens_sup_gar_mutua_ComAcomp_Dez2009.pdf

Fonseca, M., Dias, D., Sá, C. and Amaral, A. (forthcoming) Waves of dis(satisfaction): effects of the numerus clausus system in Portugal.

GPEARI, Ministry for Science, Technology and Higher Education (2011a) http://www.gpeari.mctes.pt/?idc=21&idi=507088 (accessed 12 April 2011).

GPEARI, Ministry for Science, Technology and Higher Education (2011b) http://www.gpeari.mctes.pt/?idc=21&idi=507095 (accessed 12 April 2011).

GPEARI, Ministry for Science, Technology and Higher Education (2011c) http://www.gpeari.mctes.pt/index.php?idc=21&idi=507091 (accessed 12 April 2011).

Guichard, S. and Larre, B. (2006) 'Enhancing Portugal's human capital', Economics Department Working Papers No. 505, OECD, ECO/WKP(2006)33.

MCTES (2006) *Tertiary Education in Portugal*. Background report to support the international assessment of the Portuguese system of tertiary education, Lisbon: MCTES.

Observatório de Emprego e Formação Profissional (2010) *Aspectos Estruturais do Mercado de Trabalho*, Lisbon: OEFP. www.oefp.pt (accessed on March 14 2011).

OECD (2010) *Education at a Glance 2010. OECD Indicators*, Paris: OECD.

Tavares, D., Orlanda, T., Amaral, A. and Justino, E. (2008) 'Students' preferences and needs in Portuguese higher education', *European Journal of Education*, 43, 1: 107–122.

Teixeira, P., Amaral, A. and Rosa, M.J. (2003) 'Mediating the economic pulses. The international connection in Portuguese higher education', *Higher Education Quarterly*, 57, 2: 18–203.

Teixeira, P., Madalena, F., Amado, D., Sá, C. and Amaral, A. (2009) 'A regional mismatch? student applications and institutional responses in the Portuguese public higher education system', in K. Mohrman, J. Shi, S.E. Feinblatt and K.W. Chow (eds) *Public Universities and Regional Development*, Chengdu: Sichuan University Press, pp. 59–80.

Chapter 6

Sweden

Higher education and lifelong learning in Sweden

Camilla Thunborg and Agnieszka Bron

Introduction

In this chapter, we will describe both the development of higher education in the last decade in Sweden and some aspects of lifelong learning. In Sweden, political reform in relation to access to higher education has been on the agenda since the 1950s resulting in significantly increased student numbers. Specific to the Swedish case, however, is the high level of drop-out from higher education. We will argue that participation in higher education in Sweden is characterized as a 'drop-in, drop-out' system which makes the university not only an institution for obtaining a formal degree, but also for lifelong learning. In the Nordic countries, the combination of lifelong learning and the importance of non-formal education is a significant component in the post–compulsory sector overall. At the same time, the value of higher education, as a place for knowledge creation and critical thinking, seems to be challenged by becoming increasingly an arena for instrumental learning, which is also underpinned by the demands of the labour market. A diploma from higher education does not seem to have the same value as it used to. The motivation for students to finish their studies, as well as for under-represented groups to even start, is thereby decreasing. Our conclusion is that widening access to higher education is not enough. Academic knowledge needs to have a greater value in society, and especially in the labour market, to maintain its high visibility and status in the wider society. Working-class men, particularly those from rural areas and immigrants from Africa, should be able to take advantage of the open system in Sweden, if they really think that higher education would make a difference in their lives.

Sweden: a short description

Sweden has a small population with about 9.4 million people living on nearly 450,000 square kilometres. The population density is low, with declining numbers in rural areas (especially in the northern part of four of the Swedish counties) in contrast to an increasing population in Stockholm. Migration

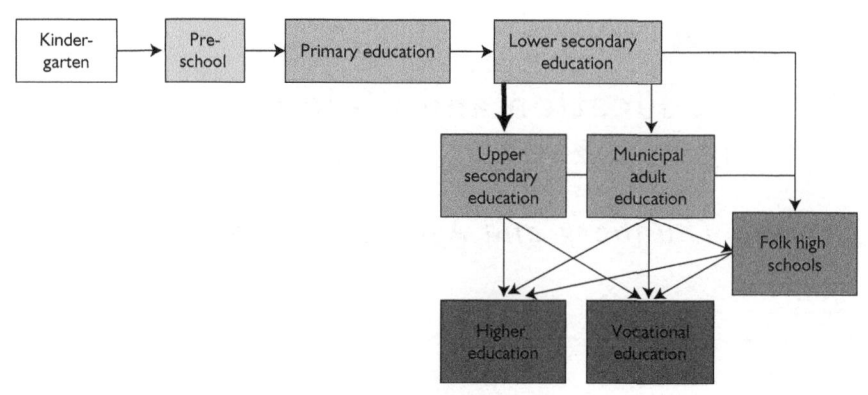

Figure 6.1 The Swedish education system

to Sweden is also increasing. In 2009, 98,644 people obtained permission to stay, 10 per cent more than in the previous year. The three most common nationalities came from Iraq, Somalia and Poland (Migrationsverket 2010). In the last decade, most of the applicants were related to those with 'permission to stay' people searching for political asylum; but the numbers of students and workers from outside the EU also increased. Since 2007, there has been a specific aim to increase the number of working immigrants because of the problem of an ageing population (Sveriges offentliga utredningar 2005: 50).

The Swedish educational system

Sweden has had an integrated school system since 1962 (Bron and Agélii 2000). The Swedish formal education system is sketched in Figure 6.1.

Through the integration of the educational system, its different parts were merged into a relatively coherent structure. Primary and lower secondary education together make nine years of compulsory school, followed by a voluntary upper secondary level where both vocational and academic programmes are organized in the same institution. There is also optional pre-school education from the age of six, which aims to give all children an equal start. Since the late 1980s, primary and secondary education has been organized by municipalities, while the state is responsible for curricula and evaluation (Bron and Agélii 2000). In recent decades, publically financed private or free schools have been organized as an alternative to public schools. Taking all levels as a whole, public schools are the most common, but at upper secondary level the private free schools – the most common choice in 2009 in the Stockholm area – are increasing in popularity all over the country (Skolverket 2010).

Upper secondary education has changed over the last 20 years. In 1993 upper secondary education was organized in 16 different three-year national programmes sharing the same general curricula. All programmes conferred basic eligibility for further studies in higher education. During the last decade, this reform has been discussed and amended. Two reasons are given for these changes: first, many students failed to graduate, especially in core competences like Maths, English and Swedish (Sveriges offentliga utredningar 2008: 27); second, different political views were put forward on the question of who should be eligible for entry to higher education. In the new reform, a firm distinction is made between vocational and academic programmes. Altogether, there ought to be 18 national programmes, six academic and twelve vocational programmes whereas apprenticeship is supposed to be optional in the vocational programmes. Some general subjects are included in all the programmes, but there are different requirements for academic and vocational programmes (www.skolverket.se).

Formal competence from upper secondary education is also available in municipality adult education (KOMVUX) and through Folk high schools. The Folk high school has a long tradition in Sweden and provides, to a large extent – despite being non-formal – eligibility to higher education.[1] During the 1990s vocational education after upper secondary level was formalized, and from 2009 situated under the Vocational college authority (YH) (Myndigheten för yrkeshögskolan, 2010), earlier called qualified vocational education (KY). Besides coordinating vocational education and training the YH authority deals with formally validating competences. In 2009, 42,000 students participated in 905 educational courses of differing lengths. Altogether, 46 per cent of the students were men and 54 per cent women. Economy, administration and marketing were the largest subjects (ibid.).

Participation in upper secondary school, as well as in non-formal education, is amongst the highest in Europe (Eurostat 2010). About 85 per cent of the Swedish population graduated from upper secondary school (Högskoleverket 2010a). Sweden also has the highest participation in non-formal education in Europe 2010 (ibid.). It is estimated that there are 1.9 million participants in popular adult education, mostly in study circles (276,000 study circles in 2008). In 2009, nearly 200,000 participants took part in courses organized by 148 Folk high schools (www.folkbildning.se).[2] Participation in higher education has increased since the 1950s and reached its highest-ever level in 2007, with about 94,000 new entrants (Högskoleverket 2010a).

The role of information and communication technologies in education

Internationally, Sweden is seen as a well-developed IT country. In 2010, it was ranked first in the world in the readiness and conditions for successful IT use in three respects: ICT development (i.e. internet use); network readiness (i.e. the IT environment offered by the country and society – individuals, companies and government); and digital economy (i.e. the economic, legal, political and social conditions relevant to the development of IT). In Sweden in 2010, 85 per cent of the population over 16 years of age had internet access at home, 97 per cent of them through broadband. The internet is used by all age groups even though people born between the 1940s and 1990s are dominant. The daily use of the internet has increased from 25 per cent in 2003 to 66 per cent in 2010 (Findahl 2010).

The use of ICT is not regulated in the formal school system, but nevertheless 95 per cent of the teachers use ICT in their classes, which in a European perspective is high – especially given that the pupils themselves are using it more than teachers in their daily schoolwork. During 2009, about 8,000 people in Sweden studied in 750 distance courses, and the number of courses offered by Folk high schools in Sweden and the number of participants is increasing (Statistiska Centralbyrån 2009). The greatest increase, however, is related to higher education. In Sweden, distance education is provided by mainstream institutions for higher education (Högskoleverket 2011). The definition of distance education has, in the last decade, become more diffuse as most campus-based courses also use learning platforms for students to be able to handle most of their studies at a distance (ibid.).

Higher education and changes over the last ten years

The Swedish system of higher education is considered to be open (Schuetze and Slowey 2000) and relatively uniform as it comprises all types of post-secondary education including professional programmes such as, for example, nursing and teacher training. In recent decades it has gone from elite to mass education and the participation in higher education as well as the number of institutions, programmes and courses, are all increasing. However, over the last ten years we can see changes concerning the openness of the system towards young students (19–24 years of age) and decreasing opportunities for mature students (partly due to changes in the 24+5 access route).[3]

Another major change in Swedish higher education policy is the pan-European standardization of higher education through the so-called Bologna process. As higher education is decentralized in Sweden, government only suggested that institutions could voluntarily implement changes in accordance with the Bologna process. However, most of the leading institutions, including Stockholm University (the largest), implemented the policy, starting in 2007.

A further change is the allocation, since 2001, of research funds only to strong research environments, which resulted in an imbalance between the disciplines. Humanities in particular are suffering, which with students' lack of interest in applying to arts and humanities, contributed to the closing down of many departments.

Higher education is publicly funded and cost about 2 per cent of the Swedish GNP in 2006, which is higher than the average in OECD countries. It is free of charge, but from 2011 fees will be charged for students from outside Europe, which is a total new situation for higher education institutions (Eurostat 2010). Since 1945, when a special commission looked at the opportunities for students from low-income backgrounds (Richardsson 1983), access to higher education has been an issue, and in the late 1960s special loans and aids for all students were implemented (Nilsson 1986). Swedish higher education consists of professional programmes, academic programmes and free courses both on campus and in the form of distance education. From 1990 to 2005 student numbers in Sweden grew from 150,000 to 330,000 (Holzer 2009). From 2002/03 to 2008/09 participation in distance education increased by 100 per cent, and by 2009 about 14 per cent of the participation in higher education was through distance education. Seventy per cent of distance education is offered as free courses. In 2008, 3,510 courses, 90 professional programmes and 129 academic programmes were available through distance learning (Högskoleverket 2011).

Within the Swedish higher education system, educational programmes with a duration from two to six years and single courses are available. Students have the opportunity to put together a Bachelors degree or a Masters degree to suit their interests as long as certain criteria are met (Högskoleverket 2009a). In total, there are 60 institutions of higher education, 14 state universities, 22 state university colleges, 3 private universities and 24 small, special institutions focusing upon certain areas, for example, theology, psychotherapy and art (Högskoleverket 2009b). In relation to high and low status respectively, Holzer (2009) makes a distinction between old and new universities. Universities established before 1977 are referred to as old universities and those that were established after 1977 as new universities. However, there also seems to be a difference concerning status related to disciplines where, for example, medicine has high status and nursing low, even if they are situated at the same university. The differentiation is in this respect more within than across institutions. Universities are also merging into bigger entities. In 2008 the Institute of Education (the teacher training college in Stockholm) merged with Stockholm University (Högskoleverket, 2009b), and in 2010 the University of Växjö and the University College in Kalmar were integrated and became Linneaus University. To achieve a better economy, the trend has been to centralize higher education (Högskoleverket 2010a). Sweden, like the rest of Europe, is suffering from recession, but has so far come out better than expected. Nevertheless, the unemployment rate increased from 6 per cent at the beginning of 2009 to 11.4 per cent in September 2010. Higher education has been used as an instrument for the labour market (Statistiska Centralbyrån 2010c) with an increase in the numbers of students in programmes leading directly to employment. The government increased the number of places in higher education for 2010 and 2011 by 10,000. Also aid and loans for students increased. Another aspect of the government's decision was to increase the level of resource allocated to research (Regeringskansliet 2009).

Several political reforms for widening access to higher education have been undertaken since the 1950s (Bron and Agèlii 2000). Since 2001, there has been a law stating that universities must have 10 per cent of non-traditional students, but in practice some universities do not accomplish this and lecturers do not often recognize having non-traditional students in their departments (Bron, Edström and Thunborg 2010). Holzer (2009) points out that the new universities have helped to widen access to higher education. The local university is seen as a possible alternative to entering the local labour market, especially for groups whose parents had upper secondary school as their highest educational level (Holzer 2009). Despite the differences in status between new and old universities there are no differences in the participation of non-traditional students.[4] The reason for this is that even elite universities offer shorter educational programmes. The differences seem instead to be related to the status of educational programmes and disciplines. Thus, medicine and law have the lowest and teacher education the highest proportion of working class students (Högskoleverket 2008b).

Even if the numbers entering higher education are high, only about 40 per cent of students end up with a degree after seven years. However, students in 'older' universities are more likely to get a degree than those attending new universities. Some students move to an old university in their final year to finish their degree (Holzer 2009). Thirty-four per cent of the Swedish population between the age of 25 and 64 has a higher education qualification, which is above the average in relation to OECD countries. Interestingly, the median age for starting to study in higher education, together with Iceland and Denmark, is the highest in the OECD (Eurostat 2010). In the academic year 2009/10 the median age for those entering higher education was 20.9 which is relatively high in an international context, but low from a historical Swedish perspective (Högskoleverket 2011).

The number of students entering higher education also varies in relation to conditions in the labour market. In a longer perspective, however, the percentage of a specific age group entering higher education is quite stable. Moreover, the number of distance students is increasing (since 2002), but most are studying for less than a year. As mentioned above, many students are taking free courses, with no relation to a specific educational programme. These courses are chosen by students starting higher education, as well as by those taking it as a part of continuing education who already have a diploma or as a part of professional development supported by employers. The participation in free courses has increased by 9 per cent, but the largest increase has been in general programmes, an increase of 13 per cent (Högskoleverket 2010a, 2011).

Non-traditional students in HE

In the Swedish context, there is no explicit definition of non-traditional students and the term is used differently in different contexts (Bron and Agèlii 2000). In one respect, the term could be used for under-represented groups in higher education. In relation to this definition, students with lower socio-economic status, ethnic background other than Swedish, with disabilities and mature students could be defined as non-traditional. Women, who traditionally were under-represented, are today highly over-represented in higher education in almost all subjects (Bron and Lönnheden 2004). According to the available statistics, there are some changes concerning overall participation in the last decade. The number of younger students has increased; students having well-educated parents are still highly over-represented, and students from working class homes under-represented, despite all the reforms aimed at widening access. Amongst the beginners in higher education under 35, 34 per cent had parents with at least three years in higher education, which represents 20 per cent of the population. In relation to gender, 38 per cent of the men and 32 per cent of the women had parents with a higher education qualification (Statistiska Centralbyrån 2010b).

The number of students with an ethnic background other than Swedish is also increasing. In the study year 2008/09, 18 per cent of the beginners in higher education had another ethnic background, compared with 12 per cent in 1999/2000. Despite this increase, these groups remain under-represented. There are, however, large differences between different ethnic groups. In 2008/09, 60 per cent of the Iranians in Sweden at the age of 25 had been or were enrolled in higher education, compared with 45 per cent of the Swedes and only 16 per cent of the Somalians. In comparison with the ten most common ethnic backgrounds in the population, students from Iran and Poland have the highest representation in higher education. Women are over-represented in these groups as well – 62 per cent of the beginners with a background other than Swedish entering higher education were women (Högskoleverket 2010a). Furthermore, there are differences in enrolment between geographical areas in Sweden. In the university cities and rich municipalities more than 50 per cent of the 24-year-olds are enrolled, but in rural areas, especially in the north, the enrolment is rather low. Danderyd, which is an upper class municipality in the Stockholm area, has the highest enrolment in relation to its population. Nearly 76 per cent of 24-year-olds were or had been enrolled in higher education, while in Arjeplog, a small municipality in a rural area in the northern part of Sweden, the proportion was only 11 per cent. There seem to be differences between men and women in rural areas in the north as well. In Västernorrland, for example, 55 per cent of the 24-year-old women but only 34 per cent of the men were or had been enrolled. In university cities the gender differences are the average for Sweden at 16 per cent (Högskoleverket 2010c). Distance education has been one of the means for widening access to higher education for non-traditional students. It has increased the participation of mature students, of students with parents with lower educational background, and for students with children younger than 18. However, most of the students studying at a distance have previous experience of studying in higher education (Högskoleverket 2011).

Higher education – a system for dropping in and dropping out

The drop-out rates for higher education in Sweden are high, compared with other countries. In 2009, for example, only 83 per cent of students completed a course or an educational programme (Högskoleverket 2010a). There are several reasons for this. First, there are differences between free courses, general and professional programmes. The completion of free courses is only about 60 per cent and is decreasing (ibid.) and in distance courses the proportion is even lower, about 56 per cent (Högskoleverket 2011). One reason for this seems to be that free courses are used as an individual lifelong learning strategy where students are dropping in, changing between courses before deciding what to do in their lives, or returning to continue to learn or changing their life course (Thunborg, Edström and Bron 2011). As an example, amongst the 240,000 that were enrolled in new courses and programmes during autumn 2010, 177,000 had previously been enrolled in higher education, 17 per cent of these had been away from studies for two years or more and 26 per cent had a previous diploma from higher education (Statistiska Centralbyrån 2010a). The completion rate in general programmes is about 80 per cent and in professional programmes more than 90 per cent (Högskoleverket 2010a). The completion rate is decreasing in general programmes and free courses, but is stable in professional programmes.

In a report from the National Board of Higher Education, drop-out from general and professional programmes is further analysed (Högskoleverket 2010b). One of the conclusions drawn in this report is that professional programmes giving certificates needed for employment have the highest completion rate. Men within technical educational programmes are more likely to drop out during their last year, largely because they have obtained employment before completion. For women, and in other fields, drop out seems to take place during the first semester. Women are more likely to change educational programmes, and are therefore not actually dropping out of higher education, while men who drop out seem to leave higher education totally. Completion could also be related to the type of diploma they are aiming for. In Sweden, students have to apply for a diploma after finishing a programme or the amount of the European Credit Transfer and Accumulation System Credits (ECTS credits) they need. A Bachelor degree consists of 180 ECTS credits and 120 credits for a Master level. In 2008/09, 27,000 Bachelor diplomas were awarded, and 20,000 of the students were women; at the Masters level 24,000 were awarded of which 14,000 were women. Overall, there was a gender difference in the region of 25 per cent. In terms of age difference, 25 per cent of the year group born in 1974 have a diploma from higher education at the age of 35. This is an increase compared with the year group born in 1962, where 11 per cent have a diploma. Within the statistical reports there are no analyses concerning drop out and/or completion of non-traditional students.

Lifelong learning

There is a shift in educational policy in Sweden from upper secondary education for all towards mass higher education, by allocation of places and funds. In this way, the goal of lifelong learning is being continuously implemented in Sweden.

Lifelong learning as a concept, which came to prominence in the 1990s in Sweden, replaced the notions of 'recurrent education' (Rubenson 1987) and 'lifelong education'. It centres on the belief that individuals can, and should, learn throughout their lives. It assumes that an individual takes responsibility for their own learning and should be actively looking for knowledge, not only at educational institutions but also in the work place and in everyday life. According to Rubenson (1996), the principles underlying the new concept are significantly different than those it replaced. Nevertheless, adult educators tend to interpret the new concept as being synonymous with adult education. The philosophy associated with lifelong learning is, however, more closely connected to the economy.

Sweden has been affected by both global and European policies of lifelong learning by taking into consideration the Hamburg Declaration on Adult Learning of 1997 and the EU Memorandum on Lifelong Learning of 2000. The Hamburg Declaration on adult education stated that learning throughout life is one of the keys to the 21st century:

> It is both a consequence of active citizenship and a condition for full participation in society. It is a powerful concept for fostering sustainable development, for promoting democracy, justice, and scientific and economic development, and for building a world in which violent conflict and war is replaced by dialogue and a culture of peace. Learning throughout life implies a rethinking of content and approach to education at all levels including adult education, to open up opportunities for learning for all.
> (CONFINTEA 1997: 1)

The Hamburg Declaration was quite easy to implement in Sweden due to its long tradition of popular adult education. In non-formal adult education, the participation rate is the highest in Europe.

Sweden has effectively implemented the EU Memorandum of 2000, which stated that 'Lifelong learning is no longer just one aspect of education and training; it must become the guiding principle for provision and participation across the full continuum of learning contexts' (EU 2000: 3). Two important goals are taken into account in this document: employability and active citizenship, 'two features of contemporary social and economic change are interrelated. They underlie two equally important aims for lifelong learning: promoting active citizenship and promoting employability' (ibid.: 5). These two key words unite questions about working life and 'bildning'. The latter includes people's opportunities to exercise their rights and obligations as citizens and be able to influence their own situation. The Memorandum provides guidance to the EU members to strengthen the European economy particularly vis-à-vis the United States, with lifelong learning being viewed as a competitive factor and instrument of growth. The fact that active citizenship is included as a goal of the EU's policy for lifelong learning proves that there are efforts to develop democracy, even if the economic vision dominates. However, the adult education community of researchers and practitioners criticized the major focus on the economic motive as the key driver. In Sweden, the criticism was connected to the emphasis on individual effort to get education and to increase cultural capital – as opposed to a focus on the common or social aspects of lifelong learning.

Even if Sweden has a long tradition of active democratic citizenship, which is fostered by popular adult education, the question of employability is a crucial consideration for the State's policy. Thus, the State's efforts to strengthen the opportunities for both young people and adults to acquire education, which enable them to be included in working life, are a priority. This was possible through the provision of courses and programmes arranged by Municipal adult education (KOMVUX) which enabled adults to obtain upper secondary education and seek higher education. In addition, the Adult Education Initiative (Kunskapslyftet), started in 1997 to give adequate upper secondary education to mostly unemployed adults, was regarded as a success.

Recently, there has been an emphasis on lifelong learning in Sweden, not only in higher education but also more generally in the whole educational system. In educational policy, a continuing argument is used, emphasizing the need for well-educated citizens and the need to integrate people with different backgrounds (ethnic, class, gender and disability) into society in order to achieve equal, cross-cultural and democratic relations. Opening higher education to the new groups is a main purpose of State policy. A clear connection between inclusion, integration and learning in the multicultural and democratic state of Sweden is evident in this policy (see Bron and Lönnheden 2004: 186).

For its population, Sweden has advanced considerably towards increasing access to higher education, however,

> there is still much more to be done, to include groups who are not sufficiently represented in the tertiary system. Providing for access is only one factor which contributes to inclusion at the entry level. Other issues and questions that remain include: What happens to non-traditional students once they are enrolled in the system? What kind of difficulties do they have in their studies and how can we overcome these difficulties? What is the 'process of learning' for them and how do we adapt to their specific learning needs? Entry is not enough; it is only then when students are successful in their learning that we can talk of a real inclusion policy and lifelong learning.
>
> (Bron and Lönnheden 2004: 186)

Knowing about the impact of higher education and its contribution to lifelong learning and inclusion to society could be facilitated by looking at graduates' critical thinking skills. Bron and Lönnheden (ibid.) ask:

> Do they (students) learn how to reflect critically and how to make critical judgements? Are they prepared to continue learning after graduation? Our limited research outcomes have proven that they do and are capable of these things. They give evidence of this by demonstrating a better understanding of their own capabilities, through a willingness to continue their engagement in societal and political questions, and by becoming a link to encourage others to take a step toward higher education.
>
> (ibid.: 186)

However, we are not sure if the objective of enabling adults to reflect critically on societal issues and critically judge the research outcomes and scientific propositions, is really possible in the current environment. The dominance of the instrumental approach towards learning is detrimental to the promotion of reflexivity and critical approaches towards knowledge and personal development. Interpretations of lifelong learning which place the emphasis on individual effort and employability reinforce this instrumentalism.

Bron-Wojciechowska (1995) argues that education as a value in itself was not emphasized by Swedish participants in the educational system in the 1980s, but was treated instrumentally as a means to getting employment and practical skills. In a new report concerning students' attitudes in Europe (Högskoleverket 2010d), students in Sweden claim that it is more important that the educational programme in higher education offers a sound preparation for their future careers than for their personal development. We can also notice, in the report, a strengthening of the instrumental and employability approach at all levels in education, even in higher education.

Conclusions

In conclusion, we will first claim that the role of higher education in relation to lifelong learning has a long tradition in Sweden, which is mostly due to the expansion of popular adult education in the nineteenth century, and its definitive success in creating opportunities for learning for a large proportion of the population. The Swedish educational system makes it possible to obtain access to the next level in the educational system and there is complementary adult education, both formal and non-formal, for being able to get access to higher education. As both formal upper secondary, community education (KOMVUX) and non-formal education, such as Folk high schools, are giving eligibility to higher education, there are indeed several options for people with different life paths to enter higher education. From this point of view, Sweden can be said to be relatively successful in creating opportunities for lifelong learning.

The drop-outs, or non-completions, could be discussed both as a success and as a failure. On the one hand, students have, and use, their opportunities to change between courses and educational programmes in relation to their different needs and wishes through their life span. For men studying technology, drop out is related to obtaining employment. On the other hand, higher education is about to fail in positioning itself as an important institution for knowledge, learning and 'bildung'. It risks becoming reduced to a means for employability, for supporting the labour market, where learning and knowledge are treated in an instrumental way.

The Swedish higher education system, on the one hand, is used as a strategy for lifelong learning by people returning to higher education several times during their life course, in a continuous process (Thunborg and Edström 2010), and for people to move between formal and non-formal educational institutions that increase their opportunities for learning. From this perspective, higher education could be seen as successful in the number of participants and that it is also used as an institution for 'bildung' all through the life course in parallel with other forms of education and training. As Bron and Lönnheden (2004) point out, people engaging in education are better equipped to engage with society and be part of a democracy.

On the other hand, the dominance of the focus on employability in higher education, together with other forms of education such as the vocational training schools, the changes in upper secondary school, and the increasing participation in work-place training activities, seem to be more prominent than ever. For students choosing higher education, knowledge directly related to future work becomes more important and aspects of 'bildung' of less importance. This may well create a more instrumental attitude towards learning (Bron-Wojciechowska 1995; Högskoleverket 2010d).

However, even more important seems to be the low completion rate in higher education which might show a tendency to a decreasing value placed on diplomas from higher education in Swedish society. In this chapter we have seen some features that seem to have an impact in this respect. One could argue that the widening of access and expansion in participation has decreased the perceived value of higher education by making it less exclusive; or that some higher education programmes do not lead – as they did in the past – to a higher income; or that students are obtaining employment before they complete their studies. Or, that the moves to recognize vocational education equally with higher education seem to change the status of academic knowledge in relation to employability. Our main conclusion is that while Sweden has been successful in widening access, on its own this not sufficient to obtain real equality for certain sections of society such as young men from working-class backgrounds, men from rural areas or immigrants from Africa. One reason for this may be that education, including higher education, is viewed instrumentally by public policy, the labour market and indeed by students. As the lifetime income of graduates in Sweden is not necessarily a great deal higher than that of the general population, it may not be perceived by some groups as being 'worth the effort'. The value placed by society as a whole on higher education therefore warrants serious and urgent discussion.

Notes

1 For Folk high schools to be able to get their financial support from the State, they are obliged to organize and run private courses compensating for participants who did not finish upper secondary education.
2 In Spring 2009, in total 100,800 students participated in Folk high school courses, of which 27,500 students were in long courses with a duration of at least 15 days, and in the autumn term there were a total of 89,700 participants of which 29,600 were in long courses. The numbers for short courses (1–14 days) and open activities were: spring term 2009, 58,400 students; autumn term 2009, 51,200 students. Also, 5,100 students in the spring term and 2,700 students in the autumn term participated in courses commissioned by outside bodies apart from the Swedish National Council of Adult Education (Statistiska Centralbyrån 2009).
3 For information on the 24+5 scheme see Bron and Agèlii (2000).
4 Södertörn University College, which is a new university, has the largest proportion of students born in another country or with two parents born in another country (39 per cent), followed by Karolinska Institutet (KI) which is seen as an old elite university (37 per cent). The most common educational programmes for these groups are shorter courses in engineering, occupational therapy, social work, teaching and nursing.

References

Bron, A. and Agélii, K., 2000. Sweden: Non-traditional Students in Sweden: From Recurrent Education to Lifelong Learning, pp. 83–100. In Schuetze, H and Slowey, M. Eds, *Higher Education and Lifelong Learners. International Perspectives on Change*. London: Routledge/Falmer.
Bron, A. and Lönnheden, C., 2004. Higher Education for Non-traditional Students in Sweden – A Matter of Inclusion. *Journal of Adult and Continuing Education*. 7, pp. 175–188.
Bron, A., Edström, E. and Thunborg, C., 2010. Forming Learning Identities in Higher Education. In ESREA (European Society for Research on the Education of Adults), *6th Adult Learning in Europe – Understanding Diverse Meanings and Contexts*. Linköping, Sweden, pp. 23–26.
Bron-Wojciechowska, A., 1995. Active Citizenship and the Value of Education – The Case of Sweden. *International Yearbook of Adult Education*, 23, pp. 200–219.
CONFINTEA, 1997. Unesco. Adult Education. The Hamburg Declaration the Agenda for the Future. 5th International Conference on Adult Education. Hamburg, Germany, 14–18 July 1997.
EU, 2000. *Memorandum on Lifelong Learning*. Bryssel: EC.
Eurostat, 2010. *Europe in Figures – Eurostat Yearbook 2010*. Luxembourg: Publications Office of the European Union.
Findahl, O., 2010. *Swedes and the internet 2010*. Stockholm: SE.

Högskoleverket, 2008b. *Universitet och högskolor. Högskoleverkets årsrapport 2008.* Rapport 2008:19R. Stockholm: Högskoleverket.
Högskoleverket, 2009a. *Swedish Universities & University Colleges.* Short version of annual report 2009. Report 2009:23 R. Stockholm: Högskoleverket.
Högskoleverket, 2009b. *Universitet och högskolor. Högskoleverkets årsrapport* [Swedish Universities and University Colleges]. Rapport: 2009:12. Stockholm: Högskoleverket.
Högskoleverket, 2010a. *Årsrapport 2010. [Yearbook 2010 from the Swedish National Agency for Higher Education].* Rapport 1010R. Stockholm: Högskoleverket.
Högskoleverket, 2010b. *Orsaker till studieavbrott. [Reasons for non-completion].* Rapport 2010: 23R. Stockholm: Högskoleverket.
Högskoleverket, 2010c. *Statistisk analys: Stora regionala skillnader i påbörjade högskolestudier bland ungdomar. [Statistical analyses: Huge differences between regions in entering higher education amongst young people].* Statistical analyses. 2010/2. Stockholm: Högskoleverket.
Högskoleverket, 2010d. *Eurostudent – om svenska studenter i en europeisk undersökning, hösten 2009.[Eurostudent – About Swedish Students in a European Study].* Rapport 2010-20R. Stockholm: Högskoleverket.
Högskoleverket, 2011. *Kartläggning av distansverksamheten vid universitet och högskolor. [Mapping distance activities at universities and university colleges].* Rapport 2011: 2 R. Stockholm: Högskoleverket.
Holzer, S., 2009. *University choice, Equality and Academic Performance.* PhD Acta Wexionensia. Economics, 1404–4307, 188. Växjö: Växjö University.
Migrationsverket, 2010. *Migration 2000–2010.* Rapport 2010: 2. Norrköping: Migrationsverket.
Myndigheten för yrkeshögskolan, 2010. *Årsredovisning för myndigheten för yrkeshögskolan 2009.* [Yearbook for the Vocational College Authorities 2009]. Dnr: YH 2010/144. Available through: www.yhmyndigheten.se/hem/ arsredovisning_716/ [accessed 2 May 2011].
Nilsson, A., 1986. Studiemedel, arbetsmarknad och rekrytering till högre utbildning. [Studyfinancing, labour market and access to Higher Education]. *Forskning om utbildning* [Research in Education], 4, pp. 18–31.
Regeringskansliet, 2009. Fler utbildningsplatser och förstärkta arbetsmarknadsåtgärder. [More places in education and labour market measures]. *Promemoria*, 2009-08-06. Green paper. Stockholm: Regeringskansliet.
Richardsson, G., 1983. *Drömmen om en ny skola: ideer och realiteter i svensk skolpolitik 1945–1950.* [The dream of a new school: ideas and realities in Swedish educational policy, 1945–1950]. Stockholm: Liber.
Rubenson, K., 1987. Återkommande utbildning: A moving target. In Rubenson, K., ed. *Återkommande utbildning – idé och strategi.* [Recurrent education – idéas and strategies]. Institutionen för pedagogik och psykologi. Vuxenpedagogiska forskningsgruppen, Linköping: Linköpings universitet.
Rubenson, K., 1996. Livslångt lärande – Mellan utopi och verklighet. In Ellström, P.-E, Gustavsson, B. and Larsson, S. Eds., *Livslångt lärande.* [Lifelong learning]. Lund: Studentlitteratur.
Schuetze, H. and Slowey, M., 2000. Traditions and new directions in Higher Education: a comparative perspective on non-traditional students and lifelong

learners. In Schuetze, H. and Slowey, M. Eds. *Higher Education and Lifelong Learners. International Perspectives on Change.* London: Routledge/Falmer.

Skolverket, 2010. 'Storstäder och friskolor lockar allt fler gymnasieelever'. [Big cities and free schools attract upper secondary students] www.skolverket.se/2.3894/ publicerat/arkiv_pressmeddelanden/2010/storstader-och-friskolor-lockar-allt-fler-gymnasieelever-1.96922

Statistiska Centralbyrån, 2009. *Sveriges Officiella Statistik.* [Swedish Public Statistics]. Statistiska meddelanden, UF 22 SM 1001. Örebro: Statistiska Centralbyrån.

Statistiska Centralbyrån, 2010a. *Higher Education. Applicants and admitted students to higher education at first and second cycle studies autumn term 2010.* Statistiska meddelanden, UF 46 SM 1001. Örebro: Statistiska Centralbyrån.

Statistiska Centralbyrån, 2010b. *Higher Education. Level of parental education among university entrants 2009/10 and first time students at third circle studies 2008/09.* Statistiska meddelanden, UF 20 SM 1003. Örebro: Statistiska Centralbyrån.

Statistiska Centralbyrån, 2010c. *Information om utbildning och arbetsmarknad.* [Information about education and labour market], 2010: 2. Örebro: Statistiska Centralbyrån.

Sveriges offentliga utredningar, 2005. *Arbetskraftsinvandring till Sverige – befolkningsutveckling, arbetsmarknad i förändring, internationell utblick. Delbetänkande av Kommittén för arbetskraftsinvandring till Sverige.* [Influx of foreign labour to Sweden – the development of demography, changing labour market, international perspectives. Partial report from the Committee for the influx of foreign labour to Sweden]. Stockholm: Fritzes, p. 50.

Sveriges offentliga utredningar, 2008. Framtidsvägen– *en reformerad gymnasieskola. Betänkande av gymnasieutredningen.* [The future way – a reformed upper secondary school]. Stockholm: Fritzes. Statens offentliga utredningar, p. 27.

Thunborg, C. and Edström, E., 2010. Changing learning identities in higher education. In Merrill, B. and Monteagudo González, J., Eds. *Educational Journeys and Changing Lives. Adult Student Experiences. Vol 1.* Sevilla: Édición Digital@ Tres.

Thunborg, C., Edström, E. and Bron, A., 2011. RANLHE (Access and Retention the Experiences of Non-traditional Learners in Higher Education Conference). Motives for entering, dropping out or continuing to study in higher education. Seville, Spain, 7–8 April.

Chapter 7

United Kingdom

Universities and lifelong learning in the UK – adults as losers, but who are the winners?

Michael Osborne and Muir Houston

Introduction

The role of universities in lifelong learning is a function of national socio-economic context and related policies, and of historical circumstance. Sections from the UK's report to UNESCO's Sixth International Conference on Adult Education set a useful context for the UK's socio-economic position.

> The overall UK population continues to grow, although Scotland's population may be about to decline ... The main driver for population expansion is rising life expectancy. As a result of major improvements in the health of people aged 60–80, 21% of the population is now over 59, and this proportion is expected to continue rising for the foreseeable future.
> Economically, the decade 1997–2007 saw the longest recorded period of continuous growth, allowing Government to make major increases in public expenditure, concentrated particularly on education, health, and overcoming social exclusion. The employment rate has grown to almost 75%, one of the highest rates in the EU, and especially strongly among women. The rise in labour demand (and other factors) has led to an increase in effective retirement ages, with 1.3 million people still in work after State Pension Age in 2007. It has also supported a surge of immigration from Eastern Europe following the expansion of the EU in 2004. This has led to a growing cultural, linguistic and ethnic diversity in the population, with migrants increasingly dispersing from urban enclaves to smaller towns and rural communities. However, in early 2008 the UK economy was showing signs of slowing down. The 0.3% rise in GDP in the first quarter was the weakest in three years and the annual growth rate had been revised downwards to 2.3%.
> (McNair *et al.* 2009: 18)

Subsequent to this time, as Osborne (2011) has noted in the UK's national report on the EC's Action Plan on Adult Learning, the UK's economic prospects have declined further, and there were huge impacts in 2010 of a government public debt estimated at some £170bn. Only areas such as health, policing and school education have been immune from swingeing cuts of up to 25 per cent. Therefore, like other areas covered by public funding, universities are suffering drastic declines in support. And since the provision of lifelong learning opportunities in universities is discretionary, activity in this domain is one of the soft targets for cuts.

This provides some background to much of what follows, an account that suggests that increasingly universities have re-trenched in the face of economic pressure and decline of public funding to the core missions of mainstream undergraduate and postgraduate teaching and research. At the same time they are challenged to find new income streams, which inevitably means non-EU international students paying high fees. Providing opportunities for adults becomes a lower priority, despite its social desirability and obvious community benefits in terms not only of economic well-being, but also of health, social inclusion and civic participation, as demonstrated in the recent report of the Independent Enquiry into Lifelong Learning in the UK (Schuller and Watson 2009). Unfortunately, there is often an absence of leadership in higher education. As Watson (2009) indicates in a sector paper for the Inquiry, 'university leaders won't do what they know they should unless and until there is a special fund to support it, and they stop as soon as the so-called "initiative" ends'.

We begin this chapter by providing a brief overview of the history of lifelong learning in UK universities, outlining their role for most of the 20th century in providing extension studies for adults in the liberal adult education (LAE) tradition. In the final decades of that century and into the 21st century, this activity became relegated to a marginal activity of a few, mainly elite, universities with widening participation (WP) for traditionally non-participating groups coming to the fore. This phenomenon, which started as a way to provide *second chance* education for adults, over the decades has become manifest in a range of flexible arrangements for access, and has become a standard bearer for lifelong learning activity in the UK. It has been an expanding activity and is no longer the preserve of adult education, but much more a means to extend opportunities to all age groups, including early awareness schemes for school pupils with lower socio-economic status (SES). However despite the extensive effort and funding that has been put into WP schemes, research suggests that there have been only modest gains in equity for these groups, and many universities and disciplines remain immune from the pressures to change their recruitment practices. In this chapter we put particular focus on this area of increasing flexibility of access within the HE system, whilst also considering the full range of lifelong learning engagements of universities.

This chapter is about the UK, but readers should note that as a result of political devolution there are separate parliaments or assemblies in Northern Ireland, Scotland and Wales, and as a result different policies with respect to various matters, including higher education. The potential effect of this regionalisation was signalled in an earlier volume by Slowey (2000: 103), and it has led to different funding policies for higher education, which in turn has had an impact on provision of lifelong learning in the sector. We therefore can observe differences in *how* universities may utilise government funding and *who* pays for higher education in the different nation states. Nonetheless, these differences are not as significant as the autonomy that universities in the UK hold, and their ability to utilise resources supplied by government through national funding councils for higher education with considerable discretion. Irrespective of jurisdiction, we have seen over the last decade a shift away from the localism implied by lifelong learning. Slowey (2000) also commented on the pressures towards globalisation, and in the last decade it is internationalisation, manifest largely in the recruitment of increasing numbers of non-EU students, dictated by the impact of declining state funding, that has come to the fore.

Historical background

The role of UK universities in lifelong learning arguably is now into its third century, though the Victorian notions of learning for learning's sake, knowledge as something valuable in itself and the pursuit of absolute truths (Newman 1994: 37–43) do not appear to resonate well with the technicist approaches of 21st-century UK governments. For example, recent proposals in England and Northern Ireland that will lead to higher undergraduate tuition fees have been criticised, *inter alia*, because most arts and social sciences programmes in such a regime would not attract any government subsidy.

The first initiative that could be viewed as lifelong learning is that of *university extension* at the University of Cambridge in 1873, and was founded upon an impetus of providing university education for working men and, according to Kelly (1992: 219), the demand 'for university help in the higher education of women'. For over a century thereafter, provision by the HE sector, principally older institutions in existence prior to the re-designation of polytechnics as universities in 1992, was largely in the Liberal Adult Education (LAE) tradition. As Osborne (2003) has detailed, the offer was often evening classes of 20–30 hours in duration that were open to all who wished to participate and were offered at modest fees and without any mandatory assessment. Courses were located both within universities and in out-reach centres, often some distance from the parent institution. In many universities, provision took on a variety of other forms. For example programmes were established that focused on older adults, such as the University of the Third Age and a number of universities offered Summer Schools and Study Tours. Universities created links with movements concerned with political and social change, such as the Workers Educational Association (WEA), the

Independent Labour Party and the Co-operative Party, and created Extra-Mural Departments and later Departments of Continuing Education or Adult Education to co-ordinate LAE work. Much of this activity is described in histories of the field, including those of Kelly (1992) and Fieldhouse (1996).

It was only in the last decade of the 20th century that significant changes began to emerge in the university sector, and indeed that lifelong learning became part of the discourse. As Slowey (2000: 104) has indicated earlier, with some notable exceptions, there had 'been little evidence produced in previous decades by policy makers or by universities on students who were not direct school leavers'. The exceptions cited were the establishment of the Open University in 1969, LAE and special entry programmes for adults which can be dated back to the Department of Education and Science (DES) initiative of 1978, and a range of part-time undergraduate provision offered by polytechnics, some university adult education departments and by specialist institutions such as Birkbeck College.

The principle shift in the 1990s was the move away from LAE to WP, described elsewhere in some detail (Osborne 2003). It was in 1989 that a more transparent funding methodology for university continuing education was introduced by the then University Funding Council (UFC). Provision of funding was extended beyond LAE to other categories that were termed 'credit bearing', 'Access' and 'disadvantaged'. These latter two categories focused in a very explicit fashion on those adult students denied access to the university system for a range of situational and institutional reasons, and were forerunners to what now is more generally known as *widening participation*. This form of provision, already in existence in the non-university HE sector (polytechnics and higher education colleges in England and Wales and Central Institutions in Scotland) since the late 1970s, represented a significant challenge to the pre-1992 institutions. For some a focus on under-represented groups was a long overdue change in direction for the older universities, the LAE tradition having moved away from its 'historic values, ... particularly its targeting of the working classes and also its commitment to "social purpose" adult education' (Fieldhouse 1996). LAE was perceived as doing little to change the fundamental inequalities in access to mainstream undergraduate provision and did little to stimulate new demand for learning from traditionally non-participating and under-represented groups, particularly those with low socio-economic status, and from some ethnic minority groups.

The effects of the change in central government funding to universities were aggravated by reforms in local government, and consequent cost-cutting in this sector, which historically had financially supported significant elements of community-based university LAE. Further the focus on WP to higher education for disadvantaged groups and a greater policy commitment towards lifelong learning became much more explicit following the Dearing (National Committee of Inquiry into Higher Education 1997) and Garrick (SOEID 1997) reports of 1997 and subsequent Green Papers (DfEE 1998,

SOEID 1998 and WO 1998). Practice in recruitment within universities as a whole could not remain the same, and between 1995 and 1996, and 2007 and 2008, full-time numbers increased by over a quarter across the whole of the UK. Further, during the same period the percentage increases in part-time numbers were much greater. Notably in Scotland, part-time enrolments rose by 280 per cent.

Yet many adult and continuing education departments within universities remained wedded to LAE, and were marginalised with the expansion and widening of participation in their own institutions often being organised in other organisational units. For two decades there has been resistance (see Jones, Thomas and Moseley 2010). The initial changes of the early 1990s were accommodated by creating accredited courses of continuing education that could lead to HE level qualifications or credits that in principle could be accumulated and transferred to degree programmes. However despite the claims that this was a means in itself to widen participation, relatively few students used accredited continuing education as a vehicle to make the transition to the mainstream, and the profile of students taking these courses did not reflect under-represented groups. This was a factor in a policy change in 2007 that perhaps has led to the final demise of the tradition that dominated the 20th century. The change was the introduction of the Equivalent Level Qualification (ELQ)[1] rule in England and Wales that stops universities from drawing down government funding to subsidise adults who have already received higher education qualifications. Thereby the personal cost increases and becomes unsustainable to many. Since many of those taking accredited continuing education have already benefited from HE, recruitment to courses has inevitably declined and as a result many departments in existence for many decades have closed down.

The decline of adult education without a specific vocational purpose in universities is a reflection of wider concerns that adult education in all sectors should have a functional focus. The UK's Confintea Report (McNair *et al.* 2009: 14) states that:

> the UK has traditionally had a very extensive range of part-time 'non-vocational', non-qualification bearing adult education delivered by public and voluntary agencies at local level. This work expanded rapidly in the late 1990s, driven by a policy to use such programmes to widen participation in education generally. However, since 2004 learner numbers in this specific kind of publicly funded provision have declined significantly. This follows the new policy focus on skills and by the transition from a managed to a market led model of education for adults, which has produced rapid fee increases for many learners.

This decline is, however, a result of a deliberate policy to focus government support on priority groups and subjects, and the effect of this 'deepening' strategy can be seen in data from the Confintea Report (ibid.: 64). These show only adult learner numbers within the key Learning and Skills Council (LSC)[2] priority programmes in literacy and numeracy rising, against the broader trend of a decline of participation in adult learning.

We have in the main focused on the lifelong learning role of UK HEIs in delivering courses with a civic purpose and providing access. Whilst recognising the sometimes false dichotomy of social and vocational purpose (since adults typically have a mixture of both), as in other parts of the world, universities also offer provision that more explicitly have a continuing professional development (CPD) role. Furthermore there are a range of other engagements with their wider community. The extent of these roles is well delineated by Charles *et al.* (2010) in their work on benchmarking the regional engagement of HEIs in England. In this work the authors look at seven main groups of processes that underpin the regional development work of universities: enhancing regional infrastructure; human capital development processes; business development processes; interactive learning and social capital development processes; community development processes; cultural development; and, promoting sustainability. In any of these areas universities can make contributions through lifelong learning, and there are many schemes within the UK HE system to facilitate and encourage such practices.

Universities have been incentivised in a number of ways to engage with their regions. Currently in England it is through the Higher Education Innovation Fund (HEIF), which is constructed as a metric-based reward system to incentivise a broad range of knowledge exchange activities which result in economic and social benefit to the country. The fund was based on the Lambert (2003) Review of Business–University Collaboration. For example, in England through the Higher Education Funding Council for England (HEFCE), the Department of Industry, Universities and Skills (DIUS) is investing £148m in HE Employer Engagement to encourage employers to develop co-funded provision for high level skills as a means to help them, and their employees, improve high level skills. Currently there are more than 70 projects approved of various lengths and types. More than 10,000 places were contracted in 2008/09 against a target of 5,000.

A good example of how the vocational agenda and the thrust for greater inclusiveness has been met is found in Foundation Degrees: 2-year short-cycle higher education qualifications. These have been conceived as a key vehicle for expansion in Higher Education – they are flexible, work-focused and demand-led qualifications that the influential Leitch Report (2006) on 'world class skills' called for.

Current thinking

For those who construe lifelong learning as the modern conception of adult education, the picture painted to this point appears doubled-edged –

declines in one area are balanced by progress in another. And it is certainly the case that from the 1980s onwards, many more adults entered mainstream undergraduate provision, including through a range of widening access initiatives, and many of these adults have come from marginalised and socially disadvantaged groups. However, in the last decade WP has become increasingly focused on young people (including within schools as part of campaigns to raise awareness of HE at an early age) and this has been at the expense of adults (see Thomas *et al.* 2005). We therefore see two tendencies mitigating against adult participation in HE: the decline in LAE and its successor provision of Adult Continuing Education (ACE) and shifts towards early intervention in access to HE.

Further, the nature of universities in the UK as autonomous organisations funded only in part by the state means that there are relatively few policy levers in place to compel them to make available provision for adults. The main levers are funding incentives, and in difficult financial times more of these levers are concerned with young people and skills development than adult education for civic purposes (see Duke 2009 for an analysis). Whilst expressions of accessibility and flexibility are without exception highlighted in institutional statements, the reality in many institutions is that mature students are not a priority. WP policy at national and institutional level in the UK has shifted to broader concerns associated with the situation of younger people in areas of socio-economic deprivation. For many institutions, mature students are now part of a much bigger picture. If they aid the meeting of enrolment targets, then this is a bonus for many institutions, but it is unlikely that special arrangements will be made to attract this group given the relative merits of meeting WP targets through focusing on younger cohorts.

Flexibility and lifelong learning

We now focus specifically on this area of WP in more detail, drawing upon a recent review that we have undertaken on behalf of the UK's Higher Education Academy (Houston, McCune and Osborne 2011) with a particular focus on how flexibility in learning paths to and within HE has had an impact on lifelong learning prospects. One of the main arguments for WP in higher education has been that of social justice (Brennan and Naidoo 2008). While the term WP may be relatively new, the idea of education as transformative and as a vehicle for empowerment and social justice is not. An examination of the development of adult and continuing education in the 20th century, to which we previously alluded in the introduction to this chapter, provides plenty of examples of outreach and other activities, which sought to widen access to learning specifically among the working class. However, it was in the later part of that century that access became more significant as the HE system expanded very considerably, and that has been facilitated by flexible delivery patterns.

By flexibility we refer to both spatial and temporal matters, namely changes that allow students access to education in locations and modes, and at times that to at least a certain degree are of individuals' rather than institutions' choosing. It also refers to those mechanisms that challenge constructions of what constitutes knowledge at Higher Education level and the means by which knowledge can be acquired and demonstrated such as the recognition and accreditation of prior (experiential) learning (R/AP(E)L), and programmes of independent study, with to quote Percy and Ramsden (1980: 15) 'its stress on weakened boundaries between subject areas, on supra-disciplinary concepts, and on student control over the way in which knowledge is transmitted' (Osborne 2006: 9). It has been suggested that the use of alternative forms of delivery and the creation of flexible pathways through higher education (Outram 2009); the development of alternative programmes of study, like the introduction of Foundation Degrees in 2001 (Greenwood and Little 2008, Hicks *et al.* 2009); the use of accelerated learning (McCaig, Bowers-Brown and Drew 2007); and the opportunities made available with innovations in information and communications technology which have allowed the development of distance, blended and e-learning (Laurillard 2002, Sharpe *et al.* 2006) have, through the flexibility they allow, opened up new possibilities for WP.

Given the difficulty of fully defining flexibility, as discussed above, it is perhaps instructive to say what it is not. The traditional undergraduate experience delivered face to face in a university location, generally to school leavers, can perhaps be referred to as rigidity in the system and sector, which flexibility seeks to overcome. If WP is to be about encouraging the participation of those people or groups who are currently under-represented, then flexibility is about the underlying functions and structures of higher education systems and institutions which allow flexible solutions that attempt to overcome the limitations of the rigidity in the traditional full-time mode for under-represented groups.

Manifestations of flexibility in the UK system include:

- Flexibility in admissions. We take this to mean entry routes for those with alternative qualifications to those posited in the traditional model.
- Flexibility of mode both of attendance and of delivery, whereby students may study part-time, at a distance utilising technology or as a mix as seen in blended learning.
- Flexibility of location, which may be related to the above, or may mean attendance not at a university, but at a Further Education (FE) college,[3] a local community space, at the workplace or at home with potential transfer of credit within the aegis of a National Credit and Qualifications System.
- Flexibility in duration, with the introduction of Foundation Degrees, the use of other forms of short-cycle higher education or the option of accelerated learning or decelerated learning.

- Flexibility in recruitment where, rather than the focus being on school leavers, a variety of other interventions are utilised. In-reach projects may encourage engagement with pupils at an earlier age in order to raise aspirations of higher education or they may engage at the level of the local community in the case of outreach to adults.

So whilst the 'gold standard' in university entry qualifications remains the A-level (or Scottish Higher), over time a number of routes have been developed to allow those with other qualifications and relevant prior experience to enter higher education. It is these forms of provision that have taken on greatest significance in lifelong learning at university level in the last two decades. Alternative routes for those with vocational rather than academic qualifications have been developed, and these can successfully widen participation to non-traditional students (Hayward *et al.* 2008: 19). Other developments include the creation of specific Access courses to allow adults with no formal qualifications to progress to higher education. According to the Quality Assurance Agency (QAA) (2009), there were 349 providers in England and Wales offering 1,557 Access courses in 2007–08, with a total of 35,275 learners registered on the courses. An additional feature of Access courses is that they are often targeted at a specific subject area or discipline, e.g. Access to the Social Sciences and Access to Nursing.

In addition, there are routes which allow direct entry to later years of degree programmes for those with sub-degree qualifications including Higher National Certificates and Diplomas and Foundation Degrees, although these arrangements tend to be concentrated in or provide articulation to post-1992 institutions (the former polytechnics and Scottish central institutions). In Scotland, in particular through Further Education Colleges this is a significant component of the HE provision for adults,

Other alternative routes which allow entry to higher education include the use of Credit Accumulation Transfer Schemes (CATS) which may allow R/AP(E)L to be used to satisfy entry requirements, or programmes of work based learning (WBL) and work related learning (WRL) may allow those already in employment to gain entry to degree programmes through vocational routes. However, these may not necessarily widen participation in terms of SES and disability.

The impact of widening participation

Despite this expansion in participation, two main barriers remain consistently problematic at undergraduate level and beyond: disability and low socio-economic status. There has been a considerable focus on these two factors and a continuing interest in the perceptions and experiences of disabled students, and issues of access and participation of those from lower socio-economic groups remain firmly on the agenda (e.g. Riddell, Tinklin and

Table 7.1 Young (18 and 19 years at entry) full-time participation in UK higher education by schooling, social class and neighbourhood, 1997/8 to 2007/08 (HESA 2009)

	% State schools		% Social class IIIM, IV, V†		Low participation neighbourhood	
	1997/98	2007/08	1997/98	2007/08	1997/98	2007/08‡
UK	82.3	88.5	25.5	30.1	12.6	10.2
England	81.6	87.9	25.4	30.0	11.9	10.3
Scotland	81.5	87.5	24.2	26.6	17.0	*
Wales	88.3	93.6	27.0	30.8	15.3	9.7
N. Ireland	96.3	99.7	34.0	40.6	9.6	6.9

† NS-SEC classes 4, 5, 6 & 7; ‡ Polar2 method; * The relatively high (in UK terms) participation rate in Scotland coupled with the very high proportion of HE that occurs in FE colleges means that the figures for Scottish institutions could, when viewed in isolation, misrepresent their contribution to widening participation. Therefore, low participation data has not been produced for institutions in Scotland.

Wilson 2005; Riddell *et al.* 2007; Iannelli 2007; Public Accounts Committee (PAC) 2009).

Performance indicators for those in receipt of the Disabled Student Allowance (DSA)[4] (Directgov, 2011) were first published by HEFCE in relation to WP for students entering in 2000/01 when 1.4 per cent of all full-time undergraduates were in receipt of DSA. By 2007/08, 4.5 per cent of all full-time undergraduates were in receipt of the allowance; in absolute terms this represents a trebling to almost 49,000 over this time period. To allow some indication of under-representation, 18 per cent (or 10 million) of the working-age population in 2008 were covered by the DSA. In addition, 23 per cent of working-age disabled people have no formal qualifications compared with 9 per cent of non-disabled people (Employers' Forum on Disability (EFD) 2010).

There are some indicators of success in terms of social class and participation, though the picture is complex. As shown in Table 7.1, whilst from 1998 to 2008, the proportion of young full-time undergraduate entrants from state schools and from lower socio-economic groups increased, the participation rate from low participation neighbourhoods fell (HESA 2009). In order to provide some context, those from lower socio-economic groups make up around half the overall population of England, but only around 30 per cent of full-time undergraduates (NAO 2008). Of note is the decrease in the proportion of those from low participation neighbourhoods, especially in Wales, and the proportionally higher participation of those from lower socio-economic groups in Northern Ireland, yet the decline and relatively low participation by neighbourhood.

In relation to mature undergraduate entrants, while absolute numbers increased, their overall share fell from 25 to 21 per cent during the same time period, because the relative numbers of young entrants grew.[5] Table 7.2

Table 7.2 Mature student participation in HE by no previous HE experience and neighbourhood in first degree and in all undergraduate level courses from 1997/98 to 2007/08 (HESA 2009)

	1st degree				All undergraduate			
	No previous HE		No HE and low participation neighbourhood		No previous HE		No HE and low participation neighbourhood	
	1997/98	2007/08	1997/98	2007/08	1997/98	2007/08	1997/98	2007/08
UK	74.8	72.7	14.4	11.6	74.3	69.9	14.9	11.5
England	76.3	72.6	14.1	11.6	75.6	69.8	14.5	11.5
Wales	79.0	75.1	17.5	12.5	78.4	72.1	18.7	12.2
N. Ireland	74.1	68.1	14.5	9.2	73.0	65.4	14.7	8.7

Source: Sargant et al. (1997).

provides more detail where relevant data were available. It provides two measures: no previous HE qualification/no previous HE and low participation neighbourhood for two groups, those studying a first degree and all mature undergraduate.

In relation to socio-economic status, Woodrow (2000) reported that in the United Kingdom twice as many people from the highest social classes A and B (as measured by employment status) participate in HE than do those from the lowest classes D and E and this is confirmed in a later report (NAO 2002). The more recent Confintea report for the UK and Thomas *et al.* (2005) also state that despite the plethora of initiatives especially in WP, this divide still exists. Overall, despite enormous efforts, the social composition of students has only undergone modest changes (HEFCE 2009; HESA 2009) and despite slight improvements in participation rates, those from lower socio-economic backgrounds are still under-represented in higher education (Bekhradnia 2003, NAO 2008).[6] Furthermore, it would appear that no matter what measures we use, there has been a decrease in the proportion of mature students over the past ten years. Whilst it may be encouraging that around two-thirds of mature full-time first degree entrants have had no previous experience, the decline in those from low participation neighbourhoods is less encouraging.

We can conclude that whilst there has been success in increasing participation and providing lifelong learning to more people, there is limited evidence of progress in widening access to those groups who have previously been excluded. The difficulties in achieving genuine WP, as opposed to simply an increase in student numbers, provides a backdrop to questions relating to how flexible learning can make a meaningful contribution to WP.

A major factor is funding. Cost, particularly for provision that is not vocational and for higher education, is a serious impediment to many adults. This is despite a number of mechanisms of funding support and in part is due to debt aversion. Since the days of the Robbins Report (Committee on Higher Education 1963) when participation was 6 per cent of school-leavers, the system of student funding has undergone substantial change (Wyness 2010). The system has moved from one within which undergraduate Higher Education was free, with the government supporting students with a means-tested maintenance grant, to one in 2011 with 40 per cent participation but no such universal support, and top-up fees in England and Northern Ireland set to rise to up to £9,000. Given the increasing numbers participating in higher education, the state was no longer willing to foot the bill for student maintenance. It was decided that those who were said to benefit most from higher education (individual students) should pay for that privilege. A further complication arose with political devolution in Scotland accompanied by the decision that Scottish and EU students would be exempt from fees, and a considerable degree of divergence exists between the constituent parts of the UK.[7] While changes in Scotland to repayment regimes occurred, at present, against a backdrop of substantial increases in fees as a result of the Browne Review (2010), tuition fees still appear to be politically unacceptable in Scotland.

The impact of these changes to student maintenance in relation to WP and access are contested. For some, there has been no obvious deterrent and both HEFCE (2005) and Universities UK (UUK) (2009) suggested that the shift from grants to loans and fees had not significantly affected entrant behaviour. However, research by Callender (2003) and Callender and Jackson (2005) has suggested that after controlling for other factors, students from poorer backgrounds were more debt averse than better off counterparts.

> Debt aversion deterred entry into HE but was also a social class issue. Those most anti-debt are the focus of widening participation policies and include:
> - those from the lowest social classes;
> - one parents;
> - Muslims, especially Pakistanis; and
> - black and minority ethnic groups.
>
> (Callender 2003: 3)

Other literature from the UK on adult participation in particular, far too extensive to quote in detail here (see McGivney 1996; Davies and Williams 2001; Davies, Osborne and Williams 2002), provides further evidence of the deterrent effect of finance. Studies concerned with decision-making to access higher education by adults by Osborne, Marks and Turner (2004) are illustrative. Their findings clearly indicated there existed at that time a highly motivated cohort of mature students wishing to enter Higher Education. However, many of these individuals approached the prospect of entering HE with trepidation and uncertainty. Most mature students have multiple roles of responsibility, which carry considerable emotional and financial burdens, and this research indicated that for many, the decision to enter education, whilst high on their agenda, was highly constrained. Considerable uncertainty existed amongst potential entrants in relation to the financial arrangements for Higher Education. Whilst it was unsurprising that these adults stated that they needed greater financial support, as important was more security, more stability, and more certainty in the arrangements that currently existed at the time of that research. For mature students in particular to participate in HE, the arrangements for supporting students have to be made more transparent. This would include not only the provision of information about fees, loans and repayment schemes, but also the interface between the benefits system and study. Such information becomes more important in the light of recent changes.

With the election of a new Conservative/Liberal Democrat coalition government in May 2010, there have been some changes in the most recent plans of the former Labour administration. Amongst proposals being signposted to make HE more affordable and accessible is the possibility of FE colleges being able to offer external degrees of universities. This would potentially have an impact on adults participating in HE level provision. Most controversial have been the plans in England to raise fees in Higher Education. As a result of the Browne Review (2010), which was 'tasked with making recommendations to Government on the future of fees policy and financial support for full and part-time undergraduate and postgraduate students', the fee cap for undergraduates has been raised to £9,000 per annum. This has been the subject of intense political debate given the pre-election manifesto commitments of the Liberal partners in the UK coalition government and has resulted in a storm of civil protest against the proposals. The influential Sutton Trust (2010: 3) argues that 'with significant variation in fees, the risk is that non-privileged students will make higher education choices based on cost – or the perception of cost – rather than academic talent and that leading universities will become the preserve of the well-off'. Although the Trust's arguments relate largely to younger people, previous research clearly shows that adults are highly risk averse in relating to the financial implications of higher education (see Osborne, Marks and Turner 2004). The plans were approved in a vote of the House of Commons on 9 December 2010 amidst extensive public protest, and many universities will be charging the maximum allowable.

Recent research sought to investigate the influence of tuition fees and their impact on WP (Adnett and Tlupova 2008; McCaig and Adnett 2009). McCaig and Adnett (2009: 18) have already been critical of the way in which the current system operates and conclude:

> unsurprisingly in an increasingly market-driven system, institutions use access agreements primarily to promote enrolment to their own programmes rather than to promote system-wide objectives. As a consequence of this marketing focus, previous differences between pre-1992 and post-1992 institutions in relation to widening participation and fair access are perpetuated, leading to both confusion for consumers and an inequitable distribution of bursary and other support mechanisms for the poorest applicants to HE.

Adnett and Tlupova (2008) are also critical of the complexities of the funding system in operation in England. They conclude:

> We have found some initial evidence suggesting that the new English student finance system, particularly the expansion of institution-specific bursaries, has significantly increased the complexity of student decision-making and is providing information too late or incentives too small to significantly affect participation decisions. Many students eligible

> for financial support seem to be either unaware of their eligibility or unwilling to apply for bursaries even after starting their courses.
>
> (Adnett and Tlupova 2008: 253)

We can therefore speculate that current plans will have to be implemented with care if cost is not to deter hard-to-reach potential students even more than now. That being the case, some of the recommendations from the Browne Review in relation to support for part-time students may well prove to be beneficial in WP by providing better access to funding than previously available, for example by removing the requirement to pay upfront. However, it is too early to say if it will be successful in its aims of increasing participation.

Diversity and segmentation

Diversity and segmentation between HE providers is a key contextual issue in relation to lifelong learning in HE. It would appear that WP and access agendas are embraced more tightly by some institutions than by others. While recognising that institutions would have their own strategies for WP, Woodrow (2000) worried about creating a dual sector – where some institutions would deal with access and WP, while others went on about their traditional research-led missions. In support of Woodrow's fears, and in spite of the appearance of supportive comments in institutional mission statements, there is some evidence that there is a division among institutional types with regard to access and WP (Scottish Funding Council 2009a).

> Each institution has individual benchmarks representing the expected participation for each group, given particular characteristics (such as subject of study, age and entry qualifications) of the students it recruits. Post-1992 institutions generally perform at or significantly above their benchmarks while the English Russell Group institutions (16 of the most research intensive institutions) generally perform at or significantly below their benchmarks.
>
> (NAO 2008: 7)

Those from higher social groups have greater than expected participation rates at Russell Group and post-1992 institutions and their dominance in highly competitive subjects like Medicine and Dentistry continues (Bekhradnia 2003; Thomas *et al.* 2005; NAO 2008; SFC 2009b). This is highly significant for students' opportunities for progression in a range of careers as the final report, Unleashing Aspiration, by the Panel on Fair Access to the Professions (2009) recognises.

One consequence of aspects of flexibility on diversity may be the reproduction of existing segmentation in the sector with a concentration of WP entrants in less prestigious institutions and in specific subject areas.

Concluding remarks

Whilst vestiges of older traditions remain at some UK universities, especially in Scotland which has been immune from ELQ, overall the landscape of lifelong learning in HE has been transformed over the last 30 years. We have witnessed a transition from one form of social purpose (LAE), largely located in units marginal to the mainstream of university work to another (WP) with a similar claim, but one that has received widespread national attention. During that time the rhetoric of lifelong learning has become ubiquitous, with hardly an organisation in the UK not citing that it is a lifelong learning organisation in its mission statement. Social and economic purposes are not however dichotomous, and as the latter increasingly has dominated policy, gradually it has been those schemes with the greatest benefit that have come to the fore. Early intervention is seen as preferable to a second chance, and lifelong learning in later life has become secondary to lifelong learning for those of school age. But even young people are challenged in their aspirations as tuition fees rise. The newly appointed Advocate for Access, Simon Hughes,[8] appointed by the UK government in December 2010, has said that it is important that young people are not put off university because of 'untruths'. Whilst the reality may be that the financial position is not always as it is interpreted, lack of clarity and fear of debt are major impediments for the poor and especially for adults.

There are many things that can be improved in terms of providing lifelong learning opportunities in universities. There is a paucity of part-time opportunity in the UK system and a system of funding that is iniquitous to those whose personal circumstances or wishes determine that this mode is preferential. A similar dearth of possibility exists in distance provision or programmes that are offered in mixed mode of distance and face-to-face. Credit and qualifications systems exist and in principle there are mechanisms that allow transfer with credit from FE to HE, but these are used in a discretionary way, giving immunity to the most elite institutions suggesting that this route rather than providing opportunities is little more than a ghetto for adults and the poor (Osborne and Maclaurin 2006). There has been a massive decline in the offer made to older adults, especially those in retirement, despite the evidence of the health benefits of lifelong learning (Field 2009). It may be that in this latter case the private sector will fill the gap, but it is unlikely to be able to do so with the comprehensiveness of a university.

It is clear that the behaviour of most UK universities is determined too often by their obsession with being world class and all that entails or at least by an agenda of internationalism determined by national funding constraints, and not by a commitment to those on its doorstep. There is of course nothing intrinsically wrong with seeking international markets, but to do so whilst ignoring the needs of the local market risks not using effectively some of the best resources available in the places where universities are located. As

Watson (2009: 11) argues, 'many of the "common-sense" elements of high performance by comprehensive universities – like teaching quality, widening participation and social mobility, services to business and the community, support of rural in addition to metropolitan communities, as well as contributions to other public services – are conspicuously absent'. Many policy recommendations to change the current system of lifelong learning, including within universities, can and have indeed been made, especially by the Independent Enquiry into Lifelong Learning. It is however very difficult to see how these can be enacted in a system within which universities are so autonomous and where the state holds some financial, but few policy levers.

To conclude by comparison with 2000 when the first volume of this book was published, the position of adult lifelong learners in higher education has declined considerably. The traditional offer of extra-mural provision has declined, the focus of widening participation is the young and the share of mature students in undergraduate courses has declined. Whilst there are some positive indicators in the proportion of mature students without previous HE experience, the proportion of those from poorer neighbourhoods in undergraduate provision has also declined. Adults have definitely been losers, and although there are winners amongst lower socio-economic groups as participation has increased, widening of participation even to younger members of lower socio-economic groups has been limited. Given the increasing costs of HE and the possible contraction of the system, we cannot be optimistic that these trends will change in the near future.

Notes

1 See http://www.hefce.ac.uk/faq/elq.htm.
2 The LSC no longer exists and its functions have been taken over by a new Skills Funding Agency (see http://www.bis.gov.uk/skillsforgrowth). According to recent surveys of adult participation by the National Institute for Adult and Continuing Education (NIACE) (Tuckett and Aldridge 2009), overall the proportion of adults currently learning is at its lowest level since 1997 and findings suggest that the real gains of a modest number of the least skilled are bought at the expense of many more of the educationally marginalised.
3 Further Education Colleges are institutions of post-compulsory education in the UK offering largely vocational provision from basic skills through to higher education level, with the latter being mainly at below first degree level.
4 When examining the indicators for those in receipt of DSA, it should be remembered that those eligible to apply for the allowance are an extremely diverse group with various forms and levels of disability which require specific and in many cases trained and specialised support services (Riddell *et al.* 2007; Fuller *et al.* 2009).
5 We note however that whilst the role of performance indicators is seen as crucial in any measures of the relative success of initiatives aimed at widening participation, this is not as straightforward as it seems. Attention has been drawn to the problems of incomplete and missing data in the statistical datasets (NAO, 2008) and the difficulties of comparisons over time when variables and fields are

changed (Gorard *et al.* 2007). For some groups the data are very poor, especially in relation to students aged 21 and over. There are also issues in the mechanisms and measures used to record non-continuation. The HESA categories for listing reasons tend to obscure the complexity of explanation. In addition, students are often reluctant to give full explanations at the time of withdrawal – or have moved out of contact with the institution altogether. An overview of the development and use of performance indicators in the UK and beyond is provided by Cave *et al.* (1996), and this is updated for the UK context in the work of Draper and Gittoes (2004: 472) who carry out a sophisticated statistical modelling analysis and 'support the conclusion that real differences in quality on student progression existed among UK universities'.

6   A detailed synthesis of the research on social class and higher education is provided by Stevenson and Lang (2010).
7   The devolved Welsh Assembly has also protected Welsh students at Welsh HEIs from the level of fee increases operating in England and Northern Ireland.
8   The Deputy Leader of the Liberal Democratic Party, himself an opponent in parliament to the proposed increase in fees. See http://www.bbc.co.uk/news/uk-12087567.

References

Adnett, N. and Tlupova, D. (2008) 'Informed choice? The new English student funding system and widening participation', *London Review of Education*, 6(3): 243–254.

Bekhradnia, B. (2003) *Widening Participation and Fair Access: An Overview of the Evidence*, Oxford: HEPI.

Brennan, J. and Naidoo, R. (2008) 'Higher education and the achievement (and/or prevention) of equity and social justice', *Higher Education*, 56: 287–302.

Browne, (2010) *The Independent Review of Higher Education Funding and Student Finance.* Online. Available HTTP <http://hereview.independent.gov.uk/hereview/report/> (accessed 5 November 2010).

Callender, C. (2003) *Attitudes to Debt: School Leavers and Further Education Students' Attitudes to Debt and their Impact on Participation in Higher Education*. London: UUK.

Callender, C. and Jackson, J (2005) 'Does fear of debt deter students from higher education?', *Journal of Social Policy*, 34(4): 509–540.

Cave, M., Hanney, S., Henkel, M. and Kogan, M. (1996) *The Use of Performance Indicators in Higher Education: The Challenge of the Quality Movement*, 3rd edition, London: Jessica Kingsley.

Charles, D., Benneworth, P., Conway, C. and Humphrey, L. (2010) 'How to benchmark university–community interactions'. In P. Inman and H.G. Schuetze (eds) *The Community and Service Mission of Universities*, Leicester: NIACE.

Committee on Higher Education (1963) *Higher Education: Report of the Committee appointed by the Prime Minister under the Chairmanship of Lord Robbins 1961–63*, Cmnd. 2154, London: HMSO.

Davies, P. and Williams, J. (2001) 'For me or not for me? Fragility and risk in mature students' decision making', *Higher Education Quarterly*, 55(2): 185–203.

Davies, P., Osborne, M. and Williams, J. (2002) *For Me or Not For Me? That is the Question*, Briefing Report No. 297, London: DfEE.

Department for Education and Employment (DfEE) (1998) *The Learning Age*, London: HMSO.
Department of Education and Science (1978) *Special courses in preparation for entry to higher education*, Letter to Chief Education Officers, 2 August.
Directgov (2011) *Disabled Students' Allowance – how to apply*. Online. Available HTTP <//www.direct.gov.uk/en/DisabledPeople/EducationAndTraining/HigherEducation/DG_10034900>
Draper, D. and Gittoes, M. (2004) 'Statistical analysis of performance indicators in UK higher education', *Journal of the Royal Statistical Society A*, 167 Part 3: 449–474.
Duke, C. (2009) 'Trapped in a local history: why did extramural fail to engage in the era of engagement?' In P. Cunningham, S. Oosthuizen and R. Taylor (eds) *Beyond the Lecture Hall*, Cambridge: University of Cambridge Faculty of Education.
Employers' Forum on Disability (EFD) (2010) *Disability in the UK*, Employers' Forum on Disability. Online. Available HTTP <http//www.efd.org.uk/media-centre/facts-and-figures/disability-in-uk> (accessed 16 June 2011).
Field, J. (2009) *Well-being and Happiness*, IFLL Thematic Paper 4, Leicester: NIACE
Fieldhouse, R (1996) *A History of Modern British Adult Education*. Leicester: NIACE
Fuller, M., Georgeson, J., Healey, M., Hurst, A., Kelly, K., Riddell, S., Roberts, H. and Weedon, E. (2009) *Improving Disabled Students' Learning: Experiences and Outcomes* London: Routledge.
Gorard, S. with Adnett, N., May, H., Slack, K., Smith, E. and Thomas, L. (2007) *Overcoming the Barriers to Higher Education*, Stoke on Trent: Trentham Books.
Greenwood, M. and Little, B. (2008) *Report to Foundation Degree Forward on the Impact of Foundation Degrees on Students and the Workplace*, London: CHERI and LSN.
Hayward, Geoff *et al.* (2008) *Degrees of Success: The Transition between VET and HE. Full Research Report, ESRC End of Award Report, RES-139-25-0238*. Swindon: ESRC.
Higher Education Funding Council for England (HEFCE) (2005) *Young Participation in Higher Education*, 2005/03, Bristol: HEFCE.
Higher Education Funding Council for England (HEFCE) (2009) *Performance Indicators in Higher Education*, Bristol: HEFCE.
Higher Education Statistical Agency (HESA) 2009 *Performance Indicators in Higher Education in the UK*. Online. Available HTTP <http://www.hesa.ac.uk/index.php?option=com_content&task=view&id=2072&Itemid=141>.
Hicks, H., Lintern, M. and Dismore, H. (2009) *What do Foundation Graduates do? Part 3*, Plymouth: HELP/CETL.
Houston, M., McCune, V. and Osborne, M. (2011) *Flexibility and its Contribution to Widening Participation: A Synthesis of the Research*, York: HEA.
Iannelli, C. (2007) 'Inequalities in entry to higher education: a comparison over time between Scotland and England and Wales', *Higher Education Quarterly*, 61 (3): 306–333.
Jones, B., Thomas, G. and Moseley, R. (2010) *University Continuing Education 1981–2006 – Twenty-five Turbulent Years*, Leicester: NIACE.
Kelly, T. (1992) *A History of Adult Education in Great Britain* (2nd edn), Liverpool: Liverpool University Press.

Lambert, R. (2003) *Lambert Review of Business–University Collaboration*. Norwich: HMSO.

Laurillard, D. (2002) *Rethinking University Teaching: A Conversational Framework for the Effective Use of Learning Technologies*, London: Routledge Falmer.

Leitch, S. (2006) *Prosperity for All in the Global Economy: World Class Skills*, London: HM Treasury.

McCaig, C. and Adnett, N. (2009) 'English universities, additional fee income and access agreements: their impact on widening participation and fair access', *British Journal of Educational Studies*. 57 (1), 18–36.

McCaig, C., Bowers-Brown, T. and Drew, S. (2007) *Accelerated Learning Programmes: A Review of Quality, Extent and Demand*, York: HEA.

McGivney, V. (1996) *Staying or Leaving the Course: Non-Completion and Retention of Mature Students in Further and Higher Education*, Leicester: NIACE.

McNair, S. and Quintero, L., with Clarke, A., Eldred, J., Hallam, A., Lavender, P., O'Hagan, J., Osborne, M., Pearce, R., Tett, L., Thomson, A., Tibbitt, J., Tuckett, A. and Watters, K. (2009) *Confintea VI – UK National Report on the Development and State of the Art of Adult Learning and Education (ALE)*, Leicester: NIACE.

National Audit Office (NAO) (2002) *Widening Participation in Higher Education in England*, London: HMSO.

National Audit Office (NAO) (2008) *Widening Participation in Higher Education: Executive Summary*, London: NAO.

National Committee of Inquiry into Higher Education (1997) *Higher Education in the Learning Society. Report of National Committee of Inquiry into Higher Education*, London: HMSO (Dearing Report).

Newman, M. (1994) *Defining the Enemy: Adult Education in Social Action*, Sydney: Victor Stewart.

Osborne, M. (2003) 'United Kingdom'. In M. Osborne and E. Thomas, *Lifelong Learning in a Changing Continent: Continuing Education in the Universities of Europe*, Leicester: NIACE.

Osborne, M. (2006) 'Flexibility and widening participation: Part 1'. In M. Osborne and D. Young (2006) *Flexibility and Widening Participation*. York: HEA.

Osborne, M. (2011) *Country Report on the Action Plan on Adult Learning*. Background Paper to the Final Conference on the Adult Learning Action Plan, 7–9 March 2011, Budapest. Online. Available HTTP <www://adultlearning-budapest2011.teamwork.fr/en/background>

Osborne, M., Marks, A. and Turner, E. (2004) 'Becoming a mature student: how older potential applicants weigh the advantages and disadvantages of embarking on a university course'. *Higher Education*, 48: 291–315.

Osborne, M.J. and Maclaurin, I. (2006) 'A probability matching approach to further/higher education transition in Scotland', *Higher Education*, 52(1): 149–183.

Outram, S. (2009) *Flexible Learning Pathfinders: A Review of the Pilots' Final and Interim Reports*. Bristol: HEFCE/HEA.

Panel on Fair Access to the Professions (2009) *Unleashing Potential: The Final Report of the Panel on Fair Access to the Professions*. London: Cabinet Office.

Percy, K. and Ramsden, P. (1980) *Independent Study: Two Examples from English Higher Education*, Guildford: SRHE.

Public Accounts Committee (PAC) (2009) *Widening Participation in Higher Education*. Fourth Report of Session 2008–09, London: The Stationery Office.

Quality Assurance Agency (QAA) (2009) *Access to HE Statistics Summary (2007–08)*. Online. Available HTTP <www.accesstohe.ac.uk/partners/statistics/2009/QAAreport09.pdf>.

Riddell, S., Tinklin, T. and Wilson, A. (2005) *Disabled Students in Higher Education*, London: Routledge Falmer.

Riddell, S., Weedon, E., Fuller, M., Healey, M., Hurst, A., Kelly, K. and Piggot, L. (2007) 'Managerialism and equalities: tensions within widening access policy and practice for disabled students in UK universities', *Higher Education*, 54 (4): 615–628.

Sargant, N., Field, J., Francis, H., Schuller, T. and Tuckett, A. (1997) *A Study of Participation in Adult Learning in the United Kingdom*, Leicester: NIACE.

Schuller, T. and Watson, D. (2009) *Learning Through Life*, Leicester: NIACE.

Scottish Funding Council (SFC) (2009a) *Statistics Publication Notice – Lifelong Learning Series*, Edinburgh: SFC.

Scottish Funding Council (SFC) (2009b) *Scottish Participation in Further and Higher Education 2003–04 to 2007–08*, Edinburgh: SFC.

Scottish Office (SOEID) (1997) *Higher Education in the Learning Society. Scottish Report of National Committee of Inquiry into Higher Education*, Edinburgh: Scottish Office (Garrick Report).

Scottish Office (SOEID) (1998) *Opportunity Scotland*, Edinburgh: HMSO.

Sharpe, L., Benfield, G., Roberts, G. and Francis, R. (2006) *The Undergraduate Experience of Blended E-learning: A Review of UK Literature and Practice*, York: HEA.

Slowey, M. (2000) 'The United Kingdom. Redefining the non-traditional student: equity and lifelong learning in British higher education, 1985–2000', in H.G. Schuetze and M. Slowey (eds) *Higher Education and Lifelong Learners. International Perspectives on Change*, London: Routledge Falmer.

Stevenson, J. and Lang, M. (2010) *Social Class and Higher Education: A Synthesis of Research*, York: HEA.

Sutton Trust (2010) *Initial Response to the Independent Review of Higher Education Funding and Student Finance*, London: Sutton Trust.

Thomas, L., May, H., Harrop, H., Houston, M., Knox, H., Lee, M.F., Osborne, M., Pudner, H. and Trotman, C. (2005) *From the Margins to the Mainstream*, London: UUK/SCOP.

Tuckett, A. and Aldridge, F. (2009) *Narrowing Participation. The NIACE Survey on Adult Participation in Learning*, Leicester: NIACE.

UUK (2009) *Variable Tuition Fees in England: Assessing their Impact on Students and Higher Education Institutions*. Online. Available HTTP <www.universitiesuk.ac.uk/Publications/Documents/Variable%20Tuition3.pdf> (accessed 5 October 2010).

Watson, D. (2009) *Lifelong Learning and the Future of Higher Education*. IFLL Sector Paper 8, Leicester: NIACE.

Welsh Office (WO) (1998) *Learning is for Everyone*, Cardiff: Welsh Office.

Woodrow, M. (2000) *What is Widening Participation?* London: European Access Network.

Wyness, G.. (2010) *Policy Changes in UK Higher Education Funding, 1963–2009*. Department of Quantitative Social Science (DoQSS) Working Paper No. 10, London: Institute of Education.

Part III
North America

Chapter 8

Canada
Large archipelago, small bridges and infrequent ferries: lifelong learning and Canadian higher education

Hans G. Schuetze

Introduction

Canada, a large country with a relatively small population, typifies the difficulties of recognizing patterns, currents, structures and mechanisms in its approach to lifelong learning. Although Canada is one large landmass, a more appropriate metaphor for the Canadian learning system would be an archipelago with many islands (Myers and de Broucker 2006; Jones 2001). Different jurisdictions are responsible for education and various types of institutions provide formal learning: autonomous universities, a heterogeneous brand of non-university post-secondary education institutions, and a private sector with its work-related training programs and courses.

As pointed out in Chapter 1, the lifelong learning concept is not limited to a particular age of the learner ("lifelong") nor a particular learning place ("life-wide"), even if some places are conventionally regarded as more important. Lifelong learning in Canada can be understood as a superstructure binding together the various individual education sectors and many "non-formal" learning places: an organizational principle that provides for learning opportunities and places on all the islands and for the bridges and ferries that link them.

The main development over the last decade has been the growth in Canada's population. This growth has been uneven: the number of inhabitants (and students) has increased, particularly in Ontario, Quebec, Alberta and British Columbia while the Atlantic and Prairie provinces have grown very little. So, the number and capacity of bridges and ferries has increased substantially in some parts of the country while in others it has remained essentially unchanged.

I start this chapter with a brief summary of the context in which the changes over the last decade have occurred. Next, I map the "archipelago" of the Canadian learning system and its linkage mechanisms – the bridges and ferries. Since some lifelong learners belong to groups who are underrepresented in the formal education system, I shall look into participation rates and patterns. Finally, I will review the progress towards lifelong learning and analyze the difficulties in its development.

The context of higher education and lifelong learning – overview and changes of the last decade

Canada shares many principal features with the other countries dealt with in this volume, in other respects it is quite unique (Boshier 2011). For example, like Australia and New Zealand, it has a sizable Aboriginal population with a rich cultural background of its own, including many indigenous languages. As in those countries, Aboriginal people in Canada are socially and economically disadvantaged, and they are far less successfully participating in high school and higher education than the rest of the population.

Economically, Canada is a rich country and this shows in its excellent infrastructure and vast fabric of formal education, which, at least in principle, guarantees access to education for all. Canada shares with Germany the feature of a federal system of government that vests the responsibility for education in the provinces (Länder) so that the Canadian national system consists of thirteen provincial (or territorial) sub-systems. Unlike Germany, however, it lacks efficient mechanisms for articulation and coordination among the various provincial and territorial jurisdictions.

Another major difference concerns Canada's immigrant population that is, with only few exceptions, highly educated and leads the rest of the Canadian population with respect to participation in higher education. This also contrasts with some of the European countries such as Germany, Austria and Sweden where most immigrants are poorly educated and hence they themselves and their offspring are under-represented in higher education. Such differences are the product of selective immigration policies. In Canada, immigration has been seen as a source of qualified labor whereas Northern Europe countries tend to admit immigrants as unqualified and cheap labor or as refugees.

Canadian facts and figures

Canada, the second largest country of the world (after Russia), has a population of 34.5 million inhabitants (2011). More than 80 percent of these live in urban settings and with a few exceptions all within 50 km of the border with the United States. Thus large areas of the country are under-populated and under-developed. Reflecting Canada's history and immigration patterns, 57 percent of the population has English as their mother tongue and 21.8 percent French, the two official languages. The population is predominantly white although almost 9 percent are of Asian origin (of which more than a third are from China). This share is fast increasing as most new immigrants (approximately a quarter of a million each year) now come predominantly from East and South East Asia.

About 4 percent of Canada's population are ethnic Aboriginals, belonging to one of the three Aboriginal groups – First Nations, Métis, and Inuit – who between them speak some 60 different languages. Of particular significance for education, almost half of the Aboriginal population consists of children and youth aged 24 and under, compared with 31 percent of the non-Aboriginal population (Statistics Canada 2006).

Of the adult population (25 years and older), 7.3 percent have eight years of schooling or less, 20 percent a secondary school certificate, 33 percent a college certificate and 23 percent a university degree. That means that more than half of the population has completed a post-secondary education credential. Another 6 percent have had some post-secondary education experience without having graduated.

The labor force is about 15.5 million. As in many other industrialized countries, the unemployment level is the lowest for the best educated, with 4.8 percent unemployment rate for those with graduate degrees, 5.5 percent for bachelors, and 6.9 percent for holders of a college certificate. The overall unemployment rate is 7.6 percent.

With a GDP per capita of $39,057, Canada counts among the world's wealthiest countries. Its economy is diversified but still in part reliant on its natural resources: agricultural products, ores and minerals including diamonds, oil, and wood and wood products. In times of worldwide financial crises and volatile world markets, this makes for a relatively stable economy, especially since prices for natural resources are increasing. While not entirely unaffected by the dramatic economic turmoil of the banking and real estate sectors south of its border in 2008/9, Canada has experienced only moderate cuts in public budgets which had only a relatively small effect on education. However, the cuts have definitely affected tuition fee levels and hence educational participation, especially by those groups already under-represented in higher education.

Politics and policies

Regardless of which party forms the federal government, Canada is basically a conservative country; its only social-democratic governments have been at the provincial level. Despite this, Canada has an advanced social system. For example, its public health care system is open to all (including immigrants) and provides free access to all medical services and prescribed drugs. In addition, several provinces provide generous social and other (for example parental) benefits.

As education is a provincial responsibility, all provinces have their own unique system of education and training. Quebec, for example, historically and culturally close to France, has progressive training policies in place such as the right to paid training leave and individual assessments of skills and competences as the basis for further training. Quebec is also the only province that has adopted the (French) system of financing training through training levies from employers that do not train their own employees.

Over the last 30 years, there have been several provincial and federal policies aiming at, or claiming to implement major planks of a lifelong learning system. However, most of these concerned access to adult education and training and especially ways of financing individual participation in adult education. None has lasted or had any real major influence. One example was the announcement by the federal government of Individual Development Accounts (IDA) with the purpose of increasing the human capital of low-income Canadians by encouraging them to contribute their own funds to improve their economic situation through training. This high-level policy announcement (in the "Speech from the Throne") was not followed through. Instead a small research unit, the Social Research and Demonstration Corporation (SRDC), was commissioned to conduct a long-term feasibility study which, more than ten years later, found that the scheme had only modest effects on participation in education and training and that no direct employment effects could be observed (SRDC 2010).

The Canadian learning system

Generally speaking, Canada has a well-resourced and efficient formal education system and while there are definite differences between the provinces in terms of structures, revenues, and policies, education standards are fairly comparable across the country. This is remarkable since Canada's provinces and territories organize education separately and there are few overall mechanisms for efficient coordination across the provinces.

Early childhood education and schooling

As stressed by psychologists, pediatricians and teachers, early childhood learning is a major factor in children's emotional, social and intellectual development and, hence, highly important for their motivation and capacity for further learning. In Canada, some 50 percent of pre-school age children with working (or studying) parents are enrolled in some type of organized early childhood program. While this sounds laudable, a 2008 study by UNICEF ranked the quality of such programs in 25 developed countries in terms of accessibility and affordability and showed Canada surprisingly at the end of the list, meeting only one of ten standards (cited in CCL 2010).

In contrast, the quality of K-12 schooling is very high – if performance-based tests are an indication: Canada scores consistently among the top ten countries in OECD's PISA study. This excellent record highlights the equity of the Canadian educational system where the gap between the highest and lowest scores is one of the narrowest in any OECD country (OECD 2011). This is partly explained by the fact that the great majority of schools are public, although private non-profit ("independent") schools are slowly gaining ground (Schuetze et al. 2011). It is also due to students from immigrant families who are, in their majority, highly motivated and hard working, and to teachers who are well trained and enjoy a high status and income.

The high school drop-out (non-completion) rate that used to be a major concern has been significantly reduced over the last decade. Currently it stands at 8.5 percent, compared with an average of 14.7 percent in 25 OECD countries (Statistics Canada 2011a). A notable exception to this positive picture are Aboriginal students, whose non-completion rate is still dramatically high.

Vocational training and continuing training

The Canadian record of vocational education and training is unimpressive. Youth not interested in going on to higher education face a limited choice of options. Dual mode apprenticeships (where learning is organized to occur in two modes and places: experiential learning at a real work place and applied cognitive learning at a vocational school or college) exist but are, in spite of many initiatives by the provinces and the federal government, under-developed (Schuetze 2003) even as the numbers of apprentices has been growing in recent years.[1] Most vocational education and training either takes place in community colleges and technical institutes or with private training providers where it tends to be short-term and rarely in conjunction with actual work places. There is also some employer sponsored training relating to work, although it is considerably less than in most European countries (OECD 2003).

Adult education and learning

Canada has a long tradition of adult education and learning. As the early immigrants who settled in the country often lacked language and specific work-related skills, adult education played a pivotal role in the country's development. Early adult education promoted literacy, citizenship and culture among those farmers, miners, loggers and fishermen with little formal schooling. However, the establishment of efficient formal school and post-secondary systems changed the goals and scope of adult education and while the provision of education to immigrants still figures large, the field has diversified considerably.

Even more than formal schooling and post-secondary education, adult education in Canada resembles a veritable patchwork. Provincial policies, structures, financing and organization differ widely. Some programs are organized and (partly) financed by provincial as well as municipal governments. Even though the federal government has no formal responsibility for adult education, it provides financial support for various adult education programs, mostly literacy and short-term job training for particular groups (Fisher *et al.* 2006; Gibb and Walker 2011). Adult education providers comprise a wide array of organizations and institutions, both public and private: colleges and universities, school boards, vocational centres, adult learning centres, community groups, employers, unions, business associations, and charity and other volunteer organizations serving various disadvantaged groups.

Significant federal budget cuts in the 1990s affected a number of adult education national bodies and voluntary associations. For example, the Canadian Association for Adult Education, active in promoting adult education since the 1930s, was closed. Another more recent blow was the closure in 2009 of the Canadian Council of Learning (CCL) that had "focused on building and communicating a pan-Canadian perspective on lifelong learning" (Grace 2009: 30). As part of its activities the CCL had established five sectoral centers, one of which, the Adult Learning Knowledge Centre, became in its few short years of existence a national centre of research and action as well as pan-Canadian networking and lobbying.

Indeed, recent Canadian governments, stuck in an economic paradigm that fails to recognize or support other objectives for adult education beyond the purely economic, have withdrawn most of their support for adult education infrastructure and programs (Rubenson and Nesbit 2011). Despite this lack of government support, there is some evidence that adult education in Canada "remains a vigorous and vital activity" (Nesbit, 2011: 2), even if many activities are now organized in new contexts, with new players and under new labels.

Higher education

Canada's federal government has no direct role in education except for the education of Aboriginal people ("First Nations") on reserves and the training of the military. It assumes, however, an important indirect role in higher education, especially through three mechanisms:

- the transfer of funds to the provinces earmarked for higher education and health;
- the funding of research (through three national Research Councils) and the financing of research infrastructure in universities (through the Canadian Foundation of Innovation and the National Research Chair Program); and
- student financial assistance through a general Canada Student Loan Program and some smaller scholarship programs for specific purpose or target groups.

Canada's history of tension between French and British cultures, its geography, and its often harsh climate have fostered an intense and determined regionalism. As a result, the provincial (and territorial) higher education systems differ structurally from each other, even if they are all binary in character, i.e. have degree-granting (universities) and non-degree sectors and institutions (colleges and institutes).

The terms "university", "college" and "institute" cover considerable variations of institutions. Thus, a "college" may refer to an undergraduate institution affiliated with a university, a special purpose professional school, such as a teacher's college or a college of arts, or a "community college". "Community colleges", set up in Canada since the 1960s emulating the US model, have different mandates in different provinces. Besides providing programs or courses of general adult education, most offer vocational or job-related diploma and certificate programs. In British Columbia and Alberta, they also provide academic transfer programs consisting of the first two years of a four-year undergraduate program. Quebec has yet another model, the *Collège d'enseignement générale et professionel* (Cégep), which offer two-year pre-university programs as well as three-year vocational programs.

Over the last decade and a half, these traditional binary lines have become blurred, and colleges and institutes in some provinces offer programs in certain fields leading to "applied" academic degrees (bachelors and masters). Also in some provinces new hybrid types of institutions have been established that combine functions of community colleges and universities.[2]

Currently, Canada has 102 degree-granting institutions, and 162 colleges and institutes. The core of the university system comprises 47 universities that are usually classified into three types: research universities with medical faculties (15 in number), comprehensive (11) and undergraduate teaching institutions (21).

There are very few private (non-public) universities. These need the respective provincial government's authorization to award degrees and must be accredited by quality boards (which have different organizational forms and names in the various provinces). Overwhelmingly, private universities are religious institutions, financed by churches or other religious organizations.

Like in many other countries, the proportion of public and private funding in the public higher education sector has markedly changed. While in 2000, 61 percent of funding for the post-secondary education sector still came from public sources, in 2006 this public share had decreased by more than 10 percent and stood at 53.4 percent. Most of the larger private share of funding is the result of steep increases in student tuition. Tuition fees accounted for 12.3 percent of university operating revenues in 1978 while the government's share was 83.8 percent. In 1998 that ratio was 26.3/64.9 and ten years later, in 2008, 34.7/57.5 (CAUT 2011: Figure 1.2). It is reasonable to presume that by 2012 that ratio will be close to 50/50.

University continuing education

The provision of and the access to continuing education are important elements of lifelong learning. Traditionally in Canada, universities and colleges have assumed a major role in this field – much like in the USA, and much more actively and broadly than in Continental Europe (Schuetze 2008a).

However, continuing education is not the exclusive domain of universities (Kirby *et al.*, 2009). Many other providers, public and non-public, compete for students, as this market is lucrative and comparatively stable. Data from the Adult Education and Training Survey (AETS) and the National Graduate Survey (NGS) show that a significant share of university trained persons choose non-university programs for their continuing learning (Adamuti-Trache and Schuetze 2010).

Chapter 1 identified a range of different categories of lifelong learners. In relation to adult students these can be summarized into four broad groups:

1 Students who start their university studies as mature adults, i.e. after having worked for a substantial period of time upon completion of their initial education.
2 Students who seek a second degree, either immediately upon completing their first degree, or later.
3 Students who either have or do not have a degree but seek further knowledge for the purpose of career advancement or change.
4 Students who either have a university degree or not and who seek further education for the purpose of self-development and personal growth.

Universities in Canada serve all these groups, although the latter two groups are the specific targets for university continuing education.

Most Canadian universities have a specific unit – called variously University Extension, Continuing Education or Continuing Studies – to deliver continuing education courses, programs, workshops and lectures to the general public, usually on a non-credit basis. These units offer also "continuing professional education", which can either lead to professional Master's or doctoral degrees, or to diplomas and certificates. Some programs or courses are mandatory and required by professional associations – teachers, engineers, lawyers or physicians – in order to maintain licenses to practice.

Not all university graduates however return to university for continuing education. Research shows that 40 percent or more of graduates participate in courses and programs that offer more practical and job specific know-how, typically offered by community colleges and technical institutes (Adamuti-Trache and Schuetze 2010).

In the (recent) past, continuing education activities were either partly financed by the general university budget, or (co-)financed by revenues from degree courses. Since the 1990s this has changed and continuing education units of all universities are now either self-financing or "profit centers" that generate revenues in addition to covering their own costs. This change in the mode of financing has significantly changed not only the type of activities offered as well as the contents of continuing education activities but also the general understanding of continuing education as a central mission of the university (Nesbit, Dunlop and Gibson 2007).

Bridges and ferries: flexibility and transferability within the learning system

Having described the main elements of the formal learning system, I now explore just what makes the discrete parts of the education archipelago a "system". What are the mechanisms that provide the metaphorical bridges and ferries that connect the different parts? I consider three linkage mechanisms that are essential to a lifelong learning system: information, transferability, and recognition for prior learning.

Information

Since there is no pan-Canadian system of education (or higher education), reliable information about programs, costs, prerequisites, application procedures and deadlines is difficult to come by, especially since admission rules for graduate programs and specific target groups are sometimes set by individual departments or programs rather than uniformly by the university. As autonomous universities are free to determine their admission criteria, the process of finding relevant information is particularly difficult for would-be learners. This is especially so for those from under-represented groups such as Aboriginal or older students who either do not have valid academic access credentials or whose prior learning credentials are dated. As information on the university home pages tends to be almost entirely targeted towards school-leavers, lifelong learners who do not fit this characteristic are often at a loss, especially if they do not have easy access to the internet.

Transferability of credits

Like the USA, Canada has a well-developed modular course system that makes academic credits portable. This greatly increases learners' mobility, both between different programs within the same institution and between different institutions. This credit recognition and transfer system is therefore a criterion generally seen as important for removing some of the roadblocks on the lifelong learning highway.

This system works well as long as credits are from a recognized institution. It does not work, or not easily, when credits to be transferred are from an institution of a different type and standing. Universities are free to decide whether or not to recognize such credits. In order to determine the equivalence of a credit, for example of a first year chemistry course, negotiations are required between institutions. In some jurisdictions, for example British Columbia, a special agency has been set up, the British Columbia Council of Admissions and Transfer (BCCAT) which, based on negotiations with all post-secondary education institutions of the province, makes available a comprehensive transfer guide where students can find course-to-course agreements among, and admissions information about British Columbia's post-secondary institutions. Similar agencies exist in some of the other provinces but there is no one single agency that provides such information for all of Canada.

Assessment and recognition of prior learning

The linchpin of life-wide learning (PLAR)[3] is the assessment and recognition of prior learning, i.e. the validation of knowledge and skills that have been acquired outside the formal education system. Attempts to build up such mechanisms are being made in many countries, not least by establishing national policies for validation of prior learning or through national qualification frameworks.

No such mechanisms exist in Canada. Despite encouragement by the federal government, responsible for labor force development and worker mobility throughout Canada, support from several provinces and other interested organizations, progress has been erratic and slow. A recent study has found that, with a few exceptions, "current PLAR practice in Canada's post-secondary institutions is sporadic, fragmented, and marginalized" (Conrad 2008: 101). This description applies also to the validation of prior learning by employers (although these seem generally to be more flexible) and some of the professional bodies that establish standards for professional practice. Ironically, validating foreign credentials is a major problem, especially so in a country that regards immigration as a chief mechanism of attracting highly trained workers.

In sum, Canada evinces a lack of coordination and cohesion when it comes to mechanisms that would make the various and disparate sectors and jurisdictions parts of a coherent and transparent system. This has raised some considerable concern, both generally with regard to the qualified workforce needed in a "knowledge-based" economy and the waste of human talent (the proverbial PhD holder who is driving a taxi). However, so far, this concern has not been strong enough to overcome parochial thinking, inter-provincial competition and the autonomy of both university admission officers and professional bodies.

For lifelong learners, this situation has two sides. On the one hand, the great variety of higher education programs and modes of participation gives lifelong learners who are sufficiently familiar with the system many choices and enables them to find learning opportunities that are in line with their needs and wants. On the other hand, the highly diversified system makes it difficult, especially for those who are most in need of information, counseling, and recognition of non-certified knowledge and skills, to navigate and access the system.

Issues and higher education policies: accessibility and participation

It should not be surprising that, due to Canadian federalism and the absence of, or will for, efficient coordination, there is no provincial or pan-Canadian policy that addresses the whole gamut of a lifelong learning system. In the absence of such comprehensive policies, a look at recent reviews and reforms in some of the provinces is useful.

Provincial policies

There have been several recent comprehensive reviews of higher education in four provinces (Alberta 2006; British Columbia 2007; New Brunswick 2008; Ontario 2005; Newfoundland and Labrador 2005; Saskatchewan 2007), some leading to subsequent government action. Specifically, the review covered two of our themes – accessibility and affordability – together with accountability, quality, and institutional diversity and collaboration. Although there were important differences, all reviews showed "the pervasive influence of economic globalization which is accompanied by an increasingly utilitarian, market-oriented ideological outlook on post-secondary education's raison d'être" (Kirby 2007: xx; 2011).

With reference to the growing demand by the increasingly knowledge-based economy for highly educated and trained workers, all reviews stress that increasing the participation and attainment levels of under-represented groups is of great importance and recommend policy interventions and outreach activities for increasing participation of Aboriginal people, women in non-traditional fields, students with disabilities, from rural areas and from low socio-economic backgrounds. Many of these would also be "first generation students" since their parents did not attend post-secondary education.

Problematic, especially for potential students from these target groups, are the rising tuition fee levels. With student fees having risen quickly and disproportionally, student financial burden and debt has also risen dramatically. The average debt for students with a bachelor degree in 2010 was $37,000. Graduate student debt is even higher. For example, the debt of doctoral students rose to an average of $43,700 (CAUT 2011: Table 3.28).

This raises more generally the question of the individual costs of learning and especially the cost and financing of lifelong learning (Schuetze 2009). Although the issues of student debt and financial barriers to participation have been raised frequently by student associations and other bodies, they have not been addressed in a satisfactory way.

This issue of affordability is particularly important in Canada since, in the absence of viable alternatives, for example a well-structured and socially recognized system of vocational education and training, 85 percent of 15-year-old Canadians expect to attend university or college. Because of a highly differentiated system of post-secondary education (of which only a relatively small part is "higher education", i.e. academic and degree-awarding in nature), many will. Since most post-secondary education programs require fees, participation is often dependent on parents' ability to pay. According to a recent study (CCL 2009a), 80 percent of parents with children under the age of 18 have either saved, or were intending to save, for their children's postsecondary education (PSE) yet they had a rather unrealistic picture of how much money was needed: 40 percent of parents expected their children to receive scholarships based on academic performance, while only 15 percent of PSE students actually did. Hence, the proportion of students who rely on financing from banks, personal loans or credit cards is 2.5 times higher than parents expected.

Levels and modes of participation: under-represented groups

Access to higher education has been increasing in Canada and has now reached the level of "universal" higher education, as defined by Trow (2010). Although seemingly a contradiction, greater access can also mean greater inequality (Altbach 2010) and there are still several groups that are significantly under-represented in higher education, even if access has increased overall (Knighton *et al.* 2009).

Aboriginal people

Almost half of the Aboriginal population in Canada is under the age of 25. Among the 20- to 24-year-old Aboriginal population, 40.3 percent have not completed high school, compared with 12.5 percent in the non-Aboriginal population (Statistics Canada 2006). So the drop-out (or non-completion) rate for young Aboriginal people is still extremely high, even if serious efforts are made, partly successfully, to prevent early school leaving – which often entails an end to learning in the formal education system.

The poor results of initial schooling can be explained by a number of factors that are well known to influence school performance and, closely related, motivation and aspirations regarding further education and formal learning. Children from low-income families are less inclined to attend post-secondary institutions than children from higher income families. Census data show that about a third of Aboriginal families are living in poor (low-income) conditions, compared with 13 percent for all Canadian families.

Increasingly, broadband internet services are becoming an essential part of Canada's communication and information infrastructure. They also play a key role in fostering lifelong learning by improving access to education and learning opportunities (see below). Access to these services is particularly important for Aboriginal people, many of whom live in small, remote communities across Canada and have no or limited internet access. According to a 2007 study by the Industry Department, First Nations people living on-reserve still rely primarily on slower dial-up internet services, and only 17 percent of First Nations communities had access to broadband services compared with 64 percent of other cities and small towns in Canada (CCL 2009b).

In spite of the dismal results of schooling, Census data show an improvement in the overall levels of post-secondary educational attainment within the Aboriginal population: Aboriginal people were as likely as their non-Aboriginal counterparts to have obtained a college or trade qualification whereas only 7.7 percent of the Aboriginal population had attained a university degree, compared with 23.4 percent of the non-Aboriginal population (CCL 2009a).

Immigrants

Recent immigrants are already generally well educated when they arrive in Canada and highly motivated and ambitious for their children to do well in school. Over half (51 percent) of recent immigrants, those who immigrated to Canada between 2001 and 2006, had a university degree, more than twice the proportion of degree holders among the Canadian-born population (20 percent) and also much higher than the proportion (28 percent) among immigrants who arrived before 2001 (Statistics Canada 2006). It is therefore not surprising that first- and second-generation immigrants are more likely than non-immigrant Canadians to participate in post-secondary education; they are also more likely than non-immigrant Canadians to attend university rather than college. Thus, more than 50 percent of immigrants participated in university compared with only 38 percent of non-immigrant Canadians – yet born Canadians were more likely to go to college than immigrants (34 percent compared with 29 percent) (CCL 2010).

Adults

Adults above the age of 25 are the largest group among so-called "non-traditional" students and were the main focus of earlier studies on non-traditional learners (see for example OECD 1987; Schuetze 1987). Almost 4 million adults aged between 25 and 64 have a university degree, up 24 percent from 2001 (Statistics Canada 2006), with younger adults (aged 25 to 34) having a higher level of educational attainment than older people. Almost six out of every ten adults have completed some form of post-secondary education of which an estimated 23 percent have a university degree, 20 percent a college diploma, and 12 percent a trades certificate.

On the other end of the spectrum, 15 percent of adults have not completed high school education, with the majority without any formal educational credentials concentrated in older age groups. Twenty-three percent of 55- to 64-year-olds have not completed high school.

Because Canadians are living longer, there has been increased demand for educational opportunities from those over the age of 65. Many educational institutions now offer "seniors" or "third age" programs that provide courses of intellectual, cultural and social enrichment.

Rural students

Canada's post-secondary institutions, particularly universities, are concentrated in medium- to large-sized urban settings. Distance from a post-secondary institution is one of several factors that influence the decision to pursue PSE – in part, because distance increases the cost of attendance. Costs can be expected to be lower when rural students are using distance education to a greater extent. Because of the slow take-up of distance learning modes of participation it is too early to tell, however, what effect e-learning will have on participation.

The problem of low participation rates has several roots, however, besides distance. The high-school dropout rate for 20- to 24-year-olds living in small towns and rural areas was almost twice the rate for the same age group living in large cities (almost 15 percent versus 8.3 percent) (CCL 2009a).

Students with low socioeconomic status

In line with the situation in other countries, Canadian students from lower-income family backgrounds are less likely to pursue PSE. In 2006, less than 60 percent of 18- to 24-year-olds from families earning less than $25,000 per year participated in PSE, compared with more than 80 percent from families with an income of over $100,000. The SES background also affects the type of post-secondary education students pursue. Students from the lowest income group participated in university at a rate of 27.5 percent compared with 48.6 percent of students from the highest income group (Statistics Canada 2006).

The reasons for this are well known. Parents from this group are mostly poorly educated themselves and therefore lack the motivation to send their children on to further education, especially since they do not have the financial means to pay for their education. Because many of them are not convinced of the benefits to be reaped from post-secondary education, especially higher education, they are also more "risk averse" than other groups when it comes to taking out loans for education.

Women

The greatest leap forward regarding participation and completion of higher education has been made by women. As shown previously, women's liberation in Canada has been most successful in education where earlier gender inequalities have been reversed (Schuetze 2000). As in many other OECD countries, women now are a clear majority in almost all higher education programs with the exception of doctoral studies and a few technical fields (Vincent-Lancrin 2008).

I now consider two modes of study which are significant to lifelong learners – part-time studies and e-learning.

Modes of study

Part-time studies

Part-time studies have long been regarded as the preferred mode of study for adults (OECD 1987; Schuetze 2000). It was assumed that the great majority would be able to combine their jobs and studies. The availability of part-time study and flexible arrangements to accommodate working adults, such as flexible scheduling, modular courses, the portability of course credits, and the combination of classroom-based teaching and distance education ("blended learning") were seen as crucial elements enabling working adults and parents with children to participate and succeed.

Part-time student attendance in Canada had steadily grown until the beginning of the 1990s but then leveled off and dropped thereafter (Schuetze 2000). This trend continued during the last decade: while full-time university enrolment grew by almost 42 percent over the 15-year period between 1993 and 2008, the level of part-time enrolment in university dropped by 13.3 percent. However, important regional differences exist: while in the two central (and largest) provinces, Ontario and Quebec, part-time student numbers decreased by around 20 percent, they increased in the two western provinces, Alberta and British Columbia, by more than 45 percent.

In contrast, full-time enrolment in colleges and institutes grew during the same 15-year period by only 26.4 percent, while part-time enrolment grew by 41 percent. This time, Alberta's enrolment growth was much smaller (2 percent) and British Columbia's even dropped by 8.7 percent.

To find an explanation for this enrolment trend in the West one would need to look more closely into the policies that drove this development. To take the case of British Columbia where higher education enrolment levels had been trailing those of the other provinces, the provincial government pursued policies and substantially increased funding to increase significantly the number of available places in degree awarding programs (see Schuetze and Day 2001).

While we have data on part-time students, there are no data that would indicate the number of programs that can be pursued in part-time mode. It can be presumed that many degree level programs still require full-time participation and that undergraduate programs are less flexible than graduate studies. Therefore, the number of part-time students might be higher if more programs allowed for this mode of study.

One possible explanation, namely that fewer people combine work and studies, is clearly contradicted by evidence: the proportion of young students who work while enrolled in post-secondary education programs is increasing not decreasing. In the ten years from 1997 to 2007 the proportion of 20-year-old university students grew from 38 to 45 percent and of college students from 48 to 56 percent. This means that approximately half of the younger student population studies only part of their time whether or not registered as a part-time student.

There are two conclusions: firstly, part-time study is not (or no longer) a matter concerning mainly adult students but for students of all ages, and secondly, the flexibility of study modalities has increased to the point that work can indeed be combined with studying full time.

Distance and online learning

Internet-based distance education and learning are potentially very useful modes of learning, overcoming the problems of distance and time – a huge problem in the large but sparsely populated areas of Canada. Such programs and opportunities could potentially reach learners in remote areas, including First Nation people living on remote reserves, and would also make higher education accessible for other learners who cannot easily attend classes on campus, such as disabled learners or full-time workers.

In order to fully harness this medium, a number of problems would need to be resolved. One is the absence of readily available broadband access in remote areas. Poorer learners might not possess, or have ready access to the technology necessary for efficiently interconnecting with tutors and fellow learners. As importantly, instructors would need to fully understand the pedagogical implications of e-learning and be ready to re-design and re-conceptualize their courses accordingly. Many potential learners, neither always fully computer literate nor familiar with the techniques of using electronic data banks and libraries, would need to be coached about independent learning.

The number and proportion of courses delivered online in Canada is high (CCL 2009a). However, Canadian post-secondary institutions have been slower than in many other countries to incorporate significant online components into their programs. Bottlenecks relate to increased workloads for instructors and a lack of additional funding as well as intellectual property issues (OECD 2005).

In sum, Canada, in spite of its excellent formal education infrastructure, is not serving well all potential learners and, in spite of its shiny record of equity, is leaving many of them behind.

Despite considerable rhetoric around the importance of lifelong learning, higher education is not quite ready to play a major role in lifelong learning. The findings of the 2006 report on the availability of formal learning opportunities for older students (Meyers and de Broucker) are still valid in 2012:

> Most post-secondary institutions have policies such as flexible admission and prior learning assessment and recognition ... Some institutions have innovative programs for adult learners without high-school diplomas or other prerequisites. But there is little evidence on the implementation and effectiveness of these policies. (p. IV)

As shown above, this summary assessment is not just valid for older adults but applies to several groups who are still denied fair access and therefore under-represented in higher education.

Summary and conclusions

Summing up the Canadian learning system and especially the situation of lifelong learners in higher education, the following themes emerge:

1 Because education in Canada is a provincial responsibility, there are a great variety of structures, providers, regulations and organizational forms. Due to the lack of efficient bodies or mechanisms that would bring the provinces together in order to articulate, coordinate and make this huge non-system coherent and transparent, it is difficult to find reliable and comparable information about learning opportunities. This acts as a significant barrier to potential learners who are unfamiliar with the higher education system.
2 With the exception of early childhood education, which is relatively under-developed, Canada's schooling system is well established and endowed. Formal primary and secondary schooling are of a very high standard and provide the young with a solid "foundation" for lifelong learning. A few discrepancies exist between the provinces and especially between urban and rural schools, however the K–12 system provides very good schooling and support for students with disabilities or other learning problems. In recent years, efforts to reduce the high school dropout rate seem to have borne fruit and while the non-completion rate is still too high, it is low in international comparison. Home schooling and "distributed learning" schemes makes participation possible for remote or disabled students who cannot attend schools regularly.

3 The higher education system is not as equitable. To be sure, the great diversity of post-secondary education offers many choices in terms of programs and modes of study, but many potential learners are left behind. This is due to some structural barriers, especially the problems of finding relevant and reliable information, the absence of efficient mechanisms of accrediting knowledge and skills learned outside the formal education and training system, and the lack of outreach and preparation activities that some of the under-represented groups require.
4 Another structural barrier is that academic credit and qualifications acquired in one institution are not always recognized by others, especially by universities, which, because of their academic autonomy, set their own admission standards and program requirements. This insular approach requires a great amount of articulation and negotiation and makes inter-institutional mobility of learners difficult.
5 As the costs of higher education have gone up dramatically over the last years and governments have seen themselves incapable of maintaining their former level of funding, students and their families are left with an increasingly higher financial burden. Since student support systems have not been able to augment their loan and grant programs commensurably, this means that students have to find resources elsewhere. This is a major barrier to potential learners who come from poorer families.
6 Although there have been substantial increases in participation in post-secondary education over the last decade and a half, inequalities persist. This applies to several groups but in particular to Aboriginal (First Nation) people who are not first but last with regard to school retention and success and also under-represented in university education.
7 Besides structural barriers such as lack of information, counseling and non-recognition of prior learning, there are other causes for under-representation, especially costs and distance which affect people from rural areas, low-income families and parents who have themselves not been successful in their own formal education.
8 One potentially efficient mechanism to overcome distance, on-line learning, has not yet been fully embraced by higher education institutions. There are a number of issues that need to be resolved before an efficient internet-based higher education learning system can be established on a broad basis. Yet, given Canada's unique geography, it is surprising that Canada is not a trail-blazer in making serious efforts to overcome these problems but rather behind other countries in which distance does not play as large a role.
9 Access to higher education in Canada is universal in the sense that more than half of the traditional age group of the population (18 to 24) is enrolled in, or has graduated from higher education. However, higher

education benefits these traditional students while others are left on the margin. For a country that aspires to become a "learning society" this is not good enough. Even under the prevailing neoliberal philosophy of governments, which sees the primary objective of education as serving the economy and higher education as the basic instrument of a "knowledge-based economy", this neglect is a waste of human talent that the country cannot afford. Rather than increasing the intake of qualified immigrants, the federal and provincial governments should make efforts to facilitate access for these under-represented groups.

10 Currently, such efforts are not made, or not made as vigorously and coherently as they should be in the pursuit of both efficiency and equity. The metaphor chosen for the title of this essay, namely that bridges are too narrow and ferries too infrequent to serve the entire population of the archipelago, seems sadly appropriate.

Notes

1 Registered apprenticeships doubled between 1999 and 2009, with 85,000 new entrants in 2009 (Statistics Canada 2011b).
2 An example is the establishment of five "university colleges" in British Columbia at the end of the 1980s, which offered four-year academic programs leading to a bachelor degree while, at the same time, continuing to provide non-degree vocational education programs (they have since been transformed into full yet specific purpose universities).
3 Alternative acronyms include APEL, PLA or RPL.

References

Adamuti-Trache, M. and Schuetze, H.G. (2010) Demand for university continuing education in Canada. *Canadian Journal of University Continuing Education 35* (2) 87–108.
Alberta. (2006) *A Learning Alberta*. Edmonton: Department of Advanced Education.
Altbach, P.G. (2010) Access means inequality. *International Higher Education No. 61*, pp. 3–5.
Boshier, R.W. (2011). "Better city, better life! Lifelong learning with Canadian characteristics". In Yang, J. and Valdes Cotera, R. (Eds). *Conceptual Evolution and Policy Developments in Lifelong Learning*. Hamburg: UNESCO Institute for Lifelong Learning, pp. 77–97.
British Columbia. (2007). *Campus 2010: Thinking Ahead*. Victoria: Ministry of Advanced Education and Labour Market Development.
CAUT (2011) *CAUT Almanac of Post-Secondary Education in Canada*. Ottawa: Canadian Association of University Teachers.
CCL (2009a) *The State of E-Learning in Canada*. Ottawa: Canadian Council on Learning.
CCL (2009b) *The State of Aboriginal Learning in Canada: The Holistic Approach to Measuring Success*. Ottawa: CCL http://www.ccl-cca.ca/pdfs/StateAboriginalLearning/SAL-FINALReport_EN.PDF.

CCL (2010) *Taking Stock: Lifelong Learning in Canada 2005–2010*. Ottawa: Canadian Council on Learning.
Conrad, D. (2008) Revisiting the Recognition of Prior Learning (RPL): a reflective inquiry into RPL practice in Canada. *Canadian Journal of University Continuing Education*, 34(2) 89–110.
Fisher, D., Rubenson, K., et al. (2006) *Canadian Federal Policy and Postsecondary Education*. Vancouver: Centre for Policy Studies in Higher Education and Training.
Gibb, T. and Walker, J. (2011) Educating for a high skills society? The landscape of Federal employment, training and lifelong learning policy in Canada. *Journal of Education Policy*, 26 (3) 381–398.
Grace, A.P. (2009) A view of Canadian lifelong-learning policy culture through a critical lens. In Field, J., Gallacher, J. and Ingram, R. (eds), *Researching Transitions in Lifelong Learning*. Florence, KY: Routledge.
Jones, G. (2001) Islands and bridges: Lifelong learning and complex systems of higher education in Canada. In: Aspin, D. et al. (eds), *International Handbook of Lifelong Learning*, pp. 545–560. Dordrecht: Kluver.
Kirby, D. (2007) Reviewing Canadian post-secondary education: Post-secondary education policy in post-industrial Canada. *Canadian Journal of Educational Administration and Policy*, 65, 1–24.
Kirby, D. (2011) Strategies for widening access in a quasi-market higher education environment: Recent developments in Canada. *Higher Education: The International Journal of Higher Education and Educational Planning*, 62(3), 267–278.
Kirby, D., Curran, V., and Hollett, A. (2009) Not-for-credit adult learning programs at Canadian post-secondary institutions: Trends, issues and practices. *Canadian Journal of University Continuing Education*, 35(2), 63–86.
Knighton, T., Hujaleh, F., Iacampo, J., and Werkneh, G. (2009) *Lifelong Learning Among Canadians Aged 18 to 64 Years: First Results from the 2008 Access and Support to Education and Training Survey*. Ottawa: Statistics Canada.
Myers, K. and de Broucker, P. (2006) *Too Many Left Behind: Canada's Adult Education and Training System*. Ottawa: Canadian Policy Research Network.
Nesbit, T. (2011) Canadian adult education: Still a movement. *Canadian Journal of University Continuing Education*, 37(1) 1–13.
Nesbit, T., Dunlop, C. and Gibson, L. (2007) Lifelong learning in institutions of higher education. *Canadian Journal of University Continuing Education*, 33(1), 35–60.
New Brunswick. (2008) *Be Inspired. Be Ready. Be Better – The Action Plan to Transform Post-Secondary Education in New Brunswick*. Fredericton: Department of Post-secondary Education, Training and Labour.
Newfoundland and Labrador. (2005) *Foundation for Success – White Paper on Public Post-Secondary Education*. St. John's: Department of Education.
OECD (1987) *Adults in Higher Education*. Paris: Organization for Economic Cooperation and Development.
OECD (2003) *Beyond Rhetoric: Adult Learning Policies and Practices*. Paris: Organization for Economic Cooperation and Development.
OECD (2005) *E-Learning in Tertiary Education: Where Do We Stand?* Paris: Organization for Economic Cooperation and Development.

OECD (2011) Education: Bridging the classroom divide. OECD Observer NR. 284, Q1.
Ontario. (2005) *A Leader in Learning*. Toronto: Ministry of Training, Colleges and Universities http://www.tcu.gov.on.ca/eng/document/reports/postsec.pdf.
Rubenson, K., and Nesbit, T. (2011) CONFINTEA VI from a Canadian perspective. *International Review of Education*, 57(1/2), 127–143.
Saskatchewan. (2007) *Post-Secondary Education Accessibility and Affordability Review*. Regina: Ministry of Advanced Education and Employment.
Schuetze, H.G. (Ed.) (1987) *Adults in Higher Education: Policies and Practice in Great Britain and North America*. Stockholm: Almquist & Wicksell.
Schuetze, H.G. (2000) Higher Education and Lifelong Learning in Canada: Re-interpreting the notions of "traditional" and "non-traditional students" in a "knowledge society". In H.G. Schuetze and M. Slowey (eds), *Higher Education and Lifelong Learners: International Perspectives on Change* (pp. 127–144). London and New York: Routledge–Falmer.
Schuetze, H.G. (2003) Alternation education and training in Canada. In Schuetze, H.G. and R. Sweet (eds), *Integrating School and Workplace Learning in Canada: Principles and Practice of Alternation Education and Training*. pp 66–92. Montreal: McGill-Queen's University Press.
Schuetze, H.G. (2008a). Producers of knowledge, centres of learning, drivers of change: Universities serving their regions. In P. Von Mitschke-Collande and R. Mark (eds), *The University as a Regional Actor: Partnerships for professional development in Europe* (pp. 11–18). Hildesheim and Berlin: Tharax Verlag.
Schuetze, H.G. (2008b). Quality assurance for Higher Education in Canada: From patchwork to national policy? *Higher Education Forum (University of Hiroshima, Japan)*, 5, 113–124.
Schuetze, H.G. (2009) Financing lifelong learning. In P. Jarvis (Ed.), *The Routledge International Handbook of Lifelong Learning* (pp. 375–389). London and New York: Routledge.
Schuetze, H.G. and Day, W.L. (2001) *Access, Participation and Outcomes in Post-Secondary Education in British Columbia: The Role of Policy and Financing (1988–1998)*. Vancouver: Centre for Policy Studies in Higher Education and Training, The University of British Columbia.
Schuetze, H.G. and Slowey, M. (eds) (2000) *Higher Education and Lifelong Learners: International Perspectives on Change*. London and New York: RoutledgeFalmer.
Schuetze, H.G., Kuehn, L., Davidson-Harden, A., Schugurensky, D. and Weber, N. (2011) Globalization, neoliberalism and schools: The Canadian story. In C.A. Torres, L. Olmos and R. Van Heertum (eds), *In the Shadow of Neoliberalism: Thirty Years of Educational Reform in North America*. Oak Park, IL: Bentham Books. http://www.benthamscience.com/ebooks/contents.php?JCode=9781608052684.
Social Research and Demonstration Corporation (SRDC) (2010) *Learning to Save, Saving to Learn – Individual Development Accounts Project. Final Report*. Ottawa: SRDC. http://www.srdc.org/uploads/learnSave_final_EN.pdf.
Statistics Canada (2006) Census data. Ottawa: Statistics Canada.
Statistics Canada (2011a) *Labour Force Survey 2010*. Ottawa: Statistics Canada.

Statistics Canada (2011b). Trends in Registered Apprenticeship Training in Canada, 1991 to 2009. In *Education Matters* 8(3) http://www.statcan.gc.ca/pub/81-004-x/2011003/article/11538-eng.htm.

Trow, Martin A. (2010) *Twentieth-Century Higher Education: Elite to Mass to Universal.* Edited by Martin Burrage. Baltimore, MD: Johns Hopkins University Press.

Vincent-Lancrin, S. (2008) The reversal of gender inequalities in higher education. In Organization for Economic Cooperation and Development, *Higher Education to 2030* (Vol. 1). Paris: OECD. pp. 265–298.

Chapter 9

Mexico

Great expectations, scattered approaches, disjointed results: the rocky road to lifelong learning in Mexican higher education

Germán Álvarez-Mendiola

Introduction

In accordance with the global economic interest in preparing human resources appropriate to a knowledge-based economy, Mexico has adopted the concept of lifelong learning and its associated ideas; in doing so, the country has acted under the assumption (promoted by international organizations) that lifelong learning is an important factor in stimulating employment, economic development, democracy, and social cohesion (OECD 1996; UNESCO 1996; World Bank 2003). Along those lines, several educational institutions and agents are interested in achieving better indicators in learning, offering more educational opportunities, and promoting training rooted in lifelong learning. Regarding higher education, various policies and programs converge with some aspects of lifelong learning: policies concerning the broadening of educational coverage, the creation of new public institutions, the recent reforms to student-centered educational models, the installation of tutoring as a formal space for accompanying students during their educational careers, some programs regarding student mobility, degree equivalence and the recognition of prior learning, as well as the expansion of the not-on-site or semi-on-site educational offering. However, there is no unified approach orienting these reforms and resources toward the construction of a coordinated system of institutions and programs. The expansion of coverage is a far cry from the universalization of higher education that is required in order to foster an educational system governed by lifelong learning principles, and the reforms to educational models do not seem to have produced the desired results in terms of a solid development of students' autodidactic abilities (the key to lifelong learning).

In this chapter I analyze the situation in Mexico. The first section covers the general problems Mexico faces due to the challenges of a knowledge-based economy and educational inequality. The second presents higher education policies related to lifelong learning and discuss several problems in their implementation – specifically, that educational reforms, in spite of their explicit intention, have not managed to place students and their learning at center stage.

Educational inequality and a knowledge-based economy

According to the general postulates of lifelong learning, individuals learn at various times throughout their lives and actively participate in society and the workforce. Their ability to learn permits them to strengthen social cohesion and increase productivity through adaptation and innovation. Thus, society and a knowledge-based economy are at the same time the foundation of lifelong learning and its beneficiaries. Nonetheless, this does not correspond to the reality of education in Mexico, due to the country's high level of poverty and deep socioeconomic inequality.

Educational inequality

The high degree of income inequality is closely related to educational disparities. The number of years of education for those whose income is in the lowest decile has hardly increased and has done so slowly: in 2000, the average was 2.8 years and in 2005, 3.2. The gap between the richest sector and the sectors with the lowest income continues to be quite high: a difference of 8.8 years of education. The great inequality in Mexico can only be compared to that in Brazil, in which the distance between the poorest decile and the richest is 8.5 years of education. In contrast, the difference in Argentina is 6.5 years, and in Chile, 6.6 years of education (PREAL 2001). Given these wide disparities, it is not surprising that Mexico is in 67th place among the 145 nations of the World Bank's Knowledge Economy Index (KEI), ranking below Argentina (59th) and Chile (42nd), and far below Finland (1st) (WBI 2009).

Many of the challenges Mexico faces in education are related to improving the quality of basic education so that students can be solidly prepared for the rest of their educational careers and have a greater probability of becoming lifelong learners. Unfortunately, too many schools do not perform well, and chances are that many young people will not acquire basic skills. Though educational coverage has improved, the figures reflect setbacks on a large scale, as can be seen in the following:

- In 2009, more than 33 million people older than 15 could not read or write, or had not finished nine-year basic education – almost the same number as in 2000. Of these, around 6 million were illiterate, about 10 million had not finished primary school, and 17 million had not completed lower-secondary education (INEA 2009).
- In 2009, the average number of years of education was 8, one less than the 9 required to complete basic education, and far from the 13 necessary to finish secondary school (Presidencia de la República 2009).
- In 2010, almost a million children between 6 and 14 years of age did not attend school (INEGI 2010a).

- The lower-secondary level is still not universal, though it has been obligatory since 1993. In 2008, 1,182,000 adolescents from 13 to 15 (14 percent of their age group) did not participate in that level (INEE 2009).
- In 2010, 60 percent of the population from 15 to 24 (i.e., 12.5 million young people) did not attend school (INEGI 2010a).
- In 2010, only 22 percent of the 20–24 age group was enrolled in higher education, which means that 7,623,607 young people are outside the school system (INEGI 2010b).

This situation has implications for the transition to the labor market. The total working population is 44,255,384, of which 16 percent have not completed primary education, only 12 percent have completed lower secondary, barely 12 percent have completed secondary, and only 17 percent have completed studies at the higher education level. Student progression through educational levels poses enormous challenges in developing lifelong learning policies. Almost 45 percent of those who started basic education in 1997 had not completed it nine years later and only 28 percent went on to tertiary education.

Additionally, even if relevant factors remain unmeasured, the results of a variety of tests on a large scale, including three versions of the OECD-promoted Program for International Student Assessment (PISA) show that Mexican students are not adequately prepared with lifelong learning competencies. Some small improvements are insufficient in comparison with the performance of other countries whose economies are similar to Mexico's. It does not seem possible that these improvements will accelerate significantly in the coming years (Muñoz-Izquierdo and Ulloa 2011).

Educational policy and lifelong learning in higher education

Governed by the economic imperative of human capital, some proposals related to lifelong learning do exist in adult education, in job training and (to a lesser extent) in technological secondary education. However, in other areas of education, institutions rarely adopt strategies guided by lifelong learning perspectives, programs are often limited to merely expressing an intention to move in the direction of lifelong learning, and are not integrated into a coherent pattern of learning. In turn, educational policies tend not to envision a coordinated and flexible system of education. In the current framework, students enter higher education with almost no training related to independent learning.

In the Sector Program for Education (2007–2012) (SEP 2007), there are only very few references to lifelong learning. Nonetheless, some strategies and objectives for higher education are somewhat related to lifelong learning, such as: making programs, curricula, and study methods more flexible; centering all of these on learning; and making them fit the needs of the productive sector and of society. The federal government is also attempting to foment the development of programs with lateral or intermediate degrees that permit students to combine study and work. Its efforts for school and institutional management revolve around an effective integration of the institutions and subsystems of higher education into an open, flexible, and diversified system. Student mobility is being addressed through the internationalization of higher education and its institutions. Additionally, the government has proposed encouraging the proliferation of continuing education programs in order to provide "refresher" courses for active professionals and to stimulate their lifelong training.

Diagnosis and policies

In 2001, the federal government initiated reform in response to critiques of teaching in higher education: the majority of educational programs are rigid and specialized, favoring teacher-centered pedagogy and student passivity. The undergraduate programs are exhaustive and of varied duration. Intermediate degrees do not exist, and insufficient attention is given to the development of higher abilities. Thus, the federal government established the necessity of:

a   Updating content and developing a flexible learning-centered focus;
b   Supporting the updating of study programs and the training of teachers for the new focus;
c   Incorporating the comprehensive nature of knowledge into academic programs;
d   Favoring students' continued learning, creativity and enterprising spirit, and their use of languages and logical thinking;
e   Ensuring that students complete their studies on time, through tutoring programs, the diversification of degree options, and the simplification of the administrative procedures for graduation;
f   Establishing a system of grants for students with financial difficulties.
(SEP 2001)

These proposals have not ceased to be necessary aspects of educational reform. Currently, the number one objective of the Government's Sector Program for Education (2006–2012) (SEP 2007) is to raise the quality of education so that students can improve their level of educational achievement, possess the means by which to access greater well-being, and contribute to the development of the nation. With this objective, emphasis has been placed on supporting models centered on learning and knowledge generation.

Though these ideas are related to the precepts of lifelong learning, there are no proposals to organize them into a system. Lifelong learning policies require the arrangement of different structures and learning programs into a flexible system which learners should be able to enter and exit at different points in time. The learners' needs include basic academic skills – such as literacy, math, and a foreign language; science skills; use of information and communication technology; and social attitudes for learning and work (OECD 2001, 2005).

Moreover, the design of a lifelong learning system requires flexible policy and regulatory frameworks that permit arrangements among a wider range of actors – such as legislatures, ministries, and other public agencies at federal, State, and local levels, as well as private institutions. The federal government needs to coordinate activities, create mechanisms to certify learners' achievements, offer incentives for learners and providers, and monitor institutions and system performance (OECD 2001, 2005). In reality, no country has implemented a complete lifelong learning system, but many, at least, have accepted the idea in educational policy documents and have started down the "step-by-step" path in that direction (Schuetze 2007).

Now we will briefly examine the basic aspects of higher education policy in order to discuss their relationship with the paradigms of lifelong learning.

Broadening the offering

In the last 10 years, enrolment in higher education has grown significantly. In 2000, there were 1,718,000 students and in 2010, 2,750,000. At the graduate level, the growth was also significant, from 129,000 students in 2000 to 208,000 in 2010. Currently, the gross enrolment rate for higher education is around 30 percent of the 19–23 age group. The majority of this growth occurred in the public sector, thanks to an explicit effort by the federal government to limit the expansion of the private sector – unlike other countries, such as Brazil and Chile, whose growth has relied on the private sector (Tuirán 2011). This rate of coverage places Mexico below OECD-member countries and others, such as Argentina, with 68 percent coverage; Uruguay, with 65 percent; and Chile, with 55 percent.

The recent growth of Mexican higher education was the result of the creation of 92 institutions and the broadening of existing institutional capacity. Thus, the subsystem of technological universities (oriented toward vocational training) grew and new polytechnic and intercultural universities were created. This growth was supported by a program of grants that covers 387,000 low-income students, which has allowed almost 20 percent of young people from low-income families to study at the higher education level (Tuirán 2011). Clearly, this percentage is far from representing equal opportunity, since a young adult from the higher deciles is four times more likely to be able to study at the higher education level than someone with a low income.

"New" educational models

Academic programs in public higher education institutions must be accredited to ensure their quality, which entails curricular changes and other measures to improve the learning environment and support students. Thus, many institutions have implemented educational models which, from a pedagogical standpoint, are relatively close to some theoretical notions of lifelong learning. These models involve changes in admission requirements and mentoring for students; curriculum flexibility to diversify the potential for learning and to promote student mobility; various types of support in languages and other basic tools (computer, writing, and research skills); national and international exchange; recognition of prior learning; training for teachers in new pedagogical techniques; subject-matter refresher courses; and linkage with the labor market.

The important question is how curricular changes have been put into practice and what results have been observed. In spite of their importance, and due in part to their novelty, little is known about processes of change in educational models. There are no organized data about the implementation of such changes, and – above all – about the results in terms of learning, conditions and skills for self-study, and employability. Nevertheless, some specific research in Mexico has made some indications which allow us to understand these new processes (Pedroza 2001; Sánchez 2007; Alarcón 2008). This research demonstrates that there are no evaluations of the models' development and results; few changes are observed in classrooms; there are no policies concerning teacher and staff training geared toward managing and changing curricula according to the new vision; study plans are conceived of as the end point, not as the launching pad for future studies and work; transverse proposals are not put into practice because of limitations to institutional structure; and mimicry is detected (ANUIES 2006). In many cases, more flexibility imposes difficulties on students who also work, due to the fact that classes that meet certain "core requirements" or electives are only held at specific times.

Educational models should resolve problems derived from educational deficiencies, which can be explained by many causes, from economic and social factors to properly educational ones, produced by a scholastic culture little inclined to experimentation and innovation. Such a culture comes from a sorry educational legacy: traditional pedagogy and approaches to learning prepare students to regurgitate content, copy texts, and memorize them, but not to discover, be creative, and enjoy learning. In higher education the predominant practices favor passivity, uniformity, redundancy, anachronisms, and formalism. Since these problems of scholastic culture are contrary to the precepts of lifelong learning, institutions cannot but overcome them if they are to move towards new teaching/learning paradigms. They must recognize students' socioeconomic and cultural diversity in order to design institutional teaching policies and strategies directed at improving retention, raising graduation rates and, above all, at increasing the quality of student development (ANUIES 2003).

In order to confront many of the problems that the new educational models are seeking to resolve, it will be necessary to change the structures that have survived in spite of the reforms. A certain "grammar of schooling" (Tyack and Cuban 1995) is being imposed. In general, undergraduate programs are very long (between 4 and 5 years), require 50 or more subjects, and are highly specialized. This is out of step with what is occurring in other countries, where undergraduate programs do not exceed 4 years and the number of subjects is almost half that in Mexico. Yet the recent curricular reforms seem to operate in the other direction: the tendency is toward content expansion (De Vries 2011).

Credit transfer system

The notion of a nationwide system for credit transfers, degree equivalence, and the recognition of prior learning is a recent idea in Mexico. To that end, the Secretariat of Public Education coordinates the National System of Credits, Validation, and Degree Equivalence, whose fundamental objective is to facilitate the transfer of students from one educational institution and program to another (SEP 2009). It is hoped that this system will support student mobility among programs; nonetheless, the statistics show that the number of students who opt for this path to degree equivalence has diminished. In 2002, 11,096 applications were received and, after a significant increase in 2003, the number declined until it reached 2,256 in 2008. Though the establishment of the national system is a step in the direction of lifelong learning, the reduction in applications is just the opposite (SEP 2010b).

Continuing education and distance learning

Another requirement for lifelong learning is the continuing education that universities and other HE institutions offer through numerous courses (generally of short duration) meant to attend to training and professional "refresher" needs. They may consist of a varied offering of courses or *diplomados*[1] that do not lead to certification. On-site forms of distribution still predominate, though open and distance learning across the internet has grown in recent years. There are still no statistics on participation in these courses, despite the fact that their proliferation is evident. The market for credentials has grown enormously, and the private higher education institutions pay attention to them quickly. People of varied ages tend to attend this type of course, but the predominant group is adults older than traditional students.

The capacity of continuing education and that of distance learning are quite different. In the public sector, the National Autonomous University of Mexico (UNAM) stands out due to its facilities and equipment, and for the enormous gamut of courses it offers. In the private sector, this position is occupied by the Technological Institute of Higher Studies of Monterrey (ITESM). Since the beginning of the last decade, the variety of models has grown but there is a lack of coordination and duplication of efforts, and a need for specific standards that define and regulate the field, as well as for frameworks and mechanisms for the evaluation of programs and their results, as there is a great unevenness in the quality of programs (ANUIES 2000).

As an attempt to solve these problems, in 2008 institutions of higher education created the National System of Distance Learning (SINED), which provides information on educational offerings, designs joint programs and courses, and provides a system of indicators for the auto-evaluation of those programs. A similar project is the Common Space for Distance Higher Education (ECOES) consortium, which is supported by 40 public universities and includes the Program for Open and Distance Higher Education (ESAD), a recent initiative of the Secretariat of Public Education whose objective is to form an innovative educational system that contributes to the comprehensive education of the population throughout their lives (SEP-SES-ESAD 2010). The enrolments in non-scholastic programs offered by all higher education institutions are growing: in 2004, 131,763 undergraduate and 15,651 graduate students were enrolled in non-scholastic programs, while in 2010, 241,050 undergraduate and 32,899 graduate students were enrolled.[2] In spite of their growth, these figures are still a small fraction of total enrolment (7.8 percent and 1.1 percent respectively) (SEP 2010a).

These are all very recent efforts and it is still too early to measure their results and effects. Nonetheless, from a pedagogical standpoint, continuing education and distance learning programs are part of student- and learning-centered models, and are, therefore, important components of lifelong learning. Their importance as far as equity is concerned rests on the fact that they can contribute to broadening coverage by offering educational options to non-traditional students even if, generally, the programs lack academic and professional recognition.

There are suspicions within the academic community in Mexico that a sort of *traditionalization* of educational practices has occurred, evident, for example, in students' dependence on their advisers and "cutting-and-pasting" information from the internet. This coincides with the views of Guri-Rosenblit (2005), for whom technological development occurs quite rapidly, but not so the human ability to adapt to and appropriate new learning styles. In some countries the academic discourse points out that education over the internet is more appropriate for students with cultural capital that permits them to develop their autodidactic abilities, and that students with greater symbolic and financial resources prefer the traditional options of the most prestigious universities. In the same way, the extent to which technology can resolve teaching and learning issues is not clear. Broad access to information is not necessarily broad access to knowledge, which can only be formed by beginning students guided by teachers who are experts in creating meaningful knowledge. No less important is the fact that distance modalities are more expensive than on-site ones, which puts low-income institutions – precisely those that could benefit most from these modalities – at a disadvantage (Guri-Rosenblit 2005).

Prior learning assessment

The Mexican government has acknowledged the importance that evaluating prior learning has for the development of lifelong learning. This type of evaluation is performed for learning equivalent to basic, secondary, and higher education, as well as learning in the workplace. The recognition of prior learning at the higher education level is growing but still small.

In 2006, the number of majors that could be accredited through exams was 28. Five years later the number had grown to 37, a result of a decision by the federal government to increase the opportunities for the accreditation of prior learning and certify it with an undergraduate degree. This was reflected in the number of people who obtained their degree through this route. In 2006, 734 obtained their degree and in 2009, 1,104 new degrees were awarded.[3] This is a small number compared with the total for the regular system and, though the tendency is on the rise, it will be many years before it is numerically significant.

Structural problems

The difficulties of producing more promising results have as their backdrop two structural problems in Mexican higher education: first, the great gap in quality and, second, the complex and difficult governability of the system as a whole.

Quality assurance

Quality assurance policies do exist in Mexico but they only indirectly provide information regarding the quality of teaching, learning, and research productivity. For example, the accreditation of undergraduate programs is barely related to graduation rates, and there are no indicators that link accreditation to students' level of knowledge, and the evaluation of professors has nothing to do with their students' performance.

At any rate, it is well known that there are differences in quality among educational institutions, even at the heart of them. We can draw a picture of these inequalities using, for example, graduation rates, which, although showing some positive signs, are still extremely low: 57 percent at the national level, with great differences among institutions. For the federal universities the graduation rate was 62.9 percent, whereas that for the public technological universities was 54.2 percent in 2005, the latest data available. In contrast, private institutions had a graduation rate of 90.7 percent (II-UNAM 2005).

The fact that some universities show above-average improvement indicates that special attention has been given to low graduation rates. Most probably, these improvements are not an effect of curricular changes or tutoring programs, but rather are simply a result of changes to degree requirements.

Data related to accredited programs can also be used to show great differences in quality. The number of programs classified as "level 1" (accreditation possible in the short term) by the Inter-institutional Committees for the Evaluation of Higher Education (CIEES) or accredited by specialized bodies under the authority of the Council for the Accreditation of Higher Education (COPAES) has grown in the past decade. There are universities in which more than 90 percent of the students are enrolled in recognized programs and, on the other hand, there are universities with less than 10 percent in that sort of program. The public sector has overtaken the private in terms of the percentage of students in accredited programs: 63.7 percent in the public sector and 14.6 percent in the private (SEP-SES 2011), confirming that accreditation policies are directed at the public sector.

Governability and governmental capacity

One of the structural problems with the design and implementation of lifelong learning systems in higher education is the lack of a true system. Not even the federal subsystems (universities, technological universities, polytechnic universities, technological institutes, and teachers' colleges) can act homogeneously, since they adhere to different institutional designs and objectives. Public policy has managed to establish common objectives through special funding for institutional strengthening and quality assurance, but there are no fluid channels for student mobility and degree recognition.

Lifelong learning requires efficient coordination among the various levels of educational institutions. Continued learning and its recognition require flexible structures and agreements between education providers and certification agencies regarding the equivalence of programs, admissions criteria, and the evaluation and certification of standards and procedures. The coordination of these institutions requires articulation and agreements among decentralized State systems and within the federal departments and agencies of education.

In higher education the credits system is still immature, thus creating difficulties for students wishing to transfer between or within institutions. Some initiatives to develop institutional networks will be able to increase mobility and exchange; nonetheless, the efforts are limited, considering the number and diversity of institutions and programs. In addition, feedback and coordination concerning the relevance and content of programs that could improve the transition of graduates to the labor market are insufficient among public and private educational institutions, companies, and communities.

Because tax revenues represented only 17.5 percent of GDP in 2009 – below other equivalent Latin American countries (Brazil 38.8 percent; Argentina 22.9 percent; Chile 18.2 percent), and far below Sweden (46.4 percent) or the OECD average (34.8 percent)[4] – the government faces limited financial capacity.[5] Besides Mexico's low tax revenue, education expenditure as a percentage of GDP has not grown to the extent that was expected in the middle of the last decade. In 2007, Mexico spent 5.7 percent of GDP on education, the same as the OECD average. The public and private expenditure on education did not reach the expected 7 percent of GDP by 2005. Education received 21.7 percent of total public expenditure, the highest percentage in the OECD, but below the 23.4 percent allocated in 2000 (OECD 2010a).

Expenditure per student is poor and a high degree of inequality exists in government funding among the various educational levels. The relatively high expenditure per student in tertiary education still reflects inequality in the distributive scheme, since the gap between secondary and higher education is the largest among the OECD countries: in 2007 the expenditure per student in secondary education was US$3,070 and in tertiary education was US$6,971, while the OECD average was US$8,746 in secondary and US$12,907 in tertiary education. Compared with the OECD average, the per-student expenditure in Mexico is low, and the gap is widening (OECD average US$8,288; Mexico US$3,189) (OECD 2010b).

While expenditure in education has increased faster than the GDP, this increase is not enough to make significant investments in system capacity. Therefore, the critical issues are to broaden and diversify financial revenue, to reduce current costs, and to establish sustainable programs for secondary and higher education and training. All political actors have agreed on the need to obtain more tax revenue and invest larger sums in education. The tax system desperately needs reform, but both Congress and the federal government lack the political capacity to address this issue. Therefore, governmental programs do not offer proposals on how to obtain new resources, nor do they make the priorities for the distribution of those resources explicit.

The lack of information about educational performance has been an obstacle for accountability and the evaluation of quality. The creation of the National Institute of Educational Assessment (INEE) has mitigated the problem in basic education by means of applying, analyzing, and interpreting the various instruments for measuring educational outcomes, and by administering both national and international tests of skills and knowledge. But a system of assessment and feedback for upper-secondary and tertiary education is practically non-existent. The better-developed systems of evaluation and information for higher education are found in the public sector; otherwise, very few private institutions are subject to assessment. Nonetheless, there are no indicators of student performance aside from graduation. At the same time, there is an absence of comprehensive information regarding independent learners outside the formal school system. Such a system of information, however, could be a central mechanism for lifelong learning.

Conclusions

Like in other countries, lifelong learning is advocated in Mexico as a way of developing a knowledge-based economy as well as promoting social mobility and equal opportunity. Governments and other stakeholders must make the necessary efforts so that the system is guided by the principles of lifelong learning. This means guaranteeing basic abilities for everyone, investing in human resources, and promoting educational innovation. It is also important to emphasize the importance of recognizing prior learning, and of increased cooperation, as well as the need to develop basic quality standards, governmental and institutional transparency, and mutual trust among the various actors. Programs must offer guidance and information, and bring learning closer to home in order to increase opportunities for access. Education of this nature ought to have sufficient resources, and be organized in a systematic way.

Even if there is no country that has fully implemented lifelong learning, the concept has guided policies in several countries in Europe and other developed countries: they have made constant efforts in various areas, such as in recognizing prior learning, motivating adult learners, connecting different places of learning, and making learning financially accessible. One observes a completely different situation in Mexico and other Latin American countries, where educational deficiencies and inequalities produce societies with a low capacity for learning. Briefly put, in Mexico some efforts are being made in a lifelong learning direction, but there are no policies, institutions, and systems that promote the principle as a whole. The official rhetoric emphasizes some elements of the emancipatory model of lifelong learning (Schuetze and Casey 2006): educational opportunities would be made available and truly accessible to all, and those who are presently excluded or marginalized would be reached out to and motivated. But these elements have not been translated into effective and well-funded programs. Against this backdrop, an inclusive model of lifelong learning would be an adequate solution, one where clear and coordinated policies and targeted programs would promote the vision of a system of lifelong learning for all.

Insofar as higher education is concerned, federal reform policies have tried to implement some features of lifelong learning; however, as they are not explicitly linked to a clear notion of a lifelong learning system, they remain rhetorical and conceptual, with low practical manifestation. Issues close to lifelong learning are centering curricula on students and learning, favoring curricular flexibility, organizing tutoring systems, and offering scholarships to students with low resources and good performance. Various institutions have implemented new models, but little is known about the impact and results of these models. There is enough to realize, however, that some lifelong learning elements exist within the framework of an educational culture replete with traditionalist and degraded practices. As to efficiency, completion rates have improved (with strong variations among institutions), but the average is still low. In spite of discussions about centering education on students and learning, the emphasis has been placed on professors' development and their status and working conditions.

On the positive side, scattered evidence indicates that these policies have favored a re-articulation of practices, and the creation of opportunities and new dynamics. In some cases, they have stimulated greater debate and a questioning of traditionalist educational practices, encouraged the search for "best practices," and offered students previously non-existent support and possibilities for studying.

Given the importance and magnitude of the change that has been occurring in Mexico, there is an increasing need for conducting specific research about the articulation of policies, institutional changes, and their impact on learning.

Acknowledgement

I would like to thank Elena Torres-Sanchez, Research Assistant at Department of Educational Research of Center for Research and Advanced Studies, for her help in compiling and processing the data used.

Notes

1 These unite various smaller courses around a common problem or topic.
2 Data calculated with Álvarez and Ortega (2011).
3 Data from the General Office of Accreditation, Incorporation, and Validation, Secretariat of Public Education (DGAIR, SEP), taken from Martínez (2009).
4 Data for Argentina and Brazil taken from Heritage Foundation (2009).
5 Data for Mexico, Sweden and average taken from OECD (2010b).

References

Alarcón, E. (2008) *Los impactos del MEIF y el PRONABES en las trayectorias escolares de la Facultad de Psicología-Xalapa de la Universidad Veracruzana* [The Impacts of the MEIF and the PRONABES in Student Trajectories, Faculty of Psychology, Veracruzana University], Thesis, M.Ed., Veracruz University, Xalapa, UV, October.

Álvarez, G. and Ortega, J.C. (eds) (2011) *Sistema de Consulta de la Base 911 de la SEP* [Searching System of the SEP's 911 Database]. Mexico: DIE-Cinvestav/ Veracruz University (CD).

ANUIES (2000) *La Educación Superior en el Siglo XXI* [The Higher Education in the XXI Century]. Mexico: Asociación Nacional de Universidades e Instituciones de Educación Superior.

ANUIES (2003) "Experiencias institucionales en torno a la innovación de la educación superior," *Documento Estratégico para la Innovación en la Educación Superior* [Institutional Experiences Around Innovation in Higher Education. Strategic Document for Innovation in Higher Education]. Mexico: Asociación Nacional de Universidades e Instituciones de Educación Superior, pp. i–lv.

ANUIES (2006) *Propuesta de Innovación Educativa para la Educación Superior 2006–2012* [Proposal for Educative Innovation in Higher Education]. Mexico: Asociación Nacional de Universidades e Instituciones de Educación Superior.

De Vries, W. (2011) "La insoportable pesadez del currículum universitario" [The Insupportable Heaviness of the University Curriculum]. *Campus Milenio* no. 400, January 27, available online at: http://www.camilenio.com/400/campus%20 400/12wietsedevries.html.

Guri-Rosenblit, S. (2005) "Eight Paradoxes in the Implementation Process of E-learning in Higher Education." *Higher Education Policy*, 18, 5–29, Palgrave.

Heritage Foundation (2009) *2009 Index of Economic Freedom*. Heritage Foundation and The Wall Street Journal, available online at: http://www.heritage.org/ Index/.

II-UNAM, Instituto de Ingeniería, Universidad Nacional Autónoma de México (2005) *Estudio de la Eficiencia Terminal de las IES Mexicanas* [Study on Completion Rates in Mexican Higher Education Institutions]. Mexico: Subsecretariat of Higher Education (SES), available online at http://ses2.sep.gob.mx/aye/f1.htm.

INEA (2009) *Estimaciones del rezago de la población de 15 años y más en educación básica al 31 de diciembre de cada año* [Estimations of educational lag of 15 year old or more population in basic education in December 31st of each year], Mexico, Instituto Nacional para la Educación de los Adultos, available online at: http:// www.inea.gob.mx/transparencia/pdf/rez_33.pdf.

INEGI (2010a) *Principales resultados del Censo de Población y Vivienda 2010* [Main results of the Population and Housing Census, Mexico]. Mexico, Instituto Nacional de Estadística y Geografía, available online at: http://www.inegi.gob.mx/prod_ serv/contenidos/espanol/bvinegi/productos/censos/poblacion/2010/princi_ result/cpv2010_principales_resultadosV.pdf.

INEGI (2010b) *Características educativas de la población*. Mexico: Instituto Nacional de Estadística y Geografía, available online at http://www.inegi.org.mx/sistemas/ sisept/default.aspx?t=medu39&s=est&c=21776.

Instituto Nacional de Evaluación Educativa (INEE) (2009) P*anorama Educativo de México. Indicadores del sistema Educativo Nacional, 2009* [Educational Landscape of Mexico. National Education System Indicators, 2009). Mexico, INEE, available online at: http://www.inee.edu.mx/index.php/publicaciones/informes-institucionales/panorama-educativo/4639.

Martínez, J. (2009) *Descentralización del Procedimiento de Certificación mediante el Acuerdo núm. 286. Subdirección de Control y Evaluación*, XVIII Reunión Nacional de Control Escolar [Decentralization of Certification Procedure, through

Agreement n. 286. Sub Direction of Control and Evaluation, XVIII National Meeting of School Control], 2009, available online at: http://www.sep.gob.mx/work/models/sep1/Resource/95504/1/descentacuerdo286.pdf.

Muñoz-Izquierdo, C. and M. Ulloa (2011) "Últimos en la prueba PISA" (The Last in PISA test]. *Nexos*, no. 401, 39–41, Mexico.

OECD (1996) *Lifelong Learning for All*. Paris: Organisation for Economic Co-operation Development.

OECD (2001) *Education Policy Analysis 2001 Edition*. Paris: Organisation for Economic Co-operation Development.

OECD (2005) *Education Policy Analysis, 2005 Edition*. Paris: Organisation for Economic Co-operation Development.

OECD (2010a) *Education at a Glance 2010*: OECD Indicators Chart B4.2 (available at Statlink http://dx.doi.org/10.1787/888932310339).

OECD (2010b) *Revenue Statistics 2010*. Paris: Organisation for Economic Co-operation Development.

Pedroza, R. (2001) "El Curriculum Flexible en el Modelo de Universidad Organizado en Escuelas y Facultades" [The Flexible Curriculum into the University Model in Schools and Faculties]. *Revista de la Educación Superior*, vol. 30 (117) 115–129, Mexico: ANUIES.

PREAL (2001) *Lagging Behind: A Report Card on Education in Latin America*. Washington DC – Santiago de Chile, Partnership for Educational Revitalisation in the Americas.

Presidencia de la República (2009) *Tercer Informe de gobierno* [Third Government Inform]. Mexico, available online at: http://tercer.informe.calderon.presidencia.gob.mx/anexo_estadistico/?contenido=67.

Sánchez, P. (2007) "Autoevaluación del Modelo Académico de la UADY" [Autoevaluation of UADYS's Academic Model]. *Revista de la Educación Superior*, vol. 36 (141) 43–64, Mexico, ANUIES.

Schuetze, H.G. (2007) "Individual Learning Accounts and other Models of Financing Lifelong Learning." *International Journal of Lifelong Learning*, 26 (1) 5–25.

Schuetze, H. and Casey, C. (2006) "Models and meanings of lifelong learning: progress and barriers on the road to a learning society." *Compare*, 36 (3) 279–287.

SEP (2001) *Programa Nacional de Educación 2001–2006* [National Program for Education 2001–2006]. Mexico, Secretariat of Public Education.

SEP (2007) Programa Sectorial de Educación 2007–2012 [Sector Program for Education 2007–2012]. México, Secretariat of Public Education, available online at: http://www.sep.gob.mx/wb/sep1/programa_sectorial.

SEP (2009) *Normas Generales de Control Escolar Aplicables al Ciclo 2009–2010: Recomendaciones en Materia de Acreditación y Certificación de Conocimientos, Habilidades y Destrezas* [General Norms of School Control for 2009–2010 Term]. Mexico, Secretaría de Educación Pública, available online at: http://www.sep.gob.mx/work/models/sep1/Resource/588/1/images/normasce091030nov(3).pdf.

SEP (2010a) *Cuarto Informe de Labores* [Forth Inform of Activities]. Mexico, Secretaría de Educación Pública.

SEP (2010b) *Estadística 2010. Resoluciones de Revalidación y Equivalencia de Estudios a Nivel Federal y Local* [2010 Statistics Resolutions of Validity and Equivalencies of Studies at Local and Federal Levels]. Mexico, Secretaría de Educación Pública,

available online at: http://www.sincree.sep.gob.mx/work/sites/sincree/resources/LocalContent/203/2/revalidaciones_equivalencias%202010.pdf.
SEP-SES (2011) "Evaluación y Acreditación en cifras (diciembre 2010)," in *Consulta de Programas Educativos de Calidad*. [Evaluation and Accreditation in Figures (December, 2010), in: Searching of Educational Programs of Quality]. Mexico, Secretaría de Educación Pública and Subsecretaría de Educación Superior, available online at: http://ses.sep.gob.mx/work/sites/ses/progcalidad/01Corte31deEnero2011Esc.xls.
SEP-SES-ESAD (2010) *Misión, visión y objetivo general* [Mission, Vision and General Objective]. Mexico, Secretaría de Educación Pública, Subsecretaría de Educación Superior and Educación Superior y a Distancia, available online at: http://www.abiertayadistancia.sep.gob.mx/index.php?option=com_content&view=article&id=98&Itemid=172.
Tuirán, R. (2011) *La educación superior en México: avances, rezagos y retos* [Higher education in Mexico: advances, lags and challenges], available online at: http://ses.sep.gob.mx/work/sites/ses/resources/PDFContent/2198/VF-CAMPUS_MILENIO%5B1%5D.pdf.
Tyack, D. and Cuban, L. (1995) *Tinkering Toward Utopia: A Century of Public School Reform*. Cambridge, MA: Harvard University Press.
UNESCO (1996) *Learning: The Treasure Within, Report of the International Commission on Education for the 21st Century* (Chair: J. Delors). United Nations Educational Scientific and Cultural Organisation, Paris.
World Bank (2003) *Lifelong Learning in the Global Knowledge Economy Challenges for Developing Countries*. Washington DC, World Bank, available online at http://siteresources.worldbank.org/INTLL/Resources/Lifelong-Learning-in-the-Global-Knowledge-Economy/lifelonglearning_GKE.pdf.
World Bank Institute (WBI) (2009) *Knowledge Assessment Methodology (KAM)*, available online at: http://info.worldbank.org/etools/kam2/KAM_page1.asp.

Chapter 10

United States of America

Adult higher education and lifelong learning in the USA: perplexing contradictions

Carol E. Kasworm

Introduction

In the last twenty years, adult higher education and the broader platform of lifelong learning in the USA has evolved into a blurred landscape of innovation and competition, as well as perplexing contractions and realignments. Adult higher education, for this chapter, refers to post-secondary credit and non-credit education serving adult students, typically identified as individuals who are 25 years of age or older. Within the United States, the term lifelong learning, "has not been as strongly embraced ... particularly in the policy arena, as represented by the unfunded Lifelong Learning Act of 1976" (Kasworm, Rose and Ross-Gordon 2010: 7–8). Thus, lifelong learning, in US scholarly and professional discussions refers to those activities and engagements representing lifespan learning beyond compulsory schooling. While OECD countries and other nations with centralized governmental planning have considered lifelong learning in higher education through policy and potential funding supports, US states and the federal governments have ignored policy for lifelong learning. Further, policy for American higher education is decentralized, with its state leaders orchestrating issues of funding and broad constitution-based frameworks, and federal government offering leverage through select policies to those institutions which accept federal funding through specialized programs or financial aid student support. The base of policy development and key practices are promulgated through individual institutions, their systems, and their accreditation agencies. Thus, policy development in American higher education has been characterized as a continuum from a sophisticated multi-player chess game to a backyard sparring match among adolescents (Cook 2011; Nye 2004). With over 4,000 higher education institutions based in different histories, missions, and fiscal viability, this diversity has offered a complexity difficult to rationally capture, much less to explain in meaningful pictures, key trends and current impacts for an international audience. Thus, American adult higher education is highly diffuse in character and often more subject to institutional change than to state or federal policies.

For many, it is believed that US higher education was shaped through societal values of egalitarianism (equal educational opportunity), pluralism (of students, institutions, programs, and extension outreach), as well as individualism (emphasis of personal choice and consumerism) (Hall 1991). Current perspectives, as provided by Agbo (2000) and Gumport (2007), suggest higher education is being transformed by a changing composition of student body, flexible structures and access, economic turbulence, liberal/ neoliberal politics, and societal demand for knowledge. Specifically, most higher education leaders point to two current societal concerns which are redefining American higher education: the concern for enhancing economic development and the related concern for increasing the percentages of college-educated Americans. For example, Shaffer and Wright report that the primary role of American higher education is focused upon "marshalling each of their core responsibilities – education, innovation, knowledge transfer, and community engagement – in ways designed to spur economic development" (Shaffer and Wright 2010: 1). And as noted by Carnevale and Rose, "It is no coincidence that the expansion of American higher education occurred as the nation was enjoying economic growth and global economic domination. Education was a primary driver of that growth" (Carnevale and Rose 2011: 12). Further, in their report, *The Undereducated American,* they spotlight the problematic comparison of the United States with other nations in relation to the percentage of college completers, noting the US ranking of seventh place in Bachelor's degree completion and ninth in all degrees for the age group 25–34 years (Carnevale and Rose 2011: 12–13). Jones, Mortimer and Sathre specifically focus upon the adult population and the role of adult higher education, noting:

> The U.S. will likely be unable to regain its place of primacy [international comparisons of college completion] by 2025 if it relies solely on strategies [for college completion] focused on traditional-age students [referring to 18–24 years of age]. Attention will necessarily have to be directed at enhancing the education attainment levels of adults who have fallen into the cracks of the education system somewhere along the way. The low-hanging fruit are those individuals who started, but did not complete, a college education. There are 32,266,000 adults age 25–64 who fall into this category.
>
> (Jones, Mortimer and Sathre 2007: vii)

Thus, the United States is also being challenged to consider adult college student non-completion as part of the policy and action agenda towards future economic strength.

While higher education is challenged to expand and strengthen its impact, there has been a contradictory influence of diminishing fiscal support for higher education. In the last three years, most of the 50 state governments have faced serious revenue shortfalls. Because states are the predominant funders for public higher education, the impact has been significant, with state budget cutbacks directly impacting institutional operations. In examining various reports, the author estimates these losses have been 10–45 percent budget accumulative cutbacks in public funding for government (including higher education) over the 2007–2010 period. While public government support for higher education has decreased, individual students are facing higher tuition costs (projected 4–40 percent accumulative increases) from public and private institutions (Supiano 2008; College Board 2010).

Given this context, this chapter will briefly explore historic past eras in development of programs, national movements, and innovative structures in American adult higher education. Current demographics and trends of adult undergraduate students will further sharpen perspectives on the blurring of distinctions of adult learners in comparison to the younger college student, as well as a following section highlighting the influential dynamics of e-learning pursued by adult learners, as well as the influence of work upon adult students. In conclusion, current possibilities and conflictual realities facing adult higher education and lifelong learning in the United States will be discussed.

Historic context

From its early colonial beginnings, American higher education has provided educational opportunities to adult learners. One of the most significant early innovations was the federal education legislation of the Morrill Act of 1862 and the later Smith–Lever Act of 1914, promulgating the belief that higher education should be furnished to all citizens, with a commitment to practical public outreach service, including aligned support for non-traditional credit and non-credit course offerings (Jencks and Riesman 1969). This legislation created the concept of the land-grant university and innovative structures and programs supporting adult access and participation. There was also a societal movement supporting "democracy colleges," the development of community and municipal colleges (with open access admissions and flexible scheduling), and the dramatic expansion of extension outreach including women's programs, summer schools, teachers' institutions, and industrial/vocational training for adults (Kasworm and Blowers 1994). A key federal role supporting adult access was the "GI Bill" (Serviceman's Readjustment Act of 1944) and further federal legislation for more recent support of veterans in higher education. This unique federal initiative provided financial aid for veterans (mature students) to enroll as undergraduates in any college or university. This initial 1940s funding and subsequent surge of veterans onto college campuses provided national visibility for adult collegiate learners. Further, the dominant youth-only institutions of this era patriotically opened their doors to this new kind of student and many continued to innovate by creating separate divisions, extension programs, evening courses, and correspondence work solely for the adult population. At the same time, there was the development of the General Education Development credential (GED), a battery of assessment tests, as an alternative to the high school diploma, which provided access to many veterans, and now serves high school dropouts with an alternative assessment to enter college.

A key innovation in the 1960s, the community college, was designed as a unique institution within American higher education (Jencks and Riesman 1969; Pfahl, McClenney, O'Banion, Sullivan and Wilson 2010). The two-year community college was crafted to provide the first two years of college, as well as extending its services into the community and responding to broader educational needs of society with a variety of non-formal and informal offerings to adults. Equally powerful in shaping adult access was the 1964 Civil Rights federal legislation requiring equal access to education (ending discriminatory practices based on race, but also age exclusion practices). During this era, there was also the unique development of external degree programs (focused upon self-directed and correspondence courses with limited on-campus instruction), growth of correspondence courses offerings and extension outreach, and new forms of academic credit by examination, including DANTES (Defense Activity for Non-traditional Education Support program [now DSST] through the military) and CLEP (College Level Examination program) (Kasworm and Blowers 1994).

Starting in the mid-1970s, there were significant innovations in adult higher education which moved beyond the traditional campus and targeted adults, including distance learning (television, satellite, and computer networking); PLAR (prior learning for academic recognition through portfolio assessment, self-directed learning contracts, and competence-based models of curriculum); collaborative academic programs between colleges and business, industry, or professional associations; and collegiate institutions with a dominant mission to serve adult learners (Apps 1988; Hall 1991; Maehl 2000). In addition, larger businesses and industries enhanced their professional continuing education activities by starting corporate colleges with specific work-related degrees (Meister 1998).

In the last decade, the USA has experienced dramatic growth of e-learning distance education, specialized adult program designs and entrepreneurial adult-focused programs in private institutions. Many of the adult programs featured stylized accelerated degree programs, with cohort-based programs of 15–30 students, focused upon one course for each 4- to 6-week period (each course meeting once a week with a practitioner instructor and then a second meeting with a project class member group), and with portfolio assessment, lockstep curriculum, and a capstone research project.

These accelerated degree programs have seen dramatic growth, with over 700 degrees in 300 institutions as of 2009 (extrapolated from Wlodkowski and Kasworm's monograph 2003). Thus, across the United States, there are five categories of higher education in relation to adult undergraduate students: (1) institutions which have age-integrated classrooms and services; (2) institutions with age-integrated classrooms and specialized services for adults; (3) institutions with age-integrated on-campus programs, but also specialized programs and outreach structures which predominantly serve adults in select settings; (4) institutions with a predominant focus upon serving adults with stylized programs, policies, and services; and (5) institutions which solely focused upon traditional age college students (excluding adults by their structures and program designs, through full-time on-campus residence attendance).

Current status of adults in American higher education and lifelong learning

In 2009, American higher education institutions had 20.4 million students enrolled in 4,474 collegiate institutions (NCES 2010a). Adult students (25 years of age and older) represented 7.6 million or 39 percent of this collegiate population (both undergraduate and graduate students). During the decade 1999–2009, adult students (ages 25 and over) had increased in larger percentages than the number of younger students, and this pattern is expected to continue (Agbo 2000; NCES 2010a). National projections to 2019 suggest a rise of 23 percent in enrollments of students 25 and over with a smaller increase of 9 percent in enrollments of students under 25.

Because specific aspects of adult life roles significantly impact access and participation, American higher education has been mindful of the growing percentage of college students who are workers, who have families, and who have life conditions which significantly influence their involvement. As of 2008, adult workers represent approximately 80 percent of all adult undergraduate students and approximately 60 percent of all working undergraduates, both traditional undergraduates (17–24 years of age) and adult students (25 years of age and above) (NCES 2008; O'Donnell 2006). Approximately 54 percent of undergraduate adult students were married. In addition, the majority of adult undergraduates were responsible for dependents (approximately 56 percent) (NCES 2010b). Given these characteristics, 60 percent of adult undergraduates were part-time students, in comparison with 10 percent of traditional undergraduate students.

Adult undergraduates often experience a more fragile existence. In particular, these adults are often faced with difficult financial circumstances to support themselves, their families, and their participation in higher education. In a national study of independent students (a more nuanced variable that is linked to financial aid eligibility and includes independent traditional and adult students), 60 percent applied for aid, and of those applicants, 85 percent received assistance, averaging $4,800 (Wei, Nevill and Berkner, 2005). These individuals were most likely to have received federal grants (Pell grants), rather than state and institutional aid, and were less likely to take a federal student loan (than dependent students) (Paulson and Boeke 2006, p. 27). With this limited financial support, it is also important to recognize that approximately 40 percent of the adult undergraduate students reported annual incomes less than $25,000 (considered below the poverty level) (Cook and King 2004).

Although there are a variety of goals and motivations for adult undergraduates, most seek a college degree based upon the need to qualify for a new job or career, often due to job cutbacks, denial of continued employment or denial of promotion without a college degree (Kasworm 2010; Kasworm and Blowers,1994). Further, adult students often seek out credentials with more job opportunities; thus more than half of the undergraduate adult students in 2009 were enrolled in either health care or business fields (NCES 2010b).

Given this complexity and diversity of adult students, higher education leaders and researchers have difficulty in designing categorization schemes to differentiate adult students from the younger college student population. Many demographic participation patterns of undergraduates do not easily discriminate between these two groupings. In essence, there is a significant blurring of various enrollment patterns and behaviors across these age groupings. Although age categories are still considered one way to define the adult college population, in the last decade higher education leaders and researchers have crafted two alternative schemes to differentiate participation patterns for targeted research and intervention. These two perspectives represent the use of (1) nontraditional student characteristics and (2) lifestyle characteristics.

As in an earlier discussion by Schuetze and Slowey (2000), as well as in this current volume, the understanding of students in American adult higher education has been influenced by the Horn and Carroll (1996) analysis. Their typology defined the "nontraditional student" through six characteristics, with cumulative characteristics having a stronger cause-and-effect relationship with students' non-participation. As Choy, Geis, and Malizio noted "73 percent of all undergraduates were in some way 'nontraditional,' with financial independence as the most common nontraditional characteristic, representing 52 percent of the students in the 1999 study" (2002: 1). Although this typology has informed the diverse characteristics across traditional and adult students, it has not delineated understandings to directly influence institutional policy and practice. Thus, adult students, along with subsets of younger students are often clustered into the term "nontraditional." Unfortunately other key characteristics of the adult student, such as adult maturity influencing learning engagement and collegiate achievement, and the importance of key work and family responsibility role commitments in relation to participation, have not been adequately addressed.

The second perspective, lifestyle patterns, represents a practitioner perspective on the variability of young and old student participation in higher education. Institutions have attempted to gain insights through demographic data on their students and created related policy and services informed by lifestyle patterns. In particular, key lifestyle characteristics have focused upon: (1) part-time students; (2) workers (who are at least half time or more in a work setting); and (3) students who were married and/or with dependents (2007–2008 data). However, institutional programs and researchers have struggled with these "lifestyle definers," because of the diversity and complexity of subgroups in relation to participation characteristics. Specific lifestyle characteristics between traditional and adult undergraduates have proven to not translate into similar program participation patterns and student service needs. An example of this complexity is presented in Table 10.1.

Adult learner participation in higher education has predominantly been documented through formal credit course enrollments in higher education environments. However, a different perspective is presented through the US National Household survey, a sample of adults aged 16 and above who were not enrolled in formal education as full-time students. In 2004–2005, approximately 44 percent of adults (212 million adults) reported participating in formal adult education activities (with the presence of an instructor) in both credit and non-credit activities (excluding full-time-only enrollments of adults in college/university or vocational/technical credential programs) (O'Donnell 2006). Workforce-related learning was the highest percentage (27 percent) of participation (which could be part-time college enrollment, employer training, or other organization courses), and informal learning (personal interest activities without an instructor) represented 21 percent participation of the survey sample.

Perhaps unique to American adult higher education, adult learning activities in higher education are often categorized by credit or non-credit venues. For example, in a recent study examining credit and non-credit participation of adults in continuing education at colleges and universities, it was reported that adults were slightly more likely to pursue credit courses (53.6 percent) than non-credit courses (46.6 percent) (Pusser *et al.* 2007). Comprehensive statistics on adult participation in non-credit options are limited, because, as suggested by Sandmann, "few states and only 40 percent of individual institutions document non-credit continuing education efforts" (2010: 225). Of particular importance is the significant development of professional continuing education, undocumented in participation levels, but with a significant volume of activity. As one considers adult higher education, there are many professional disciplines, interest groups, and organizations providing highly complex offerings representing advanced knowledge. Colleges and universities are one of the predominant providers for professional continuing education, with outreach programs based in attractive access and delivery options. Dependent upon public or private institutional providers, there could also be select funding supports to professional participants based in credit-related offerings. The high volume of professional continuing education is partially encouraged by multiple laws and regulations of professional groups or state agencies requiring yearly continuing education participation for renewal of licenses or credentials.

Table 10.1 Undergraduate students in institutions of higher education in the USA by age, employment intensity, and dependency status (percentages: 2007–2008)

Student work and dependency characteristics	18 years or younger	19–23 years	24–29 years	30–39 years	40 years or older	Average age	Median age
Work/employment intensity while enrolled							
Did not work	15.8	53.1	12.4	9.5	9.3	25	20
Part-time	11.5	62.9	14.0	6.9	4.8	23	20
Full-time (35 or more hours/week)	3.4	29.7	25.6	22.4	10.9	30	26
Dependency status							
Dependent	18.1	81.9	*	*	*	20	19
Independent	0.8	13.5	36.8	27.7	22.2	32	29
Unmarried, no dependants	0.8	7.8	58.4	17.9	15.1	30	26
Married, no dependants	0.7	22	29.8	21.5	25.9	33	28
Unmarried, with dependants	28.0	23.4	28.9	28.0	18.1	31	28
Married, with dependants	0.2	7.1	22.6	37.8	32.2	36	34

* Not applicable.

Excludes work study and assistantships.
Includes students who were enrolled exclusively full time and students who enrolled both full-time and part time during 2007–2008.

Source: Adapted from National Center for Education Statistics (2010b, Table 3.3) – Percentage distribution of undergraduates' age group and average and median age (as of December 31, 2007), and selected institutional and student characteristics: 2007–2008.

Perspectives on the new forces influencing adult higher education and lifelong learning

Although there are many complex forces challenging the place and role of adult learning in society, two of the dominant influences on the current nature and focus of adult higher education represent: (1) adults as distance learners focusing upon e-learning activities, and (2) employed adults as workers and students. These two societal forces are becoming major definers of both access and related goals for participation in current policy and practice discussions.

Distance learners (e-learning) and adult higher education

Distance education, and specifically e-learning, has become the growing phenomenon in American higher education. In 2007–2008, approximately 4.3 million (20 percent) of all undergraduate students took at least one distance education course,[1] with approximately 800,000 (4 percent) of all undergraduates enrolled in an entire program through distance education. Adult students represented 97 percent of those students enrolled in an entire program of study based in distance education delivery Table 10.2.

There is a dramatic movement by both higher education institutions and students towards e-learning as a more dominant delivery system. As reported by Sandmann (2010), the specific growth in e-learning for adults is fostered by higher education's desire for innovative outreach and engaged use of technologies for learning. In particular, many higher education leaders have suggested that the downturn of the economy and the significant rise in gasoline costs for travel to and from campus have spurred significant growth and "demand for online courses, with 66 percent of institutions reporting increased demand for *new* courses and programs and 73 percent seeing increased demand for *existing* online courses and programs" (Allen and Seaman 2010: 1).

Growth in e-learning programs for adults is differentially segmented by institutional types. With a total of 436,000 students enrolled in 2007–2008 in entire distance education programs, over half of the students (245,000 students) were in distance education programs in private for-profit institutions. The next largest student enrollments were in public institutions, with four-year colleges having 146,000 enrollments and two-year institutions with 288,000 enrollments (NCES 2010b). Thus, e-learning programs have become an entrepreneurial tool for private for-profit institutions, offering ease of access to an undergraduate degree, but this access comes with more expensive tuition costs.

Adult students as workers

A second key perspective on the direction and focus of adult higher education has been the growing national recognition of undergraduates as

Table 10.2 Engagement of undergraduate students in distance education in institutions of higher education in the USA (percentage of participation 2007–2008)

Age grouping	Participated in at least one distance education course in 2007–2008	Entire program was distance education	Location of distance education courses		
			Home institution	Other institution	Both
18 or younger	10.4	1.0	77.8	11.9	10.2
19–23	16.1	1.4	74.5	11.5	14.0
24–29	25.9	5.3	71.7	12.3	16.0
30–39	30.6	9.1	72.7	8.5	16.8
40 or older	29.4	7.7	72.9	9.7	17.3

Source: Adapted from (NCES 2010b, Table 1.7). Percentage of undergraduates who took any distance education courses, the percentage who reported that their entire undergraduate program was taught through distance education, and the location of distance education courses, by selected institutional and student characteristics: 2007–2008.

workers. Even before this recent decade of major economic upheaval, adult undergraduates were predominantly focused upon work-related educational goals (an estimated 80–95 percent) (O'Donnell 2006; NCES 2009; Stokes 2006). Today, a significant number of adult undergraduates face an unstable work life and have experienced job changes, job dislocation, or difficulties in job advancement, with approximately 66 percent of a randomly selected 90 adults in undergraduate studies facing major job/career issues because of the lack of an undergraduate credential (Kasworm and Blowers 1994). However, over the last two decades, national surveys have uncovered a paradox. When adult students were asked to designate their primary role – worker or student – in relation to their participation in collegiate coursework, there were mixed findings (NCES 2003). In this study, *Work First, Study Second*, adults reported their beliefs that they were either students who worked or employees who studied. As noted by this report, "among undergraduates age 24 or older, those who characterized their primary activity as employment were older, worked more, attended school less, and were more likely to have family responsibilities than their peers whose primary activity was being a student" (NCES 2003: iv). This pattern was most dominant with the oldest grouping aged 40 years and above. There was, however, a subset of adults who were full-time workers who reported their role as "students who worked". Thus, the complexity of adult engagement in learning was partially represented by this suggested belief system anchored in a work role or anchored in a student role, independent of the number of hours of coursework or the number of hours of work (Table 10.3). Those who saw themselves first as students were more likely to pursue full-time studies while also participating as a full-time worker.

Table 10.3 Percentages of students who work and workers who study; self-defined identity of undergraduate students aged 24 or older in institutions of higher education in the USA (1999–2000)

	Full-time	Part-time
Total	42.3	57.7
Students who work	67.9	32.1
Employees who study	24.1	75.9
All students 24–29	54.7	45.3
Students who work	71.1	28.9
Employees who study	32.0	68.1
All students 30–39	40.1	60.0
Students who work	67.7	32.4
Employees who study	24.2	75.8
All students 40 or older	27.4	72.6
Students who work	52.2	47.8
Employees who study	16.9	83.1

Source: Based on full-time attendance. Full-time attendance includes those who also had mixed full-time and part-time enrollment (NCES 2003:17). Adapted from Table 6. Percentage of undergraduates aged 24 or older according to their attendance intensity, by student employee role and age group: 1999–2000.

From a broader perspective, adult participation in lifelong learning continues to be strongly influenced through the work economy. Current rhetoric in American continuing education suggests "swirling" and "churning" of work, the relationship of job access to higher education credentials, and necessity for adults to seek new careers and related expertise (Kohl and LaPidus 2000). In addition, there has been significant growth in workforce training and professional continuing education efforts, with extensive educational efforts through the US military serving 2.2 million military service members (Polson 2010). In addition, the American Society of Training and Development reported that American business and industry expended $134.9 billion on employee learning and development in 2007, with e-learning activities increasing from 30.3 to 32.6 percent of the training (E-Learning Council 2008). In the last decade there have been significant entrepreneurial and competitive efforts focused upon an expanded range of learning opportunities (often for "new markets" that bring in new revenue) featuring courses, certificates, short-courses, post-baccalaureate offerings, assessment competencies, and related professional development experiences.

Adult higher education has become part of an expansive movement by all sectors of society – governments, businesses, professional associations, and non-profit organizations – offering advanced learning programs and credentials, most often crafted for particular work requirements or skill sets.

Possibilities and conflictual realities

The future of adult higher education and lifelong learning in America will be shaped by many forces. For this discussion, five key areas of policy and practice are identified as major potential influencers of the dimension of lifelong learning associated with adult participation in higher education. These five areas include the focus upon (1) the future of adult-distinctive higher education, (2) differentiating adult access in relation to prestige and support of higher education institutions, (3) e-learning for greater access and potential peril, (4) the blurring of traditional boundaries among and between higher education institutions, and (5) the future of advanced knowledge contained solely within formal higher education. These key influencers will continue to shape the contraction and expansion of American adult higher education.

Future of adult-distinctive higher education

Historically, American higher education differentiated its policy and practices to cater to adults based on their part-time enrollment status, work commitments, gap in school/college participation, and, for some programs, curricula and instruction focused upon life experiences and maturity. In the last fifty years, the majority of public four-year institutions have provided access and academic programs to support adult learners, either through age-integrated access, or through age-targeted access utilizing continuing education divisions to offer specialized adult-oriented programs and services. These four-year institutions have served the second largest number of adult undergraduates. However, the last decade has seen the elimination of many divisions, programs, and colleges directed to adult population in public institutions, while at the same time, small private colleges, as well as private for-profit institutions have developed distinctive adult-degree programs with nontraditional formats or e-learning access. On the other hand, public two-year institutions, known as community colleges, have always presented a strong commitment to adults and continue to be the key provider for the highest number of adult undergraduates. Their student population has an average age of 28 years, with public four-year, non-doctorate-granting institutions an average undergraduate age of 24 years, and four-year doctorate-granting institutions have an average undergraduate age of 23 years (NCES 2010b). These community colleges have provided open admissions, flexible schedules and delivery systems, and a focus on coursework towards transfer into a four-year institution, as well as stylized vocational technical programs and short-term certificates. Known as second-chance institutions, these colleges view their mission as to serve the community and its needs, including the diversity of short- and long-term instructional needs of their adults. Private non-profit institutions have the third largest enrollment of adult undergraduates and private for-profit institutions have the smallest numbers, with both creating separate and unique programs and services, and targeting adult students as a specific clientele. In these private institutions, adults are predominantly served by stylized adult degree programs, accelerated degree programs, and online distance education programs. Thus, there is an uneven terrain of access and equity for adult learners. Current national themes of economic efficiencies and efforts to spur economic development will challenge all institutions regarding their mission, programs and services. Given the consolidation and reduction of programs and services focused upon adult students over the last decade, four-year public institutions will continue to scrutinize adult-distinctive programs and services. There are clear messages of national need for adult access and degree completion; however, the rationale for distinctive and specialized programs and services will continue to involve institutional scrutiny and financial justification. Through rhetoric, policy, and practice, adult-distinctive higher education is facing a challenging future.

Differentiating access in relation to prestige and support for adult students

Adults face uneven opportunities to access highly selective or prestigious institutions. As discussed in Chapter 1 of this book, institutions which are less selective, less prestigious, less research oriented, and more focused upon serving regional or community needs tend to have a higher percentage of enrolled adult undergraduate students and appear to offer a stronger commitment to adults and their communities. Thus, research-extensive universities do serve adult learners, but often in minimal numbers (an estimated 3–10 percent of the undergraduate student population are adult students). In general, highly prestigious institutions do not provide the access and flexibility required by most adult students. A subset of these institutions offer special adult-oriented units or expect the adult to conform to the institution's culture of a full-time traditional aged student. At the graduate level, select masters programs (business, education and engineering) in more prestigious institutions target working adults through executive weekend programs, evening coursework, or stylized programs with off-campus sites and distance education offerings. In addition, tuition costs are also a dominant influence on adult access to specific institutions (high tuition costs for private institutions and more costly public research-extensive universities, with less costly tuition at two-year institutions and regional universities). For most adults, their opportunities to gain quality higher education are based in equity issues of financial support, of access to institutions which offer adult-oriented support and specific academic programs, and of access to institutions with quality instruction and outcomes. Currently, there are limited national efforts to identify those types of institutions and standards. Two of the current leaders are the Council for Adult and Experiential Learning (CAEL) with their *Principles of Effectiveness for Serving Adult Learners* (CAEL 2000) and the American Council on Education with their *Principles of Good Practice for Alternative and External Degree Programs for Adults* (American Council on Education and the Alliance 1990).

E-learning for greater access and potential peril

Adult access to undergraduate studies has always been supported through specialized delivery systems – such as correspondence studies, extension sites, evening and weekend programs, television and satellite courses, and now the growing offerings of e-learning. Current enrollments suggest that young adults are more likely to seek out on-campus programs, while adult learners are the more dominant student group in e-learning programs. However, these distinctions are becoming inconsequential as there has been a significant increase in hybrid courses (components of e-learning embedded within on-campus courses) for younger and older adults. Of growing emphasis across all of higher education, e-learning and the use of technology has become an important instructional tool for both on-campus and distance education venues.

But this growth of e-learning also presents peril to the adult learner. In particular, many marketed e-learning programs misdirect, if not directly mislead, the student regarding the ease of access and success of anytime and anyplace learning. Thus, e-learning courses and programs have seen high drop-out rates ranging from 75 percent to 10 percent of adult distance education students (Tyler-Smith 2006). A number of professional associations have created benchmark standards to assess quality e-learning, and a growing cadre of higher education leaders and instructors have developed more sophisticated and complex understandings of the particular value and utility of e-learning in relation to other forms of learning delivery. In addition, the US Department of Education has released new requirements as of July 2011 for individual state approval of distance education offerings as well as other program integrity regulations as policy leverage for quality distance education course and program offerings.

Impact of the blurring of traditional boundaries among and between higher education institutions

Because of permeable boundaries among higher education institutions, there are three key areas which have exacerbated inequity of adult learners in higher education: the need for (a) centralized advisement and counseling services, as well as targeted outreach to adult learner groups through regional or consortial centers; (b) state and institution policy regarding articulation and transfer agreements; and (c) financial aid supports for adult learners.

Because of the lack of centralized structures to provide guidance and advisement of lifelong learning options, adults experience significant difficulties in identifying and accessing learning opportunities across different higher education institutions. Thus, less educated, more isolated, and more impoverished adults often lack information and expertise to make informed decisions regarding alternative programs and institutions. As noted by Cross (1978; 1981), adults require compiled information and knowledgeable advisors to aid them in identifying and selecting more appropriate educational options for their needs. Because of the lack of authoritative resources and personnel, adults have faced several significant issues – unaccredited institutions (diploma mills) who target naive adults, private institutions who do not provide accurate information regarding high tuition costs, ill-formed understanding of degree alignment to the job market, and sometimes limited access to quality four-year institutions.

Secondly, there is a need for state policies and institutional practices supporting joint institutional articulation agreements and transfer of credit hours. Because the majority of adult learners have had multiple institutional enrollments, they typically have experienced significant barriers to the transfer and articulation of course hours from previous institutions into the current home institution. Each higher education institution operates as a fiefdom regarding the acceptance and application of specific courses towards their home institution's programs and degrees. For example, students may have completed 50 credit hours of coursework at one institution, but only 10 hours will be accepted to meet the program course requirements at the new institution. Significant national and state attention is now focused upon developing institutional policies and practices to create systematic transfer and articulation policies and agreements among institutions. Select state systems (such as Florida and California) have established common core courses for the lower division general education courses. In one research project on state initiatives, articulation and transfer of credit hour policies and practices provided significant equity supports for adults. The four states in this study offered clear messages and desired outcomes, but all policy and practice were initiated through consortial gatherings of collegiate institutions, higher education and K-12 leaders. Such outcomes included: (1) greater flexibility and more options for transfer students, (2) improved transfer rates, (3) transfer students better prepared for upper-division work, (4) improved degree completion, (5) reductions in time- and credits-to-degree, and (6) cost savings for students and the state (Kisker, Wagoner and Cohen 2011).

The third major concern focuses upon financial aid for adult students. At most higher education institutions, there is minimal support funding for part-time students and specifically for full-time working students. Students who are enrolled part time are essentially "ineligible for federal financial aid except for small amounts of Pell Grants and Perkins Loan dollars" (Cook and King 2004, p. 41). State funding for student financial aid typically mirrors the federal guidelines. Proposed changes to student aid laws would specifically aid adult students, including modifying the eligibility criteria for some loans and grants and broadening tax credit eligibility rules (Bosworth and Choitz 2002). For example, in a study of working adult parents, only 3.5 percent received Pell grants with less than 0.05 percent receiving federal loans. In addition, less than 3 percent received any institutional aid, with less than 2 percent receiving state aid, private funding, private loans, or tuition waivers, and 3.8 percent receiving veterans' benefits (Bosworth and Choitz 2002). Bosworth and Choitz raise concerns about the Hope tax credit helping adult students, because these individuals needed to make sufficient income and related federal taxes to receive a tax credit, thus questioning the eligibility of many adult students for this program. In examining the Lifetime Learning Tax credit, they note that it "benefits full-time students and those at higher-cost institutions" (2002: 44).

In numerous surveys and interviews, as well as in predictive research models of adult participation and attrition, financial resources are one of the top concerns of adult learners (Kasworm and Blowers 1994; Paulson and Boeke 2006). In one survey, more than 22 percent of prospective adult learners choose not to enroll, citing cost as a key obstacle (Stokes, 2006). Further, adult learners often cite financial issues as one of the two key reasons for leaving a program of study. Thus, adult students often find that the blurring of higher education opportunities only exacerbates their ability to participate in adult higher education with limited personal financial resources.

Future of advanced knowledge contained solely within formal higher education

There is contested terrain surrounding the presumed boundaries offered by higher education institutions as the sole providers of advanced knowledge. In particular, the dramatic growth and innovation of knowledge has been identified as a major disruptive change to the orderly and historic hierarchy of knowledge and expertise within disciplines, and in relation to levels of higher education offerings. Although higher education institutions are often designated as the knowledge industry, new and innovative knowledge development is occurring beyond the academy. Thus, the boundaries of academic disciplines and knowledge are questioned, with many renegade individuals and groups suggesting different types of knowledge and knowledge generation and dissemination are valid and valuable – beyond the higher education domain. These contested arenas are particularly confusing to adult learners and to adult higher education with the commodification of higher education and the efforts to privatize knowledge. Specific signs of these issues reflect the proliferation of types and kinds of credentials and degrees, providers (both legitimate and questionable) of varied credentials, and the growing options for gaining knowledge through open sources, such as the internet. No longer can higher education suggest that it has sole ownership of distinct forms and types of knowledge or is the sole provider for expertise of advanced knowledge. These foundational understandings have devolved and a new world of possibilities and perils are now present. In particular, many adults seek out guidance regarding which providers are authentic, knowledgeable, and reputable. In the USA, these issues have proliferated with the turbulent climate of change within higher education and the entrepreneurial leadership of private entities seeking new revenues by offering packaged knowledge content units as credentials.

Thus, the future of American adult higher education presents contradictory possibilities. On the one hand, a variety of responsive programs and options in adult higher education, based upon both historical foundations and current innovations, will be needed for finding and holding on to "good" jobs. On the other hand, American higher education will face competition for leadership in economic development and innovation. The future of American adult higher education will continue to present these paradoxical realities.

Note

1 These statistics define distance education courses to include live, interactive audio- or video-conferencing; prerecorded instructional videos; webcasts; CD-ROMs or DVDs; or computer-based systems accessed over the internet.

References

Agbo, S. (2000). The United States: Heterogeneity of the study body and the meaning of "non-traditional" in US higher education. In H. Schuetze and M. Slowey (eds), *Higher Education and Lifelong Learners: International Perspective on Change* (pp. 149–169). New York: Routledge Falmer.

Allen, I.E., and Seaman, J. (2010). *Learning on Demand: Online Education in the United States: 2009*. Babson Park, MA: Babson Survery Research Group. Available at http://sloanconsortium.org/publications/survey/pdf/learningondemand.pdf.

American Council on Education and the Alliance (1990). *Principles of Good Practice for Alternative and External Degree Programs for Adults*. Washington DC: American Council on Education.

Apps, J.W. (1988). *Higher Education in a Learning Society. Meeting New Demands for Education and Training*. San Francisco: Jossey-Bass.

Bosworth, B., and Choitz, V. (2002). *Held Back: How Student Aid Programs Fail Working Adults*. Belmont, MA: FutureWorks.

CAEL (2000). *Serving Adult Learning in Higher Education: Principles of Effectiveness. Executive Summary*. Chicago, IL: Council for Adult and Experiential Learning.

Carnevale, A., and Rose, S. (2011). *The Undereducated American*. Washington DC: Center on Education and the Workforce and Georgetown University.

Choy, S., Geis, S., and Malizio, A. (2002). *Student Financing of Graduate and First-Professional Education, 1999–2000: Profiles of Students in Selected Degree Programs and Their Use of Assistantships.* (NCES 2002–166). Retrieved from http://nces.ed.gov/pubs2002/2002166.pdf April 27, 2009.

College Board (2010). Trends in College Pricing. College Board Advocacy and Policy Center (Ed.) *Trends in Higher Education Series.* Retrieved from http://trends.collegeboard.org/downloads/College_Pricing_2010.pdf.

Cook, B., and King, J. (2004). *Low-Income Adults in Profile: Improving Lives Through Higher Education.* Washington DC: American Council on Education.

Cook, S. (2011). *A Couple of Things About For-Profit Education.* Retrieved from http://www.blogtalkradio.com/higheredcareercoach/2011/04/01/a-couple-of-things-about-for-profit-education-1.

Cross, K.P. (1978). *The Missing Link: Connecting Adult Learners to Learning Resources.* New York: College Entrance Examination Board.

Cross, K.P. (1981). *Adults as Learners: Increasing Participation and Facilitating Learning.* San Francisco: Jossey-Bass.

E-Learning Council (2008). *2008 ASTD State of the Industry Report.* Retrieved from http://www.elearningcouncil.com/content/2008-astd-state-industry-report.

Gumport, P. (ed.). (2007). *Sociology of Higher Education: Contributions and their contexts.* Baltimore, MD: Johns Hopkins University Press.

Hall, J. (1991). *Access Through Innovation: New Colleges for New Students.* New York: Maxwell Macmillan.

Horn, L., and Carroll, D. (1996). *Nontraditional Undergraduates, Trends in Enrollment From 1986 to 1992 and Persistence and Attainment Among 1989–90 Beginning Postsecondary Students.* (NCES 97–578). Washington DC: U.S. Government Printing Office. Retrieved from http://nces.ed.gov/pubs/97578.pdf.

Jencks, C., and Riesman, D. (1969). *The Academic Revolution.* Garden City, NY: Doubleday.

Jones, D., Mortimer, K., and Sathre, C.O. (2007). Increasing Productivity: Is Higher Education [As We Know It] Up To the Task? *Association for the Study of Higher Education.* Retrieved November 10, 2007, from http://www.nationalcommissiononadultliteracy.org/content/nchemspresentation.pdf.

Kasworm, C. (1980). The older student as an undergraduate. *Adult Education Quarterly, 31*(1), 30–46.

Kasworm, C. (2010). Adult Workers as Undergraduate Students: Significant Challenges for Higher Education Policy and Practice. In L.E. Perna (ed.), *Understanding the Working College Student: New Research and Implications for Policy and Practice* (pp. 23–42). Herndon, VA: Stylus.

Kasworm, C., and Blowers, S. (1994). *Adult Undergraduate Students: Patterns of Learning Involvement.* Report to OERI, Department of Education, Washington DC, Knoxville, TN: College of Education, University of Tennessee.

Kasworm, C., Rose, A., and Ross-Gordon, J. (2010). Adult and Continuing Education as an Intellectual Commons. In C. Kasworm, A. Rose, and J. Ross-Gordon (eds), *Handbook of Adult and Continuing Education: 2010 Edition* (pp. 1–12). Thousand Oaks, CA: Sage Publications.

Kisker, C., Wagoner, R., and Cohen, A. (2011). *Implementing Statewide Transfer and Articulation Reform: An Analysis of Transfer Associate Degrees in Four States* (Report #11-1). Los Angeles: CA: Center for the Study of Community Colleges.

Kohl, K., and LaPidus, J. (eds) (2000). *Postbaccalaureate Futures: New Markets, Resources, Credentials.* Phoenix: American Council on Education and the Oryx Press.

Maehl, W. (2000). *Lifelong Learning at its Best: Innovative Practices in Adult Credit Programs.* San Francisco: Jossey-Bass.

Meister, J.C. (1998). *Corporate Universities: Lessons in Building a World-Class Work Force* (revised and updated edition). New York: McGraw-Hill.

NCES, National Center for Education Statistics (2003). *Work First, Study Second: Adult Undergraduates Who Combine Employment and postsecondary Enrollment* (NCES 2003-167). Retrieved from http://nces.ed.gov/pubsearch/pubsinfo.asp?pubid=2003167.

NCES, National Center for Education Statistic (2008). *Recent Participation in Formal Learning Among Working-Age Adults With Different Levels of Education* (NCES 2008-041). Retrieved from http://nces.ed.gov/pubs2008/2008041.pdf.

NCES, National Center for Education Statistics (2009). *Digest of Educational Statistics: 2008.* (NCES 2009-20). Washington: DC: Department of Education. Retrieved from http://nces.ed.gov/programs/digest/d08/ch_3.asp.

NCES, National Center for Education Statistics (2010a). *Digest of Education Statistics: 2010.* Retrieved July 25, 2011, from http://nces.ed.gov/programs/digest/d10/ch_3.asp.

NCES, National Center for Education Statistics (2010b). *Profile of Undergraduate Students: 2007–2008.* Web Pages NCES 2010-205. Retrieved from http://nces.ed.gov/pubs2010/2010205.pdf.

Nye, J. (2004). *Soft Power and Higher Education.* Paper presented at the The internet and the University Forum. http://net.educause.edu/ir/library/pdf/FFP0502S.pdf.

O'Donnell, K. (2006). *Adult Education Participation in 2004–2005* (NCES 2006-077). Retrieved from http://nces.ed.gov/pubs2006/adulted/.

Paulson, K., and Boeke, M. (2006). Adult learners in the United States: A national profile. *Informed Practice Series.* Washington DC: American Council on Education, Center for Policy Analysis, Center for Lifelong Learning.

Pfahl, N., McClenney, K., O'Banion, T., Sullivan, L.G., and Wilson, C. (2010). The learning landscape of community colleges. In C. Kasworm, A. Rose, and J. Ross-Gordon (eds) *Handbook of Adult and Continuing Education. 2010 Edition* (pp. 231–241). Thousand Oaks, CA: Sage.

Polson, C. (2010). Military Contributions to Adult Education. In C. Kasworm, A. Rose, and J. Ross-Gordon (eds) *Handbook of Adult and Continuing Education: 2010 Edition* (pp. 263–283). Thousand Oaks, CA: Sage.

Pusser, B., Breneman, D., Gansneder, B., Kohl, K., Levin J., Miliam J., *et al.* (2007). *Returning to learning: Adults' Success is Key to America's Future.* Retrieved from http://www.luminafoundation.org/publications/ReturntolearningApril2007.pdf.

Sandmann, L. (2010). Adults in four-year colleges and universities. In C. Kasworm, A. Rose, and J. Ross-Gordon (eds) *Handbook of Adult and Continuing Education: 2010 Edition* (pp. 221–230). Thousand Oaks, CA: Sage.

Schuetze, H., and Slowey, M. (2000). *Higher Education and Lifelong Learners: International Perspective on Change.* New York: Routledge Falmer.

Shaffer, D., and Wright, J. (2010). A new paradigm for economic development: How higher education institutions are working to revitalize their regional and state economies. University of Albany, State University of New York: Higher Education, Public Policy Research Arm of SUNY.

Stokes, P. (2006). Hidden in plain sight: Adult learners forge a new tradition. *A National Dialogue: The Secretary of Education's Commission on the Future of Higher Education*. Washington DC: Department of Education.

Supiano, B. (2008). Financial officers expect more big tuition increases. *Chronicle of Higher Education*. Retrieved from: http://chronicle.com/search/?search_siteId=5&contextId=&action=rem&searchQueryString=tuition+increases.

Tyler-Smith, K. (2006). Early attrition among first time elearners: a review of factors that contribute to drop-out, withdrawal and non-completion rates of adult learners undertaking eLearning programmes. *Journal of Online Learning and Teaching*, 2(2). Retrieved from http://jolt.merlot.org/Vol2_No2_TylerSmith.htm.

Wei, C., Nevill, S., and Berkner, L. (2005). Independent Undergraduates 1999–2000 (NCES 2005-151). *National Center for Education Statistics*. Retrieved March 15, 2006, from http://nces.ed.gov/pubs2005/2005151.pdf.

Wlodkowski, R. and Kasworm, C. (eds) (2003). *Accelerated learning for adults: the Promise and Practice of Intensive Educational Formats* (Vol. No. 97). San Francisco: Jossey-Bass.

Part IV

Pacific – Australia, Japan and New Zealand

Chapter 11

Australia

Intensifying performance and learner-centredness in Australian higher education

Harsh Suri and David Beckett

Introduction

In March 2008, the Australian Government initiated a *Review of Higher Education* (Bradley 2008) to examine the future direction of the higher education sector, its fitness for purpose in meeting the needs of the Australian community and economy, and the options for ongoing reform. The Review was conducted by an independent expert panel, led by Emeritus Professor Denise Bradley, and the 'Bradley Report' (2008), as it has become known, made some significant claims for the nation's efforts to increase participation in the sector, in an era of shrinking governmental resourcing. Most boldly:

> Australia is losing ground. Within the OECD we are now 9th out of 30 in the proportion of our population aged 25 to 34 years with such qualifications, down from 7th a decade ago. Twenty nine per cent of our 25- to 34-year-olds have degree-level qualifications.
> (Bradley 2008: xi)

Then Bradley drew attention to 'those disadvantaged by the circumstances of their birth: indigenous people, people with low socio-economic status, and those from regional and remote areas' (Bradley 2008: xi), and noted that '[p]articipation by these groups has been static or falling over the last decade' (Bradley 2008: xii). Moreover, in looking at educational institutions themselves,

> Higher education has changed dramatically over the last 30 years or so. It once comprised a small number of publicly-funded institutions. This is no longer the case. There are now 37 public universities, two private universities and 150 or so other providers of higher education. The public universities derive significant proportions of their income from non-government sources and some private providers receive government subsidies. The public–private divide is no longer a sensible distinction.
> (Bradley 2008: xi)

As we write, the significance and impact of the Bradley Report are still unfolding, with several initiatives being funded by the government in response to its recommendations. The Government also published its detailed and resourced response to the Bradley Report, entitled *Transforming Australia's Higher Education System* (DEEWR 2009b), which is making a significant impact on policy and practice in higher education. Drawing mainly on these two documents, what follows is an account of evolving participation patterns in higher education, and what is starting to be done about some of the main patterns of under-representation. The Australian historical and sectoral context is also described, then we link this to lifelong learners, especially to an emerging focus on student- or learner-centredness, and to the five main questions this book addresses. In the process, the characterisation of lifelong learning formulated by Candy *et al.* (1994) is introduced and drawn upon (as it was in James and Beckett 2000), as part of the policy prognosis we set out.

A nation in transition to a 'knowledge economy'

Australia is a vast island continent, sparsely populated with 21 million people. Until the 1960s and 1970s the cornerstones of national economic prosperity were primary industries – pastoral, agricultural and mining – which capitalised on Australia's abundant natural resources and advantages. However, the economy underwent substantial structural change in the latter part of the 20th century. The catchcry of the 1990s was for the 'lucky' country to become the 'clever' country.

Successive governments had begun to see Australia as economically vulnerable in global terms. The 'clever' country transition was to be achieved through a deregulated economy exposed to worldwide competition, the consolidation of robust secondary manufacturing industries, and growth in the areas of tourism and other service sectors. In addition, federal government policy in a range of portfolios was underpinned by the belief that the nation's wealth would be dependent on the production of 'knowledge' goods by a sophisticated tertiary workforce.

Along with these macroeconomic changes, the technological transformation of work and the rapid growth of knowledge in many fields contributed to the requirement for a more highly educated nation. Demand for all forms of education increased, especially post-secondary education. In universities, enrolments in postgraduate education climbed steeply: tight labour markets and more sophisticated workplaces initiated the re-entry to formal education of people in early- or mid-career seeking retraining or to gain career advantage.

Since the 1990s the Australian geopolitical environment has become less Anglo/Eurocentric. The cultural and economic future of Australia was now depicted in the context of South-East Asia, and Australian higher education has become a prominent industry in the region, with most universities benefiting from the revenue provided by fee-paying international students – in the main, citizens of neighbouring Asian countries, principally Singapore, Malaysia, China (including Hong Kong), Indonesia, India and Vietnam. The majority of international students reside in Australia during their studies, however technological delivery and collaborative arrangements with Asian universities rose in the late 1990s and off-shore campuses have been established in many Asian cities.

Official figures provide this 2009 snapshot of student enrolments in Australian higher education providers (HEPs) which include universities as well as non-university providers:

1. The number of domestic plus international students enrolled at all HEPs reached 1,134,866 in 2009, an increase of 6.5 per cent from 2008.
2. There were 813,896 domestic students in 2009 – comprising 71.7 per cent of all students – an increase of 5.4 per cent from 2008. Overseas student enrolments increased by 9.1 per cent to 320,970 in 2009.
3. The number of postgraduate students increased by 6.5 per cent to 307,973 while the number of undergraduate students increased by 6.3 per cent to 790,810.
4. More than half of all students enrolled were female (55.4 per cent).
5. More than two-thirds (70 per cent) of students were studying full time.
6. The majority of students were enrolled at public universities. Public university enrolments increased by 5.6 per cent in 2009 (1,058,399 students in 2009, up from 1,002,003 in 2008), while private provider enrolments increased by 19.3 per cent (76,467 students at 77 providers in 2009, up from 64,092 students at 73 providers in 2008).

(DEEWR 2009a)

Which Australians traditionally have been less likely to participate in higher education? There is an egalitarian spirit among Australians, who do not like to admit to the existence of class divides, yet socioeconomic differences in the Australian population, which possibly broadened in the 1990s, are closely associated with persistent patterns of educational advantage and disadvantage. People of lower socioeconomic backgrounds are significantly under-represented in universities and there are marked variations in higher education participation between metropolitan, rural and remote regions.

Though Australia is a vast continent, it is highly urbanised and most Australians are city-dwellers concentrated along the south-eastern seaboard. About 30 per cent of Australians, however, are classified as living in rural or remote areas. Large distances from major cities, dispersed populations, and depressed rural microeconomies create difficulties in the provision of education and health services. School retention rates are lower in rural areas and fewer rural and remote dwellers on a per capita basis attend university.

Ethnicity also shapes a definition of the non-traditional student. Australia is a poly-ethnic nation. Underpinning this poly-ethnicity is a unique indigeneity. Its indigenous people are the descendants of people who lived on the continent for 40,000 years prior to European settlement in 1788. Indigenous people live in both urban and rural Australia, many in remote areas. The conditions for many indigenous communities, especially in the distant outback, are far from acceptable. They have poor access to amenities and infrastructure, and educational participation is low. Health problems are acute and life expectancies are appallingly low. The policies of successive Australian governments have failed to make major inroads into these problems.

The nation's poly-ethnicity is also the outcome of various waves of immigration in the post-World War Two period. Immigrant recruitment on labour market and humanitarian grounds brought people from Europe and more recently from Asia, Central America and Africa, producing a cosmopolitan society. About 20 per cent of Australians have a first language other than English; about 40 per cent of Australians have at least one non-English-speaking parent. It is quite common for schools in the metropolitan areas of the major cities to have astonishingly diverse populations, with perhaps several dozen immigrant languages represented in a school population of a few hundred (Beckett 1997).

This brief description of the social, cultural and economic context of Australia flags some of the major influences on higher education at the end of the first decade of the 21st century. The concept of a non-traditional learner invites a number of interpretations in Australia. It is not circumscribed solely by age, since factors such as socioeconomic background, ethnicity, and geographical location historically have been potent factors in the likelihood of tertiary educational participation. With the expansion of the higher education system, much headway has been made in removing barriers and improving the perceived relevance, attainability and outcomes of university study for non-traditional students. However, persistent patterns of educational disadvantage remain. As we argue in this chapter, the Australian higher education system is in transition, marked by the rhetoric of the knowledge economy, not by references to 'lifelong learning' or the 'learning society', although these latter phrases are implicit in ubiquitous lists of generic 'graduate attributes'.

The Australian higher education system

Australia is a federation of six states. The states have responsibility for schooling, which is free in public sector schools, and the federal government substantially funds and has responsibility for higher education. In addition, the federal government plays a policy-coordinating role with the states in the provision of vocational education and training. Unlike the position in the United Kingdom and the United States, there is no involvement of local government in educational provision.

Australia's early nationhood was a cultural transplant of the British Isles and many aspects of Australian life were modelled on English examples, including the first universities and the early 'grammar schools'. The first 'sandstone' universities were established in Sydney and Melbourne in the 1850s, as were some small technical schools – for mining, domestic arts and industrial technology. The university system expanded massively following World War Two, and a further large expansion took place in the 1960s. In 1964, the Martin Report was the basis of federal legislation that consolidated a divide between liberal and vocational curricula, the establishment of the so-called 'binary' system of vocationally-orientated Colleges of Advanced Education and Institutes of Technology alongside the traditionally academically-oriented universities.

More sweeping changes were ahead. In 1987, the federal government dissolved – through a series of mergers and amalgamations – what was by then a binary system of 19 universities and 69 Colleges of Advanced Education, creating a Unified National System, and in 2008 the Bradley Report identified 39 universities (only two of them private) each of which is a teaching and research institution, though they are highly differentiated (by research intensity, technology and regionality).

It is in the massive upheaval involved in the formation of the Unified National System, which was justified on both social justice and human capital grounds, that we see the beginnings of the current push towards a 'knowledge economy'. The architect, John Dawkins, then federal minister for higher education, sought to remove endemic participation imbalances while at the same time significantly expanding the nation's knowledge and skill base (Dawkins 1988). The Dawkins reforms ambitiously attempted to build a higher education system with a capacity to provide education and training commensurate with a new economic environment. The alignment of higher education with national economic objectives heralded a new era of vocationalism in universities.

The expansion from an array of elite universities, towards a mass system of providers where some were more research intensive than others, ushered in dramatic changes in funding arrangements. Fees had been abolished in 1974 but this constrained the revenue available to fund expansion. In response, the government crafted the Higher Education Contribution Scheme (HECS), a unique income contingent loan scheme. Australian students who are typically undergraduates, but may be graduates taking a course in professional formation, are eligible for 'Commonwealth supported places' (CSPs). This means either an up-front or deferred payment under the HECS-HELP, or the FEE-HELP schemes. The HELP in each case is a loan for the debt incurred whilst a student, and repaid through the taxation system after graduation once income has reached a threshold level, which is AUD 44,912 in the 2010–11 income year and AUD 47,196 for the 2011–12 income year. Although the total operating grants to universities increased through the period following

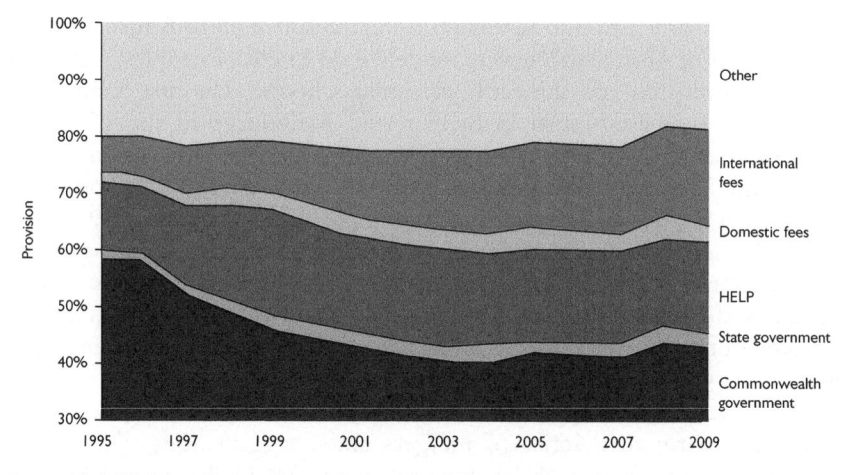

Figure 11.1 Higher education revenue proportion by sector
Source: Universities Australia 2011: 12

the creation of the Unified National System, a steadily shrinking proportion of Gross Domestic Product was allocated to higher education. The graph in Figure 11.1, generated by Universities Australia (2011) based on DEST and DEEWR Finance statistics, depicts how the proportion of higher education revenue from different sources varied from 1995 to 2009. While the proportion of funding from the federal government was shrinking, the universities increased their funding from students, particularly in the form of international student fees.

In the face of declining public revenue, the modern Australian university has become adaptive and entrepreneurial in order to diversify its revenue base. New technological opportunities have hastened the imperative for internationalisation, with online global provision by overseas consortia being viewed as a threat to lucrative markets in the Asian region. Domestically, universities compete vigorously for students and course marketing is extensive. At the same time, paradoxically, collaborative and cooperative arrangements between universities and other educational and commercial organisations have grown. Universities have a new interest in vocational programmes, alliances with industry and workplace-based training. Increasingly, universities conceptualise the student as a client and are reaching out to non-traditional markets and non-traditional students.

TAFE (Training and Further Education) was born in 1974. Commonwealth legislation that year established state-specific systems of technical and further education, provided in close connection with industry, and intending to service apprenticeship and other training programmes, as well as broader social justice, access and bridging courses. Despite a history of flexibility and responsiveness to student and industry needs, TAFE has had a perennial image problem. Sandwiched between the top end of liberal studies secondary schools preparing students for academic and professional futures, and the 'higher' tertiary destinations which would fulfil those futures, mainstream TAFE courses have always led to lower-status outcomes – despite these outcomes having traditionally underpinned earning a living. In diverse ways, TAFE meets the needs of school-leavers and of adults seeking to upgrade their employability. This is achieved through courses in pre-employment skills, such as in literacy and numeracy, and in employment skills in para-professional work and apprenticed trades. In addition, TAFE provides recreation and personal fulfilment courses, not directly vocationally orientated. Until quite recently, modest fees, or none at all, were charged.

Since the early 1990s a national 'training reform agenda' has required TAFE to integrate into national vocational education and training policies, primarily through the exposition and development of competency-based curricula and assessment. Legislation in 1992 established a new peak body to administer the total Australian governmental provision of vocational education and training, both nationally and in each state: the Australian National Training Authority (ANTA) shaped and funded, in partnership with each state, the field of vocational education and training (including TAFE and adult and community education).

Like the Dawkins reforms in higher education, the training reform agenda was also intended to galvanise new global market initiatives through a more sophisticated labour force, characterised by new skills and competence. The convergence of common imperatives in both higher education and vocational education and training – and the establishment of unified national approaches in both areas – has raised new questions about the relative roles, responsibilities and status of the two sectors, and blurred them.

Equity of access, meaningful participation, and finally, successful outcomes for traditional and new claimants upon both TAFE and higher education studies, are all policy areas that confront the new political imperatives. It is increasingly apparent that globalisable enterprises require the widest possible pool of talent from which to shape the new 'knowledge-based' markets – and universities are caught up in this, in two ways. First, they are themselves players in such globalised markets, since academia is itself a knowledge-based industry. Second, their students-as-graduates are increasingly expected to demonstrate their acquisition of self-directed or lifelong learning capacity.

These trends, in particular the new vocationalism and enhanced industry linkages, bring universities into close alignment with the major public providers of vocational education and training, and of workplace skill formation in general, all under the responsibilities of the Federal Department of Education, Employment and Workplace Relations (see http://www.deewr.gov.au). A number of tertiary institutions are dual sector, such as RMIT University, offering both higher education courses (crudely, for the award of degrees) and TAFE courses (for the award of diplomas as well as non-award programmes in Technical and Further Education). By 2010, we also see the emergence of TAFE providers offering Bachelor degrees, such as Box Hill Institute, in eastern metropolitan Melbourne. Traditionally, TAFE courses were lower rungs on the ladder of qualifications, and only a few managed to climb up to the heights – this defined 'higher' education (it was above 'lower'). In recent years, however, the Australian Government has been encouraging 'articulation and connectivity' between the two systems to 'improve pathways and movements between sectors' in both directions (DEEWR 2009b: 43).

Within this context, the Australian Government committed an additional funding of $5.4 billion over a period of four years to:

> support high quality teaching and learning, improve access and outcomes for students from low socio economic backgrounds, build new links between universities and disadvantaged schools, reward institutions for meeting agreed quality and equity outcomes, improve resourcing for research and invest in world class tertiary education infrastructure.
> (DEEWR 2009b: 5)

Resourcing such a broad and ambitious agenda as this is still unfolding, but already we have enough promised, or realised, to provoke some discussions of under-represented groups, within a policy environment where the ideals of lifelong learning and the knowledge economy bump up against each other. We turn to this now.

From lifelong learning to the knowledge economy

Lifelong learning had become an umbrella term in Australia by the end of the 20th century, but now it has been supplanted by the discourse of the knowledge economy. Traditionally, it was used to signify intellectual autonomy and non-reliance on formal educational participation. On the other hand, it evoked a diametrically opposite concept, that of repeated engagement with education and training programmes, whether in educational organisations or in the workplace. This led to a frequent contradiction in the portrayal of the lifelong learner. He or she was someone whose learning is independent of educational organisations. Equally, he or she was also someone who is motivated and able to engage in formal learning throughout his or her lifespan. The breadth of the concept had made it a convenient rhetorical slogan and its over-use had exhausted its explanatory value.

It is, nonetheless, worth recalling its potential. The report *Developing Lifelong Learners through Undergraduate Education* (Candy, Crebert and O'Leary 1994), prepared for the then National Board of Employment, Education and Training, was a landmark in the discussion of lifelong learning in Australian higher education. The authors responded to a brief to identify and describe the characteristics of undergraduate education, which enable and encourage graduates to participate in formal and informal learning throughout their lives (Crean 1994). The report adopted a curriculum focus, being concerned in the main with the teaching and learning conditions that create the skills, dispositions and capacities for learning after graduation, yet the 'profile' they outlined has interest and significance well beyond university experiences.

A profile of the lifelong learner: key attributes

- An inquiring mind
- Helicopter vision
- Information literacy
- A sense of personal agency
- A repertoire of learning skills.

(Candy, Crebert and O'Leary 1994: 43–44)

These proposed attributes of the lifelong learner suggested that learning across the lifespan relates the processes and the products of learning intimately. Traditionally, universities have not paid much explicit attention to the processes of learning, but have insisted on the integrity and standing of the product. Yet learners of any age, and with almost any sort of involvement with the labour market, bring to their daily activities a rich array of attributes, not many of which have been highly regarded by universities. Many of these attributes are the kind of thing that can be learnt (or at least strengthened by learning, especially by formal learning through sustained, systematic encouragement). Equally these attributes in turn enrich learning processes, whether formal, non-formal or informal. That is, these attributes make learning processes more likely to be educational. So process and content interact dialectically, and do so right across the human age span.

Following the 'Candy' profile of the lifelong learner, the Karpin Report (1995) also influenced thinking in higher education. Similar to Candy, but from a different perspective, Karpin advocated a holistic managerial model of workplace learning, especially in the overt support given to the 'higher order social and cognitive competencies', which Karpin calls 'soft skills'. These are the interpersonal and communicative capabilities of strategic thinking, vision, flexibility and adaptability, self-management, team membership, problem-solving, decision-making and risk-taking. Of course these capabilities – or attributes – are not adequately characterisable as merely cognitive in a narrow sense, since they involve the social and affective. Indeed the tag 'soft skills' is a pejorative misnomer. It is quite difficult to educate for these capabilities, and even more so to have them count in corporate structures for productivity and promotion outcomes, yet lifelong learning at its broadest is about acquiring these capabilities and exercising them in a sophisticated fashion.

So in both the education and the corporate world in Australia in the early to mid-1990s there was an emergence of interest in more sophisticated and more holistic adult learning capabilities and strategies. In the years following the Candy and Karpin reports the concept of lifelong learning centred less on curriculum and more on structural issues. For instance, a study funded by the Department of Education, Science and Technology (DEST) identified the following four distinguishing features of the lifelong learning policy agenda:

- The recognition of both informal and formal learning;
- The importance of self-motivated learning;
- An emphasis on self-funded learning; and
- The idea that participation in learning should be universal.

(Watson 2003: viii)

In recent years, attention has shifted – arguably narrowed – to the institutional arrangements that encourage and allow entry and re-entry to formal learning at various stages in life and career. And now we have ubiquitous lists of 'graduate attributes', which are meant to reassure prospective employers – and some graduates – that higher education does 'deliver': various desiderata, broadly similar to Candy's and Karpin's. In the globalising labour market, graduates are expected to be team builders and players, confident communicators and resourceful decision-makers, all of this within a 'project' mentality (Beckett 2010).

Participation

But how inclusive has higher education been, in the march towards these desired, and, it must be said, desirable, outcomes? Three broad observations can be made about these data. First, while participation rates increased considerably during the late 1980s and early 1990s, expansion stalled in the late 1990s, and this has been taken up by the federal government as a policy priority, as explained below (Bradley 2008; DEEWR 2009b). Second, though there have been major gains in access for identified equity target groups, some groups still remain seriously under-represented in participation share (DETYA 1999a, 1999b; DEEWR 2009a). Third, substantial differences are apparent in the social and demographic composition of the student populations across fields of study and across institutions (Baldwin and James 2010; DEEWR 2009a; James *et al.* 1999). Let us now unpack these trends.

The higher education student population rose dramatically in Australia during the last twenty years, most steeply in the late 1980s soon after the Dawkins reforms. In the last two decades of the 20th century, universities coped with a massive expansion in student numbers. In 1987, there were 394,000 university students; by 1997 this had climbed to 659,000 (all data from DETYA 1998 unless indicated otherwise). The number of undergraduate students grew by 58 per cent, from 330,500 to 521,500. The strongest growth, however, was in postgraduate education. The number of coursework students more than doubled, rising from 49,000 to 102,500 during this period. The number of postgraduate research students grew even faster, climbing by a staggering 145 per cent – from 14,500 in 1987 to 35,000 in 1997. This growth is reflected in qualifications achieved, but an ambitious new target has been identified, in the light of Australia's slump in OECD rankings from 7th to 9th:

> Over the last 20 years, there has been an increase in the rate of students obtaining bachelor level qualifications, primarily due to the reforms during the late 1980s and early 1990s as part of the move to mass participation in higher education. The current attainment rate for bachelor degrees for 25 to 34 year olds stands at around 32 per cent. The Government has therefore announced its ambition for growth in higher education attainment, so that by 2025, 40 per cent of all 25 to 34 year olds will hold a qualification at bachelor level or above.
> (DEEWR 2009b: 12)

Despite the growth in the system, there has been mixed success with regard to non-traditional students overall. Since the late 1980s federal policy has identified equity target groups, including women, particularly in non-traditional areas. With the expansion of access to higher education as the 20th century came to a close, the higher education participation rates of all groups improved, but the relative participation share of some had altered little. The rising participation of women in undergraduate education is a success story which has continued into the 21st century. By 1997, women occupied 55 per cent of all higher education places, slightly above their population share of 52 per cent, and this is still true (DEEWR 2009a).

Higher education has also been successful in attracting people from non-English speaking backgrounds, though equally it could be said that some ethnic communities and families have been very successful in the aspiration to gain 'first generation' higher education entry for their children. Overall, students from non-English speaking backgrounds are presently slightly over-represented on population share, but there are marked differences between ethnic groups – especially newly-arrived sub-groups, for example from the Horn of Africa – that may require closer monitoring.

There has been less success with other subgroups. Indigenous people, people from low socio-economic (SES) backgrounds and people from remote and regional parts of Australia are seriously under-represented in Australian higher education (Bradley 2008). Even though 2.2 per cent of the Australian population is indigenous, only 1 per cent of commencing students are indigenous as evident from the following federal data:

- Aboriginal and Torres Strait Islander students comprised less than 1 per cent (10,465) of all enrolments in 2009, and 1 per cent (4,832) of

commencements. The number of Aboriginal and Torres Strait Islander students increased by 9.8 per cent for all students and 11 per cent for commencing students between 2008 and 2009.
- Increases in Indigenous student numbers were recorded across all broad fields of education, with the largest increase being in Mixed Field Programmes (up 45.6 per cent to 753 students) and Engineering and Related Technologies (up 29.9 per cent to 243 students).
- The main fields of education in which Indigenous students were enrolled were Society and Culture (3,406 students, or 32.5 per cent of the total Indigenous students), followed by Education (2,017 students) and Health (1,802 students).

(DEEWR 2009a: 1)

People from lower socioeconomic backgrounds are defined as 25 per cent of the national population. However, '[t]he proportion of low SES students enrolled in higher education in Australia has remained static at about 15 per cent over the last two decades' (DEEWR 2009b: 12) and this has led to the following policy goal:

By 2020, 20 per cent of higher education enrolments at the undergraduate level will be of people from a low SES background ... In 2010, the funding provided will be about 2 per cent of teaching and learning grants, and will increase to about 3 per cent in 2011. By 2012, equity funding will be broadly in line with the recommendation of the Bradley Review to increase it to 4 per cent of teaching and learning grants.

(DEEWR 2009b: 13)

Links with schooling and VET providers will seek to diversify pedagogies, and to provoke market forces:

The Government has therefore allocated $108 million over four years for a new partnerships programme, to link universities with low SES schools and vocational education and training providers. The intention is to create leading practice and competitive pressures to increase the aspirations of low SES students to higher education ... [by providing] financial incentive to expand their enrolment of low SES students, and to fund the intensive support needed to improve their completion and retention rates ...

Better measures of low socio economic status will be developed which are based on the circumstances of individual students and their families and performance funding will be based in part on how effective institutions are in attracting these students.

(DEEWR 2009b: 13–14).

The situation for people from rural and remote areas is only slightly better. In 2007, even though 25.4 per cent of the general population was from rural/regional Australia, their participation rate in higher education was only 18.1 per cent. Similarly, although 2.5 per cent of the general population was from remote areas, the participation rate of people from remote areas in higher education was only 1.1 per cent (Bradley 2008).

Regional TAFE participation does not offset lower university participation rates, despite speculation there might be some substitution in rural areas. Variations in university participation between regions in metropolitan areas, according to socio-economic profile, are as substantial as the variations between rural and metropolitan regions. Partly to address these variations, regional universities have taken up e-learning and more diverse forms of course delivery, but, even so, the 'knowledge economy' version of the lifelong learning acknowledges that life and livelihoods need to be paid for, and this is increasingly difficult in rural and regional Australia. In 2011, the federal government has commissioned a review to explore the viability and potential impact of a model of student income support to increase higher education participation levels of rural and regional students (DEEWR 2011b).

These imbalances show that, despite expansion and progress towards equity goals, there remains significant social stratification in higher education participation. Indeed, aggregate figures mask important variations in the patterns of the participation of non-traditional students' participation by institution and by field of study. Overall, non-traditional students, broadly defined as 'under-represented' by sub-group, as we are discussing here, are more likely to apply and to gain access to the newer, lower status universities, and are significantly under-represented in the more prestigious professional fields (James 2007).

But common to all higher education is the rise in paid (but part-time) employment amongst students who are, at least officially, 'full-timers'. The quality of what is therefore known as 'first year experience' has become a topic of some debate (James, Krause and Jennings 2010). Its significance for this analysis lies in the extent to which engagement with studies is affected, and perhaps even compromised, by students' need to earn a subsistence living. In this circumstance, rural and regional students are a more dramatic example of a general social phenomenon: if students cannot, or choose not to, subsist on parental or governmental welfare, or by working casually in the labour market, then pressures are on higher education to develop learning management systems, and provide amenable campus experiences which dovetail, rather than conflict, with this motivation. James and his colleagues found in their survey of first-year students across nine universities in 2009 that 61 per cent engaged in part-time work averaging 13 hours a week. This is growing: their 2004 survey found that 55 per cent were working part time.

The new significance of student choices

Given the overview of the recent couple of decades, as outlined above, we see that in general the higher education sector has become more responsive to the needs of under-represented students. Four trends are discernible.

First, an emphasis on quality assurance has brought *a new client focus* to universities and enhanced efforts to monitor student feedback and to adapt programmes according to student needs and expectations.

Second, contemporary Australian universities are aware of and sensitive to *socio-cultural diversity*, in its many manifestations, and evident in the extensive access and support programmes offered by all institutions. For example, every university has a 'disabilities' support office and staff for engaging a wide range of challenges to normalised assumptions about the typical learner. Similarly, policies and debates about sexual, religious and dietary allegiances and lifestyles enliven many campuses, in the general direction of increased sensitivity to diversity.

Third, the concept of *flexible, or blended, delivery* is a defining feature of curriculum planning in many institutions, with the objective of providing learning in a manner, time and place that suits the individual learner, especially when the casual labour market claims so much of the typical week. The communication capacity of new technologies has provided much of the impetus for this trend.

Fourth, universities have taken steps to *improve articulation* – especially between higher education and TAFE – and to encourage and recognise two-way student movement, or even a non-linear 'hopping around'. These developments include the introduction of collaborative higher education and TAFE courses, and the growth of degree courses, such as nursing and hospitality, as we mentioned earlier.

It is worth noting that this last point engages three education sectors: higher education, TAFE, and schooling. In Australia, federal government policy in the vocational education and training sector is designed to filter down to senior secondary school, in that adolescents are encouraged to blend part-time studies with part-time work and part-time training – all alongside each other in the typical week! Coupled with this is additional encouragement to undertake subjects with count for 'dual recognition'. This means that English, for example, perhaps re-badged as Communication, is available both for tertiary entry calibration, and simultaneously as a subject on the first rung of a vocational credential pathway, leading towards a certificate, then a diploma and so on, with employability as the target.

The net effect of these two initiatives at the top end of secondary school is to free up the exclusively academic tertiary focus – which generates the traditional full-time school-leaver entry route to universities – in favour of a looser set of non-traditional arrangements.

Taken together, all four of these trends mark the ascendancy of *student-centred thinking* in higher education. The university is increasingly the catalyst for self-guided learning and academics are conceptualising their roles as supporters and mentors in addition to their subject expertise. 'Projects' on campus, and community-based, and overseas, semesterised exchanges are much more common in the curriculum. Pedagogically, small-group work, and IT-friendly 'café'-style work places mark the appearances of many university campuses, not forgetting the way libraries on those campuses now provide varied social, as well as silent, zones for studies. Curricula forego ever-expanding content in favour of transferable and generic investigative skills, and information acquisition and analysis skills. In some cases, students have been handed the opportunity to shape their own programmes, and frequently work-based studies such as co-operative, sandwich, or intern courses are built into degree structures. By and large the philosophy underpinning these trends is congruent with the Candy profile of the lifelong learner, since the educational ideal, in more than a single sector, is the preparation of autonomous learners with the capacity to pursue learning outside the guidance (and constraints) of formal educational programmes, but taking full advantage of the power of sociality, as shown informally in team-work and projects, on- and off-campus, and increasingly through e-learning.

But even beyond transferable and generic attributes, universities are reforming their substantive curricula. With one eye on the Bologna Process, and another eye on the typical United States structure of a broad liberal education, followed by 'grad school' as professional formation, some universities in Australia are reforming their degree structure and content. The most prominent reforms are occurring at the University of Melbourne (where we each work) which, from January 2008, replaced over 100 Bachelor degrees with just six 'liberal' degrees (see http://our.melbourne.edu.au/students.html#ourmodel).

These are followed by a range of professional formation degrees as two-year or more Masters programmes, such as the MTeaching, MAccounting, MNursing and so on. Doctoral programmes, mainly the PhD, follow the two earlier stages. Bologna requires a '3+2+3' year structure, and this Melbourne Model provides one way to encourage a more mature deliberation of one's career choice, rather than assume that, at the point of school leaving (typically aged 18), one's choice of vocational preparation is well-considered.

The Australian Government has intensified its focus on institutional performance and accountability to assist students in making more informed study choices from high quality options. A comprehensive framework for quality assurance of higher education providers is being set up with four distinct elements. First, an independent Tertiary Education Quality and Standards Agency (TEQSA) is being established with regulatory powers to monitor quality and ensure standards of higher education providers. Second, all Australian higher education providers will now be required to register on a national register. Third, a higher education standards framework has been developed to cover five domains: registration standards, qualification standards, information standards, teaching and learning standards, and research standards. Fourth, it is intended to establish a 'My University' website by January 2012 where each institution is expected to build its profile to assist prospective students in making informed choices (DEEWR 2011a).

In acknowledging these institutional developments, we do not wish to overstate the extent or rate of change. The trends outlined are not universal. Not all Australian universities have reshaped their cultures and pedagogical practices. Many admission procedures, teaching practices and assessment methods would be instantly recognisable to students of the 1960s and doubtless earlier. Flexibility in provision, and responsiveness to student choices, have nonetheless made great progress, and the trajectory – towards 'self-directedness' in learning – is promising.

But self-direction can be pushed even further – into the choice-making of *personalised learning*. Learners of any age can expect and appreciate self-direction from their education providers, but can these providers rise to the challenge of more finely granulated learning? By this we do not mean self-centredness, or the 'loneliness of the long-distance runner' – or PhD student, for that matter. Instead, we wonder if the knowledge-production ethos under-recognises the ways in which personalised learning should be engaged by higher education. In short, can universities strive to engage *everyone's* unique interests, needs and aspirations, not merely those who are under-represented?

An answer to that question is beyond this chapter. However, we can still claim that arguably, the major curriculum and pedagogical challenge that confronts the Australian academic community is understanding and responding to student diversity. An implicit assumption of the elite era was that university teachers taught cohorts with roughly comparable levels of preparedness and 'ability'. Greatly expanded access has diversified the lecture room in tangible ways. Indeed, it has de-centred the 'lecture' itself, and made the room a fairly fragile dwelling-place of knowledge. In a more virtual world, social networking has become the focus of youthful energy, and pedagogically, even emails and static learning management systems are looking inert. Facebook and Twitter are universally available, and growing exponentially. These personalised *experiences* are immediate, ephemeral and, since they involve the whole person and some IT, holistic. Shouldn't the conversion of these experiences to *learning* be the *first* focus, now, of higher education?

This epistemological challenge is urgent because it is ubiquitous. Both under-represented and over-represented students, alike, are coming to higher education unfamiliar with both the culture of universities, and the model of reified knowledge upon which these institutions were traditionally established, and such students may be less pedagogically deferential. This is arguably a good thing! A critical stance is at the heart of Western education – and universities have been its main vehicle for the last thousand years. Now the criticality could be turned upon the providers. Obviously, the complexity of academic teaching has risen and a broader set of educative understandings and skills is needed. This creates daily stresses and strains at the academic–student interface. Under-represented students may be most strongly identified with these tensions and may continue to bear the label of the 'weaker' student, whereas in fact it may be the inability of academics to recognise the vitality and fidelity of such experiences as the basis for pedagogy and assessment, which is the main emergent problem. Profound epistemological, pedagogical and academic challenges lie ahead!

An important demographic point should now be made. There are no reliable figures on the so-called 'mature-age' version of the challenges just described. That is to say, reliably when non-school leavers enrol for higher education, it is not possible to measure the extent to which these mature-age people, who are typically part-timers, are *entering, as opposed to re-entering*, the sector. Higher education (structured so that a Bachelors is regarded as a good preparation for a Masters degree), even within a Bologna process, is not the same as higher learning (since life itself brings experiences which generate more sophisticated approaches to learning within formal settings, within a Bachelors-level subject undertaken by a mid-career learner). And neither higher education *nor* higher learning are necessarily congruent with the wisdom thought to come from learning across the lifespan!

These conceptual considerations, and the lack of data to contribute to them, are central to any discussion of extent of participation in university studies by reference to lifelong learning, as well as to any resort to Australia as a 'knowledge economy'. On the 'Candy' profile of lifelong learning, which centres upon the self-direction of generic learning capabilities, what else these students (both the school-leaver part-timers, and the mature-age part-timers) are doing can be factors in the likelihood of their success once they engage in higher education. But a narrow definition of lifelong learning – more institutional, less experiential – assumes that 'lifelong' is the propensity of certain groups to dip in and out of formal studies. This latter definition runs the risk of remaining self-serving: to those students who have much, more will be given. Participation debates then are reducible to outcomes data. A similar fate may face 'knowledge productivity' as a justificatory ethos for participation. Who amongst any under-represented group would justify a better deal on the basis alone of increased productivity? We argue that educative ideals above and beyond the merely reductive should be retrieved, and we look to this debate with enthusiasm. A genuinely 'knowledgeable' society would strive to spread personalised learning (constructed as we have done, through sociality and including networked technology) through its higher education institutions, and in that way, grapple with the conversion of myriad and powerful experiences into *a new epistemology of practical pedagogy – better learning for all.*

What is overlooked so far, at least in Australia, is how life and work experiences mediate access in the first place (at whatever age the access is sought), and upon any second and subsequent points of access. A wider definition of lifelong learning such as Candy's acknowledges this depth and breadth of experience, and the enrolment trends, towards part-time studies right from school leaving onwards, signal that challenges in participation may start with the very conceptualisation of the issue. Hence our scepticism that a 'knowledge economy' version of higher education participation may leave untouched and unexamined the fundamental, and legitimately lifelong, aspirations of learners, beyond the real or assumed productivity ascribed to them, as knowledge workers, by the federal government.

Drawing it all together

What can be said from an Australian perspective in answer to some of the key questions posed in Chapter 1 of this volume?

1. *Does the term 'adult student' retain much that is distinctive?* In Australia adult students as a special category, distinctive from school-leaver students enrolled in higher education, has basically lost its meaning. We have set out the circumstances of students in terms of their reliance upon part-time, or even full-time work, and the substantial flow-on effect this has for what we used to rather glibly call the 'campus experience'. The campus is not often a Monday-to-Friday experience now. Australian students of any age will be constrained as students by their own need to be in productive employment. This will range from 'Mac-jobs' for school-leavers, often of over 13 hours a week, to mid-career professionals, who are squeezing in professional development alongside mortgages, parenting and promotions. The reforms of university curricula, such as the Melbourne Model (with its 'liberal' degrees at the start) or more vocational pathways (in dual-sector institutions like RMIT University), tend to enhance this trend by blurring the distinctions between origin of applicant by age at intake. Students will be of any age, but less exclusively only learners – they will also be tax-payers, spouses, managers and leaders, in their respective communities and in the labour market. They will be lifelong learners whether or not they acknowledge that in themselves.
2. *What are the equity implications of growing differentiation within the higher education sector?* Differentiation within higher education in Australia has only really been officially encouraged in this century. In the 1990s, the Unified National System we described earlier brought about a rush towards the traditional model of the research-intensive university. The absurdity of 'one size fits all' and the severe and worsening research funding ostensibly to be spread around produced segmentation into four parts: the 'Go8' ('Group of Eight' traditional 'sandstones'), a Technology Network group, a group of comprehensive post-1960s

universities, and a group with diverse regional missions. Add to this the more recent growth in vocational institutions outside higher education, such as TAFE which can award degrees, and a vast number of private providers of low-level training (e.g. in IT, hairdressing, catering) for the visa-focused international market, and we have a melting pot of offerings, with complex equity considerations. 'Know how' (Beckett and Hager 2002; Beckett 2009, 2010) is at centre stage, but its depth and delivery will vary dramatically as infrastructural and relational resources will vary widely. Does an industry co-operative or sandwich programme come with access to the Big End of town? Does a catering or hospitality certificate or degree come with access to high quality facilities? Hot-desking hairdressing or IT equipment does not lead to better experiences, whether these be on campus, or in a corporate workplace.

3 *Does e-learning have a dramatic impact?* In Australia, our vast distances, small population, large number of universities, and high urbanisation provide a strong case for sophisticated e-learning. But the take-up is patchy, largely because we do not have a national culture of mobility. At first glance, this would seem to encourage e-learning, as it means students of any age or circumstance could enrol and study at a distance. And this does happen. But it has also meant a vast and persistent expenditure on geo-physical campuses. One of the great markers of rural and regional identity is a 'local' higher education campus. And one of the great expectations Australians persist with – even in the state capital cities – is that there will be such a campus near where they live. Only now are higher education institutions coming to understand some ways that campus and e-learning possibilities can be melded, so that the 'eros' of learning is apparent (Beckett 2000). And, in that respect, it must be said that more sociable forms of synchronous technology now make for more holistic (less lonely, less 'print-on-screen') and lifelong learning.

4 *What does any blurring of public and private provision mean for learners?* Because public funding of Australian universities has been declining for decades, it is perhaps better to call the 38 'public' universities something else. Our university (Melbourne) now describes itself as 'public-spirited'. The blending of Commonwealth Sponsored Places (government money) and fee-bearing places (for international students) has meant some long vocational or professional courses, such as medicine, can incur huge debts for later repayment through taxation (for Australian citizens), or can shorten the queue for entry in favour of the very wealthy.

5 *What is distinctive about 'higher' education in Australia?* Epistemologically, we see a focus around research-informed teaching as continuing to be important. The differentiation debates are often

about the range and vitality of specific research themes, such as primary industry in rural institutions, or marine biology along the Great Barrier Reef. 'Teaching-only' institutions are unlikely to enjoy 'higher' esteem, as this would retrieve the old binary system from its Dawkins-dug grave. But there is great interest across the sector in 'applied' research, which, in a technology university, for example, is a genuine epistemologically creative endeavour: it can generate 'higher' claims on learning, because the impact of applied research can flow through to the teaching – or the learning experience in general – and to the formation of graduates who can make innovation work well in the vocational and professional worlds (Beckett and Mulcahy 2006; Beckett 2011).

In conclusion, we claim that under-represented Australians will participate in a student-choice market in higher education. Indeed, progress has been made in the last decade. In 2000, James and Beckett were 'uncertain' about the prospects of that. Although the ideology of knowledge production masks the uneven and spasmodic representational changes that are occurring, and with renewed federal policy initiatives will continue to occur, underpinning such an ideology is a more substantial focus on student, or rather, learner, choice-making. Each of the five responses above has the quality of learner choice-making at its heart. Personalised learning is being acted out as grassroots decisions are made household by household about initial and continued participation in 'higher' studies. Campuses, debts, timetables, practicals and projects: these are increasingly what sway personal decisions to sign up for studies. For this reason – the overall growth of learner-centredness – we believe the future for better participation in Australian higher education looks promising.

Although James and Beckett concluded a decade ago that the federal government was 'unable to find a way to fund a truly mass higher education system, with broadly-based lifelong learning principles at its heart' (James and Beckett 2000: 192), we believe that even within the knowledge production ideology, lifelong learning, advanced through participation in higher education, is emerging implicitly in learners' personal preferences. The sector is grappling with fundamental epistemological, pedagogical and structural changes, as it seeks to engage and enhance this choice-making capacity.

References

Baldwin, G. and James, R. (2010) 'Access and equity in higher education', in P. Peterson, E. Baker and B. McGaw (eds), *International Encyclopedia of Education*, 4: 334–340, Oxford: Elsevier.

Beckett, D. (1997) 'Case study: Australia, Project: Vocational education and training in foreign countries', in U. Lauterbach, W. Huck and W. Mitter (eds), *Internationales Handbuch der Berufsbildung* [International Handbook of Vocational Education],

German Institute for International Educational Research, Carl Duisberg Gesellschaft, and Bundesminister für Bildung und Wissenschaft: Frankfurt.
Beckett, D. (2000) 'Eros and the virtual: Enframing working knowledge through technology', in C. Symes and J. McIntyre (eds) *Working knowledge: The new vocationalism in higher education* (Research into Higher Education series), Open University Press: UK.
Beckett, D. (2009) 'Holistic competence: Putting judgments first', in K. Illeris (ed.), *International perspectives on competence development*, Routledge: London.
Beckett, D. (2010) 'Adult learning: Philosophical issues', in B. McGaw, P. Peterson and E. Baker (eds) *International encyclopaedia of education*, 3rd edn, Elsevier: Oxford, UK.
Beckett, D. (2011) 'Learning to be at work', in L. Scanlon (ed.) *Becoming a professional.* Lifelong Learning Book Series. Springer: Netherlands.
Beckett, D. and Hager, P. (2002) *Life, work and learning: Practice in postmodernity.* Routledge International Studies in the Philosophy of Education 14, Routledge: London.
Beckett, D. and Mulcahy, D. (2006) 'Constructing professionals' employ-abilities: Conditions for accomplishment', in P. Hager and S. Holland (eds) *Graduate attributes, learning and employability*, Springer: New York.
Bradley, D. (2008) *Review of Australian higher education: Final report*, DEEWR. Online. Available HTTP: <www.deewr.gov.au/he_review_finalreport > (accessed 20 February 2011).
Candy, P., Crebert, G. and O'Leary, J. (1994) *Developing lifelong learners through undergraduate education*, Commissioned Report No. 28, National Board of Employment, Education and Training, Canberra: Australian Government Publishing Service.
Crean, the Hon. Simon (Minister for Employment, Education and Training) (1994) *The enabling characteristics of undergraduate education: Advice of the National Board of Employment, Education and Training and its Higher Education Council*, Canberra: Australian Government Publishing Service.
Dawkins, the Hon. J.S. (1988) *Higher education: A policy statement (The white paper)*, Canberra: Australian Government Publishing Service.
DEEWR, Department of Education, Employment and Workplace Relations (2009a) *Summary of the 2009 higher education student statistics.* Online. Available HTTP <http://www.deewr.gov.au/HigherEducation/Publications/HEStatistics/Publications/Pages/Students.aspx> (accessed 16 May 2011).
DEEWR, Department of Education, Employment and Workplace Relations (2009b) *Transforming Australia's higher education system.* Online. Available HTTP <http://www.deewr.gov.au/HigherEducation/Pages/TransformingAustraliasHESystem.aspx> (accessed 16 May 2011).
DEEWR, Department of Education, Employment and Workplace Relations (2011a) *The four elements of the new quality and regulatory arrangements for Australian Higher Education.* Online. Available HTTP <http://www.deewr.gov.au> (accessed 24 April 2011).
DEEWR, Department of Education, Employment and Workplace Relations (2011b) *Review of student income support reforms.* Online. Available HTTP <http://www.deewr.gov.au/HigherEducation/Programmes/YouthAllowance/Pages/RSISRSubmissionProcess.aspx> (accessed 24 April 2011).

DETYA (1998) *The characteristics and performance of higher education institutions*, Occasional Paper Series, Higher Education Division. Canberra: Australian Government Publishing Service. Online. Available HTTP <http://www.detya.gov.au/highered/otherpub/characteristics.pdf> (accessed 28 January 2000).

DETYA (1999a) *Students (preliminary) 1999: Selected higher education statistics*, Canberra: Australian Government Publishing Service.

DETYA (1999b) *Equity in higher education*, Occasional Paper Series, Higher Education Division, Canberra: Australian Government Publishing Service. Online. Available HTTP <http://www.detya.gov.au/highered/occpaper/99A/equityhe_all.pdf> (accessed 28 January 2000).

James, R. (2007) *Social equity in a mass, globalised higher education environment: The unresolved issue of equitable access to university in Australia*. Paper prepared for the University of Melbourne Faculty of Education Dean's Lecture series, 18 September. Online. Available HTTP <http://74.125.155.132/scholar?q=cache:OobsmJN0wR0J:scholar.google.com/+James+Social+equity+in+a+mass,+globalised+higher+education+environment&hl=en&as_sdt=0,5&as_ylo=2001&as_vis=1> (accessed 24 April 2011).

James, R. and Beckett, D. (2000) Australia: Higher education and lifelong learning: An Australian perspective, in H. Schuetze and M. Slowey (eds) *Higher education and lifelong learners: International perspectives on change*, pp. 173–194, RoutledgeFalmer: London.

James, R., Krause, K. and Jennings, C. (2010) *The first year experience in Australian universities: Findings from 1994 to 2009*, The University of Melbourne. Online. Available HTTP <www.cshe.unimelb.edu.au/research/FYE_Report_1994_to_2009.pdf> (accessed 24 April 2011).

James, R., Wyn, J., Baldwin, G., Hepworth, G., McInnis, C. and Stephanou, A. (1999) *Rural and isolated students and their higher education choices: A re-examination of student location, socioeconomic background, and educational advantage and disadvantage*, Canberra: Australian Government Publishing Service. Online. Available HTTP <http://www.detya.gov.au/nbeet/publications/hec/studentchoices.pdf> (accessed 28 January 2000).

Karpin Report (1995) Enterprising nation: Report of the industry task force on leadership and management skills (D. Karpin, Chair), Canberra: Australian Government Publishing Service.

Universities Australia (2011) *Universities Australia submission to the higher education base funding review*, The Universities Australia website. Online. Available HTTP <www.universitiesaustralia.edu.au> (accessed 24 April 2011).

Watson, L. (2003). *Lifelong learning in Australia*, DEST. Online. Available HTTP <http://www.dest.gov.au/sectors/higher_education/publications_resources/profiles/lifelong_learning_australia.htm> (accessed 24 April 2011).

Chapter 12

Japan
Lifelong learning and higher education in Japan

Shinichi Yamamoto

Introduction

Lifelong learning (*Shogai-Gakushu*) has for long been prominent in debates about the future of education systems in Japan. The discussion about lifelong learning was especially active when the Ad-hoc National Council on Educational Reform (*Rinkyoshin* in Japanese) issued four reports between 1985 and 1987. 'We should transform our education system into a system of lifelong learning' was the most important conclusion of the *Rinkyoshin* exercise. This was because, in addition to preparing for the education system of the 21st century, a key objective of the reform process was to solve a serious educational problem referred to at the time as the 'examination hell'. This referred to a concern about the fierce competition for the admission into universities. Excess competition was regarded as causing serious damage to primary and secondary education, endangering foundation learning and the well-balanced development of the children (Ad-hoc Council on Education 1987).

At the same time, however, people believed that graduation from prestigious universities guaranteed them, by finding employment at large companies, a promising future with many economic and social benefits. By contrast, a university diploma did not give adult learners much of a benefit because they were too old to find permanent employment with tenure at those companies. The *Rinkyoshin* was convinced that, by eliminating this unwholesome relationship, university education would become more valuable for adult learners and the 'examination hell' problem would be mitigated. The number of adult learners in higher education is therefore one of the important indicators of the success of lifelong learning in Japanese higher education.

In this chapter, I first briefly depict the historical development of higher education in Japan as this is important as the backdrop for the discussion of the role universities have played, and are still playing, for older students. I then discuss the meaning of lifelong learning in Japan which is markedly different than in most other industrialized countries, followed by a summary of higher education reforms in the 1990s and the first decade of the 21st century. Finally, I outline some future perspectives for lifelong learning at Japanese universities.

Higher education and its development in Japan

Development of higher education beginning in Meiji

In Japan, the modern higher education system started in 1877 when Tokyo University was established, to be reorganized a little later (1886) and re-designated as an Imperial University. The Imperial University had special missions which were mandated by the state, especially to introduce the most advanced knowledge and technology from advanced countries in Europe and North America, which was regarded as essential for the purpose of modernization, and to train a small number of young men from the ruling elites, who were expected to serve and lead the country as politicians, bureaucrats, scientists and engineers. No other imperial university was established until 1897 when the Imperial University Kyoto was founded. Later, between 1907 and 1939, another five imperial universities were set up in Sapporo (Hokkaido), Sendai (Tohoku), Nagoya, Osaka and Fukuoka (Kyushu). These imperial universities played a leading role not only in the modernization of Japan but also as an effective devise for recruiting good talented students from established families as well as poorer ones.

In addition to these imperial universities, the government established other types of higher education institutions as national schools as well as accredited local public and private institutions. They were technical and commercial colleges for training personnel for industry and business, higher normal schools for training middle school teachers, preparatory high schools connected to universities, medical colleges for training physicians and dentists, and so on. Private and local public 'universities' were not allowed and national universities other than 'imperial universities' were not established by the government until the enactment of the University Order in 1918. Since then, higher education in Japan began to expand. The emerging system was a hierarchy, with imperial universities at the top, other universities in the middle, and the rest in the lower middle and at the bottom. The division of roles within the hierarchy was clear.

In 1940, there were 47 national universities (including the imperial universities), 193 technical and commercial colleges, 32 preparatory high schools, and 4 higher Normal schools for teacher training. In 1943, Normal schools for elementary school teachers were upgraded as higher education institutions by law. There were 56 Normal schools in 1944, which became part of new national universities after World War II.

Massification of higher education after World War II

After World War II, the Japanese education system was completely transformed by adapting structures and terminology to the American system. The school education system was simplified and primary education was now called elementary school, junior and senior high school stood for secondary education, and university for higher education. Thus 'university' became the only type of higher education institution. To become universities, institutions had to be approved by the Minister of Education. Although this approval was not easy to obtain for pre-war non-university higher education institutions, the number of universities sharply increased from 47 in 1940 to 201 in 1950. Also, the government temporally approved some pre-war higher education institutions as 'junior colleges', which were two-year higher education institutions. There were 149 junior colleges in 1950 and the number increased to 264 in 1955. The junior college system was perpetuated in 1962 along with the creation of colleges of technology as the third category of higher education institutions.

The post-war 'American-style single-track' secondary education system, and the enormous growth in the Japanese economy in the 1960s and 70s, triggered rapid increases in post-secondary education enrolment. In 2009, 98 per cent of students advanced to senior high schools. Now, all graduates of senior high schools became eligible to enter higher education institutions, provided they passed the appropriate entrance exam. This expansion of graduates from upper secondary school and the strict hierarchy of higher education are at the origin of the so-called 'examination hell' phenomenon mentioned above.

Beginning in the mid-1960s, higher education enrolment increased massively with the effect of the transformation of higher education into a mass system. 'Massification' of higher education, however, entailed not only quantitative expansion of the system but also systemic change. The 1963 Report of the National Council on Education, an advisory body to the Education Minister, warned that problems arising from massification could be solved only by greater diversification of the higher education system. Between 1960 and 1975 participation ratios among 18-year-olds jumped from 10 per cent to 39 per cent, mainly by expansion of the private sector. Private universities and colleges (including two-year junior colleges) increased in number from 525 in 1960 to 933 in 1975, while the number of national universities grew only from 72 to 81 during the same period. Participation ratios were stabilized in 1975–85 by the introduction of a strong government initiative, called the Higher Education Plan, which aimed at enriching the quality of university education by restricting the further expansion of universities and colleges. However, participation grew again after the late 1980s.

Today, more than half (57 per cent) of the 18-year-old population attends universities and colleges, and if we include non-university institutions in the system, 78 per cent participate in higher education. To accommodate such a huge number of students (about 3 million) takes some 1,200 universities and colleges, including 395 two-year junior colleges (Table 12.1). The private sector represents about three-quarters of higher education institutions – 595 universities and 378 junior (two-year) colleges – while more than half (54 per cent) of graduate studies takes place at the 86 national universities, where the bulk of research is conducted.

Table 12.1 Number and type of higher education institutions and students in Japan, 2010

	Total	Universities	Junior colleges	Technical colleges
Institutions				
Total	1,231	778	395	58
National	137	86	0	51
Local public	125	95	26	4
Private	969	597	369	3
Enrolment				
Total	3,102,229	2,887,414	155,273	59,542
National	678,653	625,048	0	53,605
Local public	155,681	142,523	9,128	4,030
Private	2,267,895	2,119,843	146,145	1,907

Source: Calculated by the author from the School Basic Survey data by the Ministry of Education (2010).

Lifelong learning and higher education

Higher education for the youth

Before the *Rinkyoshin* reports, lifelong learning in Japan had been understood in a different way than in other advanced industrialized countries where it is an important tool of up-grading for employability and careers. By contrast, Japanese people regarded lifelong learning as a joyful pursuit for seniors in order to acquaint themselves with Japanese classical literature, such as 'Genji Tales' and 'Haiku Poems' or develop skills for their hobby, such as painting and crafts. Thus most of the lifelong learning programmes were supplied by local governments, including education commissions, and private companies, called 'culture centres'. The university sector did not play any major role in this regard except for a few university extension programmes that were related to this kind of activity. Apart from these programmes, very few adults studied in formal programmes of higher education in the 1970s and 80s.

This separation of lifelong learning from higher education, especially university programmes, is evident even today. The Ministry of Education, Sports, Culture, Science and Technology (hereafter 'MEXT') announced in 2010 that university freshmen over 25 years old were only 2 per cent of total entrants in 2008, an extremely low ratio compared with other OECD countries, where around 20 per cent was the average (Figure 12.1). Thus, Japanese higher education caters only for the young and they know that higher education is valuable for them only when they are young. But why do only the young study at universities and why do so few adult students enrol?

Several distinctive features of the Japanese higher education and employment system explain the extremely low participation of older students. First, the Japanese higher education has been set up, from its beginning, to train young people required for the rapid modernization and industrialization of the country, and thus had no mandate or no interest in educating adults.

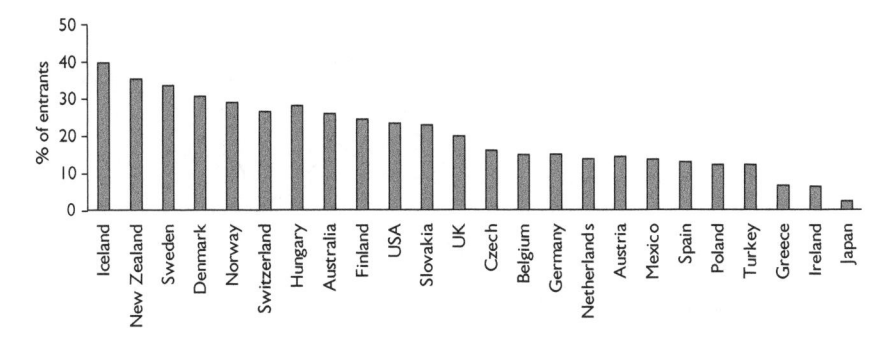

Figure 12.1 University entrants aged 25 years and older
Source: Calculated by the author from the report by the Ministry of Education (2012).

Second, industry has regarded higher education, or rather the extremely difficult entrance examinations, as an effective screening device for their own recruitment, and thus they have preferred to recruit young students who show good exam results, even if they had no job experience or particular job-related skills. In the eyes of industry they were promising students because they had passed the hurdle of the entrance exams, and their proven intelligence and resilience suggested that they would be hard working and trainable so that industry would give them the needed practical training later. This attitude is related to so-called 'Japanese employment practice' according to which Japanese leading companies recruit new personnel into full-time and tenured jobs only when they have graduated from universities (*Shinsotsu* in Japanese) and are under 25 years old or so. These young graduates thus selected are supposed to work for the company all their working life to be promoted later to be managers in these companies.

Thus a student's chance of finding employment in a leading company after four years study at university totally depended on their success at the university entrance exams. An OECD study team once criticized that 'the university which one enters, especially if it is either Tokyo or Kyoto, has a decisive importance for one's future career, and entrance is decided by a single examination taken at or about the age of 18' (OECD 1971: 50). This criticism is still valid today because many university students start their job search in their junior years and thus there are a lot of formally dressed ('Recruit Suits' in Japanese) students to be seen on weekdays walking around the main streets of central Tokyo, where the main offices of leading companies are located. They sacrifice time for their studies to find a tenured job far in advance of their graduation. This tendency has intensified recently because of the rising youth unemployment rate (Figure 12.2) due to the recession and also due to the changing policy of companies that have reduced the numbers of tenured employment (Arimoto 2007).

Third, the lifelong learning system thus tended to focus on non-formal education, learning outside of schools, especially of universities and colleges,

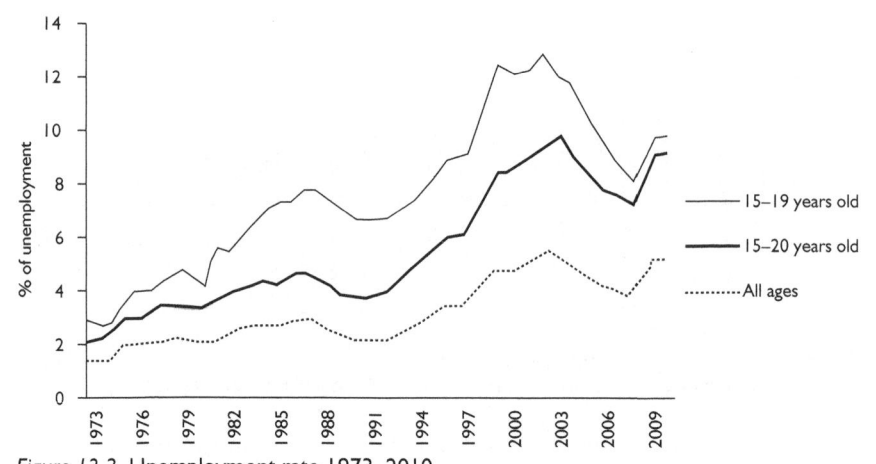

Figure 12.2 Unemployment rate 1973–2010
Source: Calculated by the author from the data by the Ministry of General Affairs, 2010.

and had little, if any, role with regard to training skills and acquiring knowledge necessary for various kinds of job. The OECD concept of 'recurrent education' (OECD 1973) was therefore quite new for Japanese scholars and policy makers and did not fit with the Japanese concept of lifelong learning. Thus, understanding the lifelong learning system as it was seen in Japan contributes to understanding the Japanese higher education system.

Educational policy making within the Ministry of Education

Regarding the policy of higher education and lifelong education, until 1988 MEXT had two departments: the Higher Education Bureau and the Social Education Bureau. The former dealt with education at universities and colleges, while the latter dealt with non-formal education mainly provided by educational commissions of local governments. It was called 'social education' and had little relationship with school education in terms of degrees and credits. Due to the growing importance of lifelong learning and the recommendations of *Rinkyoshin*, however, MEXT reorganized its departments in 1988. The Bureau of Social Education was reformed to become the Bureau of Lifelong learning and was situated as the first and thus top bureau of the MEXT, where previously the Bureau of Primary and Secondary Education had been located. This new location indicated that the government and MEXT now regarded lifelong learning as having the highest priority in educational policies. They also understood that lifelong learning should be developed in close relationship with formal education, especially higher education. Reflecting this new priority, a Lifelong Education Promotion Law was enacted in 1990, although the law mainly aimed at building a system of lifelong learning at the level of local government.[1]

Higher education for adult learners

As mentioned above, the relation of lifelong learning with higher education had not been strong until the *Rinkyoshin* reports on educational reform, published in 1985–87. That was partly because traditionally, as mentioned, higher education institutions were for the young who would study and upon graduation seek employment and future career chances with large companies or the public service, while lifelong learning was seen as activities for adults that would be pursued outside of higher education. Although universities and colleges accept adult students, about 95 per cent of freshmen enter universities and colleges at the age of 18 or 19 and nearly 90 per cent of them finish their undergraduate programmes four years later.

Graduate programmes attract a greater proportion of adult students than undergraduate programmes. According to a 2008 survey by MEXT, about 20 per cent (12 per cent in master's programmes and 34 per cent in doctoral programmes) of the entrants were adult students and the number has been increasing recently. Why do more adult students study at graduate rather than undergraduate programmes? One of the reasons is that many of them already have a bachelor's degree, another that graduate programmes offer more professional education and training and therefore are more attractive for those who have already found work but wish to upgrade their skills and career chances. On the other hand, many young students prefer to finish their study after getting bachelor's degrees because, if they go on to graduate schools, they are becoming too old, as mentioned already, to find good jobs under the practice of Japanese-style employment, believing that it is very difficult to find full-time and tenured jobs at big companies if they are 25 years old or older. This is the principal reason why graduate study is not so popular among young students. A few exceptions are those who wish to become academics and engineers. The former positions require doctoral degrees and, as of recently, engineers are required to hold master's degrees.

Policies that encourage adult students to study at universities

Since the 1990s the MEXT has implemented several policies which aim at increasing the number of adult students at universities and colleges. These include:

1 easier admission to graduate schools (as of 1989);
2 evening courses for those who have daytime jobs (1989 for master's programmes and 1993 for doctoral programmes);
3 utilizing various media for instruction (1998);
4 flexibility regarding time to degree (1999).

There are also other policies to encourage adult students to study:

5 financial support for adult students to study some recognized vocational subjects;
6 a tax reduction for small and medium companies who send employees for study at universities;
7 special incentives and support for government officers who study at universities;
8 an increasing number of correspondence courses;
9 a new study scheme that allows students to study flexibly, i.e. by taking course modules in some selected subjects and accumulating their course credits in order to eventually graduate with a degree.

These policies aim at reducing barriers for adult students to study at graduate programmes as well as undergraduate ones, which were hitherto organized and scheduled to fit young full-time students.

In 2004, the government introduced professional schools as a part of the graduate schools system. Professional schools (*Senmonshoku Daigakuin*) aim at training students to become lawyers, managers and accountants. These professional programmes are different in the way in which they train future professionals compared with traditional graduate programmes, which aim at research training and teaching advanced knowledge of academic disciplines. Although professional schools are not for adult students alone, many adult students are studying at these professional schools to upgrade their future career.

A typical case in terms of adult learning is the newly created Law Schools (for more details, see Saegusa 2007). Before the introduction of the law school system, the National Bar Examination in Japan, the passing of which is required to become a lawyer, judge or public prosecutor, had been extremely difficult. The pass rate was 2–3 per cent and the exam was called the Modern 'Keju', the term for the exam required to become a bureaucrat in imperial China. Many talented young people failed the Bar Exam. Since many who tried and failed several times were 30 years old or older and had nothing to show for their studies in terms of a recognized qualification, this system was seen to be a waste of human resources. At the same time, the profession failed to attract promising people due to the tough exam. The idea of creating Law Schools was to remedy this situation as the law school exam would be easier and the pass rate would be 70–80 per cent.

Together with the new law school system, introduced in 2004, other professional schools were set up such as business, accounting, and technology management. For the people who had already started their work at companies, study at the law and other professional schools seemed very attractive because they could study towards a recognized professional qualification, the promise and expectation of more income and social status.

In the case of the law schools, this new professional graduate school model attracted unexpected numbers of adult applicants and led to an unexpected number of new law schools. More than 70 schools, including schools that had no experience of running law faculties, were established and total enrolment reached more than 7,000.

However, the number of graduates who passed the exam remained at the level of 2,000–3,000. This bottleneck was due to two factors: the capacity of internship training which was administered by the Ministry of Justice, and the opposition of the Bar Association, which was reluctant to increase the number of potential competitors. The pass rate of the exam after finishing the law school programme was very disappointing for the adult students because many of them had sacrificed their jobs in order to study at law school and also had paid expensive tuition fees. Some students who failed the exam complained that they would lose their future career chances because of this situation.

Thus in Japan, adult programmes in universities will be successful only to the extent that the diploma is useful for adult learners in their future career, but as the example of the new law schools demonstrates, it may still be very difficult to attract students to these programmes if the labour market is not ready to accommodate newly qualified entrants.

Recent higher education reform

Higher education before the 1990s

The 1990s and 2000s were decades of substantial higher education reform in Japan. The thrust of most of these reforms was that universities must play a more important role with respect to the knowledge-based society and the globalization of the economy. Until the 1990s it was rare for individual institutions to be urged to introduce changes. While there were many government initiatives for higher education reform such as reforms of the graduate education system, the establishment of 'new universities' like Tsukuba, and the control of private higher education through the newly issued 'Higher Education Plan', were aimed at the systemic level and did not directly influence change in individual institutions.

Although the higher education system was seen as having many problems, for most individual universities and colleges the reforms seemed to be very far from their daily management and for them the system worked quite well as long as they could attract sufficient numbers of applicants. Also they felt it would be difficult to introduce changes at the institutional level, many of which would have to be implemented against strong opposition by faculty who had enjoyed academic freedom and university autonomy. However, from the beginning of the 1990s higher education reform extended to individual institutions as well as systemic reform. It is fair to say that, within ten years, many reforms were successfully implemented.

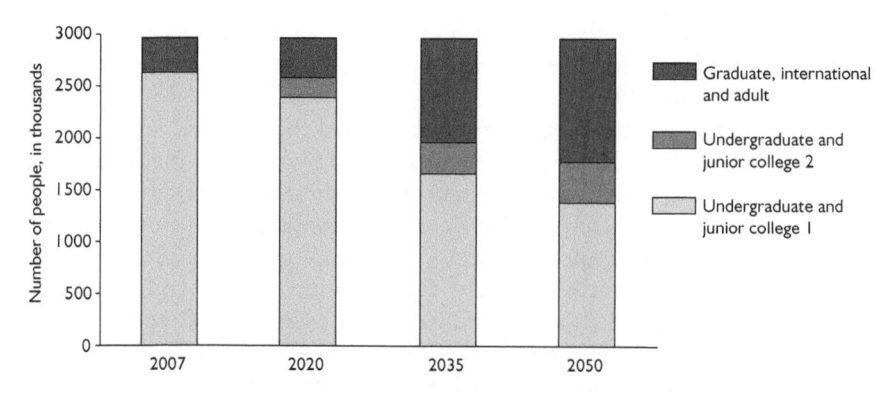

Figure 12.3 University enrolment: implications of demographic trends and projections for the future (to 2050)
Note: 'Undergraduate and Junior College 1' is the estimated figure if the participation ratio into universities and colleges keeps stable at 53% in 2007. 'Undergraduate and Junior College 2' is the figure if the participation ratio increases to 60% in 2020, 65% in 2035 and 70% in 2050. 'Graduate, international, and Adult' is the rest of enrolment if we keep the same total enrolment as in 2007.
Source: Yamamoto, 2009.

The reform of universities and the background

The 1990s saw sweeping socio-economic changes that followed the end of the Cold War, which changed the political environment domestically as well as internationally, and the collapse of the 'bubble economy' in Japan which resulted in far-reaching changes of the economic, industrial and employment system. The higher education sector was no exception. The faculty-led 'old university autonomy' was replaced by a manager-led 'new university autonomy' that was to be accompanied by greater accountability and responsibility.

In addition, the population of 18-year-olds started to decline dramatically in the 1990s. This cohort, the traditional age group of university students, shrank by 40 per cent, from 2,050 thousand in 1992 to 1,200 thousand in 2010, and it is estimated that this population will continue to decline to around 700 thousand in the mid-21st century. The impact of this on higher education is huge because universities and colleges in Japan had depended entirely on this population of 18-year-olds, and not so much, as explained before, on older students. More than half of the private institutions now cannot recruit enough students and thus face a difficult situation due to the lack of revenue from student tuition fees. Figure 12.3 shows that universities and colleges in Japan must attract far more non-traditional students besides the traditional 18–19-year-old cohort if they wish to maintain the current enrolment level of 3 million. Non-traditional students in Japan are graduate and adult students whose numbers are at present quite small. Not least, therefore, participation of adult students into university programmes is strongly encouraged. To accomplish this, higher education must become more attractive for adult students. However this depends not only on internal reforms to better accommodate demand from these groups of students but also on various factors external to higher education, especially the recruiting and employment practice of big companies.

Direction of higher education reform

Current higher education reforms cover a variety of changes, from administrative and managerial matters to teaching and research methods and contents. However, from the middle of the first decade of the 21st century, there is concern by MEXT and also by universities themselves about the quality of education. Concretely this relates to university evaluation (which was introduced in the 1990s) and accreditation. A new accreditation system was introduced in 2004, the same year as the introduction of the incorporation of national universities. Under the new accreditation system, every institution, whether national, local public or private, must be evaluated by the authorized accrediting agency and the results of this evaluation must be laid open to the public.

Although this new accreditation system, along with other policy measures to assure the quality of university education, has no direct connection to the encouragement of lifelong learning, these policies will make universities attract more adult students. First, universities need more adult students to maintain their level of enrolment. Second, if quality of education is assured by an authorized agency, it will be a great help for adult students at universities and colleges. With the advancement of a knowledge-based society and globalization, the role of higher education has been gradually but steadily changing from a screening device for the young to an educational opportunity for a wider variety of students including adults.

Conclusion and future perspectives for lifelong learning

Figure 12.4 shows the current population of learners, enrolled in both the formal education sector and the non-formal education sectors. There are many people who study and learn at various kinds of institution and programmes. As can be seen from Figure 12.4, higher education does not yet play a major role in serving lifelong learners. Traditional young students dominate enrolment in the formal higher education sector, indicated by the long black bar. Outside formal education, there are variety of opportunities to study, indicated by white bars, and it is here where the majority of learners are supposed to be adults.

However, there are many benefits of studying at higher education institutions, not just in terms of the quality of the programme, teaching staff and educational facilities, but also the opportunity of obtaining a degree which

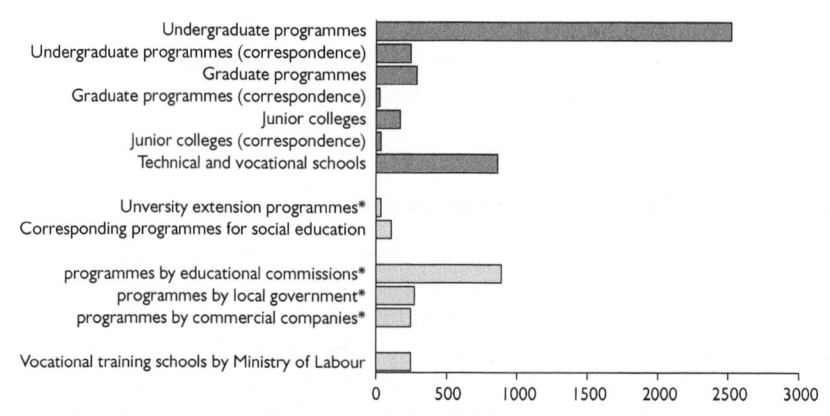

Figure 12.4 Numbers of learners in different types of programmes (thousands) 2007†

* Numbers of learners are modified by length of study compared with school education.
† MEXT uses several different sources of data, thus some data are older than 2007.
Source: MEXT data modified by the author (NCE 2008).

enhances future employment and career prospects. With the development towards a knowledge-based society and facing increasing globalization, the need for lifelong learning will be growing. Higher education, especially universities and colleges, must respond to this new situation. This is very important for them not only to respond to the needs of lifelong learners but also for their own reform that will enable them to play a leading role in this new prospective knowledge-based society. With the higher education reforms of the last two decades in Japan, such efforts have just started.

Notes

1 Some conceptions of lifelong learning include vocational training outside school education, which was dealt with by the Ministry of Labour and Social Welfare in 2001. However, due to the focus on lifelong learning in *higher education*, vocational training is not dealt with in this chapter (but see Yamamoto, Fujitsuka and Honda-Okitsu 2000).

References

Ad-hoc Council on Education (*Rinkyoshin*) (1987) *Policy Recommendations on Future Education System in Japan*, Tokyo: Government of Japan.
Arimoto, A. (2007) 'Recent reforms of higher education in Japan: A sociological study of the relationship between social system and higher education system', *University Studies (University of Tsukuba)*, 35: 1–16.
Ministry of Education (2010) The School Basic Survey (Gakko Kihon Chosa), 2010 Report. [Online] Available at: http://www.e-stat.go.jp/SG1/estat/List.do?bid=000001028876&cycode=0.

Ministry of Education (2012) To increase the number of adult students into universities (Daigaku ni okeru Shakaijin no ukeire no sokushin). [Online] Available at http://www.mext.go.jp/b_menu/shingi/chukyo/chukyo4/houkoku/1293381.htm.

Ministry of General Affairs (2010) Basic Survey of Labor Power (Rodoryoku Kihon Chosa). [Online] Available at http://www.stat.go.jp/data/roudou/sokuhou/tsuki/index.htm.

NCE, National Council on Education (1963) *Policy Recommendations on Improvement of University Education*, Tokyo: MEXT.

NCE, National Council on Education (2008) *Policy Recommendations on Lifelong Learning in Japan*, Tokyo: MEXT.

OECD (1971) *Reviews of National Policies for Education, Japan*, Paris: Organization for Economic Cooperation and Development.

OECD (1973) *Recurrent Education: A Strategy for Lifelong Learning*, Paris: Organization for Economic Cooperation and Development.

Saegusa, M. (2007) 'Japanese universities' high policy implementability: The introduction of the Japanese law school system', *University Studies (University of Tsukuba)*, 35: 67–79.

Yamamoto, S. (2007) 'Doctoral education in Japan', in S. Powell and H. Green (eds) *The Doctorate Worldwide*, SRHE and Open University Press, Ch.15.

Yamamoto, S. (2009) 'Future enrolment of higher education in Japan (Koto Kyoiku no Shorai Kibo)', *Higher Education Report (Monbu-Kagaku kyoiku-Tsushin)*, 221: 38–49.

Yamamoto, S., Fujitsuka, T. and Honda-Okitsu, Y. (2000) 'Japan: From traditional higher education to lifelong learning: Changes in higher education in Japan', in H., G. Schuetze and M. Slowey (eds) *Higher Education and Lifelong Learners*, pp. 195–216, London: Routledge.

Chapter 13

New Zealand
Lifelong learning and higher education in Aotearoa New Zealand

Brian Findsen

Introduction

The notions of 'lifelong learning' and 'higher education', both concepts with potentially multiple meanings, are enmeshed in the historical and cultural context of Aotearoa New Zealand. In this chapter, the ideological and historical components of New Zealand (tertiary) education are examined prior to discussion on the character of lifelong learning and adult learning/ education. The focus of this chapter is placed on post-compulsory education in a lifelong learning framework, particularly what constitutes 'tertiary education'. Respectively, this chapter discusses adult students in tertiary education, the structure of and differentiation within tertiary education, the roles of principal providers (universities, polytechnics, whare wānanga), and issues of access and equity within the system and ICT developments. As appropriate, changes since the rendition from Boshier and Benseman (2000) are given precedence.

New Zealand education in historical context

New Zealand was colonised by the British (at least initially) and was established as a Commonwealth country as part of European imperialism, and consequently in contemporary times has many of the hallmarks of this cultural conquest – a cultural heritage and an education system which echoes British structures, processes and systems (Dakin 1996). Yet this country is very much a modern-day Pacific nation where the indigenous Māori have special rights as *tangata whenua* (people of the land). In accord with the Treaty of Waitangi signed in 1840 between the British Crown and local Māori *iwi* (tribes), the Crown agreed to provide citizenship to iwi in exchange for protection of *taonga* (treasures such as language), partnership in mutual endeavours (such as education) and full participation in society (consistent with equality of educational opportunity). These principles of protection, partnership and participation are significant in contemporary education policy.

From earlier colonial beginnings, Aotearoa New Zealand has evolved in a more sophisticated, predominantly urban, well-educated, bi-cultural and multi-cultural society. It is bi-cultural by dint of the special relationship emergent from the Treaty (and acknowledged by many in the increasingly common use of the title of 'Aotearoa New Zealand'); it is multi-cultural by the reality of the diverse character of its inhabitants after significant migration from the Pacific in the 1960s and more recent immigration from South-East Asia. Today the multi-ethnic composition of the population of around 4.2 million is as follows: European, 67.6 per cent; Māori, 14.6 per cent; Pasifika Peoples, 6.9 per cent; Asian, 9.2 per cent; other, 1.7 per cent (Ministry of Education 2008). The creative tension between bi-culturalism and multi-culturalism is played out in policy development in economic, social and cultural spheres, including education.

Lifelong learning and adult education

As in most Western countries, the education of adults has played second fiddle to compulsory education. Adult education has been subject to political whims of Government in terms of credibility and funding and has had its social purpose mission blunted by neoliberal imperatives. The issues faced by a developing field in a small country were those familiar to other nations too: the expansion of both liberal and technical/vocational education without privileging one over the other; the degree of centralisation required in a relatively small colony when regions wanted maximal autonomy; the ways to serve the least privileged members of society under the ideology of equal educational opportunity; how to grow a professional cadre of adult educators without distancing them from the people that are intended to serve. Boshier and Benseman (2000) argue that a 'cult of efficiency', in line with rampant market forces, has typified the New Zealand education landscape.

Tobias (1996: 42) identifies what he considers as the five main sub-fields of Adult and Community Education (ACE):

- Adult basic education;
- Second-chance education opening the way to further formal education, training and/or employment;
- Personal development education which enables an individual to live in a family, group or community;
- Cultural education which enables a person to participate in life in their community;
- Education to facilitate group and community development.

In this description of the field, at least the non-vocational side of it, both individual and collectivist perspectives are incorporated. Especially in a New Zealand where the population base is less dominated by white Europeans, the increasing proportions of Māori and Pasifika nations' peoples creates urgency in all forms of education (early childhood; compulsory schooling; tertiary) to operate in innovative and authentic ways to meet the learning needs of these collectivist communities.

One of the most significant reports focusing on the role of adult and community education was compiled by a Government working party in 2001. In its definition of ACE, the five perspectives enunciated by Tobias (1996) were retained and the following were added:

- English language and social support programmes for speakers of other languages;
- Revitalisation of Māori language and culture;
- Education for social and environmental justice.

These additions reflect the need to better meet the needs of new migrants coming from a more diverse geography; the demands to keep *te reo Māori* (Māori language) to the forefront of societal consciousness, given that Māori is an official language of the country and not spoken elsewhere; the desire to retain both the radical tinge of adult education and to support the moves towards environmental renewal in line with this country's 'clean and green' image so important for tourism. The role of ACE also incorporates strong links to New Zealand's international connections (e.g. our role in the Asian South Pacific Bureau of Adult Education, ASPBAE).

The working party was adamant that the special character of ACE be retained (AECLWP 2001). The recommendations of *Koia! Koia! Towards a Learning Society*, simplified here, were related to addressing five central issues:

1 Sector recognition for a fragmented field: that ACE be given a place in the Ministry of Education;
2 Meeting community education needs through the establishment of ACE learning centres, local ACE networks and greater monitoring and evaluation;
3 Māori development through greater Māori control of knowledge, information and funding;
4 Funding of $13.9m be protected (ring-fenced), better long-term strategies and emphasis be given to 'priority learner groups';
5 Sector capability enhancement through planned professional development and research.

While this report was published a decade ago, it was seminal in providing a stronger structure for ACE in a lifelong learning framework. This structure, until recently (especially under a Clark-led collation), has ensured that ACE has been incorporated into mainstream Governmental priorities. Yet, the current Key-led Government has implemented cuts to adult and community education in schools (80 per cent reduction in Equivalent Full-time Students funding for 2010) and in universities (around 50 per cent for 2011). In effect, this has decimated the field in terms of liberal education. The stronghold for ACE is currently adult literacy and numeracy which is one of the Tertiary Education Commission's priorities, along with provision for Māori and Pacific peoples. The networks established to disseminate funding at the local level are in disarray and the ACE Aotearoa (the umbrella membership organisation for ACE), given that it too is under the auspices of the TEC, struggles to provide adequately for a disparate and desperate field.

In previous studies, Benseman (2005a) has outlined developments in lifelong learning in this country. He argued that lifelong learning in the halcyon days of the 1980s and 1990s faded in a questionable era within the new millennium. The over-arching economic-political context aligned to globalisation has necessitated retrenchment and a re-assessment of Government priorities for tertiary education generally, including ACE. Amid Benseman's observations about changes in the most recent decade, he includes a continuing confusion about the definitions of lifelong learning (and subsequent uncertainty of Government commitment), the over-emphasis on individualism and the appearance of neutrality in educational policy. On the other hand, the previous support for non-traditional learners in policy declarations has been enhanced.

The links between adult education and lifelong learning are obvious; at times one is used as a synonym for the other. While the meaning of lifelong learning remains problematic, it has been strongly aligned to economic rationalism where education is a key means of up-skilling the workforce to enable New Zealand to compete internationally in a global market. As commented in the international literature on lifelong learning, the term has been most closely associated with a nation's economic performance but has broader meanings to include personal fulfilment, active citizenship and social inclusion (Coffield 2000; Field 2002; Jarvis 2007). As summarised by Benseman (2005b), lifelong education in the 1980s was identified with Skill New Zealand, the crown agency largely responsible for workplace education and unemployment programmes. While the Faure report of 1972, *Learning to Be*, had been widely accepted in this country, ostensibly because of its acknowledgment of the importance of non-formal and informal learning in a democratic context, in the latter part of the twentith century it was buried under a vocational training and skills agenda. Further, New Zealand had been a partner in international literacy surveys (the OECD International Adult literacy Survey, IAL, of 1996/1997; the Ministry of Education's Adult Literacy and Life Skills Survey, ALL, of 2006/2007) which revealed an underclass of struggling adults in basic literacy and numeracy. The Government undertook a review of industry training, *Skills for a knowledge economy* (Ministry of Education 2001a) in which workplace learning assumed greater significance as a strategy to address under-performing companies/organisations.

The New Zealand Qualifications Authority and Qualifications Framework

In the 1980s and 1990s the Government made considerable efforts to make education accessible to a wider range of people and to breakdown artificial barriers between academic and vocational (work-based) learning. In an attempt to (further) democratise access to education, the New Zealand Qualifications Authority (NZQA) was established with its associated National Qualifications Framework (NQF), originally set at eight levels, later extended to ten. The new framework was designed to provide a flexible, modularised system, where achievement is recognised through competencies known as unit standards. Level 1 is equivalent to year 11 in high school (former fifth form); level 5 is equivalent to the first year of university study. On the surface this framework enabled previously poorer performers to gain success and satisfaction from their competency-based achievement. In particular, initially at least, it appealed to providers of education for Māori and Pacific peoples. The framework has been used by high schools around the country and by most tertiary education providers to enable greater portability of achievement/qualifications. However, the universities have never embraced the strategy on the basis that learning cannot readily be reduced to predetermined outcomes; higher level reasoning should not be captured in this way and excellence in achievement is insufficiently validated in this framework (Peddie 1996).

The structure of tertiary education in Aotearoa New Zealand

While the term 'higher education' is seldom used, it was formerly equated with the university sector and perhaps stretched to include polytechnics. Today the term 'tertiary education' has been adopted by Government to encompass a very wide array of providers of post-compulsory education. As mentioned in the Ministry of Education's national report of 2008 on Adult Learning and Education, two important changes have taken place early in the new millennium: the introduction of the Tertiary Education Strategy (TES) as a mechanism for Government to set priorities and strategies; and the establishment of the Tertiary Education Commission (TEC) as a body responsible for planning and funding tertiary education in New Zealand (Ministry of Education 2008: 6). As stated in the TEC's Annual Report 2010, the main task is to instigate the TES 'through the funding and monitoring of tertiary education organisations, and advising on tertiary education policies and priorities' (TEC 2010: 11). This sector includes literacy and numeracy education (as part of foundation studies), part-time and full-time study, work-related training and doctoral research. The Tertiary Education Strategy 2010–2015 is fundamental, according to Government, in achieving this country's economic, social, cultural and environmental goals.

There are over 700,000 students engaged in structured learning in over 800 organisations under the umbrella of the TEC. In particular, the following organisations are funded by the TEC and constitute the tertiary education sector:

- eight universities (Auckland; Auckland University of Technology, AUT; Waikato in Hamilton/Tauranga; Massey in Palmerston North, Albany and Wellington; Victoria in Wellington; Canterbury in Christchurch; Lincoln in Christchurch; Otago in Dunedin);
- 20 institutes of technology and polytechnics (ITPs) focusing on technical/vocational programmes;
- 348 private training establishments (PTEs) (e.g. language schools, business, hairdressing, hospitality, religious-based agencies);
- 38 industry training organisations (e.g. dairy, automotive industries);
- three wānanga (Aotearoa with multiple campuses; Awanuiarangi in Whakatane; Raukawa in lower North Island);
- 365 schools supporting ACE, foundation literacy and numeracy, training opportunities programmes, youth training, workplace literacy;
- 14 other tertiary providers (OTPs) (e.g. the National Association of ESOL Home Tutors Schemes; Literacy Aotearoa Inc., Workbase Education; NZ Playcentre Federation);
- 44 other providers.

(TEC 2010: 5)

This multitude of providers engage in a wide philosophical variety (humanist, progressive, vocational, radical) but more stringent funding rules have effectively narrowed the range of acceptable options to those more directly linked to economic performance. There was Governmental concern over the quality and relevance of provision. Accordingly, reforms changed the model to one where investment-led funding would be the norm and provision is explicitly linked to Government priorities and those of education stakeholders in the community. An example of this strategy has been how literacy and numeracy education has assumed major importance. After the relatively negative results from New Zealand's participation in the 1996 International Adult Literacy Survey (IALS), when this country's espoused position of near to full literacy was exposed as defunct, a comprehensive plan was adopted by Government. Boshier and Benseman (2000) referred to these unexpected learning outcomes as a 'literacy crisis'. The policy report, *More than words: the New Zealand adult literacy strategy* (Ministry of Education 2001b), sought to address this embarrassment, involving workplace initiatives and other schemes to improve access to and quality in provision. In a more recent budget (2008) a five-year Literacy, Language and Numeracy Action Plan (LLN) has been put in place. Energy has been channelled into improving what happens in the workplace but also to the idea of embedding literacy and numeracy in all low level tertiary education study (levels 1 to 4 on the NQF), particularly in polytechnics. Clearly, the Government is putting many eggs of increased baseline learning performance into the literacy and numeracy basket.

In a recent report from Government, the TEC (2010: 2) has identified what it considers to be key issues in tertiary education. Within the context of fiscal restraint and greater accountability, decisions are increasingly being linked to a performance-based funding system. In this report the TEC identified issues as:

- the system moving from being uncapped to being capped;
- a performance basis for funding research and research-based teaching;
- fee increases are subject to controls rather than being set entirely by providers;
- the cost to Government of student loans has increased as interest payable by borrowers was phased out.

The Student Achievement Component (SAC) of funding to institutions is now agreed by the TEC in Investment Plans. In this regime school leavers are given pride of place in universities, and mature-age students, previously having access to open entry at age 20, are now in the lowest category in a revamped 'managed entry' system operating in universities.

Adult students in the tertiary education system

Arguably anyone entering a tertiary education provider at the age of 16 might be considered 'adult', but the more generally accepted understanding of the term is that of students of 25 years or above. The term 'mature-age student' is usually applied to such students. In line with the massification of higher education internationally (Duke 2005; Oduaran and Bhola 2006; Thompson 2000), the diversity of students has expanded including a sizeable proportion of adult students, many of whom study part-time while working full-time.

Older students (those 40 years or above), a subset of mature-age students, constitute an increasing proportion of the nation's population with half of those over 15 in this category. Understandably, the demand for education continues for those primarily from the middle-class who are used to plentiful educational opportunity. In terms of tertiary students, over 30 per cent are older students (Ministry of Education 2006: 1). Nearly 8 per cent of all New Zealanders aged 40 or over are enrolled in formal study at a tertiary provider. However, older students are also more likely to be studying at sub-degree level in certificates and diplomas. According to the Ministry of Education, there has been a major trend of older Māori taking up study, with 25 per cent of people in bachelor-level studies enrolled in 2005 over the age of 65 being Māori.

In an overview of adults in education, Scott (2010) summarised some key points concerning adults in education:

- Nearly half (or 48 per cent) of New Zealanders aged 25 to 64 were in some form of study in 2006.
- Women were slightly more likely to participate in non-formal study than males.
- Participation decreased with age for formal study but peaked in the 45–54 age group for non-formal study.
- Adults with higher-level qualifications were more likely to participate in formal or non-formal study than those with no or lower-level qualifications.
- Employed adults were less likely to participate in formal study than non-employed adults, but were twice as likely to participate in non-formal study as non-employed adults.
- 77 per cent of those who did non-formal study in 2006, did so for job reasons. This rate was higher for men, the employed, and those with higher-level qualifications.

(Scott 2010: 1)

Given this country's historic reputation for an open, flexible system (extra emphasis provided by the implementation of the NQF) there have been significant numbers of older students entering the system at sub-degree level who had no previous qualification. In 2005, 42,000 students were in this category and one in three was a first-time tertiary student. The Ministry of Education reports that while the completion rates of older students are marginally below those of students younger than 25 years, after adjusting for part-time study and lower school qualifications, completion rates actually increased with age until the mid-fifties. This fact reinforces the belief that age is largely irrelevant in terms of older students' readiness to engage with formal education (Findsen and McCullough 2008; Withnall 2010).

In a project initiated by Davey, Neale and Morris-Matthews (2003), the focus was upon 'education in mid to later life', where the researchers analysed patterns of participation and emergent issues for older learners at Victoria University in Wellington. Essentially, the study looked into the circumstances surrounding older people's entry and engagement in university studies – their motives, the incentives and barriers experienced en route, their actual learning experiences and outcomes. At the time of the study, the following general characteristics of people over the age of 40 who participate in education in New Zealand were identified:

- Two-thirds are women;
- Three-quarters study part-time;

- Nearly half are women studying part-time;
- Four out of five are aged 40 to 59;
- Only one in 20 is aged 60 or more.

(Davey *et al.* 2003: 16)

Since this study the economic situation in this country has worsened but it is not expected that this profile will have changed significantly.

The Victoria study consisted of 70 per cent female with two out of three in the 40–49 age group and fewer people in the older age cohort. In terms of ethnicity, the majority (87 per cent) were Pakeha (European), with only 8 per cent Māori, 5 per cent Asian and 3 per cent Pacific Island students. While four out of five had family members who had been to university, this was more likely to be siblings or children rather than parents. Hence, many were first generation students in families. In terms of study patterns, a quarter were full-time (in comparison with 60 per cent for all Victorian students), 65 per cent were studying in the humanities/social sciences, 22 per cent in commerce, 7 per cent in law and 6 per cent in science. Education was by far the most popular subject. Overall, four out of five were in some kind of paid work with 72 per cent in professional/technical and 16 per cent in administrative occupations. Perhaps unsurprisingly, the main motives were either work-related – getting better qualifications to improve job performance – or personal fulfilment. This snapshot at one university provides some insights into the special character of university-based study for mature-age students and demonstrates the prevalence of part-time study, the importance of older students in terms of lifelong learning policy in practice and typical gender biases in subject choice.

At a more generalised level, the Government quite clearly sees tertiary education, including the widening of access, as an investment – 'the ability of graduates to obtain employment, contribute to the growth in the economy and receive higher wages in return' (TEC 2010: 8). However, the return of a qualification in New Zealand does not necessarily translate into higher comparative wages in comparison with electricians, plumbers and carpenters, for instance.

At the time of writing there is considerable turmoil in tertiary education and mature-age students are especially affected. In further marginalisation of the marginalised (those outside the 'traditional' student of the capable school-leaver), the TEC has stressed the importance in institutional Investment Plans of priority given to under-25s, Māori and Pacific Island students. Under 'managed entry' operating in all universities at present, admission criteria will be more rigidly and systematically employed than in the past so that students without advanced academic standing will be waitlisted in long queues. The days of 'open entry' to mature-age students are numbered and a historical legacy of open access is under severe threat.

Tertiary education in New Zealand: differentiation and stratification

The four original 'colleges' (later fully autonomous institutions) in Aotearoa New Zealand provided the academic backbone in the higher education system. Overall, there are 135,200 Equivalent Full-time Students (EFTS) across the university system (Universities New Zealand 2011: 2). Most people would attest to the relative equality of standards across the eight publically funded universities while their individual characters have been moulded by international and local imperatives. However, the University of Auckland with 31,700 EFTS, is the highest ranked university in international league tables and is a member of the Universitas 21 club, thus differentiating itself from the others in terms of status. While all universities have internationalisation, research and post-graduate study as major drivers, there are considerable differences across the universities in these domains, with the four 'traditional universities' still enjoying strong public support.

Increasingly, 'performativity' (documentation of teaching and compliance to pre-determined learning outcomes) governs what is possible in the classroom, with innovative teachers as mediating agents between systemic demands and responsive teaching. The function of universities as critics and conscience of society remains on the statutes, but many people would argue that the challenging voices of dissent have been effectively curbed in a neoliberal regime. In addition, the line between universities and larger polytechnics is increasingly blurred as the latter expand their curricula and engage in research and postgraduate study (e.g. UNITEC in Auckland).

Undoubtedly, the Government views universities as sites of innovation and commercialisation and a central contributor to an enlightened workforce. All of the universities have established commercial outlets for research worth $350 million, according to Universities NZ. As remarked in a recent review of universities in terms of economic value, 'increased productivity generated by university research and education helps to boost incomes and provide a better quality of life for New Zealanders' (NZIER 2010: 1). Unsurprisingly, the TES is focused on increasing labour force skills and generating innovative research. This is clearly a human capital agenda with some spin-offs for social capital (Field 2003). This same report identifies four areas of significant public and private benefit from education: productivity, labour force participation, social cohesion and health.

Bridging and foundation studies

One heavily contested arena amid the different types of providers (universities, polytechnics, private training establishments, and wānanga) is that of bridging and foundation studies. These terms, closely aligned to adult literacy, language and numeracy (LLN), have varied definitions and underpinning ideologies. Benseman (2005b) suggests a three-way typology of adult literacy perspectives: a functional technical approach; social action, reflecting a perspective derived from Freirean notions of 'reading the world'; and literacy as social practices, embedding literacy in the social and cultural contexts of learners (e.g. the family).

Foundation skills (or LLN) has incorporated adult literacy, second-chance education, basic skills, English for speakers of other languages (ESOL) and adult basic education. The International Adult Literacy Survey of 1996 and the more recent Adult Literacy and Life Skills Survey of 2006 have revealed sub-groups of the population who are disproportionately represented in the lower levels of literacy proficiency, particularly non-native speakers, Pasifika, Māori, unemployed and low-skill workers, low-income people and older adults. These politically charged results have no doubt helped to fuel the recent TES focus on under-25s, Māori and Pacific peoples. There is no doubt that current government policy favours foundation programmes to be offered by ITPs and PTEs rather than universities, given that the bulk of these courses are in levels 1–3. In 2007 there were 36,800 students in foundation education in Tertiary Education Institutes (TEIs) of which 58 per cent were enrolled in wānanga, 37 per cent in ITPs and the remainder in PTEs and universities. Students are mainly part-time and the age of students is relatively high (nearly 50 per cent aged over 40 years) (Ministry of Education 2008).

Bridging education programmes tend to be a subset of foundation studies and more explicitly function to take learners from one level to the next, sometimes across providers. These programmes, both credit and non-credit, have historically been strong in universities but are now under threat. They have been either oriented towards developing academic skills for the masses or developed specifically with a particular sub-group under social equity imperatives (e.g. mature-age Māori students). Managed entry in universities has increased the stakes of admission for all students and since demand far exceeds supply under a capped EFTS environment, the need for such programmes is called into question in a university context.

The ITP sector within tertiary education has been more closely linked than universities to technical, vocational and workplace learning. There is a huge range of sizes of these institutions which are frequently the only Government-funded local option for youngsters leaving school who are not destined for university study. As ITPs have embraced the NQF, there are significant numbers of students in levels 1–3 who subsequently enter low-level jobs or stay on for degree studies. In some instances, ITPs collaborate with other tertiary providers to ensure a fuller range of opportunities than if working in isolation.

The wānanga are unique institutions to Aotearoa New Zealand specialising in programmes of direct relevance to Māori students employing a *kaupapa Māori* approach (preferred Māori way of learning and teaching), using predominantly

Māori teachers and Māori language, as appropriate. These institutions form part of on-going Māori *tino rangtiratanga* (self-determination) in economic, cultural and political affairs and were originally spurned by the state (see McCarthy 1996) but ultimately legitimated by the Government in the TEC funding regime. Two of the stated TEC priorities for 2009–2011 are to 'increase Maori achievement in tertiary education' and 'improve literacy and numeracy' both strongly intertwined ideologically and practically (TEC 2010: 7). The three wānanga provide a viable alternative for Māori school leavers and Māori mature-age students in predominantly lower level qualifications and complement what is offered in other tertiary education institutions.

Participation in tertiary education

At a broad level, the Ministry of Education reports that in 2008 over 102,000 New Zealanders gained a tertiary qualification with one-third at bachelor degree level or above. The Ministry interprets this completion rate as a measure of the country's skills acquisition capability and as an indicator of internal efficiency. However, 'completion', like the term 'dropout', is emotionally loaded and easily misconstrued. Given that completion refers to completion of a qualification (rather than a course) then there is considerable under-estimation of participation. To the credit of the Ministry, it recognises that 'completion goals cannot be viewed in isolation from access goals' (Education Counts 2009: 1). In other words, the lower status institutions, which tend to attract more students with minimal familial history of post-compulsory education and consequently are potentially 'higher risk', should not be assessed for completion using the same criteria as high status universities (Hodgson 2000). In the New Zealand context, wānanga are conspicuous in this regard, as they attract disproportionately large numbers of Māori older students who are first-timers in tertiary education.

In the early 2000s there was substantial growth in completions for level 1 to 4 certificates principally associated with ITP and wānanga growth, but from 2005 to 2008 enrolments and completions declined as a result of the Government's policy of improving relevance and increasing the numbers of under 25s in the system. This 'hardening' of the policy environment is also demonstrated by the increased numbers of completions for doctorates by 555 between 2000 and 2008 (Education Counts 2009). Historically, New Zealand has one of the highest levels of part-time study amongst OECD countries. Under managed entry into universities, it will be prudent to track the admission and completion rates of older students in the wake of stronger policy supporting younger students.

The participation rate of females in tertiary study has exceeded that of males. According to Ministry of Education figures, the gap has actually increased from 15 per cent to 21 per cent. Before we draw too many conclusions from this bare statistic, we need more refined data for discrete kinds of learning activity. In terms of ethnicity, surprisingly, Māori participate at a higher rate than non-Māori. However, Māori have more engagement at the sub-degree level while non-Māori are highest at degree level and above. As in other countries (e.g. the USA), proportionately more Asians are studying for tertiary qualifications at first and postgraduate degree levels than other ethnicities, what some commentators have dubbed 'the over-achievement' of Asian students. In accord with Government policy to build capacity at higher levels of qualification, postgraduate students increased by 9 per cent from 2002 to 2008 (Education Counts 2010: 3).

Māori tertiary education

Māori and Pasifika Peoples, traditionally disenfranchised groups from success in education (Jenkins and Ka'ai 1994), have battled to gain equality of access and outcomes from the Pakeha-European biased system. While participation levels are higher than for other groups, they are concentrated in lower status areas. In Ministry of Education statistics for 2005, Māori students by subsector reveal that 34 per cent were studying in wānanga, 26 per cent in ITPs, 18 per cent in universities, 18 per cent in PTEs and the remainder in other providers (Ministry of Education 2007: 2). Hence, while levels of participation are healthy, the eventual outcomes in terms of future workforce engagement are more dubious.

A specific policy and programme aimed at Māori students' achievement in all learning locations is entitled *Ka Hikitia: Managing for Success, Education Strategy 2008–2012*. It is a 'broad reaching five-year strategy aiming to transform and change the education sector, ensuring Māori are able to enjoy education success as Māori' (Education Counts 2011a: 1). It is a target-driven research-informed strategy for transformative change, not an incremental response to Māori aspirations. It focuses on four areas: foundation years, young people engaged in learning, Māori language education and organisational success (beginning with the Ministry itself).

Pasifika Peoples' Tertiary Education

While education for Pacific peoples is not linked to a Treaty as for Māori, it is a serious area of concern for the New Zealand Government. Pasifika Peoples constitute 6.9 per cent of the New Zealand population and live mostly in heavily urbanised areas such as Auckland and Wellington. In June 2006, the Pasifika Education Plan 2006–2010 was released. Its focus is on:

- Participation and quality in early childhood education;
- Strong literacy and numeracy foundations in schooling, and making sure students are engaged in learning;
- More effective engagement with parents;

- Transitioning students into higher levels of learning and achievement in tertiary education. (Education Counts 2011c: 1)

The plan embodies the expected aspirations of increased participation at all levels of the education system, improving retention and encouragement of Pasifika students to enter advanced degrees. While some issues for Pasifika Peoples are similar to those for Māori (alienation from a British-dominated education system; inappropriate curriculum in schools; insufficient teachers of Pasifika descent in the overall system; persistent under-achievement), Pasifika Peoples are not indigenous to New Zealand and came as new migrants to be assimilated into mainstream society and have suffered on-going marginalisation (Mara *et al.* 1994).

International students in Aotearoa New Zealand

As part of New Zealand's 'export education', international students are invited into this country to provide additional funds for tertiary education providers. Unlike domestic students, they are ineligible for student loans and can boost substantially the financial coffers of individual institutions. Of course, the policy of internationalisation in the tertiary sector means much more than money – enrichment of the education context by international perspectives is very important, helping to prevent a myopic view of the world by New Zealanders. However, the cultural enrichment argument for recruiting overseas students tends to be swamped by the economic imperative. Most institutions aim for a diverse mix of students to avoid over-dependence on any one market and to embellish the experience of these students in a foreign environment. Ministry of Education figures reveal that from 2007 to 2008 there were 39,800 international students across the system after a peak of 50,394 in 2004. The New Zealand Government is keen to eliminate current barriers for entry (such as notorious waiting times for visa approvals) to maximise export education and keep their own funding to tertiary education limited. The incorporation of international students into the TES is significant as it signals the importance of internationalisation in New Zealand education and boosts the financial coffers for TEIs. Further, significant numbers of these students gain residency and subsequently contribute to a competitive workplace.

ICT and tertiary education

As New Zealand is a small country where geographical distance is less of a barrier for communication than in many other countries, distance learning was not developed as rapidly as in Canada and Australia. Even so, this mode of learning, especially through Massey University initially, has been incorporated into TEIs' regular practices as part of flexible learning programmes. In the ITP sector, the Open Polytechnic leads the way but all institutions have engaged positively with e-learning. Online learning has become an accustomed practice and developments within institutions and platforms such as Moodle enable teachers to use a wider array of methods than in the past. In most publically funded tertiary institutions professional development for novices and experienced teachers provides on-going possibilities for engaging with new information and communication technologies, exemplified at the University of Waikato through its Teaching Development Unit.

One of the realities faced by cash-strapped tertiary providers is that some high schools, especially the more financially comfortable private schools and leading public secondary schools, have resources which are not readily matched. There are significant gaps between decile one schools (lower socio-economic) and decile ten (schools located in affluent areas) in what can be provided to students; similarly, in the TEI system, there is considerable differentiation between institutions. The Ministry of Education commissions research and evaluation on e-learning practices in education. This includes assessment of e-learning practices, particularly those that make a real difference to students' learning and support for innovation and reflection upon formative pedagogical decision-making (Education Counts 2011b).

Concluding comments

This chapter has traversed the unsettled territory of tertiary education in Aotearoa New Zealand. It is a dynamic, constantly changing arena, subject to global economic and cultural trends, yet steadfastly retaining a distinctive New Zealand flavour, reflective of this country's location in the South Pacific and its colonial history. While many institutions retain aspects of a British identity, increasingly the system is contextualised in a post-colonial era where European influences are weaker and Asian–South Pacific–American influences stronger. Recent Governmental policy through the Ministry of Education, the TEC and the NZQA, has emphasised the need to address overt disparities in educational opportunity. Since 2000, Governmental policy has been preoccupied with under-25-year-olds, Māori and Pacific Peoples' life chances.

In the past decade the rhetoric of lifelong learning has been incorporated into much of Government's educational policies but has seldom been translated into funding that really makes a difference for adult and community education. ACE has always been a Cinderella sector and its status has changed little since it was embedded into the TEC after the *Koia! Koia!* report. The core of ACE is now in the foundation skills domain where funding is more plentiful; outside of increasingly narrowing priorities in literacy, numeracy and foundation skills, the struggle for resources continues. In the latter part of the first decade of the 2000s, contestability for funding has increased and greater differentiation is occurring between different types of TEIs.

Consistent with worldwide trends towards greater accountability for Government spending, increased surveillance of education and a move towards performativity within institutions, a straitjacket is being imposed on providers to adhere to Government priorities. Yet the pluralism evident in tertiary education gives some credence to optimism – there is still a range of pathways for students to achieve their educational goals; open entry to universities, while under a dark cloud, may be preserved in part through institutions' initiatives in collaboration with partners. The uptake of tertiary education by previously-excluded marginalised groups (Māori, Pasifika) is laudable though currently located in lower-status institutions and programmes. Given the Government's priorities, other groups may unintentionally be disenfranchised such as mature-age students. This 'mixed' report is reflective of a tertiary education system dealing with at times contradictory objectives related to wider tensions between market liberalism and social equity outcomes.

References

AECLWP (2001) *Koia! Koia! Towards a learning society: The role of adult and community education*, Report of the Adult Education and Community Learning Working Party, Wellington.

Benseman, J. (2005a) 'Paradigm regained? The re-emergence of lifelong learning in New Zealand in the late 1990s', *New Zealand Journal of Adult Learning*, 33 (1): 21–39.

Benseman, J. (2005b) 'Foundation learning in New Zealand: an overview', in J. Benseman and A. Sutton (eds) *Facing the challenge: Foundation learning for adults in Aotearoa New Zealand*, 11–25, Wellington, Dunmore Publishing.

Boshier, R. and Benseman, J. (2000) 'The impact of market forces in the quest for lifelong learning in New Zealand universities', in H.G. Schuetze and M. Slowey (eds) *Higher Education and lifelong learners: International perspectives on change*, 217–234. London and New York: RoutledgeFarmer.

Coffield, F. (2000) (ed.) *Differing visions of a learning society* (2 vols), Bristol: Policy Press.

Comparative Education Research Unit (2007) *The Adult Literacy and Life Skills (ALL) Survey: An introduction*, Wellington: Ministry of Education.

Dakin, J. (1996) 'Looking back', in J. Benseman, B. Findsen and M. Scott (eds) *The fourth sector: Jult and community education in Aotearoa New Zealand*, 21–37, Palmerston North: Dunmore Press.

Davey, J.A., Neale, J. and Morris-Matthews, K. (eds) (2003) *Living and learning: Experiences of University after age 40*, Wellington: Victoria University Press.

Duke, C. (2005) (ed.) *The tertiary moment:Jhat road to inclusive higher education?* Leicester: NIACE.

Education Counts (2009) *Completion of tertiary education*, Wellington: Ministry of Education.

Education Counts (2010) *Participation rates in tertiary education*, Wellington: Ministry of Education.

Education Counts (2011a) *Māori education*, Wellington: Ministry of Education.

Education Counts (2011b) *E-learning research and evaluation*, Wellington: Ministry of Education.
Education Counts (2011c) *Pasifika education*, Wellington: Ministry of Education.
Faure, E., Herrera, F., Kaddowa, A., Lopes, H., Petrovsky, A., Rahnema, M. and Ward, F. (1972) *Learning to be: The world of education today and tomorrow*, Paris: UNESCO/Harrap.
Field, J. (2002) *Lifelong learning and the new educational order*, Stoke on Trent: Trentham Books.
Field, J. (2003) *Social capital*, London: Routledge.
Findsen, B. and McCullough, S. (2008) 'Older students' engagement with further and higher education in the West of Scotland: Final report to the West of Scotland Wider Access Forum', University of Glasgow: Department of Adult and Continuing Education.
Hodgson, A. (2000) 'The challenge of widening participation in lifelong learning', in A. Hodgson (ed.) *Policies, politics and the future of lifelong learning*, 51–68. London: Kogan Page.
Jarvis, P. (2007) *Globalisation, lifelong learning and the learning society: Sociological perspectives*, London: Routledge.
Jenkins, K. and Ka'ai, T. (1994) 'Māori education: A cultural experience and dilemma for the state – a new direction for Māori society', in E. Coxon, K. Jenkins, J. Marshall and L. Massey (eds) *The politics of learning and teaching in Aotearoa New Zealand*, 148–179, Palmerston North: Dunmore Printing Co.
Mara, D., Foliaki, L. and Coxon, E. (1994) 'Pacific Islands education', in E. Coxon, K. Jenkins, J. Marshall and L. Massey (eds) *The politics of learning and teaching in Aotearoa New Zealand*, 180–214, Palmerston North: Dunmore Printing Co.
McCarthy, M. (1996) 'He Hinaki Tukutuku: The baited trap' (Whare wānanga: Tensions and contradictions in relation to the state), in J. Benseman, B. Findsen and M. Scott (eds) *The fourth sector: Adult and community education in Aotearoa New Zealand*, 81–94, Palmerston North: Dunmore Press.
Ministry of Education (2001a) *Skills for a knowledge society: Nga mohiotanga me to kohanga whai matauranga*, Wellington: Ministry of Education.
Ministry of Education (2001b) *More than words: The New Zealand adult literacy strategy*, Wellington: Ministry of Education.
Ministry of Education (2006) *Older students*, Wellington: Ministry of Education.
Ministry of Education (2007) *Māori participation in tertiary education 2005*, Wellington: Ministry of Education.
Ministry of Education (2008) *The Development and State of the Art of Adult Learning and Education: National Report of New Zealand*, Wellington: Ministry of Education.
NZIER (2010) *The economic value of University investment: Report to Universities New Zealand (Te Pōkai Tara)*, Wellington: NZIER.
Oduaran, A. and Bhola, H. (eds) (2006) *Widening access to education as social justice*, The Netherlands: Springer.
OECD (2007) *Literacy skills for the knowledge society: Further results from the International Adult Literacy Survey*, Paris: OECD and Human Resources Development Canada.
Peddie, R. (1996) 'A framework for lifelong learning? Adult and community education and the NZQA', *Access: Critical perspectives in cultural and policy studies in education*, 15 (2): 53–66.

Scott, D. (2010) *Non-formal and formal learning – adults in education*, Wellington: Ministry of Education.

TEC, Tertiary Education Commission (2010) *Tertiary Education report: Introduction to the key issues in Tertiary Education*. Online. Available <http://www.tec.govt.nz/Documents/Publications/BoM%20Introduction%20to% key%Issues%20 Tertiary%20Eduation> (accessed 21 January 2011).

Thompson, J. (2000) (ed.) *Stretching the academy: The politics and practice of widening participation in Higher Education*, Leicester: NIACE.

Tobias, R. (1996) 'What do adult and community educators share in common?', in J. Benseman, B. Findsen and M. Scott (eds) *The fourth sector: Adult and community education in Aotearoa New Zealand*, 38–64, Palmerston North: Dunmore Press.

Universities New Zealand (2011) *The NZ University system*, Wellington. Online. Available <http://www.nzvcc.ac.nz/nz-university-system> (accessed 24 January 2011).

Withnall, A. (2010) *Improving learning in later life*, London: Routledge.

Part V
Perspectives from two 'BRICS' countries

Chapter 14

South Africa

Higher education in lifelong learning in a middle-income country:[1] but by the grace of champions?

Shirley Walters

Overview

Lifelong learning in a middle-income country like South Africa exists between the political and economic pressures of a large proportion of young people, on the one hand, and the need for ongoing access to learning opportunities throughout life as the 'front-end loading model' of schooling is inadequate for the majority of impoverished people. This chapter reflects back over the last ten or so years of higher education in lifelong learning, using both a national study on the impact of the South African Higher Education Qualifications (Sub)Framework on adult learners (DLL 2010a) and a case study of one historically black university, the University of Western Cape. It describes the competing social, economic and political currents which foreground the essential role of adult and lifelong learning champions in keeping equitable spaces open for adult learners.

Introduction

The commitment made in the South African Higher Education Policy document of 1997, that the education system would 'open its doors, in the spirit of lifelong learning, to workers and professionals' (DoE 1997: 17) raised expectations in South Africa that provision for the education of adults would be taken seriously. Yet one finding of the study by Buchler *et al.* (2007) was that adult learners remain poorly served at all levels of higher education institutions, and that this problem was exacerbated by the shortage of information on adult students and programmes that have large numbers of adults or cater specifically for them. The study on 'Equity, Access and Success of Adult Learners' (Buchler *et al.* 2007) set out to investigate whether a higher education system that facilitates access, equity and success for adult learners exists or is being formulated. It asked: What is the place of adult learners in South African higher education policy? What has been the actual impact of the National Qualifications Framework in facilitating the democratization of knowledge? What is the place of the different components of the South

African education system in producing the skills and knowledge required for equitable socio-economic development? The study concluded that adult learners are seemingly not a high priority at a time of scarce resources and competing challenges. However, the authors urge that:

> the education of adults in a society such as South Africa is a political, moral, historical and economic issue – and it is not merely one of these, but all of them. Adults have a critical role to play in the development of South Africa because of their accumulated knowledge and experience, which can be mediated by educational processes to strengthen it and make it socially useful.
> (Buchler et al. 2007: 152)

Since then, little seems to have changed. As a submission to the Summit on Higher Education Transformation, called by the South African Minister of Higher Education and Training, in April 2010 suggests:

> from a broad systems point of view, in the five years since the study, little seems to have been done to improve the lot of adult learners in the universities. This includes those students who have entered via recognition of prior learning (RPL). In fact, there may well be unintended consequences of certain policies to work against access, equity and success of adult learners within a lifelong learning philosophy and approach.
> (UWC 2010: 2)

The South African situation is certainly not unique. (With South Africa having been recently invited to join the Brazil, Russia, India and China (BRIC) economic configuration, hopefully it will become more possible to test this assertion more systematically over time.) However, it is reasonable to assume that within low- and middle-income countries, the spaces for encouraging and supporting adult learners to fully embrace higher education opportunities can easily close down in the face of resource constraints, political pressures from large proportions of youth in our societies, and the resilient picture that holds most higher education systems captive, and which is contradicted by the facts, that it is mainly serving young, full-time, able-bodied, middle-class, urban youth, who have good health, resources and time to concentrate solely on their studies.

In this chapter, I begin by setting the scene for lifelong learning in higher education in South Africa, posing the question as to who are 'adult learners' in this context. I highlight in particular the demographic profile of the country and the implications this has for understanding priorities in education and training. I draw on a case study of the University of Western Cape that has been at the forefront of advocating lifelong learning in higher education, to shine light on critical tensions for lifelong learning in higher education in

South Africa. These are also refracted through the study[2] into the impact of the Higher Education Qualifications Framework (HEQF) on adult learners (DLL 2010a). But first, as a backdrop I provide a thumbnail sketch of higher education in South Africa.

The Higher Education Act of 1997 made provision for a unified and nationally planned system of higher education and created a statutory Council on Higher Education (CHE), which provides advice to the Minister and is responsible for quality assurance and promotion. The Act aimed to transform the previous racialized and unequal system of apartheid to one which embraced redress, equity and quality. Between 2003 and 2005 there was major restructuring of public higher education institutions (HEIs) resulting in 36 HEIs being merged into 23: 11 universities, 6 comprehensive universities and 6 universities of technology. Between them in 2009 they enrolled 837,779 students in total with 684,419 undergraduate students and 128,747 postgraduate students. The institutions vary greatly in terms of size, scope and history. There is also a growing private higher education sector which occupies niche areas. In 2011, there were 87 registered and 27 provisionally registered private higher education institutions (see www.che.ac.za accessed 26 April 2011).

In 2008, it was reported that although the higher education system had made major advances towards greater equity and efficiency, the legacy of apartheid lingered on. Participation rates of black youth remained low, and they were not performing as well as other 'population groups'. The authors stated that, 'Students are dropping out of higher education at alarming rates often because they cannot afford to stay at university' (Breier and Mabizela 2008: 278).

In 2009 a new policy was introduced to build a differentiated post-school system (CHE 2009). The Department of Education was split into the Department of Higher Education and Training and the Department of Basic Education, which oversees schooling for youth. As Cosser (2010) stated, the unbundling of the departments paved the way for redrawing the post-school landscape and forced a re-examination of the entire education and training pathway system. He highlighted major problems in the system relating to a dearth of intermediate education and training opportunities. He pointed to the estimated 2.8 million 20–24-year-olds not in employment, education or training, who are a major concern for politicians and are creating a lever for certain immediate policy imperatives that have implications for adult learners in the system. In total, 51 per cent of the 48 million people in South Africa are under 25 years of age.

Who are adult learners?

It is commonly accepted that lifelong learning is for people of all ages and stages of life, even though in popular parlance it is often assumed to be referring to adult or 'non-traditional' learners. Using Schuller and Watson's (2009: 1) four stages, higher education caters primarily for those in the latter part of stage one (0–25 years) and the second stage (25–50 years). In the first stage, writing about the UK, Schuller and Watson suggested that all people should have claims to learning and development. Learning in the second stage should aim at 'sustaining productivity and prosperity, but also at building strong family lives and personal identity'. As they said, 'this is a new mosaic of time with different mixes of paid and unpaid work and learning time'.

Defining adult learners in the context of South African higher education is no easy task. Bourgeois, Duke, Guyot and Merrill (1999: 3) defined 'mature adults' as having had 'a significant break, with other life-[experience] and work-experience, prior to entering higher education'. Furthermore,

> More than half of those in modern [Higher Education] systems are adults in the sense of having left full-time education for other roles before returning later to full-[time] or part-time study. Such students commonly combine study with other major life roles: work, family and community. Their dedication to the business of being a student is less exclusive. On the other hand their occupancy of the student role may be more single-minded and purposeful: getting a degree, not living the life of a student who is growing up.
> (Bourgeois *et al.* 1999: 17–18)

In the literature on lifelong learning, the changing age profiles particularly in highly developed economies are key drivers of debate. From an international perspective, the question of the changing demographics raises interesting, paradoxical issues for lifelong learning.

A key observation in a middle-income country like South Africa is the very large proportion of young people. The age profile and trend is very different to that of most of the highly developed economies. For example, the 0–14-year-olds in Australia comprise 20 per cent of the population, in Brazil 28 per cent, in India 33 per cent, South Africa 32 per cent and the UK 18 per cent. The proportions of 60-year-olds-plus are: Australia 18 per cent, Brazil 9 per cent, India 8 per cent, South Africa 7 per cent and the UK 21 per cent. In addition, life expectancy at birth in South Africa in 2007 was 50 years. This compares with UK figures for 2004–2006 of 77 years for men and 81 years for women. These figures are also highly determined by social class and race/ethnicity; whereas middle-class people's demographic profile may be similar to that in the UK, the majority of people who are poor will carry the burden of ill health and premature death (Walters 2008).

This is a challenge for researchers in the low- and middle-income countries. The fundamental demographic differences between countries of the political 'South' and of the political 'North' is very significant because of the colonial histories and the common practices of people in the South deferring to those in the North from where the majority of literature in the field is generated and sourced. The logic of systems' development therefore needs to be carefully interrogated so as to avoid inappropriate borrowing of theories and practices between North and South.

Having said this, there are situations in the South which can benefit greatly from some of the theories emanating from the North. A case in point is Schuller and Watson's (2009) four life stages approach to lifelong learning systems' development and resource allocation. I will elaborate on this by focusing on the reality of the HIV and AIDS pandemic that is having an impact upon aspects of people's lives, and in doing this I hope to illuminate one crucial aspect of the South African higher education context, which will in all likelihood resonate for other low- and middle-income countries who have poverty and ill health as overwhelming realities.

One of the most telling situations which challenges the notion of 'front-end loading' of the education and training systems, and stresses the importance of a lifelong learning philosophy and approach, is the impact of the HIV and AIDS pandemic. In South Africa, 5.6 million people are HIV positive with cumulative AIDS deaths at around 2.5 million to date. A 2005 study of teachers revealed that 21 per cent of 25- to 34-year-olds and 13 per cent of 35- to 44-year-olds tested HIV positive.

The impact on life of HIV and AIDS is graphically described in a study by Steinberg (2008). He shows how caring for the sick, dealing with the loss of economically active members of the family, mobilizing to advocate and educate people around the epidemic, are all-absorbing for many women, men and children in HIV and AIDS saturated communities. There are more and more grandparents, and particularly grandmothers, who have to educate and support their grandchildren with their own children dying prematurely. This calls on social, economic and lifelong learning systems to support them.

At the same time, HIV and AIDS calls into question what it means to be an 'adult' or more specifically an 'adult learner' aside from the notion of chronological age. The most significant dimensions in defining an 'adult' appear to be that adult learners carry 'adult responsibilities' through their economic, family or community commitments. They bring complex life experiences to the learning environments and their time is often very constrained, precisely because of their multiple roles and responsibilities. The growing numbers of child-headed households, through loss of parents to AIDS or other illnesses, raise key questions as to who are 'adult', given that the children will be carrying out 'adult responsibilities'. This then poses challenges for provision of learning opportunities for both children and adults. Contexts like this raise fundamental curricular questions for which capabilities are needed at each of the four life stages to attain sustainable livelihoods (Walters 2010).

At the same time, for many of the school-going youth, because of poor economic circumstances, they enter school late or stop out and re-enter, so finish school as older than their middle-class contemporaries. This therefore makes the definition of 'adult' complex, and using chronological age only is a problem. For the study on the impact of the HEQF on adult learners, this dilemma was not resolved as it required far more detailed research. But taking a cue from the Cape Higher Education Consortium (CHEC) Adult Learning Group, the working definition adopted of adult or mature learners was characterized by one or more of the following: 'an adult learner is someone who carries multiple responsibilities; is over 25 years old; frequently working while studying; has had significant time out from study and has had work or community engagement experience; and often lacks formal access requirements' (DLL 2010a).

As mentioned above, of the 48 million people in South Africa, 51 per cent are below the age of 25 years with the majority being black and poor. In total, 70 per cent of South Africans over 20 years have not completed secondary school. It is not surprising, given the racialized history of South Africa, that the distribution of education levels is least favourable to black people and most favourable to white people. Having said this, the level of education amongst all adults is improving significantly. The younger the adults, the more likely they are to have received at least a primary education (Walters 2008: 25).

Because of these demographic realities, the definition of 'adult learners' cited above has relevance as it recognizes the strong possibility of people lacking formal access requirements to higher education, and it takes into account experience of community engagement, in addition to other work. This definition is used therefore as a touchstone in this chapter.

I turn now to sketching the position of adult learners in higher education in South Africa, before looking in more detail at one case study.

So what about adult learners in higher education in South Africa?

As the study by Buchler *et al.* (2007) states, one of the first acts of the new South African government was to establish the South African Qualifications Authority (DoE SAQA Act 1995). SAQA was established to oversee the implementation of the National Qualifications Framework (NQF), which in turn was to assist in the creation of an integrated education and training system that would overcome the fragmentation and inequalities of the past. The development of an NQF in South Africa was strongly influenced by qualifications framework discourses and practices elsewhere, and was accompanied by notions of lifelong learning, the recognition of prior learning (RPL), flexibility and portability of credits and qualifications that have generally come to characterize NQFs around the world. The NQF's development had strong roots in the labour movement and the struggle of the Congress of South African Trade Unions (COSATU) to have workers' knowledge recognized (Lugg 2009; Parker and Walters 2008).

With specific reference to policy change and transformation in the higher education sector in South Africa, references to broadening the base of higher education have been explicit and frequent in the key higher education policy documents emanating from government over the last 15 years and more. A key feature of the projected new system has been that it would reflect 'a broadening of the social base in terms of race, class, gender and age'. In addition, 'The system will open its doors, in the spirit of lifelong learning, to workers and professionals in pursuit of multi-skilling and re-skilling, and adult learners whose access to higher education had been thwarted in the past' (DoE 1997: 17). These sentiments were direct political responses to the inherited disparities of access, opportunity and resources for staff, students, and institutions across racial, gender, class and geographical lines.

Following the earlier documents, the National Plan for Higher Education (DoE 2001) advocated an increase in the general participation rate in public higher education in South Africa, with the aim of facilitating lifelong learning, developing the skills base of the country, and redressing historical inequities in the provision of education. The National Plan for Higher Education (NPHE) acknowledged that in the short to medium term, a shortage of qualified school leavers made the targeted increase (from 15 per cent to 25 per cent of the population, over a period of 10–15 years) unlikely. The NPHE suggested that participation rates in public higher education in South Africa could therefore be augmented by recruiting increasing numbers of 'non-traditional' learners, identified as workers, mature adults, women and disabled people. This should be 'an important policy goal in its own right' but the NPHE noted that institutions had done little to initiate RPL opportunities or 'programmes to attract workers, mature learners, in particular women, and the disabled, who were denied access to higher education in the past' (DoE 2001). It further noted that there was a 'large potential pool of recruits' indicated by the 1996 census data: 1.6 million adults with a school leaving certificate were then in the 25–39 age group.

However, the NPHE was finalized during the period of a rapid increase of total higher education student numbers, and concerns emerged in government and bodies like the Higher Education Quality Committee (HEQC) about the effects of this growth on quality of provision, and the impact on throughput rates. One response by government has been to review growth rates and to insist that in the short term, at least, the system focused on retention (including quality of provision and improvement of throughput) and not growth. More recently there has been a shift in this approach because of the political concern of the growing numbers of school leavers who are not in employment and not studying. Pressure to expand access for young people in particular is therefore an urgent political issue and can be witnessed in the long queues of prospective, expectant students snaking around many higher education institutions in January 2011 at the start of the academic year.

So what about the adult learners? Buchler *et al.* (2007) found in a study conducted in 2004 and 2005, that the percentage of adult learners in the system was far higher than anticipated with over 50 per cent of students (80 per cent being at undergraduate levels) who were over 23 years of age. However, as they argued, access to higher education in large numbers was not sufficient, as adult learners also raised pedagogical challenges that needed to be confronted more fully by HEIs. This was an important issue for society, because it spoke to the question of whose and what knowledge was privileged, and how accumulated experience was used as part of collective social knowledge. They argued that to attain access, equity and success for adult learners in higher education, deep transformation was required from the micro teaching/learning relationships, to the meso institutional cultures, to the macro provincial and national environments.

The study, through detailed interrogation of three case studies of higher education institutions, found great unevenness in the recognition and treatment of adult learners. I turn now to one case study, which also formed part of that study, to shed light on contemporary trends.

Case study: University of Western Cape (UWC)

UWC is a historically black university that was founded in 1960 to fulfil the needs for 'coloured bureaucrats and professionals' to service the apartheid political vision. In 2010 it had about 17,000 students with a student profile of primarily black, poor and working-class students, nearly 60 per cent being women. From the beginning, offering evening classes to working students was part of its mandate.

An analysis of UWC as a lifelong learning institution has been undertaken previously (Walters 2005), where I used the key categories identified in the Cape Town Statement on Characteristic Elements of Lifelong Learning Higher Education Institutions (DLL 2001). I do not intend rehearsing the arguments here, but rather reflect briefly on some trends since then. I do this with the hope that this may well have resonance for some institutions in similar economic contexts elsewhere.

To recap briefly, the six categories from the Cape Town Statement indicate a systemic awareness of the interconnections between the macro environment, the meso organizational context and the micro cognitive and affective learning interactions. As noted previously, a lifelong learning framework forces our gaze both inwards towards individual and organizational learning and outwards towards relationships in the broader society (Volbrecht and Walters 2000).

In a recent brochure on lifelong learning at UWC the following highlights are given as worthy of note: approximately 45,000 students have enrolled at UWC as part-time students over the last 20 years; the Division for Lifelong Learning, which is a small advocacy, service and research unit working across all faculties, was established in 1999 to promote the lifelong learning mission of the institution; the Senate Lifelong Learning Committee, chaired by the Rector and initially other senior leadership representatives, was established in 2005; the recognition of prior learning (RPL) services to thousands of students through advice, counselling and the portfolio development course, and is seen as leading the way nationally; over 200 registered and quality assured continuing education courses are run annually; dedicated services to the part-time students, who make up about 20 per cent of the total number, have increased through an innovative After Hours Study Zone; three general graduate attributes have been adopted for all students, one of which is for all students to acquire the capabilities of becoming lifelong learners; and lifelong learning awards are made annually at the graduation ceremony to four categories which include inspirational students who are studying part-time, come through alternative access routes, or are over 50 years old (DLL 2010b).

While there has been significant progress in embedding a philosophy and approach to lifelong learning at the university, the understanding of what this means continues to shift and change. For purposes of this discussion, I will highlight three key tensions in ongoing support for adult learners:

1 Mainstreaming of lifelong learning to include all students;
2 Blurring of the lines between part- and full-time students;
3 Exploring and expanding 'flexible provision'.

As mentioned above, the political lever in the higher education system at present is the large proportion of young people who are unemployed or not in education or training. They constitute a 'political time-bomb', therefore great political pressure is being exerted to absorb as many of them as possible into the universities. Given that there are few intermediate institutions in the post-secondary school system to absorb the students, they want to access the universities. This poses major problems for institutions like UWC, who have most students coming from HIV and AIDS saturated communities, and from poor and working-class schools. These schools are not able to prepare students for university. The government, in turn, is not funding universities adequately for the academic development and support that is required to assist them to succeed. With the pressure of numbers from the schools, there is a tendency amongst some faculties to argue to discontinue their part-time or after-hours classes. As it is primarily part-time and adult learners who attend these classes, including those who have come through alternative access routes, this has major implications for the future provision for adult learners.

Simultaneously, there are interventions to strengthen the quality of teaching and learning at the university and in the system more broadly. This is partly because of the new funding formula, which is emphasizing efficiency and successful throughput which can work against the idea of part-time adult learners coming in and out of learning over a longer time period. The assumption can reasonably be made that the perceptions of the implementation of the funding formula are in fact working against the lifelong learning intentions of the policy.

The UWC teaching and learning strategy includes the introduction of 'graduate attributes' for all students. These relate to 'scholarship and the development of a critical attitude to knowledge'; 'critical citizenship and the social good'; and 'lifelong learning which describes an attitude or stance towards themselves' (UWC Charter of Graduate Attributes, November 2009). The introduction of the graduate attribute of 'lifelong learning' has opened a space for staff and students across the campus to engage more fully with the concept of lifelong learning. For many, it had previously been perceived as the concern of adult learners or part-time students. While this greater openness is welcomed by the staff of DLL, the small unit faces the dilemma of how far to be drawn into support for the full-time and mainly younger students, potentially jeopardizing the amount of support it can offer the more marginalized adult learners.

At the same time, there is a gradual blurring of the lines between 'full-time' and 'part-time' students. On the one hand there is ambiguity in the definitions of 'full-time' and 'part-time' as they are categories that are self-selected by students, and the motivation for categorizing themselves as one or the other is driven by a complex set of economic and social factors, for example relating to access to accommodation, insurance cover or student financing. It cannot be used as a reliable indicator of the study load of the students, the time of day they study or whether or not they are in full-time or part-time work.

In addition, increasingly full-time students are attending the after-hours classes. While there is a high correlation between being a part-time student and studying during after-hours, an evaluation of the after-hours booking statistics of 2008 shows that up to 30.4 per cent of the classes during after hours are listed as 'full-time'. This emphasizes the confusion that exists in the naming of courses as 'part-time' or 'full-time', and the ambiguity around this continues, although it has been pointed out on numerous occasions that it is the students not the courses that are full-time or part-time. The after-hours teaching programmes are offered from Monday to Friday between 16h30 and 21h00, on weekends and during dedicated block periods in academic holidays (DLL 2010c).

During 2010, a proposal to undertake action research into a more systematic development of 'flexible provision' for the university was adopted (DLL 2010c). Why this interest in flexible learning provision? In recent years there have been significant advances in South Africa in the development of technology, as has been the case in most countries of the world. While internet access is significantly less in lower- and middle-income countries compared with the highly developed economies (Walters 2008), there is rapid progress in becoming connected. These advances have provided new opportunities for teaching and learning, but have also created new demands on institutions to prepare students for working and learning in a rapidly changing world. In addition the boundaries between creators and sources of knowledge are continually being blurred. As in many parts of the world, students are changing with those coming straight from school to UWC belonging to a generation loosely called 'generation y', the millennium generation, or the 'net generation'. What separates this group from previous generations is that they are familiar with the internet and all the gadgets that accompany it. Cell phones, iPods and other electronic devices are regarded as basic staples of existence for many of them – for example, 85 per cent of South Africans across all social classes have access to cell phones. Simultaneously UWC also attracts students from previous generations of learning/teaching environments; students who are used to 'chalk and talk' learning and for whom knowledge is accessed on their own from books.

The interest in 'flexible provision' relates also to increasing pressure on the use of the physical space. In 2010 the full-time numbers at UWC increased by 2,438 students, creating tremendous pressures on the teaching capacity, particularly in the Economic Management Sciences (EMS) and Natural Science Faculty. EMS has a 1st year Information system group of 1,200 students. In order to accommodate these large numbers the first 800 students attended the module in the 1st semester and 400 students attend in the second semester. Science serves students across faculties and has to teach groups of similar sizes, outstripping the capacity of the newly built Life Sciences Building. The Dean of Science proposed to change the length of the lecture period and the length of the term in order to gain seating capacity by freeing up space in the timetable. The Science faculty already uses all lunch hours and extends the hours of practical sessions until 19h00. They are aware of the problems that students face with public transport which stops after 19h00, so the late afternoon slots will mainly be filled by students from the campus-based residences. Without additional, mainly human resources, the already overstretched Science faculty will struggle to deliver.

So this large increase in full-time students has posed venue capacity problems and necessitates a rethink on how the facilities are to be used more efficiently. As mentioned previously, this pressure puts the after-hours provision under threat. The paradox is that this is being considered at the same time as 'flexible provision' is being discussed. Clearly, the after-hours classes are an important form of flexible provision. In order to keep the 'doors of learning open', the scope of promoting the full use of the hours available (including from 16h30 onwards, weekends, block courses, third semester) has to be explored as well as the full range of modes of delivery (face-to-face to mixed mode, including e-learning).

The blurring of lines between various constructs is leading to increasing numbers of scholars theorizing 'flexibility' – what it means; why the concept has such currency; and what the implications are for understandings of our changing practices. There are debates about 'knowledge wars', which were highlighted by Fenwick (2010), who uses actor network theory (ANT), cultural historical activity theory (CHAT), and complexity theory, to discuss and theorize the 'blurry lines' between concepts of 'full and part-time study'; 'traditional and non-traditional students'; 'distance and face-to-face teaching'; 'day time or after hours study'; what it means to 'work'/'not work'; whose knowledge counts, when, where, and in whose interests; 'open source' versus proprietary approaches to information and knowledge and so on. Lifelong learning is right in the middle of these theoretical developments. These are generative theoretical developments which move beyond what Fenwick refers to as 'tired theories'.

In summary, the picture for adult learners at UWC is mixed – it is riddled with contradictory pushes and pulls. There have been important gains in the embedding of a lifelong learning philosophy and approach so that it is becoming more mainstream, however in the process, the future of quality support for adult learners is fragile and it is reliant on ongoing advocacy and support from a small group of champions in the institution.

In order to update ourselves on how far this is replicated in other parts of the country, we at the DLL undertook a preliminary study into the intended or unintended consequences of the Higher Education Qualifications Framework (HEQF) for adult learners (DLL 2010a). It is to the outcomes of this study that I now turn.

But by the grace of champions?

The purpose of the preliminary study was to investigate intended and unintended consequences of the HEQF for adult learners and to catalogue any existing prejudicial factors with a view to making recommendations on how to better support adult or non-traditional students. It set out to capture a schematic history of the development of the HEQF, to analyse those documents and catalogue findings in relation to adult learners, and to identify case studies as examples of 'typical' programmes for adult learners as 'test' cases. The study involved perusal of key documents and interviews with various people who were involved in or related to the construction of the HEQF, or are working a lot with adult learners in Higher Education Institutions (HEIs).

In summary, the key findings were:

1 The majority of prejudicial features relating to the HEQF are not in the framework as such but in the way individual academics and administrators interpret and seek to enact it.
2 There are no incentives or mechanisms for encouraging and supporting institutions that attempt to address issues outside the norm, such as

part-time study and working adult students. Within universities, part-time studies are for the most part the 'poor cousin'.
3 As long as RPL is an unfunded mandate within the system, many potential adult learners will not be able to access HE with or without the HEQF.
4 There are some serious problems and anomalies with regard to credit accumulation and transfer within and across HEIs.
5 The equity or social justice dimension of programmes seems to be reliant on particular champions who work hard, against the odds, to transform their practices and support others who do likewise. Even if the rhetoric of mission statements of HEIs include a commitment to transformation and social justice there is a reluctance to offer financial support and incentives to such 'champions'; indeed, many confront what they describe as an 'uphill battle'. Generally, there seems to be a shift away from addressing social justice by paving the way for adults to study at HEIs, towards what can be interpreted as a 'financial efficiency model', i.e. 'time to degree' has become central to the funding formula.
6 More research is needed to gain a more accurate picture of what the costs and benefits for adult learners are to the HE system, the society and the individuals, from multiple perspectives, of providing successful access and progression through higher education.

(DLL 2010a)

These findings are not unexpected, given the dominant economic paradigm within which the country and the world at large is operating; the political pressures coming from the large number of poor, unemployed, and poorly educated youth; and the 'knowledge wars' over whose knowledge and what knowledge counts as really useful.

The South African situation is certainly not unique. However, as suggested above, it is reasonable to assume that within low- and middle-income countries, the spaces for encouraging and supporting adult learners to fully embrace higher education opportunities can easily close down in the face of resource constraints, and political pressures from the large proportions of younger age groups in such societies. However, with poverty and health issues like that of HIV and AIDS, a lifelong learning philosophy and approach is very relevant.

The roles of the 'champions' in the system are therefore crucial to holding and incrementally enlarging and transforming the higher education space for lifelong learners (in the full sense of the term). The scholar-activists must therefore support and encourage them to continue against difficult odds and, as Watson (2010) in a Presidential Address to the Society for Research into Higher Education (SRHE) urged, be simultaneously more humble and assertive. We have to speak truth to power, but we also have to speak truth to ourselves. Our analyses can be of use to those who have to make difficult political decisions, including distributional decisions that affect our daily lives. We should also become less precious, less fatalistic and more self-critical in seeking to understand the communities in which we are essentially participant observers.

Notes

1 Refer to World Bank definition and Action Plan for MIC in Africa, www.worldbank.org sourced 26 April 2011.
2 This preliminary research has been done through the Division for Lifelong Learning (DLL) at the University of Western Cape (UWC), with valuable input from members of the Adult Learning Working Group of the Cape Higher Education Consortium (CHEC), with financial support from the South African Qualifications Authority (SAQA). It was conducted by Professor Astrid Von Kotze during September–November 2010, in close consultation with the author.

References

Bourgeois, E., Duke, C., Guyot, J.L. and Merrill, B. (1999) *The Adult University*, Buckingham: SRHE and Open University Press.

Breier, M. and Mabizela, M. (2008) 'Higher education', in A. Kraak and K. Press (eds) *Human Resources Development 2008*, 278–299, Cape Town, HSRC Press.

Buchler, M., Castle, J., Osman, R. and Walters, S. (2007) 'Equity, access and success: adult learners in public higher education'. in Council on Higher Education, *Review of Higher Education in South Africa*, 124–156, Council on Higher Education, Pretoria.

CHE, Council on Higher Education (2009) 'Higher Education Monitor: The state of higher education in South Africa', *Higher Education Monitor*, 8, October, Pretoria.

Cosser, M. (2010) 'Creating new education and training pathways: How do we expand and differentiate post-schooling opportunities?' in *Review of Education, Skills Development and Innovation*, November, 4–6, Human Sciences Research Council (HSRC), Pretoria.

DLL, Division for Lifelong Learning (2001) *The Cape Town Statement: The characteristics of a lifelong learning higher education institution*, University of Western Cape, Bellville, South Africa.

DLL, Division for Lifelong Learning (2010a) *The HEQF and adult learners: But by the grace of champions in Higher Education Institutions? Questions and concerns: Research Report*, University of Western Cape, Bellville, South Africa.

DLL, Division for Lifelong Learning (2010b) *Lifelong learning at UWC Brochure*, University of Western Cape, Bellville, South Africa.

DLL, Division for Lifelong Learning (2010c) *Clearing the ground: Towards understanding and implementing flexible learning/teaching provision at UWC: Update Report on Research*, October, University of Western Cape, Bellville, South Africa.

DoE, Department of Education (1995) *South African Qualification Authority Act.* No 1521 4. Online. Available HTTP <http://education.pwv.gov.za/content/documents/236.pdf>.

DoE, Department of Education (1997) Education White Paper No.3: A programme for the transformation of higher education. *Government Gazette* 386 (18207). Online. Available at <http://education.pwv.gov.za/content/documents/178.pdf>.

DoE, Department of Education (1997/1999/2000/2002) *Higher Education Act 101 of 1997.* Online. Available HTTP <http://education.pwv.gov.za/content/documents/65.pdf>.

DoE, Department of Education (2001) *National Plan for Higher Education,* Pretoria, South Africa.

DoE, Department of Education (2007) 'The Higher Education Qualifications Framework', Government Notice No. 928. *Government Gazette,* 30353.

Fenwick, T. (2010) *'Knowledge wars': Let the river run,* University of Western Cape Vice Chancellor's Julius Nyerere Lecture on Lifelong Learning, October.

Lugg, R. (2009) 'Making different equal? Rifts and ruptures in state and policy: The NQF in South Africa', in L. Cooper and S. Walters (eds) *Learning/work: Turning work and learning inside out,* HSRC Press, Cape Town, South Africa.

Parker, B. and Walters, S. (2008) 'Competency based training and national qualifications frameworks: Insights from South Africa', *Asian Pacific Education Review* 2008, 9 (1): 70–79.

Schuller, T. and Watson, D. (2009) *Learning through life,* NIACE, Leicester, UK.

Steinberg, J. (2008) *The 3 letter plague,* Cape Town: Jonathan Ball.

UWC (2010) *Equity, access and success of adult learners in universities in South Africa: What still needs to be done?* Submission to the Summit on Higher Education Transformation, 22 April, Ministry of Higher Education and Training.

Volbrecht, T. and Walters, S. (2000) 'Re-imagining a picture: Higher education in lifelong learning', in *Adult Education and Development Journal* No 55 IIZ/DVV, Hamburg, Germany.

Walters, S. (2005) 'Realising a lifelong learning higher education institution', in P. Sutherland and J. Crowther (eds) *Lifelong learning: Concepts and contexts,* Routledge Falmer, UK.

Walters, S. (2008) *South African National Report of the Development and State of the Art of Adult Learning and Education,* June 2008, Research Report for Commission on Lifelong Learning, NIACE, UK.

Walters, S. (2010) 'The planet will not survive if it's not a learning planet: Sustainable development within learning through life', *International Journal of Lifelong Education,* 29 (4): 427–436.

Watson, D. (2010) *Higher education through the age of austerity,* Presidential Address for the Society for Research into Higher Education (SRHE) Annual Conference, 14 December.

Chapter 15

Brazil

Lifelong learning and the role of the university in Brazil: some reflections

Ana Canen

Introduction

This chapter analyses how lifelong learning, as developed in the context of universities in Brazil, has been interpreted in recent Brazilian educational policies. Our particular focus is the final *Conferência Nacional de Educação* (National Conference for Education) document (CONAE 2010), which is the basis for the Brazilian government's ten-year *Plano Nacional de Educação* (National Educational Plan), or PNE, which is supposed to guide the national educational system from 2011 to 2021.

The PNE argues that lifelong learning as an explicit policy paradigm is still missing in Latin America, but lifelong learning does exist in various forms (Carnoy and Wagner 2005) as technical training for out-of-school youth, in-firm training, university level adult distance education (teachers for example), and as other forms of continuing education (mainly for adults with higher education). Therefore, it is a valuable exercise to analyse what opportunities are available for lifelong learning in the rapidly growing higher education system (with the focus on the 'university') of a large economy such as Brazil, whether lifelong learning is expanding within that system, even if it is taking place in an implicit, indirect, and rather fragmented way, and where the potential for further expansion lies in higher education.

To do this analysis, we propose a framework for understanding the role of lifelong learning in which the university is characterized as a multicultural organization geared towards promoting lifelong learning within and outside its geographical limits, particularly in the context of highly multicultural and unequal societies as in Latin America. Two questions move the chapter: Given the university's current role in lifelong learning, what could be a transformative framework for lifelong learning in that current role? To what extent do the university's fragmented activities that are not visibly lifelong learning oriented have the potential to serve as lifelong learning under a broader view of lifelong learning? The chapter suggests that the university still has some way to go for generating and boosting lifelong learning as a goal with culturally diverse students. The study is relevant comparatively insomuch as it can contribute to the debates about the role of the university for the development of lifelong learning in a new, Brazilian/Latin American model, which hopefully may contribute to the debates about lifelong learning in other multicultural countries throughout the world.

Lifelong learning in recent Brazilian policies

How have universities helped or hindered lifelong learning in a culturally diverse environment and student body as found in Latin America and particularly in Brazil? What specifically is lifelong learning and what could lifelong learning be in a Latin American context? Can lifelong learning work in Latin America in the same way as in European countries, for example? How could lifelong learning work in a framework that actually takes diverse cultures into account?

In order to answer those questions, it is interesting to provide a cursory view of Higher Education (HE) in Brazil. Maculan (2010) points to the coexistence of public HE institutions (government supported, at the federal, state and city levels), and private ones (non-profit, such as religious, philanthropic and communitarian; and for-profit ones). Also, HE institutions in Brazil can be classified as: universities, university centers, isolated higher education schools, technology higher education centers, and integrated higher education schools. It should be noted that universities – particularly the government supported ones (federal, state and city ones), as well as Catholic private, non-profit ones – have been associated with the role of knowledge production through a strong research-oriented perspective. Furthermore, those institutions have also been recognized for a strong social commitment translated in initiatives geared towards linking their activities to societal needs. In that sense, universities should arguably be the natural sites for the development of lifelong learning in Brazil, and therefore they are the focus of the present study.

Considering that Brazil's economy has been steadily growing, the need for a skilled workforce and the ensuing key role of continuing and lifelong education has been highlighted both in the press and in scholarly debates. However, when talking about continuing and lifelong education in Latin America and, more specifically, Brazil, the expression lifelong learning seems to continue to be an invisible concept. It is associated with adult education and therefore reduced to a separate line of action or goal rather than an embracing category (CONFITEA 2009). In fact, as claimed in the CONFITEA document, expressions such as 'adult education' and 'continuing education' seem to be the most familiar in the region, even though a series of international conferences and scholarly research have systematically pointed to the relevance of focusing on learning, rather than on teaching, which is the underlying idea in the word 'education'. One of the possible reasons that the lifelong learning terminology appears to be more widespread in English-speaking Caribbean countries than in Latin America may have to do with the fact that 'lifelong learning has not been properly and consistently translated into Spanish and Portuguese, where the equivalent is a long phrase, and learning continues to be interchangeable with education' (CONFITEA 2009, p. 22).

Terminology in discussing adult opportunities for acquiring further knowledge is also an issue in an important recent document of the CONAE (National Conference for Education in Brazil) (2010). This document defines goals and rationales for educational principles that undergird the upcoming ten-year National Educational Plan (2011–2021). It attempts to develop the groundwork for an integrated and coherent Brazilian National System of Education. CONAE does not use the expression 'lifelong learning' (*educação permanente*) in any of the six axes around which it is structured – namely the role of the State in ensuring the right to a quality education; education quality, democratic management and evaluation; preparation and valuing educational professionals; educational financing and social control; and social justice, education and work: inclusion, diversity and equality. If, however, the key words are changed to 'continuing education' instead of lifelong learning, the document highlights some sentences referring to the relevance of distance education courses to provide for the continuing education of teachers and other educational actors. In addition, if the key words are changed to 'adult education', about ten pages are dedicated to stressing the importance of providing adult education that ensures dignity, citizenship and the valuing of diversity for that group of Brazilians who are unqualified or lacking in formal education credentials and who therefore deserve a compensatory 'second chance' educational opportunity. Looking at the CONFITEA and CONAE documents, it therefore seems to be clear that no framework exists in Brazil for lifelong learning. Basic and foundational skills and competencies are the most stressed target in Brazil and Latin America, which seems to underlie the trend towards thinking about lifelong learning as the acquisition of a 'second chance' for educationally unqualified marginalized groups.

Such an emphasis is understandable, given some worrying educational indicators. In fact, Schwartzman (2004, p. 13) argues that 'the main problems with Brazilian education are those related to the quality and retention of students in the public systems'. The author points to 'inequity in the access to good quality education, which affects mostly the poorer segments of the population', as well as 'the large number of persons who leave education before getting their certificates, without acquiring the knowledge and skills they were supposed to have'. As a result, 'a huge waste of resources [has been] spent on keeping in schools older students who should not be there' (ibid.).

In line with those comments, it is important to note that even though access to primary education has been universalised in Brazil, the same cannot be said concerning secondary and tertiary education, which are characterized by high drop-out rates, and in the case of tertiary education, limited access, particularly for children of families in the lowest 60 per cent of income (CONFITEA 2009). According to the World Bank (2010) report, Brazil has only one quarter of the relevant population group attending a higher education institute, which is reflected in the very small proportion of the labour force with tertiary level qualifications (8 per cent). The report goes on to argue that access to universities, especially the most prestigious ones, 'is heavily skewed against students from low income families [and] there are also serious regional disparities' (World Bank 2010). If anything, the World Bank greatly understates the problem. Almost 80 per cent of students in Brazil attend private higher education institutions, which all charge fees, many of which are for profit, and most of which are of low quality, although many are rather efficient from an economic standpoint. Drop-out rates from all higher education institutions are high, and much higher for private universities.

As stated before, the primary and secondary education system also suffers from severe quality problems, including the fact that most (new) teachers are poorly trained in low-quality higher education teacher training programmes, and that there are severe shortages in important teaching fields such as mathematics. Poor-quality primary and secondary education results in weak academic preparation of students relative to the academic requirements of most public supported (free of tuition) universities' entrance exams. The lower the socioeconomic background of students, the more likely that they will have poorly prepared teachers and weaker preparation. This forces the mass of secondary graduates into the fee-paying higher education system, where most lower-income students cannot afford to pay. Despite higher entrance requirements, a higher fraction of lower-income students attends public universities, but even so, 60 per cent of private university and more than 50 per cent of public university students are from the top income quintile. More than half of the students attending public universities attended private secondary schools. The CONAE (2010) document itself seems to recognize that fact, by stressing that access to universities in Brazil is still biased towards the mostly academically prepared (and high income) groups, to the detriment of the majority of the population.

Such an unequal educational scenario seems to be the basis for a type of lifelong learning associated mainly with the concept of providing a remedial, compensatory second chance of formal education for young and older adults in Brazil and throughout Latin America (CONFITEA 2009). This concept equates lifelong learning with 'adult education'. On the other hand, the job training perspective seems to get increased attention in Latin America as an alternative economic model that generates alternative approaches to education and training linked to production, commercialization, barter and other income-generation activities (CONFITEA report 2009), even though it goes unnoticed in the Brazilian CONAE (2010) document. Indeed, the CONFITEA (2009) report gives some illustrations in Brazil, citing the

'Fishing Letters Programme' (*Programa Pescando Letras*), which provides literacy for artisanal fishermen and women, and the 'Literacy Inclusion Project' (*Projeto Alfa-Inclusão*), provided by the Ministry of Education and the Bank of Brazil Foundation, which links literacy teaching and training to entrepreneurial activity with a view to generating income and sustainability in rural and marginal urban communities.

In addition to those initiatives targeted at low-income and educationally marginalized groups, the trend toward on-the-job lifelong learning at the other end of the educational spectrum, namely for higher education graduates working in organizations, is also noteworthy. Lifelong learning for graduates focuses on tailor-made educational and training packages for specific job needs, generally following diagnostic data regarding skills and competencies needed to improve their work performance. However, in the CONAE (2010) document, the 'on the job training perspective' is only mentioned either in connection with continuing education for teachers, or when referring to vocational perspectives in formal schooling, in which the fostering of partnerships between secondary schools and enterprises is highlighted so as to provide students with internship placements and opportunities that likely put them in touch with the real world of work. Other programmes and dimensions related to job training and the potential role of universities in that training are overlooked in the CONAE document.

What then would be the role in this seemingly 'lifelong learning-free' environment for the university in promoting lifelong learning? If we were to take only the narrow view as discussed before and gleaned from the analysed documents, the role of the university would be highly limited in Brazil and Latin America. In the context described, the university would contribute (i) to preparing teachers to teach in adult education, in order to promote the development of core competencies and skills, particularly in basic literacy and numeracy; (ii) to preparing pedagogues to work in organizations and enterprises coordinating continuing training programmes in those organizations, as expressed in the National Guidelines for Pedagogical Courses; and (iii) to promoting continuing education programmes in partnership with organizations and enterprises, as well as with federal, state and district authorities in order to provide for broadening and enhancing knowledge, competencies, and skills of teachers, school managers and organizational employees in general. Such courses have indeed been offered under different formats, structured in flexible ways, generally for those working in graduate education and for organizational employees.

However, universities should see themselves, and be seen as, sources of continuing education and training beyond this more narrow definition of lifelong learning. I discuss the extent to which such a broadening of perspective could take place in Brazil and in Latin America in the next section.

Potential contributions of university systems towards a future lifelong learning framework

Our analysis of major documents defining educational policies in Brazil reinforces the notion that a dichotomized approach exists to lifelong learning in Brazil, confirming Carnoy and Wagner's (2005) study, which concluded that

> The main argument of the Brazil case study is that lifelong learning is an 'invisible non-system,' that is, it is not counted as part of the formal education system, nor taken into account at all in national statistics, nor taken into account for public policy purposes in terms of labour, education, or social policy, nor subject to any central coordination. Thus, a lifelong learning system exists, and its potential clients—employers, entrepreneurs, and the unemployed—know where and how to look for it, but it is very difficult to assess for research, planning, evaluation or other public policy purposes.

That also seems to hold for Latin American countries in general, where lifelong learning, or even a framework of adult learning, has not been the focus of policies in the region, which continue to focus on adult education and on literacy acquisition (CONFITEA 2009). Indeed, the Government of Brazil needs to elaborate a lifelong learning strategy and qualifications framework to establish better linkages and bridges among all providers of education and training services (World Bank report 2010, p. 4).

Moving beyond explicit discourses in order to try and gauge lifelong learning possibilities embedded in university activities, breaking down these activities into various categories could arguably tell a more complete story about how the university in Brazil, and more generally in Latin America, could contribute to a lifelong learning framework. This way of analysing this potential role for the university should not be seen as an attempt to see a visible system of lifelong learning where none exists. Rather, it intends to identify possible ways that the university can be involved in a possible coherent future lifelong learning framework that could arguably make for a more integrated approach to education in Brazil. Building on that view, three areas seem to be key in understanding potential university contributions towards lifelong learning, as discussed in the CONAE (2010) document and drawing on anecdotal evidence in Brazilian universities' bylaws and other documentation.

The first area refers to *access to university in Brazil*. Schwartzman (2004, p. 30) suggests that Brazilian higher education 'should expand much more than the current level of less than 10% participation of the relevant age group', adding that 'this can only be done through continuous diversification, pluralism, deregulation, and the creation of mechanisms to curtail credentialism and stimulate quality and pertinence' (p. 30).

In that sense, some programmes have been developed by government in order to provide more equitable access to university, among them ProUni and individual public university affirmative action programmes that have created entrance quotas for black, indigenous and poor students who attend public secondary schools. The ProUni (*Programa Universidade para Todos* – 'University for All') aims to place academically qualified low-income students into private tertiary education institutions, after they have been approved in a national end-of-secondary examination (ENEM). They receive scholarships depending on the economic level of their family. The private institutions where they are placed are benefited in two ways: they expand their enrolment with subsidized fee-paying students who otherwise would not be able to pay; and private, for-profit institutions get tax exemptions in return for accepting scholarship students. The public university affirmative action programmes vary from university to university, but in general they benefit students who attend public secondary schools and are members of demographic groups that have lower levels of education and lower income, such as blacks, mulattos, and indigenous people.

The ProUni programme has produced mixed feelings in Brazil: on the one hand, it has been praised as a step forward in equalizing opportunity to learn in that it allows higher numbers from under-represented groups to reach university where previously they would not have been able to. As argued by Schwartzman (2004, p. 30), in Brazil the private sector 'is already responsible for two-thirds of the enrolment, and it would be impossible to reverse this situation in the foreseeable future'. On the other hand, critics argue that the resources given to private institutions could instead be shifted towards public institutions to increase their capacity to increase enrolment. As mentioned before, a high fraction of the enrolment increase at the tertiary level in the 2000s has been in private institutions, so that there is an argument to shift the increase back to public institutions. Yet, since, on average, private institutions cost less per student, it could be argued that the government is wise to contribute the much smaller subsidy needed to provide access for low-income students to private institutions.

Affirmative action in the form of quotas for black, indigenous, and poor students gives them an incentive to do reasonably well on a public university examination and helps them gain access to a university education. According to the CONAE (2010) document, only 12.1 per cent of the population aged between 18 and 24 years old attends university, and in the last entering group (2010), almost 80 per cent attend private institutions. CONAE points out that whites represent 52 per cent of the Brazilian population, but are 73 per cent of higher education students; those of mixed race represent 41 per cent of the general population, but only 20 per cent of higher education students; whereas those who identify themselves as blacks represent about 6 per cent of the population but only less than 4 per cent of higher education students.

The CONAE (2010) document supports affirmative action for public universities geared towards students that studied in public schools, developing quotas that conform to the proportion of black and indigenous groups in each Brazilian state. It suggests that affirmative action should be seen as a temporary remedy, recommending that such programmes be limited to ten years. The autonomy guaranteed by the Brazilian Constitution (1988) to public universities in Brazil means that any of these recommendations are not compulsory, leaving it up to each institution to decide if and how they want to implement these programmes. Indeed, as mentioned, affirmative action programmes have to be implemented on the initiative of individual universities, and cannot be prescribed by the government as State policy.

Again, this policy recommendation has been producing mixed feelings and contentious debates, particularly because Brazil views itself ideologically as a mixed race society, and it is often difficult to tell who is black or miscegenated and therefore who is entitled to benefit from the quota. Some universities have been adopting a mix of race and social and economic criteria, but even then with results that are far from producing a consensus. The other typical problem with affirmative action policies is that the drop-out rates of students admitted under the programme tend to be higher than those of students who get in without benefit of extra points. Many affirmative action admissions arrive at the university with poor foundational skills. Therefore, in a lifelong learning framework, the equity programmes for access should be accompanied by other initiatives that should ensure both financial and academic support, which public universities are not always prepared to offer, unless they receive extra government funding to provide compensatory programmes.

A second area that is fundamental for a lifelong learning perspective in higher education refers to *curriculum and pedagogy*. The CONAE (2010) document emphasizes the need for a national curricular framework that ensures the learning of basic cultural, artistic and scientific national and regional values. Such a view has been informing the national curricular guidelines that have been issued for various programmes in the university. Also, a national curricular framework seems to underlie the moves towards evaluation policies that have stressed the need to assess higher education in terms not only of the diverse projects that characterize such differentiated institutions, but also the degree to which students have been prepared in what government and career specialists deem as the core skills and competencies to be delivered by the university. That aspect is emphasized in the CONAE (2010) document. It reinforces the role of national evaluation policies aligned with the national curriculum framework of schools and HE, in order to assess the efficiency and efficacy of those systems vis-à-vis their curriculum development.

This national perspective seems to be nuanced in that the CONAE (2010) document stresses the need to ground curriculum practices and pedagogy in cultural diversity (the document talks about education tailored for rural areas, indigenous populations, and so forth). Therefore, it highlights the need for the university to prepare teachers to deal effectively and competently with cultural plurality. In fact, the document proposes curricular initiatives that should expose students to Brazil's rich ethnocultural diversity and the history which produced this diversity. It suggests that students should understand ethnic and racial relationships in Brazil and purge themselves of any racial prejudices. Such a curricular perspective may be relevant to lifelong learning, insomuch as it takes into account the need to adapt national guidelines to the diversity of students in Brazilian society (including those from marginalized and under-represented gender, race, and ethnic identities, among others). Hence, it may arguably contribute to reducing academic failure and drop-outs in the university, apart from making students from different cultural and ethnic backgrounds feel valued as they see their histories and identities represented in curriculum and pedagogy. However, the way in which core curricular content, competencies, and skills listed in the national curricular guidelines could be linked to cultural diversity is not mentioned, leaving a tension between the intention to make curriculum and pedagogy more flexible in a lifelong learning perspective, and the evaluation of the university and its students based on the national, homogeneous curricular guidelines.

In addition, when considering lifelong learning, the flexibility in curriculum development and delivery is a key dimension, providing as it does room for diverse students of different ages, interests and cultures to frame their curricular choices accordingly, with differentiated certifications according to the chosen courses. The CONAE (2010) document consolidates this view of plural paths in the university that could challenge rigid undergraduate course structures and provide for short-term 'technological courses', averaging two years study, aimed at preparing future professionals for work in diverse fields. It should be noted that in Brazil it is the private higher education sector that seems to be more active in embracing these plural paths; public universities are resistant, valuing more traditional undergraduate courses.

It should also be noted that whereas ethnic identities seem to be the main focus of the CONAE (2010) document when considering issues related to curriculum and pedagogy geared towards cultural diversity, it is silent with respect to older adults or those with other (marginalized) cultural identities wishing to enhance their skills, knowledge, and competencies in a lifelong learning perspective. There is no mention of curricular perspectives, pedagogy or any other educational measures to meet those needs. Again, the CONAE (2010) document suggests the concept of adult education as a compensatory programme geared towards those that are illiterate or that failed to complete their formal schooling in earlier phases of their lives. That issue needs to be confronted, particularly considering that there are already some public universities (for example, in Rio de Janeiro) where courses for the so-called 'third age' are flourishing. This programme is known as 'university for the third age', configuring an encouraging although still isolated path towards a possible enlarged lifelong learning framework for higher education in Brazil.

Further, the CONAE (2010) document explicitly notes that Brazil is a multiethnic and unequal society and that a national system of education should prioritize the eradication of prejudices and discrimination, as well as guaranteeing educational equity and increased access to higher education. Indeed, it clearly states that higher education should be recognized as a social and public right, as well as a universal human right, therefore reinforcing the role of the State in guaranteeing its provision. Indirectly, then, the CONAE (2010) document seems to contribute to a possible lifelong learning framework for university when it claims that

> [University] expansion with quality, and its commitment towards society should underlie policies in the area ... the need to promote equitable access to higher education of under-represented groups in night courses, as well as in day or whole day courses (the latter mostly attended by students from elite groups) should be grounded in the enlargement of state and federal universities and the construction of new ones in the interior of Brazil ... as well as the guarantee that less economically privileged students should be the object of national plans for assistance and affirmative action.
>
> (CONAE 2010, p. 74)

A third area that is key to the contribution of the university to lifelong learning refers to *extension and continuing education courses* it provides to organizations, State and district authorities, schools and other groups as a token of its social relevancy. Such courses are flexible, and since they have been developed in different formats by different faculty members in diverse departments in the universities, they arguably represent an important dimension of the university towards a lifelong learning framework. Such an extension perspective has allowed universities to undertake partnerships with organizations, both governmental and non-governmental, as well as public and private institutions and district and State educational authorities. For example, courses for teacher professional development in a multicultural perspective have been successfully developed (Canen and Santos 2009). Universities have also developed programmes geared towards researching logistics and management in organizations (Canen and Canen 2005). Such an extension perspective has been compulsory for universities, which have been moving into that area with new paradigms that bring a social relevancy component to their activities, by making them interact with society through these programmes that involve groups outside the university.

This area is not mentioned in the CONAE (2010) document. CONAE does not seem to recognize its value and its possible impact on greater equity in access to the university, especially since some of the projects for continuing education include professional development of primary and secondary school teachers and managers, which are fundamental in raising the academic capacity of public schooling. Considering that affirmative action is being viewed as a temporary solution to the academic and economic disadvantage suffered by certain groups in Brazilian society, 'the single most important lever to increase equity in tertiary education access will be to improve the quality of public secondary education (World Bank 2010, p. 4). Such an argument has also been stressed by Carnoy and Wagner (2005), who claimed that the more that those who attend secondary education (or equivalent adult education) complete their studies and the better their preparation, the more likely the opportunities for relevant post-school lifelong learning in the workplace or in the vocational training system.

Thus, the university has already been involved in all three areas we have discussed and could arguably represent steps towards a broader lifelong learning framework. That broader framework could move lifelong learning beyond traditional concepts of adult education and job training that now continue to dominate government policies and restrict the development of a larger and more diverse approach to lifelong learning.

Conclusions and recommendations: towards a multicultural framework for lifelong learning

The present chapter has presented an overview of the university's role in providing lifelong learning in Brazil, as gleaned from the discourse in the upcoming national educational plan. The analysis also tried to make some comparisons of the Brazilian situation to the rest of Latin America. The explicit meanings of lifelong learning in Brazil seem to be split into two parts of the broad lifelong learning spectrum: on the one hand, it is viewed as a second chance for the acquisition of core and basic competencies and skills for youth, adults and elderly people who did not complete their primary or secondary schooling; and on the other hand, it is viewed as equivalent to on-the-job or professional training for employees who work in schools, firms, and other production and service organizations. This conforms to Carnoy and Wagner's finding that no country in the Latin American region has really developed policies within a lifelong learning framework.

Recent policy discourses suggest, therefore, that lifelong learning is still an invisible system in both Brazil and the rest of Latin America, and this carries over to universities in those countries. However, as a way of discovering possibilities to make lifelong learning more visible, I have highlighted some current university activities, namely in the areas of improving access to higher education, in university curriculum reforms that focus on multiculturalism, and in continuing education as university extension. Such efforts to provide equitable access and permanency to culturally diverse students, as well as the extension of knowledge-acquisition activities for adults, suggest that there are lifelong learning development possibilities in Brazilian universities, albeit in an implicit rather than explicit way.

Carnoy and Wagner (2005) argued that a more explicit lifelong learning framework could help to guide policy development in ways that address inefficiencies and gaps in the present patchwork of provision. We argue that a transformative framework for lifelong learning should take into account the plural cultural identities of learners in Brazil and Latin America; and it should integrate those activities in the three university areas mentioned in the last section under a more coherent, explicit lifelong learning framework, based on a multicultural perspective. Such a view is particularly relevant for Brazil and Latin America, with their multicultural and highly heterogeneous learner populations.

In order to achieve this more explicit framework, a multicultural ecological approach (Borrero and Yeh 2010) can help in viewing the university as a multicultural organization (Canen and Canen 2005, 2008) that deals with an array of cultural views and social and ethnic diverse backgrounds that impinge on university life. Such a multicultural framework (Canen 2008; Canen and Peters 2005) considers that lifelong learning is the core of identity formation, in that it instils the idea that all of us, throughout our lives, need to be interested in continuing learning. Moving beyond such noble intentions, the university could achieve that goal as long as it does not focus exclusively on those students that already have cultural capital similar to that embraced by the university formal curriculum. The university system needs to incorporate as part of its specific policy plans students from under-represented and marginalized groups. As contended by Borrero and Yeh (2010), minority individuals find themselves in a position of having to navigate different relationships and styles of interaction in their lives. Therefore, the right learning context is needed, as they should feel comfortable speaking their native language, having their cultures valued, and, at the same time, having to learn dominant cultural values and norms.

In that sense, the equity-oriented perspective that undergirds the upcoming Brazilian National Educational plan could arguably be a starting point towards that framework. Whereas the policies proposed do not explicitly mention a lifelong learning paradigm, a lifelong learning framework could more coherently integrate equity-oriented ideas by focusing on the learners' cultural plurality and on the need to foster an approach that enhances their continuing learning experiences. In order to do so, flexibility and autonomy are key words for universities in Brazil, so that their academic research can be integrated with teaching and continuing educational activities in extension services, and thus be more equipped to develop lifelong learning in a broader framework.

Hopefully, future policies in Brazil and Latin America will not be a hiding place for lifelong learning, but develop an original and culturally based Latin American project that contributes to a new lifelong learning vision. This study is comparatively relevant insomuch as it stirs the debates about the role of universities in the redefinition of lifelong learning not only in the region but in other societies as well.

References

Borrero, N.E. and Yeh, C.J. (2010), Ecological English Language Learning Among Ethnic Minority Youth, *Educational Researcher*, v. 39, n. 8, pp. 571–581.

Canen, A. (2008), *Teacher Education and Competence in an Intercultural Perspective: some reflections in Brazil and the UK*. Köln: Lambert Academic Publishing.

Canen, A.G. and Canen, A. (2005), *Organizações Multiculturais*. Rio de Janeiro: Ed. Ciência Moderna.

Canen, A. and Peters, M. (2005), Editorial: Issues and Dilemmas of Multicultural Education: theories, policies and practices, *Policy Futures in Education*, Oxford, v. 3, n. 4, pp. 309–313.

Canen, A. and Santos, A. R. (2009), *Educação Multicultural*. Rio de Janeiro: Ed. Ciência Moderna.

Carnoy, M. and Wagner, A. (2005), *Lifelong Learning and Training Policies in Latin America*, World Bank report.

CONAE (Conferência Nacional de Educação) (2010), Construindo o Sistema Nacional Articulado de Educação: o Plano Nacional de Educação, diretrizes e estratégias de ação [National Conference in Education in Brazil, 2010]. Brasília: Ministério da Educação (MEC).

CONFITEA (2009) *International Conference on Adult Education (CONFINTEA VI), Regional Synthesis Report* 'From Literacy to Lifelong Learning: Towards the Challenges of the XXI Century', organized by UNESCO-UIL/INEA (Mexico, 10–13 September 2008), compiled by Rósa Maria Torres.

Maculan, N. (2010), Globalization and Higher Education: perspectives on policy and practice in a BRIC country (Brazil). Lecture delivered at Dublin City University, 8 December.

Schwartzman, S. (2004), The Challenges of Education in Brazil. In: Brock. C. and Schwartzman, S. (eds), *The Challenges of Education in Brazil*. Oxford: Symposium Books, pp. 9–40.

World Bank (2010), *Tertiary Education and Lifelong Learning in Brazil*, report organized by Jamil Salmi with Chloë Fèvre (pdf).

Part VI
Epilogue

Epilogue

Chapter 16

Afterword
A look around the corner

Maria Slowey and Hans G. Schuetze

Higher education and lifelong learners

Taken together, the fourteen rich and varied country case studies in this book offer a distinctive contribution to the conceptual development of the topic of lifelong learners and higher education. But this is no abstract discussion. The structures and processes examined result in significantly different distributions of opportunities for learners of different ages and socio-economic backgrounds to gain access to higher education over their lifecourse.

There is much to be learnt from the reflections of the situation in different societies, and each chapter stands as a case study in its own right. In this brief Afterword, therefore, our intention is not to provide a comprehensive summary, but rather to reflect on a cluster of important thematic issues. We draw on perspectives emerging from the case studies that are useful in progressing our understanding of a number of key issues discussed in Chapter 1. All chapters show higher education systems in the 21st century as subject to an extraordinary range of competing pressures. The situation in most, if not all, is highly volatile, making accurate projection impossible. Nevertheless, we conclude by tentatively pointing to some directions for the future.

We highlight three key areas in our 'look around the corner': first, the question of country groupings and degrees of responsiveness of different systems and different parts of systems to lifelong learners; second, the issue of the not-yet-realized potential of e-learning; third, we briefly revisit the inter-relationship of the twin concepts of the 'learning society' and 'lifelong learning' – both of which are fluid and multi-faceted. Finally, we take a tentative look ahead.

Thematic groupings of countries

The countries covered in this book are different with regard to traditions, structures and policies. But beyond the obvious, can we find commonalities that make some countries more similar in comparison with others? In our 2000 book we identified three groups of countries based on the degree of openness and responsiveness to non-traditional learners. Sweden and the USA demonstrated the most flexible arrangements for accommodating adult and other 'non-traditional' students; the Anglophone countries (with the exception of Ireland) showed some degree of openness, often with extensive opportunities for part-time study; whereas the central European countries and Japan (where the university system is, in several respects, comparable to Germany and Austria) were the most rigid and least 'friendly' to such students.

Subsequently, 'paired' or 'family groups' comparisons have been developed by others connecting educational access with overall levels of equality. For example, analysis by Green (2006) identifies four groups of countries with respect to skill formation strategies, competitiveness, economic success and social cohesion: namely, the USA and Anglo-Saxon (English speaking) countries; core (central) European countries; Southern European; and Nordic countries.

The country case studies in this book – extended beyond our earlier work to include important perspectives from middle-income countries – examine lifelong learning policies and strategies. They offer insights into those features of higher education we have identified as being conducive to successful participation by the different categories of lifelong learners outlined in Chapter 1. These include, in particular: wider access, active outreach to groups under-represented in higher education, flexible organization of credit, recognition of prior learning (RPL) which permits, in fact encourages, mobility in and out of the system over time ('drop-in', 'drop-out') and/or mobility between institutions (at regional, national or international levels), part-time and distance learning opportunities, continuing education, financial and logistical support – including impartial educational advice and guidance for people over their entire lifecourse.

Revisiting our original group of ten countries a decade later, we find that, despite continuing expansion of their higher education systems, and increases in participation rates, the composition of our three broad country groupings remains relatively unchanged. We do, however, also find challenges and contradictions that might be described as 'one step forward and two steps back'. This particularly applies to the crucially important opportunity for lifelong learners to study on a part-time basis. Even in countries where flexibility has been fairly well embedded in the system of higher education (for example, Sweden, the UK, Australia, New Zealand and the USA), part-time provision, a cornerstone of access for many categories of lifelong learners, is under pressure. There are many reasons for this apparently counterintuitive finding. Our analysis of the country case studies draws attention to three in particular.

- Firstly, the global financial crisis and associated pressures on public finances for higher education teaching is leading to a (re)enforcement of 'full-time' students in many systems as the core source of institutional funding. Even in public institutions, part-time students (especially at the postgraduate level) are increasingly being viewed as important fee-paying 'customers' in a quasi-market environment.

- Secondly, the marked increased emphasis on research output (and associated rankings criteria – to which we return below) places increased pressures on academic staff, relegating the teaching of 'marginal' students to a low priority.
- Thirdly, there is an increased focus at national and international levels (including the Bologna Process in Europe) on universities and other institutions of higher education achieving greater 'efficiency', 'throughput' and graduation rates. While desirable from certain financial and educational perspectives, a – probably unintended – consequence is that this emphasis is leading to a reduction in the genuine flexibility for lifelong learners to drop-in and drop-out of higher education (as in the Swedish model) as suits their learning requirements at different stages over their lifecourse.

For the future, better and more consistent data than we presently have on participation and completion rates of students, their age, background, and family status, and on financing and other support available, would enable us to achieve a better understanding of the differences and communalities. To obtain a fully rounded picture we would need not only to include data on the structure of, and participation in, the pre-school and school system (K to 12). This is of particular importance when including, as we have started to do here, middle-income countries in the framework. The inequalities are stark: for example, in the developed countries, such as Sweden, Germany and Japan, on average young people have 14 years in formal education, compared with an average of 10 in Mexico and Brazil and even less in South Africa.

This imbalance provokes the larger question as to whether lifelong learning may be a concept which is applicable only to rich countries. At one level, the three chapters on South Africa, Brazil and Mexico suggest such a proposition. Portugal appears also to fall in this category because of the legacy of dictatorship and associated inadequate formal education infrastructure (even if it has greatly profited from considerable financial subventions for education from the EU). More importantly perhaps is the larger question as to whether a lifelong learning model which is dominated by a narrow human capital approach may have the unintended consequence of contributing to a continuing strategy for under-development and asymmetry of power relations between the North and the South (see, for example, Preece 2009).

The perspectives from the South provide a crucial, constant reminder of the gross levels of global inequalities in relation to access to even basic levels of education, yet alone higher education. More than this, however, their experience offers valuable new insights and challenges. To take just one example from the chapter on South Africa: from an educational perspective, what does it mean to be an 'adult learner' when life expectancy is low, and when a young person of 12 years of age may have to take on responsibilities as head of a family due to the impact of a disease such as AIDS? In such circumstances, education has to be extended over a longer period of time as it fits around work and domestic responsibilities, throwing into question traditional notions of what it means to be a 'student' in higher education.

The not-yet-realized potential of e-learning

One of the more surprising outcomes of the country case studies is the lack of any sizeable progress in the use of online technology. Most countries do indeed report a significant increase in the use of new technology for 'regular' higher education students, and for niche areas such as continuing professional development. However, given the explosion in the use of social media as well as of the internet, a greater role of internet-based independent-learning programmes, especially in countries like Australia, Canada, Mexico and Brazil where distances are so vast, might have been expected.

Reflecting on the potential of new technology for the enhancement of learning in higher education, Martin Trow foresaw the internet as making possible

> what was once merely an educator's dream: that is, the possibility for all people in a society to have access to education all their lives, in subjects of their own choice and at times and places of their own convenience.
> (Trow 2010: 519)

It also, he suggested, pointed to a new stage of development from his original conception of 'universal access' from 'higher levels of enrollment' in colleges and universities by students of traditional college age

> to a conception of access as participation in lifelong learning by people in their homes and workplaces ... (This) will surely have revolutionary consequences for our existing institutions and systems of higher education.
> (Trow 2010: 519)

The country case studies report on many innovations in the use of technology with a view to enhancing teaching and learning in higher education. There is also certainly an increase in online courses – mainly at the postgraduate level or in the for-profit sector – and some development associated with the 'open courseware' (OCW) movement. However, these do not – as yet – amount to the major step change foreseen by many analysts.

Our analysis of the cases in this book points to a number of key barriers. Specifically, issues around the design and pedagogy of online programmes, access to IT from remote areas, and the lack of familiarity with IT of lifelong learners from different socio-demographic and economic backgrounds are still formidable barriers to the full use of the technological possibilities of IT and help explain why the potential of online learning has not yet been realized.

Higher education and lifelong learning: building blocks of the 'learning society'?

The concepts of 'learning society' and of 'lifelong learning' are often used in close connection, and sometimes even as a synonym. However, the main agent of lifelong learning is the individual – or, in the neoliberal policy context, the 'consumer'. The principal agent of the 'learning society' is society – traditionally, the collective of individuals, organized at a national level through the state.

There is a debate about the various component parts that make a country a learning society (for example, Schugurensky 2007). Certainly, universal access to higher education is an important factor. Using Trow's classification whereby a higher education system is universal when 50 per cent or more of the typical age cohort is enrolled is, as he himself admitted, no longer a valid measure since distance education and independent learning in various combinations of formal and non-formal education arrangements are often not, and cannot be, counted.

The question then is whether, in the absence of the large-scale use of internet-mediated programmes, as still seems to be the case, other criteria, such as the age participation rate of school leavers are adequate to define the learning society. Most authors in this book draw attention to one or both of the main conceptions used by us in our previous volumes: that is, adult learners (OECD 1987) and/or non-traditional learners (Schuetze and Slowey 2000). But we also see evidence, to varying degrees, of the more expanded typology of lifelong learners we developed in Chapter 1: (i) second chance learners, (ii) equity groups, (iii) deferrers, (iv) recurrent learners, (v) returners, (vi) refreshers, and (vii) learners in later life.

Overall, despite the fact that it may be virtually impossible to quantify their number, we suggest that a focus on 'lifelong learners' is a core perspective to understand the constitution of a learning society, or a system of lifelong learning.

A look ahead

As discussed in Chapter 1, the concept of lifelong learning is contested: for some it is effectively seen as a synonym for 'adult education' (Jarvis 2009); or a neoliberal perversion of 'lifelong education' (Boshier and Benseman 2000); or a concept that perhaps is just too complex to be suitable for translation into concrete policies (Field 2006).

Given the fluid nature of the concept, the quest for clarity, and perhaps in some quarters a nostalgia for the past, this critique is understandable but, based on the evidence in this book, erroneous. While our specific focus is on higher education, the importance of both horizontal and vertical linkages between different elements of the education and training 'system' cannot be overstated in any discussion of lifelong learning. Motivation and ability for further learning are very closely connected with the earlier learning phases in life: in fact, to a considerable extent, they lie at its very foundation.

This importance of building connections across systems thus emerges as a significant theme in a comprehensive review of tertiary education policies in 24 countries (OECD 2008). A subsequent analysis of policy implications from this study recommended that each country should review the extent to which

> the tertiary education system is contributing effectively to lifelong learning and assess the flexibility of the system, relevance of provision and funding arrangements are suited to lifelong learners.
> (OECD 2011: 8)

Shifting the focus of attention from the *systemic* dimension of lifelong learning to the potential impact of higher education policy and practice on the *lifelong learner*, and the opportunity to gain access to higher education at different points over her or his lifecourse are, we suggest, possible ways to escape this morass of conceptual confusion.

Shifting the focus to the lifelong learner also places differentiated higher education institutions in the broader landscape of lifelong learning. This is represented in Figure 16.1. The constituent elements of this figure are essentially the same as those we identified in our 2000 book. However, the underlying dynamics of the wider learning environment in which higher education operates has altered significantly as a result of the ubiquitous role of information and communications technology. While all higher education institutions are inevitably connected with their wider social environment, the country case studies show that, from the perspective of lifelong learners, it tends to be those institutions at the upper part of the inverted pyramid which are the most engaged and accessible.

Why should the more elite institutions remain largely inaccessible to most categories of lifelong learners? At one level the answer is obvious and relates to selectivity and socialization. A new though related dimension, however, lies in the growing significance of national and international 'league tables' over the last decade (Marginson and van der Wende 2006; Hazelkorn 2011). As Watson (2009) points out, most criteria for defining 'world class' universities actually *exclude* precisely those elements which are 'vital for the effective support of lifelong learning' (p. 102). Important omissions relevant to lifelong learning are: assessment of teaching quality; widening participation and social mobility; services to business and the community; and contribution to other public services.

In relation to a 'system' of lifelong learning, perhaps the same might be said as a comprehensive review of higher education commented about 'world class' universities: 'everyone wants it, but no one knows what it is'

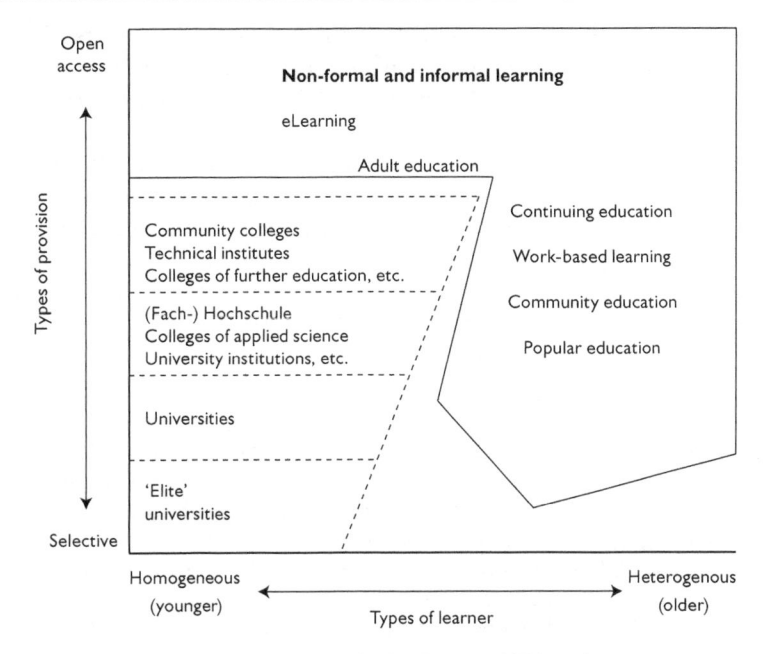

Figure 16.1 Higher education in the broader landscape of lifelong learning
Source: adapted from Schuetze and Slowey (2000, Figure 1)

(Altbach *et al.* 2009). One attempt to envision such a system is provided by Scott (2010). *Inter alia* it would encompass: the radical extension of the scope of higher education to include existing and new types of informal learning and learning in communities and workplaces; more significant roles for voluntary organizations (representing civil society) and commercial organizations (representing the market); 'challenging redefinitions' of academic standards in teaching and research; and, most significantly from our perspective,

> the re-focusing of attention on the continuing education of more diverse social groups and older students (so ending the dominant focus on the initial, and terminal, education of, generally privileged young adults).
> (Scott 2010: 24)

Despite their different demographic profiles, this issue is relevant not only to the rich countries of the North but also to the poor countries of the South. Lifelong learning in middle-income countries exists, as Walters puts it (Chapter 14) 'between the political and economic pressures of a large proportion of young people, on the one hand, and the need for ongoing access to learning opportunities throughout life as the "front-end loading model" of schooling is inadequate for the majority of impoverished people'.

Certainly these issues are complex and the broader vision of a lifelong learning system of higher education, while dynamic and exciting, is not without risk. The country case studies in this book show elements of higher education systems which are at a point of crisis – not just in financial terms but, even more importantly, also in terms of their self-definitions of purpose and role.

However, while challenging for systems and institutions, our analysis of the country case studies leads us to believe that finding ways of meeting the diverse educational needs of lifelong learners is far from being the 'problem'. On the contrary, drawing on the rich work and life experience and motivation of lifelong learners may well in fact form part of the *solution* to the current global malaise in higher education.

References

Altbach, P.G., Reisberg, L. and Rumbley, L.E. (2009) *Trends in Global Higher Education: Tracking an Academic Revolution*, Boston: Boston College CIHE.

Boshier, R. and Benseman, J. (2000) 'The impact of market forces in the quest for lifelong learning in New Zealand universities', in H.G. Schuetze and M. Slowey (eds) *Higher Education and Lifelong Learners: International Perspectives on Change*, London: RoutledgeFalmer,

Field, J. (2006) *Lifelong Learning and the New Educational Order.* 2nd edn, Stoke-on-Trent: Trentham Books.

Green, A. (2006) Models of Lifelong Learning and the 'Knowledge Society'. *Compare*, 36(3), 307–325.

Hazelkorn, H. (2011) *Rankings and the Reshaping of Higher Education: The Battle for World Class Excellence*, London: Palgrave Macmillan.

Jarvis, P. (2009) 'Lifelong learning: a social ambiguity', in P. Jarvis (ed.) *The Routledge International Handbook of Lifelong Learning*, London: Routledge, 9–18.

Marginson, S. and van der Wende, M. (2006) *Globalisation and Higher Education*, Paris: OECD.

OECD (1987) *Adults in Higher Education*, Paris: OECD.

OECD (2008) *Tertiary Education for the Knowledge Society*, Paris: OECD.

OECD (2011) *Tertiary Education for the Knowledge Society: Pointers for Policy Development*, Paris: OECD.

Preece, J. (2009) *Lifelong Learning and Development: A Southern Perspective*, London and New York: Continuum.

Schugurensky, D. (2007) 'The learning society in Canada and the US', in M. Kuhn (ed.) *New Society Models for a New Millennium – The Learning Society in Europe and Beyond*, Frankfurt and New York: Peter Lang.

Scott, P. (2010) 'Access in higher education in Europe and North America: trends and developments', *Bologna Handbook 16.* Berlin: European Universities Association and Raabe.

Schuetze, H.G. and Slowey, M. (eds) (2000) *Higher Education and Lifelong Learners: International Perspectives on Change*, London: RoutledgeFalmer.

Trow, M.A. (2010) *Twentieth-Century Higher Education: Elite to Mass to Universal*, Baltimore: The Johns Hopkins University Press.

Watson, D. (2009) 'Universities and lifelong learning', in P. Jarvis (ed.) *Handbook of Lifelong Learning*, London: Routledge, 101–113.

Index

The abbreviation HE stands for higher education. Cross-references in the form *see (below)* or *see also (below)* point to a later subheading under the same main heading.

Abitur 43, 44, 45, 46, 49, 56, 57
Aboriginal people
   Australia 205–6
   Canada 136–7, 145, 146–7, 152
access to HE
   admission models 50–51
   challenge of democratizing access to knowledge 77–8
   in individual countries *see under specific countries*
   and lifelong learning 40, 43–57, 71–4
   and the need for a qualified workforce 45, 51, 52, 54–5
   non-traditional routes 43–57
   numerus clausus 43, 55, 88
   and prestige and support for adult students 185–6
   and social origin 33
Adnett, N. and Tlupova, D. 125–6
Adult Continuing Education (ACE) 118, 231–3, 235, 244
African Union Harmonisation Strategy 8
Age Participation Rate (APR) 6
AIDS 14, 255
American Council on Education 186
ANKOM programme 53–4
Aontas 70
Aotearoa New Zealand *see* New Zealand
apprenticeships 34, 45, 52, 55, 99, 139
Argentina 158, 161

Auckland, University of 239
Australia 195–214
   e-learning 207, 209, 213
   higher education 195–214; access 201; articulation 208; blurring of public and private provision 201, 213; Bradley Report 195–6, 199; Candy Report 202–3; differentiation and equity 212–13; flexibility 208; HECS (Higher Education Contribution Scheme) 199; Karpin Report 203; and lifelong learning 14, 202–4, 207, 209, 211–12; participation 204–7; quality assurance 208; revenue 199–200; and socio-cultural diversity 208; student choices and their new significance 208–12; system 198–202, 212; Tertiary Education Quality and Standards Agency (TEQSA) 209; *Transforming Australia's Higher Education System* 196; Unified National System 199–200, 212
   knowledge economy: and lifelong learning 14, 202–4, 207, 211–12; transition to 196–8
   lack of change in HE 17–18
   lifelong learning 211–12; 'Candy profile' 202–3, 209, 211, 212; *Developing Lifelong Learners through Undergraduate Education* 202–3; and the knowledge economy 14, 202–4, 207, 211–12
   Martin Report 199
   poly-ethnicity 198
   population percentage of 0–14 year olds 254

socio-economic inequalities 197
students 204–7, 212; ethnicity 198; financial aid 199; indigenous 205–6; international 197; of low socio-economic status 206; new significance of student choices 208–12; non-traditional 205–7; part-time study 207, 208, 211, 212; from rural/remote areas 207; working 207
TAFE (Training and Further Education) 200–202, 207, 208, 213
universities 196–7, 199–200, 203, 204, 207, 208–9
vocational education 201, 206, 208, 213
Australian National Training Authority (ANTA) 201
Austria 25–40
access to HE 33, 34, 40
continuing education 31, 39
HE culture 27–9, 39–40
HE policy: Bologna Process 28–9, 31–2; changes in the 2000s 25–32; at a crossroads 39–40; and employers 28, 29; impacts on study conditions 31–2; non-recognition of part-time undergraduate study 16, 29, 32, 39; transition to two-tier system 28–9
lifelong learning 39–40; and the establishment of a university of continuous education 30–31; as a study motive 36–7
Matura 33, 40
students: with alternative entrance qualifications 33–4; with children 37–8; female 32, 33; foreign 33; late beginners and senior students 34; in new sectors of higher education 38–9; non-traditional 25–40; part-time 29, 32, 39 *see also (below)* working; with special needs 27, 38; statistical portrait in the 2000s 32–9; study motives 36–7; surveys 41n3; working 27, 29, 32, 34–6, 37, 41n4
tuition fees 29, 30, 31, 32
universities: 1993 University Organisation Act 26–7; 2002 Universities Act 27, 38; Childcare in Universities project 37–8; control of admission 39, 40; Danube University Krems 31, 39; establishment of private university sector 30; *Fachhochschulen* 26, 28, 32–3, 34, 36, 37, 41n2; governance 26–8; Humboldtian tradition 27, 28, 29; and massification 39; new public management 26; *Pädagogische Hochschulen* 32–3, 37, 41n2; rectors 26, 27–8; and the state 26

BCCAT (British Columbia Council of Admissions and Transfer) 144
Begabtenprüfung 51
Benseman, J. 233, 240
Berufsakademie 46
Berufsfachschule 45
Birbeck College 115
Bologna Declaration 7–8, 52
Bologna Process
 Austria 28–9, 31–2
 Germany 46–7, 52–3
 Ireland 64, 65
 Portugal 95
 Sweden 100
Borrero, N.E. and Yeh, C.J. 277
Boshier, R. and Benseman, J. 231, 235
Bosworth, B. and Choitz, V. 188
Bourgeois, E. *et al.* 254
Box Hill Institute, Melbourne 202
Bradley, D., *Review of Higher Education* 195–6, 199
Brazil 266–77
 CONAE (National Conference for Education) 266, 268, 269, 270, 271, 273–5
 CONFINTEA (International Conference on Adult Education) 267–8, 269–70
 continuing education 266, 267–8, 270, 275, 276, 277
 higher education 267; growth and the private sector 161
 lifelong learning 266–77; potential contributions of university systems 271–7; in recent policies 267–70
 PNE (National Educational Plan) 266, 268, 277
 population percentage of 0–14 year olds 254
 ProUni programme 272
 tax revenues 167

British Columbia Council of Admissions and Transfer (BCCAT) 144
Bron, A. and Lönnheden, Ch. 106–7, 108
Bron-Wojciechowska, A. 107
Browne Review 124, 125, 126
Buchler, M. *et al.* 251–2, 256, 258

CAEL (Council for Adult and Experiential Learning) 186
Callender, C. 124
  and Jackson, J. 124
Cambridge, University of 114
Canada 135–53
  Aboriginal people 136–7, 145, 146–7, 152
  community colleges 139, 141, 142
  credit transferability 143–4, 152
  demographics 136–7
  economy 137; knowledge-based 144, 153
  e-learning 150
  higher education 140–41, 151–3; Aboriginal people 146–7, 152; access 145–6, 152; adult participation 147–8; assessment and recognition of prior learning 144–5; distance and online learning 150–51; immigrant participation 147; and lifelong learning 135–53; overview and changes of the last decade 136–43; participation levels and modes of under-represented groups 146–9, 152; part-time studies 149–50; rural students 148; university continuing education 141–3
  immigrant population 136, 147
  Individual Development Accounts 138
  learning system 138–45, 151–3; accessibility and participation 145–9; adult education and learning 139–40; continuing training 139; distance and online learning 150–51; early childhood education and schooling 138–9; flexibility and transferability 143–5; higher education 140–43; information 143; part-time studies 149–50; provincial policies 145–6; university continuing education 141–3; vocational training 139

lifelong learning in HE 135–53; overview and changes of the last decade 136–43
politics and policies 137–8
Quebec 135, 137, 141, 149
students: Aboriginal 145, 146–7, 152; adult 147–8; decline in undergraduate part-time numbers 16; immigrant 147; of low socio-economic status 148; rural 145, 148; women 149
universities 141–4
Canadian Association for Adult Education 140
Canadian Council of Learning (CCL) 140
Candy, P. *et al.* 202–3
  profile of lifelong learning 202–3, 209, 211, 212
Carnevale, A. and Rose, S. 174
Carnoy, M. and Wagner, A. 271, 276, 277
CATS (Credit Accumulation Transfer Schemes) 120
Charles, D. *et al.* 117
Chile 158, 161, 167
China 6
Choy, S. *et al.* 178
Clancy, P. 64, 74
Clark, B. 9
CLEP (College Level Examination program) 176
Collins, T. 78
Common Space for Distance Higher Education (ECOES) 164
community colleges 6
  Canada 139, 141, 142
  US 176, 184–5
Composite Learning Index 12
continuing education 282, 287
  Adult Continuing Education (ACE) 118, 231–3, 235, 244
  Austria 31, 39
  Brazil 266, 267–8, 270, 275, 276, 277
  Canada 141–3
  Germany 46, 47, 48, 50
  Ireland 75
  lifelong learning *see* lifelong learning
  Mexico 160, 163–5
  Portugal 91
  South Africa 259
  Sweden 102

UK 115, 116, 118
US 176, 179, 183, 184
continuing professional development (CPD) 13, 117, 284
Co-operative Party 115
Copenhagen Process 52, 53
credit transfers
   Canada 143–4, 152
   Credit Accumulation Transfer Schemes (CATS) 120
   European Credit Transfer System (ECTS) 8, 29, 41n1, 53, 104
   from FE to HE 127
   Mexico 163

DANTES (Defense Activity for Non-traditional Education Support program) 176
Danube University Krems 31, 39
Davey, J.A. *et al.* 237–8
Davies, P. and Feutrie, M. 9
Dawkins, J. S. 199
deferrers 15, 49
distance education 8, 13, 49, 53 *see also* e-learning
   Canada 150–51
   Distance University Hagen 56
   Ireland 74, 75, 76
   Mexico 163–5
   open and distance learning (ODL) 76
   Portugal 91
   Sweden 100, 101, 102, 103, 104
   US 176, 181, 182Tbl., 185, 186
distance students 4, 75, 102
Dublin, Trinity College 65, 66
Dublin City University 65, 74
Dublin Region Higher Education Alliance (DRHEA) 76–7

ECOES (Common Space for Distance Higher Education) 164
ECTS *see* European Credit Transfer System
e-learning 13, 284
   Australia 207, 209, 213
   Canada 150
   Ireland 77
   New Zealand 244
   Portugal 94
   South Africa 261
   UK 119
   US 176, 181, 183, 184, 185, 186

ELLI (European Lifelong Learning Index) 12
ENLACES (Latin American and Caribbean Area for Higher Education) 8
equity
   and differentiation 212–13
   groups 15
   and lifelong learning in HE 3, 4, 7, 64–9, 71–4
Equivalent Level Qualification (ELQ) 116
ESAD (Program for Open and Distance Higher Education, Mexico) 164
European Credit Transfer System (ECTS) 8, 29, 41n1, 104
   for VET (ECVET) 53
European Higher Education Area (EHEA) 7–8
European Lifelong Learning Index (ELLI) 12
European Qualifications Framework (EQF) for Lifelong Learning 53
European Social Fund (ESF) 90, 91
European Union (EU) 7–9
   Memorandum on Lifelong Learning 105–6
   Portugal's entry 82, 94
European Universities Association (EUA) 65
European Year of Lifelong Learning (1996) 70
Expert Group on Future Skills Needs 70

Fachhochschulen
   Austria 26, 28, 32–3, 34, 36, 37, 41n2
   Germany 46, 51
Fieldhouse, R. 115
Forfás 70

Germany 43–57
   Abitur 43, 44, 45, 46, 49, 56, 57
   access to HE 43–57; admission models 50–51; changing policies for non-traditional students 51–5; current state of non-traditional access 55–6; and the need for a qualified workforce 45, 51, 52, 54–5; *numerus clausus* 43, 55
   ANKOM programme 53–4

Index

apprenticeships 52
Begabtenprüfung 51
Berufsakademie 46
Berufsfachschule 45
Bologna Process 46–7, 52–3
Conference of the State Ministers of Education (KMK) 55
Copenhagen Process 52, 53
excellence initiative 47
Fachhochschulen 46, 51
Gymnasium 43, 44–6, 49
HE reforms 46–7
institutional context of HE 44–7
Länder 44, 45, 46, 50–51, 56
lifelong learners in HE 43, 47–51
non-traditional students in HE 43, 47–51; and access 51–6
qualified workforce 45, 51, 52, 54–5
universities 51
vocational training 45, 49, 52, 53
Global Report on Adult Education and Learning 10–12
globalization 84, 95, 114, 145, 201, 204, 225, 227, 228, 233
Guri-Rosenblit, S. 164
Gymnasium 25, 43, 44–6, 49

Hagen, Distance University 56
Hamburg Declaration on Adult Learning 105
higher education (HE)
 access *see* access to HE
 Age Participation Rate 6
 Bologna: Declaration 7–8, 52; Process *see* Bologna Process
 and the changing role of universities 5
 culture 4; Austria 27–9, 39–40; Mexico 162, 169
 e-learning *see* e-learning
 and employers 14, 28, 29
 factors in international statistics 6
 global development and trends 3, 5–12
 growth 6, 14
 in individual countries *see under specific countries*
 and the 'learning society' 153, 232, 285
 and lifelong learning, looking ahead 285–8
 marketization 5
 massification 39, 218–19, 236
 new learning technologies 16–17, 77 *see also* e-learning; ICT role in education 100
 in non-university institutions 6, 14
 overview of country case studies 9–12
 policy steering 8
 polytechnics *see* polytechnics
 privatization in 5
 relevance of the concept of lifelong learning in twenty-first century to 13–16
 resources 5
 shift in knowledge Modes 14
 slow adaptation to lifelong learning 4
 students *see* students
 tuition fees *see* tuition fees
 typology of lifelong learners in the early twenty-first century 14–16
 universities *see* universities
Higher Education Innovation Fund (HEIF) 117
Higher Education and Lifelong Learners: International Perspectives on Change (2000) 3, 4, 43, 47, 60, 62, 100, 178, 285, 287
HIV 14, 255
Horn, L. and Carroll, D. 178
Hughes, Simon 127

ICT (Information and Communication Technologies) 99–100, 243–4
Imperial University, Tokyo 218
Independent Labour Party 115
INEE (National Institute of Educational Assessment, Mexico) 167
Information and Communication Technologies 99–100, 243–4
Institutes of Technology Act (Ireland, 2006) 65
International Adult Literacy Survey (IALS) 235, 240
Ireland 60–78
 distance education 74, 75, 76
 economy 61, 62, 63–4, 67, 70, 77, 78
 Expert Group on Future Skills Needs 70
 higher education: 1997 Higher Education Act 65; 2000–2010 62–9; 2006 Institutes of Technology Act 65; access 71–4,

77–8; Bologna Process 64, 65; e-learning 77; 'Fourth Level Ireland' 67; growth 66–7; lifelong learning in *see (below)* lifelong learning in HE; *National Strategy for Higher Education to 2030* 61, 70, 75–6; Newman's establishment of 60; open and distance learning 76; participation levels 60–61, 65–9, 70, 71, 74–5; part-time study 67, 68–9Tbls, 72, 74–6, 77; performance 61, 66, 73, 74, 76; policy 60–66; Programme for Research in Third Level Education 64; recognition for prior learning 70
lifelong learning in HE 61–78; and the challenge of democratizing access to knowledge 77–8; and equity 64–9, 71–4; and innovative modes of study 74–7; interpretations 70–77; and the National Plan for Access 71–4
migration patterns 62–3
National Development Plan 67
National Framework of Qualifications 65, 70
National Plan for Access 71–4
National Skills Strategy 70
Science Foundation Ireland 64
students 65–7; ages on entry 73; enrolment trends 66–9; gender equality 72; mature 72, 73; non-traditional 72–4; part-time 67, 68–9Tbls, 75–6; women 66–7, 72
unemployment 63; by level of education 64Tbl.
universities 60, 65, 66–9, 74; enrolment trends 66–9
Irish Universities Association 67
Irish Universities Quality Board 65

James, R. 207
and Beckett, D. 214
Japan 217–28
employment 217, 221
higher education 217–28; 1963 Report of the National Council on Education 219; before the 1990s 225; for adult learners 221Fig., 223–5, 226–7; development beginning in Meiji 218; direction of reform 227; institution numbers and types 219, 220Tbl.; and lifelong learning 217, 220–25, 227–8; massification after World War II 218–19; Plan 219; policies encouraging adult study at universities 223–5; policy making within Ministry of Education 222; quality 227; recent reform 217, 225–7; for the youth 220–22, 223
knowledge-based society 225, 227, 228
Law Schools 224–5
learners in different types of programmes 228Fig.
learning in later life 16, 220
lifelong learning 217, 220–25; future perspectives for 227–8; Lifelong Education Promotion Law 222
MEXT (Ministry of Education, Sports, Culture, Science and Technology) 220, 222, 223–4, 227
population decline of 18-year-olds 226
professional schools 224
Rinkyoshin (Ad-hoc National Council on Educational Reform) 217, 222, 223
students 220Tbl., 226; adult 221Fig., 223–5, 226–7; employment prospects 217, 221
universities 218–19, 220Tbl.; accreditation system 227; and adult learners 221Fig., 223–5, 226–7; entrants aged 25 years and older 221Fig.; policies encouraging adult study at 223–5; projected enrolment at 226Fig.; reform 226–7
youth unemployment 221, 222Fig.
Jones, D. *et al.* 174

Karpin Report 203
Kelly, T. 114
knowledge Modes and forms 14
knowledge-based economies 4, 7, 14, 17, 54, 61, 67, 70
Australia 14, 196–8, 202–4, 207, 211–12
Canada 144, 153
Japan 225, 227, 228
Mexico 158, 168
Krems, Danube University 31, 39

Latin American and Caribbean Area for Higher Education (ENLACES) 8
learners in later life 16
Learning for Life (White Paper) 75
learning technologies 16–17, 77 *see also* e-learning
ICT role in education 100, 243–4
Learning: the Treasure Within 12
Leitch Report 117
Liberal Adult Education (LAE) 114–15, 116
lifelong learners
 in individual countries *see under specific countries*
 life stages 13
 typology in HE in the early twenty-first century 14–16
 and university entrance selection 40
lifelong learning 3–4, 6–9, 39–40, 286
 and access to HE 40, 43–57, 71–4
 Age Participation Rate 6
 articulation 4
 continuing education *see* continuing education
 coordination 4
 and diversity 126
 European Qualifications Framework for 53
 European Year of Lifelong Learning (1996) 70
 factors in international statistics 6
 'first generation' 6–7
 and flexibility 118–20, 126; and the broader landscape 16–17
 global developments in HE relevant to 5–12
 human capital model 4, 7, 17
 in individual countries *see under specific countries*
 and innovative modes of study 74–7
 and the 'learning society' 285
 and the life stage of the learner 13
 and the mode of study 13
 and the organization of provision 13
 outlook in HE 17–18, 285–8
 'recurrent education' 90, 105, 222
 relevance of concept to HE in twenty-first century 13–16
 'second generation' 7
 and segmentation 126
 slow adaptation of HE to 4
 social justice and equity model 4, 7
 and thematic groupings of countries 281–4
 and the type of programme 13
 and university entrance selection 40

Maculan, N. 267
Māoris 230, 231–2, 233, 236, 238, 240–41, 242
marketization 5
Martin Report 199
Matura 33, 40
mature students 4, 6, 48
 Ireland 72, 73
 Portugal 92–3
 senior students 34, 50
 Sweden 100, 103
 UK 118, 121–3
McCaig, C. and Adnett, N. 125
McNair, S. *et al.* 112, 116
Melbourne, University of 209
Mexico 157–69
 Common Space for Distance Higher Education (ECOES) 164
 educational expenditure 167
 educational inequalities 13, 158–9
 educational policy and lifelong learning in HE 157, 159–68; 2001 government reform 160–61; broadening the offering 161; continuing education 160, 163–5; credit transfer system 163; distance learning 163–5; governability and governmental capacity 166–8; "new" educational models 162–3; prior learning assessment 165, 169; quality assurance 165–6; structural problems 165–8
 HE culture 162, 169
 HE growth 161
 knowledge-based economy 158, 168
 National Institute of Educational Assessment (INEE) 167
 National System of Distance Learning (SINED) 164
 Program for Open and Distance Higher Education (ESAD) 164

Sector Program for Education 159–60
students 161
tax revenues 167
traditionalization of educational practices 164
universities 161, 163–5, 166; polytechnic 161, 166
Morrill Act (1862) 175
motivation 36–7
Myers, K. and de Broucker, P. 151

National Autonomous University of Mexico (UNAM) 164
National Strategy for Higher Education to 2030 (Ireland) 61, 70, 75–6
neoliberalism 4, 7, 67, 153, 174, 231, 239, 285
Nesbit, T. 140
new learning technologies *see* learning technologies
new public management (NPM) 26
New Zealand 230–45
  Adult Continuing Education (ACE) 231–3, 235, 244
  adult education: adult students in tertiary education 236–8; and lifelong learning 231–3, 238, 244–5
  education in historical context 230–36
  e-learning 244
  institutes of technology and polytechnics (ITPs) 235, 240, 241, 242, 244
  International Adult Literacy Survey (IALS) 235, 240
  international students 243
  lifelong learning 231–3, 238, 244–5
  Literacy, Language and Numeracy Action Plan (LLN) 235
  Māori language 232, 241, 242
  Māoris 230, 231; ACE 231–2, 233; tertiary education 236, 238, 240–41, 242
  More than words report 235
  multi-cultural society 231
  National Qualifications Framework (NQF) 234, 237
  part-time study 234, 236, 237–8, 240, 241
  Pasifika peoples 231, 233, 238, 240, 242–3
  polytechnics 234, 235, 236, 239, 244
  private training establishments (PTEs) 235, 240, 242
  Qualifications Authority (NZQA) 234, 244
  Skill New Zealand 233
  tertiary education: adult students 236–8; bridging and foundation studies 239–41; differentiation and stratification 239–43; and ICT 243–4; Māoris 236, 240–41, 242; participation 241–2; Pasifika peoples 238, 242–3; structure 234–6; TEC (Tertiary Education Commission) 234–5, 236, 238, 244; TES (Tertiary Education Strategy) 234, 239, 240
  universities 233, 234, 235, 239–40, 242, 245; managed entry system 236, 238, 240, 241
  Waitangi Treaty 230, 231
  wānanga 235, 239, 240–41, 242
  women students 237, 238, 241
Newman, John Henry 60, 78
non-traditional students
  access to HE 43–57
  Australia 205–7
  Austria 25–40
  definitions 25, 48–50
  Germany 43–57
  Ireland 72–4
  Portugal 92–4
  Sweden 102–3
  US 178
NPM (new public management) 26

OECD (Organisation for Economic Co-operation and Development) 7, 12, 74–6, 77, 286
  Program for International Student Assessment (PISA) study 138, 159
  recurrent education concept 222
OECD countries *see also specific countries*
  average percentage of university entrants over 25 years old 220
  demographic shifts 4
  graduations 6
  HE participation rates, equity and access 3
  high school drop-out rate 139
online learning *see* e-learning
open and distance learning (ODL) 76
  see also distance education

Open University 115
O'Riain, S. 63, 78
Osborne, M. 112–13, 114
　et al. 124
O'Toole, F. 63

Pädagogische Hochschulen 32–3, 37, 41n2
part-time study/students 6, 13, 282
　Australia 207, 208, 211, 212
　Austria 16, 29, 32, 39
　Canada 16, 149–50
　Ireland 67, 68–9Tbls, 72, 74–6, 77
　New Zealand 234, 236, 237–8, 240, 241
　South Africa 258, 259–60
　UK 16
　US 177, 183Tbl., 184
Pasifika peoples 231, 233, 238, 240, 242–3
Percy, K. and Ramsden, P. 119
PISA (Program for International Student Assessment) study 138, 159
PLAR (prior learning for academic recognition) 144–5, 176
polytechnics 6
　Mexican polytechnic universities 161, 166
　New Zealand 234, 235, 236, 239, 244
　Portugal 85–6, 88, 89, 90, 92, 93Tbl., 94
　UK 115, 120
Portugal 82–95
　Comprehensive Law on the Education System 89
　economy 84, 85–6
　educational attainment 82–3, 84; and unemployment 84–5
　employment 83–4; Portuguese National Employment Programme 90–91
　entry into EU 82, 94
　and the European Community 90
　and the European Social Fund 90, 91
　higher education 82–95; access 88, 92–4; Bologna Process 95; country-specific context 83–5; e-learning 94; expenditure 89; and family income 88; and the former political regime 82, 83; graduation rate 86; New Opportunity Programme 91; for non-traditional adult students 92–4; overview of national system 85–9; participation levels 82, 84, 94–5; performance 83, 86–7, 95; performance-based contracts 94; policies for lifelong education 89–91; Technological Specialization Courses 91–2; tuition fees 88
　labour cost differentials 85
　lifelong learning 84, 89–91
　National Commission for Lifelong Education and Learning 90
　polytechnics 85–6, 88, 89, 90, 92, 93Tbl., 94
　students 82–3; enrolments 86Tbl., 92; graduation rate 86; loans 89; mature 92–3; non-traditional 92–4; social support system for 88–9; women 92–4
　unemployment 84–5
　universities, enrolments 86Tbl., 92
　and the World Bank 85–6
prior learning
　Mexico 165, 169
　PLAR (prior learning for academic recognition) 144–5, 176
　R/AP(E)L (recognition and accreditation of prior (experiential) learning) 119
　RPL *see* recognition for prior learning (RPL)
privatization 5, 188
Program for International Student Assessment (PISA) study 138, 159
Programme for Research in Third Level Education (PRTLI) 64
PUSH provisions 49–50

Qualifications and Quality Assurance Ireland 65
quality assurance 65, 83, 165–6, 208, 209, 253
Quebec 135, 137, 141, 149
Quinn, Ruairí 66

recognition for prior learning (RPL) 15, 282 *see also* prior learning
　Ireland 70
　recognition and accreditation of prior (experiential) learning (R/AP(E)L) 119
　South Africa 252, 256, 257, 259, 263

'recurrent education' 90, 105, 222
recurrent learners 15
refreshers 16
returners 15–16, 49
RMIT University 201, 212
Rothblatt, S. 78
RPL *see* recognition for prior learning
Rubenson, K. 105

Sandmann, L. 179, 181
SAQA (South African Qualifications Authority) 256
Schuller, T. and Watson, D. 254, 255
Schwartzman, S. 271
Science Foundation Ireland (SFI) 64
Scott, D. 237
Scott, P. 287
Scottish higher education 116, 120, 121Tbl., 123–4, 127
second chance learners 15
senior students 34, 50
Shaffer, D. and Wright, J. 174
SINED (National System of Distance Learning, Mexico) 164
Skilbeck, Malcolm 76
Skill New Zealand 233
Slowey, M. 115
Smith–Lever Act (1914) 175
social justice 118, 199, 200, 263, 268
    and equity model of lifelong learning 4, 7
South Africa 251–64
    adult learners 253–8
    Council on Higher Education (CHE) 253
    e-learning 261
    Higher Education Act (1997) 253
    higher education in lifelong learning 251–64; adult learners 253–8; HE system 251–3; HEQF (Higher Education Qualifications Framework) 253, 256, 262–3; National Plan for Higher Education 257; participation 253; roles of the champions 262–4; UWC case study 258–62
    HIV and AIDS 14, 255
    life expectancy 254
    National Qualifications Framework (NQF) 256
    population percentage of 0–14 year olds 254
    recognition for prior learning 252, 256, 257, 259, 263

SAQA (South African Qualifications Authority) 256
Southeast Asian Ministers of Education Organisation 8
Steinberg, J. 255
students
    distance 4, 75, 102
    ethnicity 103, 109n4, 198, 238
    female *see* women students
    of individual countries *see under specific countries*
    international 197, 243; PISA (Program for International Student Assessment) study 138, 159
    loans 89, 101, 178, 188
    of low socio-economic status 103, 113, 115, 120, 123, 145, 148, 206
    mature *see* mature students
    non-traditional *see* non-traditional students
    part-time *see* part-time study/students
    from rural areas 103, 145, 148, 207
    senior 34, 50
    tuition fees for *see* tuition fees
    women *see* women students
    working *see* working students
Sutton Trust 125
Sweden 97–109
    demographics 97–8
    distance education 100, 101, 102, 103, 104
    educational system 98–9; ICT in 100
    Folk high schools 99, 100, 107, 109nn 1–2
    higher education 97–109; access 97, 101–2, 103, 106, 107–8; Bologna Process 100; changes over the last ten years 100–102; discipline imbalance 100; funding 100–101; and lifelong learning 13, 105–7; participation levels 99, 102; as a system for dropping in and dropping out 97, 104
    ICT role in education 99–100
    lifelong learning 13, 105–7; EU Memorandum on Lifelong Learning 105–6; Hamburg Declaration on Adult Learning 95

Municipal adult education
(KOMVUX) 99, 106, 107
students: ethnicity 103, 109n4;
and the labour market 102; loans
101; mature 100, 103; non-
traditional 102–3; women 99,
103, 104; young 95, 100
unemployment 101
universities 101, 109n4
vocational education 99

Technological Institute of Higher
Studies of Monterrey (ITESM) 164
Thomas, L. *et al.* 123
Tobias, R. 231
Tokyo University 218
*Transforming Australia's Higher
Education System* 196
Trinity College Dublin 65, 66
Trow, M.A. 284
Tuijnman, A. 10
tuition fees
Austria 29–30, 31, 32
Portugal 88
UK 114, 124

UNESCO 6, 7, 77
Learning: the Treasure Within 12
UNICEF 138
United Kingdom 112–28
Adult Continuing Education 118
Confintea VI report 112, 116–17,
123
Department of Industry,
Universities and Skills (DIUS)
117
e-learning 119
FE colleges 125
higher education: Employer
Engagement 117; Equivalent
Level Qualification 116; external
degrees 125; factors against adult
participation 118, 127; funding
113, 114, 115, 117, 118, 123–4;
inclusiveness 117; Leitch Report
117; and lifelong learning *see
(below)* universities and their role
in lifelong learning; recent growth
in HE 14; recognition and
accreditation of prior (experiential)
learning 119; Scotland 116, 120,
121Tbl., 123–4, 127; tuition fees
114, 124; widening participation

(WP) 113, 115, 116, 118–19,
120–26, 127
Independent Enquiry into Lifelong
Learning in the UK 113, 128
Learning and Skills Council (LSC)
117, 128n2
Liberal Adult Education 114–15, 116
lifelong learning *see (below)*
universities and their role in lifelong
learning
polytechnics 115, 120
population percentage of 0–14 year
olds 254
socio-economics 112–13
students: decline in undergraduate
part-time numbers 16; on Disabled
Student Allowance 121; mature
118, 121–3; socio-economic status
123; young full-time entrants 121
Tbl.
universities and their role in lifelong
learning 112–28; and continuing
professional development 117;
current thinking 117–20; and
diversity and segmentation 126;
flexibility in 118–20, 126; and
funding policies 114, 123–4; and
government funding cuts 113;
historical background 114–17;
impact of widening participation
120–26
University Funding Council (UFC)
115
United States of America 173–89
1964 Civil Rights federal legislation
176
American Council on Education 186
CLEP (College Level Examination
program) 176
community colleges 176, 184–5
continuing education 176, 179,
183, 184
Council for Adult and Experiential
Learning (CAEL) 186
DANTES (Defense Activity for
Non-traditional Education Support
program) 176
e-learning 176, 181, 183, 184, 185,
186
General Educational Development
(GED) credential 176
GI Bill (Serviceman's Readjustment
Act of 1944) 175

HE access 185–6
HE and lifelong learning 173–89; and adult students as workers 181–4; current status of adults 177–9; differentiating access in relation to prestige and support for adult students 185–6; distance education 176, 181, 182Tbl., 185, 186; future of adult-distinctive HE 184–5; future of advanced knowledge contained solely within formal HE 188–9; historic context 175–7; impact of blurring of traditional boundaries among and between HEIs 186–8
HE categorization by credit or non-credit venues 179
Morrill Act (1862) 175
PLAR (prior learning for academic recognition) 176
Smith–Lever Act (1914) 175
students 177–9, 180Tbl., 181–4, 185–6; financial aid 178, 187–8; non-traditional 178; part-time 177, 183Tbl., 184; working 177, 181–4, 185, 187, 188
work economy 183
universities
and changes in HE systems 5
childcare in 37–8
control of admission 39, 40
entrants aged 25 years and older 221Fig.
European Universities Association (EUA) 65
governance 25, 26–8
of individual countries see under specific countries and specific universities
and Newman 60
polytechnic see polytechnics
private university sector 30
rectors 26, 27–8
social opening up of 51
students see students
University Funding Council (UFC) 115
University of the Third Age 114
University of Western Cape (UWC) 258–62

vocational training 45, 49, 52, 99, 139, 201, 206, 208, 213
vocational education and training (VET) 53, 139

wānanga 235, 239, 240–41, 242
Watson, D. 17, 113, 128, 286
Watson, D. and Taylor, R. 70
WEI (World Education Indicators) Programme 6
women students
Austria 32, 33
Canada 149
gender equality 72
Ireland 66–7, 72
New Zealand 237, 238, 241
Portugal 92–4
Sweden 99, 103, 104
Woodrow, M. 123, 126
Workers Educational Association (WEA) 114
working students 258
Australia 207
Austria 27, 29, 32, 34–6, 37, 41n4
US 177, 181–4, 185, 187, 188
World Bank 7, 77, 85–6, 269
World Education Indicators (WEI) Programme 6